THE TWO HEADED QUARTER

THE TWO HEADED QUARTER

*How to See Through Deceptive Numbers
and Save Money on Everything You Buy*

Joseph Ganem

To Mary,
Best Wishes,
Joe

chartley
publishing

Baltimore

Published by Chartley Publishing, LLC

For information contact:
Chartley Publishing, LLC
P. O. Box 6705, Baltimore, MD 21285
www.ChartleyPublishing.com

ISBN-10   0-9677551-3-1
ISBN-13   978-0-9677551-3-7
Library of Congress Control Number: 2006907121

Book Cover Writing: Graham Van Dixhorn, Write to Your Market, Inc.

Publisher's Cataloging-In-Publication Data
(Prepared by The Donohue Group, Inc.)

Ganem, Joseph.
  The two headed quarter : how to see through deceptive numbers and save money on everything you buy / Joseph Ganem.

   p. : ill., charts ; cm.

  Includes bibliographical references and index.
  ISBN-13: 978-0-9677551-3-7
  ISBN-10: 0-9677551-3-1

1. Finance, Personal. 2. Consumer education. 3. Saving and investment. I. Title.

HG179 .G36 2007
332.024   2006907121

For Sharon

and our children

Thomas, Katherine, and Claire

"It has been my experience that competency in mathematics, both in numerical manipulations and in understanding its conceptual foundations, enhances a person's ability to handle the more ambiguous and qualitative relationships that dominate our day-to-day financial decision-making."

—Alan Greenspan
Former Federal Reserve Chairman

CONTENTS

Preface

This book is meant for more than reading. It should be put to use for the rest of your life. In it I will address many common questions that confound and frustrate people in their financial lives, such as the following:

Why is it so difficult to get out of debt?
What is the best approach to take when negotiating a car purchase?
Should you purchase extended warrantees?
How can women be treated "equally" and still lag behind men on the company pay scale?
What are the conditions necessary to make money gambling?
Why do the rich get richer?

Surprisingly, the answers to these questions originate in financial math and once you understand why you will be able to make the math work for you. But this book goes beyond just being an exposé. Along with general questions like these, this book will also address more specific questions such as these:

Do you have any way of knowing how truthful the lender is when you sign a loan agreement?
Should you take the 0% financing offer or the rebate on a new car purchase?
Can you save money on credit cards by chasing introductory teaser rates?
If you know the monthly payment you can afford on a house or car, what is the highest purchase price you can pay?
How much do you need to save each month to meet your retirement goals?

These are just some of the many questions we encounter in our day-to-day financial decision-making. This book provides the tools you need to answer these questions and others like them. If you are shopping for a car or house, negotiating your salary, deciding on credit card offers, or considering a potential investment, the information I present will allow you to make an informed decision and avoid costly pitfalls. You will be able to do your own financial planning. Just grab a calculator, read one of the examples, fill out one of the worksheets provided in the Appendix, and look up the answer in one of the book's tables.

Along the way to understanding the answers to all these questions we will also gain some behavioral insights, such as the answers to these questions:

What behavior do teachers, corporate accountants and real estate salespeople share?

Why does the average investor do so much worse than the market averages?

Why do different presentations of the same choice affect the decision people make?

The answers to these questions might surprise you but they relate to conflicts between psychological needs and requirements for mathematical truth.

Math is a subject most people prefer to avoid, but the banks, finance companies and retailers are math savvy. They have become creative at mathematical deception, which I define as *making claims that satisfy the conditions for mathematical truth but at the same time are intentionally misleading*. To the mathematically naïve, an exact number or equation carries a prestige that is difficult to challenge. The idea that mathematical claims can be both true and deceptive is difficult to grasp. But a recurring theme throughout this book is that individuals and corporations use meaningless and deceptive mathematical truths to avoid responsibility for intentionally misleading claims and practices.

Since I have studied, taught, and used math my entire life, I see deceptive mathematics every day. I see people misled into making costly choices that could have been avoided. Over the years I've collected examples and included them in this book. Many of these examples are calculations I performed so that I could make informed choices on my own finances. To use this book you need to know how to do arithmetic with a calculator. No other math expertise is needed. I explain the technical terminology—each term, each concept, and its relevance. I have also peppered the book with example stories, many from my own life and many from current events. I hope that you will find this book useful, informative, and entertaining.

—Joseph Ganem
Baltimore, Maryland
June 2006

Deceptive Math

True and False

"The trouble with people is not that they don't know but that they know so much that ain't so."

—Josh Billings
19th century American humorist

This book has a twofold purpose: (1) to serve as a guide for making common personal financial decisions and (2) to expose common mathematical claims related to financial decision-making that are both true and deceptive.

This book is not intended to discuss outright fraud. Embezzlement, skimming, "cooking the books" are not what I consider mathematical deceptions; they are criminal acts that can land their perpetrators in jail. However, the book does give examples of mathematical cues that should alert you to fraud and profiles some fraudulent practices where these cues have appeared.

The art of making statements that are both true and misleading is a legitimate form of expression in our culture. We are bombarded with advertisements every day, and many of them fall into this category. With experience we have learned to see through many of the sales pitches. However, sales pitches framed in mathematical language are often equally creative at being both true and misleading and are much more difficult to see through. Worse, the mathematical parlance often lends many of these claims a false aura of respectability.

Most mathematical deceptions do fall into recurring categories. These are as follows:

• *Re-labeling:* Using a different name that seems nicer than it actually is. Want to advertise an eye-catching low finance rate? Call your finance charges a transaction fee. This will also make comparison-shopping for finance rates next to impossible (unless you read the chapters in this book on loans).

• *Use of counter-intuitive results*: Math is difficult in part because results are not always what our "common sense" would lead us to expect. Presenting people with questions involving measurements, averages, statistics, and probabilities will expose widespread fallacious beliefs. As a result people make wrong and costly decisions on many issues (insurance, investments, public policies, testing practices). Believing something to be true when it is false is even worse than ignorance. You willingly act against your own interests.

• *Carefully chosen framing:* An extensive body of psychological research dating back to the 1950s demonstrates that people respond to identical choices differently depending on how the choices are presented (framed). More people, for example, will respond favorably to a "get two for the price of one" sale than "buy 2 and get 50% off." From a financial point of view, the two propositions are identical, but the first presentation leads people to think they are getting something for free.

•*Ignorance of number size:* A million, a billion, a trillion: a common attitude is that all these numbers are equally large. Not a good attitude when considering investment decisions. Whether you are buying stock or starting your own business, you need some idea of the market size for the product or service being delivered, the cash flow it will generate, and a reasonable estimate of the growth rate. It is easy to fantasize about becoming rich on some new business venture or stock purchase, but often a few simple estimates and calculations will tell you the most likely profit potential before you begin.

This book is divided into four parts. The first part—Daily Deceptions—examines numerical comparisons in a wide variety of contexts. Every day we engage in buying decisions where the sellers bombard us with impressive claims stated in numerical terms. You will learn that many of the numbers thrown at you every day are either deceptive or meaningless. Topics in Part I include deceptive numerical comparisons encountered when shopping, how the presentation of prices affects the outcome of automobile and real estate negotiations, and how averages are used to manipulate and deceive. The use of charts to support quantitative arguments is also examined. I will show how the exact same numerical data can be pictured differently in charts. Two opposing politicians for example, will show charts that look completely different as a way of arguing opposite sides of an issue, but the data shown on the charts will be in complete agreement.

The second part—Income—discusses earning, saving, investing, gambling, and risk-taking. The chapters that discuss earning, saving and investing contain tables and worked examples that are designed for use with the worksheets in Appendix I. The examples illustrate common financial planning scenarios such as negotiating salaries, projecting future income and expenses, planning for retirement, adjusting for inflation and choosing investments. With the aid of a calculator and the worksheets you can adapt the examples to your personal financial situation and have the ability to make informed choices.

In the chapters on gambling and risk-taking, the difference between the two activities is explained. We will learn why gambling should be avoided, but risk-taking is unavoidable because it is inherent in most financial decisions—even "safe" choices have more risk than you might think. Risk-taking exposes conflicts between psychological needs and mathematical requirements for success. Because of the psychology, people are inherently prone to making mathematically bad choices when confronted with decisions that involve risk. Whether choosing an investment or purchasing insurance, it pays to be aware of the psychological needs within all of us—myself included—that result in poor choices and cost us money unnecessarily.

The third part—Loans—contains numerous tables that can be used to answer many common questions that relate to decisions about borrowing money. For many people, debt is unavoidable and debt management a constant struggle. This part of the book has more examples, tables and worksheets than any other part. But I believe that these resources can become a lifetime guide for anyone because the use of borrowed money is so prevalent in our society. The mathematics of debt is highly counterintuitive, and finance companies take full advantage of deceptive math in their constant bombardment of consumers with loan offers. The tables and worksheets in Part III are easy to use and will be valuable to you when making any kind of purchase that involves borrowed money.

Misunderstood math is the subject of part four. This final part of the book will take a scientific excursion. It will teach how a professional scientist, such as myself, uses and interprets numerical information. Then I will contrast the scientific understanding with how numerical data is distorted by the media and describe the misunderstandings that result. Numbers that result from a measurement have several attributes that need to be understood before making any decision based on the numerical data. The attributes of precision and accuracy (Chapter 11), size (Chapter 12) and confidence (Chapter 13) are explained. People have naïve notions of numerical precision and accuracy, number size, and how probability and statistics relate to the degree of confidence in a measurement. Whether voting, reading the newspaper, deciding on workplace policies, or making a medical decision, costly bad decisions are often the result of knowing a little about something, but not actually understanding the math. I will examine and clarify common misunderstandings and relate them to some current events.

Throughout this book, real-life examples for each subject are discussed. Many of these examples come from my own personal experiences, where I discovered that much of the marketing that uses numbers presents false choices, rigged against the consumer. Like flipping a two-headed quarter, you pay no matter which side the coin lands on because you are unaware that the coin has no tail. My goal is show how mathematical principles are used to manipulate the economic choices we make every day, whether we are aware of them or not. Of course, it pays to be aware.

Part I

Daily Deceptions

CHAPTER ONE

Shopping

Meaningless Comparisons

"What if I told you, that for $1000, you could own this building and everything in it?"

—Salesman for a "Buyer's Club"

Early in my adult life, before I had the savvy to avoid situations where high-pressure sales tactics are used, my wife and I answered a call to receive a "free" gift from a "buyer's club." The club had just opened a brand new facility in the St. Louis area, where we lived at the time; and through the offer of "gifts," prospective members were enticed to visit and learn about their services.

My wife and I arrived at our appointed time; and before we could take our "gift," a salesperson had to take us on a tour of the facility and tell us about their services. Married couples had to be present together. I learned from this experience to *never* talk with a salesperson that insists that a married couple *must* be present together. That condition *always* means that a decision will be demanded immediately after hearing the sales pitch. The last thing a high-pressure salesperson wants to hear is "Sounds good but I need to talk it over with my wife/husband and get back to you." A calm talk with a spouse that is completely free of emotional manipulation from the salesperson will inevitably doom the sale.

The salesman who greeted us had an immediate financial proposition stated in clear mathematical terms. As we walked into a large showroom filled with expensive-looking merchandise, he said, "What if I told you, that for $1000, you could own this building and everything in it? Would you accept?"

"Well, yes."

"Let me show you how that will come true."

Of course he did not offer us the whole building and everything in it for $1000. Instead he led us through an impressive amount of arithmetic to convince us that joining his buyer's club would be a mathematically equivalent financial proposition.

He began by showing the merchandise on display. Next to each item was a newspaper advertisement that showed the price of the same item on sale at another store. Next to the display, in big bold letters, was the price available to members of their Buyer's Club. In all cases the members' price was less than half the advertised sale price.

We moved to his office where he then explained that over the course of our lifetime we would "save" over $200,000 by purchasing everything that we would ever need for furniture, kitchenware, computers, televisions, electronics: in summary, everything you can image buying, including automobiles, through the club. All this savings would be available to us for a lifetime membership fee of $1000.

The offer did include restrictions. When I asked the price of some items I actually wanted to buy, not just those on the display floor, he explained that prices are kept in complete secrecy. You had to be a member to view their catalogs. All items must be ordered through catalogs, paid for in advance, and delivery charges would be applied. Secrecy was necessary because if their prices became public knowledge, every retail store in St. Louis would go out of business. In fact to keep local stores in business, laws had been passed to restrict the people to whom they could offer memberships and the time period of the offer. You had to be "nominated" to join and there were no second chances. If we left without joining, we would never be invited again. He also said, "The price to join is reduced if you nominate friends and relatives; and remember, this is a lifetime membership. We can offer these fantastic discounts because we only profit from membership fees, *not from merchandise sales."*

At that moment I realized this was a scam and asked to leave. In an instant our salesman changed from Dr. Jekyll to Mr. Hyde. He ranted about our wasting his time and said *he* would have to personally pay his boss money because *we* wouldn't take his offer. He expressed fury over my inability to understand the "lifetime" of savings, totaling hundreds of thousands of dollars that we would forfeit for lack of a measly $1000 investment. Etched in his facial expression was utter contempt for my short-sighted stupidity.

We accepted our "gift"—an inexpensive copper pot—and hastily left. Six months later I saw a report on the local television news. The State Attorney General's office had launched an investigation into this buyer's club. It had mysteriously closed, and its employees and management had vanished. Not only had the members been deprived of their "lifetime" of savings; many had paid in full for merchandise listed in the club catalogs that had never been delivered.

The experience reminded me of a story told by Whitey Herzog, who at the time (1986) managed the St. Louis Cardinals baseball team. The Cardinal's owner, Gussie Busch, a man in frail health and well into his 80s, offered Herzog a "lifetime" appointment as manager. Herzog's response was "Whose lifetime are we talking about?"

Elements of Deceptive Math

I am certain that many adults have experienced similar high-pressure sales tactics and can recount similar stories. But, my reason for re-telling this experience is not because of the high-pressure sales tactics. My interest is the sales pitch. I tell this story to open my discussion because this Buyer's Club has a sales pitch with some of the mathematically deceptive elements that will be discussed in the chapters that follow.

For example, the sales pitch ignores the consequences of "saturation," an effect that will be discussed in greater detail in Chapters 3 and 5. The effect of saturation means that a "lifetime" of savings cannot be funded entirely by membership fees. I knew that as soon as the St. Louis market for new members "saturated" —meaning no more people available to purchase memberships —no more money would be made by this company. The market must saturate because St. Louis, although a large metropolitan area, has a finite number of people. Of course the salesman and all the other people running this club do not work for free. Once all available people have been sold memberships, they will move on to look for another income source.

The business model described in the sales pitch also fails the "reasonability test" that I will describe in Chapter 3. Their business is not reasonable because it is essentially a "pyramid scheme." In a pyramid scheme, goods and services are not profitably sold. The business profits solely by recruiting additional partners who contribute money. It is clear, that like a pyramid scheme, this Buyer's Club will need a constant influx of new members to hold off financial collapse. They have a good financial reason for wanting you to "nominate" your friends and relatives. Legitimate buyer's clubs, such as Sam's Club, or B. J. Wholesale, charge nominal membership fees; the bulk of their income comes from selling the merchandise.

The sales pitch also violates the "mediocrity assumption" that I will state in Chapter 3. There is no reason to believe that I am special in a way that justifies an extraordinary one-time offer. There is no reason to believe that my $1000 won't be accepted if I return a few days later. Clearly his allusion to "laws" being in place to protect other retailers is complete nonsense.

However, I tell this story to open my discussion on shopping because the salesman's use of price comparisons in his presentation is common. When confronted with a decision, consumers routinely make numerical comparisons, not only of prices, but also of product specifications. Salespeople have a variety of techniques for "framing" comparisons so that their product appears favorable. Usually the "frame," which refers to the context provided for the comparison, is mathematically true, but it is either completely meaningless or it cleverly disguises important facts. For example, the salesman in this incident showed heavily marked-down prices on a *few* selected items to imply that *all* items were heavily marked down. When questioned further he had elaborate nonsensical reasons for not showing me the price of all the items. His comparison might be impressive, but without all the facts it doesn't mean anything. It will be a theme in this chapter and throughout the entire book that numbers alone are meaningless. A number must have a context and only when that context is properly understood can a correct decision be made.

Comparison Shopping

Comparison of a "sale price" to a "list price" is the most common retail-marketing ploy. Visit enough stores to check prices of equivalent items, and it becomes apparent that the "sale price" is in fact the "market price." Items are rarely sold at their "list price" so the "savings" are an illusion. The going price that an item sells for is its "market price," and no single retailer can do much to alter or manipulate market prices. A "list price" is anything the retailer says, and the resulting "savings" anything their marketing department wants to claim.

While usually obvious, the list price deception does have subtler forms. Many companies use rebates to market their products. If a consumer sees two competing items, one at $25 and the other at $30 with a $5 rebate, his or her perception is that the $30 item is superior, even though the actual cost of the items is the same. Usually though, if the consumer purchases the $30 item, it will cost $30 because the $5 rebate becomes less attractive once the item is purchased and the detailed instructions to receive the rebate are examined. Many people give up when rebate forms have to be completed, bar codes cut out and receipts photocopied. The rebate benefits the company in two ways. It enhances the perceived value of the product, and the rebate money usually stays in the company's pocket.

Other variations of the "list price" scam are the agreements between healthcare providers and insurance companies. Healthcare providers routinely bill insurance companies for amounts several times what they intend to collect. A 45-minute outpatient surgery for my son resulted in bills totaling $19,887. Of this total, my insurance company paid $3228, I paid $1077, and the remaining $15,582 was a "reduction in billed charges," required by the insurance company's contract with the provider.

The scary part of healthcare is that the fictitious billing becomes real if you are uninsured. A March 5, 2006 broadcast on the CBS news show *60 Minutes* profiled uninsured hospital patients who were billed four to five times the amount paid by insurance companies for the same treatments. A spokesman for the hospital industry hid behind a mathematical deceptive argument. In an interview, she insisted repeatedly that all patients were "charged" the same amount. That was true. The difference was that for the insured patients the hospitals "accepted payments" from insurance companies for a small fraction (20-25% in some cases) of the amount charged. Uninsured patients were told the charges were "non-negotiable" and had their accounts referred to collection agencies.

Use of large numbers

Large numbers are always more attention-getting than small numbers. Here are some examples:

• America Online distributed promotional packages that advertised 1025 free hours of Internet time. It appeared that all the Internet surfing you could possibly imagine doing was free. However, read the fine print, and find out that those 1025 hours must be used within 45 days. There are a total of 1080 hours in 45 days. Unless you planned on doing nothing but using the Internet for 45 consecutive days, the 1025 hours is a meaningless number. What the promotion actually means is that you are given a 45-day free trial period. However, 45 is a much smaller number than 1025 and therefore not nearly as impressive on a brochure.

•During the 2002 tax season, H&R Block ran commercials promoting their tax preparation services. According to their sales pitch, Americans overpaid their taxes by $311 million dollars the year before. That is an impressive amount of money. But, consider that number in context. According to the IRS Website (www.irs.gov) 129,783,221 individual tax returns were filed for Fiscal-Year 2001. If H&R Block's claim of $311 million in overpaid taxes is true, that works out to an average of $2.40 per tax return. No commercial would advertise the $2.40 per return amount because H&R Block charges far more than that for preparing a single return.

•Publishers' Clearing House markets its sweepstakes so heavily that the phrase "prize patrol" has national recognition. But does the winner become an instant millionaire? According to their rules, the winner of the "$10 million super prize" receives $500,000 the first year, $250,000 every year thereafter, until the 30th year when a final payment of $2,500,000 is made. That's right; the winner must wait 30 years before receiving a check that is in excess of $1 million. The rules also stated that the winner of the Publishers' Clearing House $1 million prize receives $25,000 per year over 40 years. It is true the winner receives $1 million, but most of us would not use the term "millionaire" to refer to someone with a $25,000 annual income.

•Consider a common food label—"90% Fat-Free." The last two words will be in big bold letters and notice that 90 is a big percentage. Of course a mathematically equivalent statement is "10% of this product is fat." Doesn't sound as "fat free" anymore, does it, especially when considering that the daily recommended value for fat intake is 60 grams? Consuming 600 grams of food (about 1.3 pounds) that is "90% fat-free" will meet your daily recommendation for fat consumption. It is easy to exceed 60 grams of fat intake during a day while dining on foods that are 90% fat-free.

Dilbert: © Scott Adams/Dist. by United Feature Syndicate, Inc.

The rule of one.

To make the mathematical claim that a set includes certain items only requires the inclusion of *one* item. Here are some examples:

•A department store advertises a sale that claims everything in the store is 5% to 90% off. Translation: all items in the store are 5% off. But a few packages of ballpoint pens sold in a discount bin in office supplies are marked down 90%.

•Car dealerships often advertise used car prices from $1000 to $10,000. Translation: an old clunker with a book value of $300 is on "sale" for $1000. All other used cars start at $9999.

•A homebuilder places a large sign on a former cornfield that states "New Single Family Homes from the $190s." Translation: for $199,000 you get a frame, walls and a roof. Extras such as floors, appliances, and a driveway come at an additional cost.

Selective sample size

Hiding price and nutritional discrepancies by clever packaging is commonly used to sell foods.

On a trip to the grocery store to buy coffee, I was confronted with the choice of Maxwell House Original Blend or Maxwell House Master Blend. Each came in identically sized three-pound cans and sold for $6.79. But a closer inspection revealed that not only did the cans not contain three pounds, the amount under three pounds varied. The can of Original Blend had 2 pounds 7 ounces (39 ounces total); the can of Master Blend had 2 pounds 2.5 ounces (34.5 ounces total). On a per pound basis, the Master Blend sells for $3.15 and the Original for $2.79.

The competing brand of Folgers was no better in its packaging. On the same shelf, two identically sized packages of Folgers' French Roast and Columbian, each sold for $3.29. But the French Roast had 11 ounces compared to 12 ounces for the Columbian. One ounce is too small a weight difference to notice when you pick up the packages, so you think these are identically priced. In fact the Columbian was being sold for $4.39 per pound, and the French Roast $4.79 per pound.

Nutritional labeling also makes use of selective sample size combined with misleading imagery to fool consumers into thinking certain foods are healthy, when in fact, they are not. In the same aisle as the coffee I found 12-ounce cans of Classic Coke. The nutritional label lists 140 calories and 39 grams of sugar per serving. The ingredients list water and high fructose corn syrup as the two main ingredients, followed by caramel coloring, phosphoric acid, natural flavors, and caffeine. No surprises here: Coke has never been considered a healthy drink. On a neighboring shelf sat one-pint bottles of Minute Maid apple-cranberry-raspberry juice. The Minute Maid brand, which is owned by Coca Cola Inc., features images of fresh fruits. A check of the nutritional label shows 120 calories and 31 grams of sugar per serving. Obviously a healthier choice compared to Coke? Think again, and look more carefully at the label. The serving size for the juice is 8 ounces. The one-pint bottle actually has 15.4 ounces (0.6 ounce less than one pint) so the serving size per container is listed as "about 2." If you drink 12 ounces of the juice, you will consume 180 calories and 46.5 grams of sugar. On a per ounce basis, the juice contains 28% more calories and 19% more sugar than the Coke. If you drink the entire bottle of juice you will consume 231 calories and 60 grams of sugar, nearly twice the calories and sugar that a 12-ounce can of Coke contains.

How can fruit juice be so caloric? Don't nutritionists tell us to eat lots of fruits? The ingredients on the fruit juice list water and high fructose corn syrup, first and second, followed by "less than 1% each" of apple, cranberry, and raspberry juices. The phrase "less than 1%" is a curious mathematical expression. The label does not say "minimum of 1%," which would assure us of at least 1% fruit juice. If we lumped the small amounts of fruit juices in this drink together under the heading "natural flavors," the ingredient list becomes almost identical to one for Classic Coke. All that would be missing to make it Coke would be the nutrient-free chemicals—caramel coloring, phosphoric acid, and caffeine. In other words, from a nutritional standpoint, the only substantive difference between drinking Classic Coke and Minute Maid apple-cranberry-raspberry juice, is that the juice has 28% more calories per ounce, almost all of it from additional sugar.

Comparison to an extreme

If you want a bad product to look good, find an even worse product to compare it to.

An example of this technique was an advertising campaign for Kentucky Fried Chicken (KFC) in the fall of 2003 that promoted their original recipe fried chicken as a health food. In one of the TV commercials, a woman arrives home and says to her male partner, "Remember how we talked about eating better? Well it starts today." She brings out a bucket of KFC while an announcer explains that two Original Recipe chicken breasts have less fat than a Whopper.

A check of company Websites shows that the announcer's statement is mathematically true. A single chicken breast has 19 grams of fat, which means two breasts have 38 grams of fat compared to 43 grams of fat for a Burger King Whopper. The two breasts also have less saturated fat, 12 grams compared to 13 grams for a Whopper. What isn't mentioned is that the 38 grams of fat is 58% of the daily recommended fat intake. Also not mentioned is that the two KFC chicken breasts have 760 calories compared to 710 for a Whopper, 290 mg of cholesterol compared to 85 mg for a Whopper, and 2300 mg of sodium compared to 980 mg for a Whopper.

The mathematical truths about the fat content notwithstanding, the idea of KFC marketed as health food was so absurd that even the Federal Trade Commission stepped in with a civil subpoena that asked the fast-food chain to explain and justify its claims. Shortly afterwards KFC pulled the ads from television.

Anchoring Effects

Psychologists have extensively documented a behavioral effect known as "anchoring." When a person is asked to make a numerical estimate, he or she usually begins with a "starting value" and then "adjusts" that value to arrive at a final estimate. Anchoring is a tendency for the final estimate to be biased towards the starting value. The final estimate is determined more by the starting value than any other factor.

Psychologists Tversky and Kahneman first described anchoring. In one of their experiments, a group of students was given five seconds to estimate the value of 8 x 7 x 6 x 5 x 4 x 3 x 2 x 1. The median estimate for the group was 2250. A second group of students were asked to estimate 1 x 2 x 3 x 4 x 5 x 6 x 7 x 8. Reversing the sequence moved the median estimate downwards to 512. Because people read from left to right, 8 x 7 or 56 becomes the "anchor" for the first sequence. The starting point of 1 x 2 x 3 or 6 becomes the anchor for the second sequence. Final estimates are strongly shifted towards the anchor. As a result, *the order of presentation determines the estimate*.

Of particular fascination in this experiment is that both groups of students were anchored downward. Because all the numbers in the sequence are small numbers, it is difficult for anyone to believe that the correct answer is 40,320.

The multiplication of 8 x 7 x 6 x 5 x 4 x 3 x 2 x 1 is an obscure arithmetic problem; but place dollar signs in front of numbers and anchoring effects become costly. Consider the results of another psychological study on anchoring that dealt with the estimated values of homes provided by professional real estate agents.* Psychologists Northcraft and Neale showed dozens of real estate agents a house that had been previously appraised for $135,000. Without telling him or her the appraised value, each agent was asked to make his or her own appraisal. The agents were given twenty minutes to inspect the property and provided with a 10-page packet of information the contained all the information normally used to appraise residential property, including listings for other properties being sold in the neighborhood. Only one piece of information varied in the packet given to each agent — the listing price of the house.

When the listing price was $119,900, the average appraised value was $114,204. For listing price of $129,900 the average appraised value was $126,772. For a listing price of $139,900 the average appraised value was $125,041; and for a listing price of $149,900 the average appraised value was $128,754. By varying only one piece of information in a 10-page packet (the listing price), the average appraised valued shifted by more than 10%, which for this home amounted to more than $14,000. But only 10% of the agents mentioned listing price as one of their top three considerations in appraising the home. It is interesting that anchoring effects influence experts without their being either aware of or, at the very least, willing to admit the possibility. Also note that whatever listing price was provided, the real estate agents always considered it too high.

The Anchoring Effect

There is a strong tendency for a person to use as a
starting value the first number to which he or she is
exposed. Estimates are biased towards that first number.

---

*G. B. Northcraft and M. A. Neale, "Experts, amateurs, and real estate: An anchoring and adjustment perspective on property pricing decisions," *Organizational Behavior and Human Decision Processes,* vol. 39 (1987) pp.84-97

Because anchoring is so prevalent and so well documented, savvy salespeople and marketers are deliberate and thoughtful in the order that prices are presented. Sales presentations are rarely accidental in their ordering. But customers are often unaware of the extent to which they are being manipulated by the order.

Go on an outing with a real estate agent. Invariably, the first homes you are shown are at the top of your price range and not exactly the kind of home you want. Affordable homes that are closer to your needs are shown last. The ordering might appear inefficient. Why not start with homes you are most likely to buy and skip the others? But, by showing overpriced homes first, the high prices become your anchor. Your frame of mind while viewing the homes depends on the order in which they are shown. If the home you are most likely to buy is shown first, you lose interest when higher priced, less desirable homes are shown afterwards. Instead you think about a possible offer on the home you want. But when high-priced, less desired homes are shown first, discouragement sets in. Finally when the home you are more likely to buy is shown you feel relief because it appears to be a bargain. You can have what you want and have it for less money. Of course, "less" is always a relative term. The home you want to buy might still be overpriced, but it is so much less compared to your anchor that you are happy to pay the price. A willingness to negotiate vanishes.

In an outing with a real estate agent, he or she is usually allowed to select the homes presented and the order of presentation. Be aware of the context the agent creates with the presentation. Ask yourself how you would have reacted had the homes been shown in a different order. Do some independent research to find out what homes you were not shown.

Automobile ads also draw buyers in with an anchor. A recent ad for pickup trucks in my local paper has a sale price of $10,688 in large bold print alongside even larger sized print that states $199 per month. But the fine print in this ad states that the "sales" price includes $3000 cash or trade in from the customer. In other words, this vehicle sells for $13,688. Using the logic of this ad a sale price of $1 could be advertised provided the customer supplied $13,687 in cash. Why construct an ad based on such silly logic? The reason is that the $199 figure that the reader sees first becomes an anchor. For less than $200 per month, you can have a brand new pickup truck. According to the fine print the $199 per month is based on a 4.65% APR loan for 60 months. Financing $13,688 at the same 4.65% interest rate for 60 months results in payments of $256 per month. Readers are less likely to be drawn in to read the ad if the big bold number is $256. Again, because people read left to right, the number $199 appears almost $100 less than $256. Of course if the ad succeeds in bringing in a customer who has no cash, the salesperson will argue that for "only $50 more per month" the truck is theirs.

The Negotiation Principle

Because of anchoring, the starting point in a negotiation biases the outcome. Most negotiations begin with a starting point. A salary negotiation begins with your previous salary, even if you worked for a different employer. A negotiation for a real estate or automobile purchase begins with the seller's asking price.

The Negotiation Principle

Your strategy in any negotiation should be
to control the starting point.

If the starting point is far from where you want finish, suggest a different starting point. If your salary at your previous job is much lower than you want, don't bring it up. Suggest a salary based on what people in similar jobs do and have research to back your position. Don't automatically knock 10% off the asking price for a house for your first offer. Know the market and start with a reasonable price for a comparable piece of property. If you buy a used car, don't bargain down from the asking price. Find out the "book value," which is the cash that you would get from an insurance settlement if you totaled the car. Make the dealer justify why the price should be higher than the book value. When buying a new car, do not bargain down from the asking price, bargain up from the dealer invoice price. Book values and dealer invoice prices for almost all makes and models of automobiles are available over the Internet. See the Websites listed at the end of this chapter.

Also, learn to be creative in putting time pressure, so often used against the buyer, back on the seller. The smoothest negotiation I ever had for a car was the time I showed up on a Friday night armed with all my Internet research, one half-hour before closing. They dropped the whole salesman/sales manager charade and accepted my offer within 10 minutes. I was prepared to spend all night, but it was the end of the week and they wanted to go home.

Car buying and the dealer invoice deception

Even if you succeed in starting at the "dealer invoice" price when negotiating an automobile purchase, be aware that the "dealer invoice" is itself a mathematical deception. One common negotiating ploy used by car salesmen is to produce the "dealer invoice" and then ask what you think is a "fair" mark-up.

I find it humorous that dealers will ask customers how to run their business. How would a customer be able to judge fairness when no information is provided on their overhead and sales commissions? The point of the ploy is to convince you that the dealer invoice is the cost to them for the car and to make money they must sell the car for more than the invoice.

Actually the "dealer invoice" is not the true cost to the dealer of the car. Car dealers have agreements with manufacturers known as "Dealer Holdback." The manufacturer credits to the dealer's account a specific percentage of the price of each car sold. Usually it is 2-3% of the sticker price, MSRP (Manufacturer's Suggested Retail Price), not the invoice price which is usually 10-20% lower than the MSRP. If the MSRP on a car is $20,000 and the dealer is offering to sell it for $500 over a $17,000 invoice price, there might be 3% of $20,000 or $600 that the dealer pockets without telling you.

Also, manufacturers routinely provide bonuses in the form of cash, vacations, or additional cars to sell at no cost, if specified sales goals are met. If a salesman is giving the hard sell on a particular make and model, odds are the dealer gets a bonus from the manufacturer if enough of that model is sold. All of the complicated financial agreements between the manufacturer and dealer allow the continuation of the "dealer invoice" charade because buyers are never informed of all the manufacturer incentives that provide money above the invoice price.

Summary

While the logic behind price and product comparisons provided by salespeople and marketers is often obvious nonsense, the psychological effects are real. People do become anchored to the numbers first provided to them. The only way to protect yourself from being manipulated by someone else's anchor is to do your own research and have all the facts before making a purchase or entering a negotiation. Know ahead of time what a reasonable outcome should be and use that number as your anchor.

Advertising the Nonexistent

A current trend in advertising is to give prominent placement to what the product does *not* contain. Here are some examples:

•Many high fat foods have the words "cholesterol free" in bold letters on the label. Actually, cholesterol is only found in meat and dairy products. Almost all snack foods are cooked in vegetable-based oils. Unless meat or diary is an essential part of the product—real cheese, real butter, real eggs, or real meat—cholesterol is absent.

•The Atkins Diet craze swept through the food business in 2003. Suddenly restaurant menus had "low-carb" labels alongside their high fat, high cholesterol, high calorie meat dishes.

•Soft drinks without caffeine have that fact prominently displayed on the label. Actually, commercial soft drinks, which consist of carbonated water, corn syrup, and chemical flavors, must have caffeine added for it to be in the drink. But Coca-Cola chooses to market Coke and Caffeine-free Coke rather than Coke and Caffeinated Coke.

•Bottled water is sold as non-carbonated, low in sodium, and purified. Come to think of it, water is also low-carb, fat-free, cholesterol-free, caffeine-free and calorie-free. Water is the perfect food product to market because it has no nutritional value at all. As a result of all the marketing, people are willing to pay more for a gallon of bottled water than they are for a gallon of gasoline, even though most people have access to drinking water for free.

Using the above logic, I thought about marketing this book with large lettering on the cover stating "Not a TV Program." But, I decided to leave it to someone else to begin that trend.

Chapter 1 Resources

Scott Plous, *The Psychology of Judgment and Decision Making* (New York, NY: McGraw-Hill, 1993), provides a readable and entertaining account of how mathematical framing influences the decisions people make. Plous provides a quiz at the beginning of the book so that readers can test for their own misconceptions and biases before they are explained. He then summarizes the results of numerous psychological studies.

Daniel Kahneman, Paul Slovic, Amos Tversky, (Editors), *Judgment Under Uncertainty: Heuristics and Bias* (Cambridge: Cambridge University Press, 1982) is a collection of landmark papers from 39 different contributors on the psychology of human decision-making under conditions of risk and uncertainty. Kahneman is a psychologist who shared the 2002 Nobel Prize in Economics that according to the citation was "for having integrated insights from psychological research into economic science, especially concerning human judgment and decision-making under uncertainty."

For useful Websites for car buying and pricing, as well as tips on negotiating see:

http://www.carprice.com—Pace Buyer's Guides

http://www.kbb.com—Kelly Blue Book

http://www.edmunds.com—Edmunds Car guides

CHAPTER TWO

Averaging

Numbers In Place of Judgment

"And that's the news from Lake Woebegon, where all the women are strong, the men are good looking, and the children are all above average."

—Garrison Keillor
From his Prairie Home Companion weekly radio show

All of us want to have children who are above average, who we support with pay that is above average, from jobs where our performance is judged above average. Of course the humor in Keillor's line is that the word "average," as it is generally understood, represents the middle. There must be people below average for people to be above average. Mathematically, it is impossible for everyone to be "above average."

Or is it impossible? The mathematics of averages is prone to more manipulation than you might think. People who provide averages often have strong financial incentives to manipulate the numbers. From education, to investing, from home buying to salary negotiations, the use of "average values" is pervasive and persuasive when decisions are made. Enormous sums of money change hands because of average test scores for schools, earnings per share reports on companies, and home appraisals based on average neighborhood sale prices. In this chapter we will examine both the methods and incentives for manipulating averages. The deceptive use of averages causes financial decisions to be driven by what I call the "numerical outcome principle," rather than good judgment.

A Class Where All the Children Are Above Average

I teach college; and at the end of each semester, I am faced with the same problem that all college faculty throughout the country face. On one hand, I have a class full of students who each insist that their work is above average and want a grade that reflects their superior performance. On the other hand, there are administrators trying to combat "grade inflation," who threaten to sanction faculty members who are too easy with grades. From the faculty member's viewpoint, it is not an either/or choice on which constituency to please. Students unhappy with their grade will result in administrators who are unhappy with the faculty member. The choice is more like the proverbial one between "a rock and a hard place." Most faculty members, myself included, would rather just teach and not have to grade at all. However, grading is part of the job description, and our own performance evaluations will suffer if we do not grade in an appropriate manner.

There is a mathematical solution to the grading conundrum. If I wanted to be mathematically deceptive, I could create a situation where all the students are above average. The solution is particularly simple in my case because I teach physics. Each of my students takes a four-credit lecture course along with a one-credit laboratory course from me. Each course receives a separate grade. The solution to my problem would be to grade the laboratory especially hard and give all the students Cs. In the lecture course I could be especially easy and give all the students As. I could then report to administrators and students, that my average grade is a B. However, for any individual student who came to question me on their grades, I could point out that their Grade Point Average from my two courses is 3.6 (nearly an A- average), which is far above my average grade. All of my students would be well above average.

Two parts to an average

How is this bit of mathematical deception possible? Each time an average is computed two choices must be made. (1) What to include in the average—the sample. (2) How much each object in the sample counts toward the final result—the weighting factors. An average is not a precisely defined mathematical result. Human judgment must enter in at the beginning of the calculation when the sample and weighting factors are chosen.

At colleges, for the purposes of computing averages, letter grades are assigned numerical values. The traditional point scale is as follows: A=4.0, B=3.0, C=2.0, D=1.0, F=0.0. If there are 10 students and each receive an A and a C, the average grade is the sum of all the points (4.0 x 10) + (2.0 x 10), or 60, divided by the total number of grades (20), resulting in 3.0, which is an average grade of B.

In the above calculation, all the grades are "weighted" equally. However, equal weighting is not the method the Records Office uses to compute the "Grade Point Averages" (GPAs) that are reported on student transcripts. For a GPA calculation, each grade is multiplied by the number of credit hours for the course it represents. A student who received an A in a four-credit course and a C in a one-credit course, has a GPA that is (4.0 x 4) + (2.0 x 1) = 18, divided by the total number of credit hours (5), resulting in a GPA of 3.6. Each student will have a Grade Point Average that is higher than the average grade.

So what is the correct way of computing an average? There is no correct way of performing an average. *Each time an average is computed, a choice must be made for the weighting factors.* For computing GPA's the weighting factors are the credit hours. You might argue that no weighting factors were used in computing the average grade and therefore it is a more honest calculation. But weighting factors were used. When all grades are weighted equally, the weighting factors are all effectively equal to 1; and that is a choice.

Meaningful Averages

A better question to ask when confronted with a number that represents an average is the following: Is the averaging method meaningful? "Meaningful" is of course a concept without a mathematical definition. What constitutes "meaning" is open to human judgment. Colleges have decided that it is more meaningful to weight each grade a student receives with the number of credit hours, because that more accurately reflects student effort and achievement. The reasoning is that it takes more work to earn an A in a four-credit course than it does to earn an A in a one-credit course.

Likewise, individual professors must decide the weight to give each individual assignment when the final grade for a course is computed. Usually the weighting factors are specified at the beginning of the course—homework is 30%, the final exam is 30%, each quiz is 5%, etc. A professor who weights all grades equally, thereby attaching the three-hour final exam the same importance as a 10-minute quiz, is likely to generate howls of protests from students. The students will argue, and rightly so, that weighting every grade equally will not produce a final grade for the course that accurately reflects their work. In other words, their final "average" will not be meaningful.

Meaningful samples and meaningful weights

What constitutes a meaningful average is not always clear. Consider another example from academia. You are selecting a college and ask, on average, what percent of the teaching is done by full-time faculty members, as opposed to part-time faculty and graduate students. Most colleges have a two-tiered system for hiring teachers. There are tenured and tenure-track professors who typically hold doctorate degrees in their field of expertise and often spend most of their career teaching at a single college. Also hired are temporary teachers, usually graduate students or professional workers who teach part-time. The part-time instructors come and go as normal fluctuations in student enrollment dictate. Obviously colleges prefer to report as high a number as possible for the fraction of teaching on average, that is performed by full-time professors. Prospective students are not eager to pay thousands of dollars in tuition, if first-year graduate students teach all of their courses.

However, before an average is computed the percent of teaching performed by full-time faculty must be defined. Consider a computation for a hypothetical department with the schedule of courses shown in Table 2.1. What is the fraction of teaching performed by full-time instructors for this schedule? At first glance you might answer 70% because 7 out of the 10 course sections have a full-time instructor. However, the school might choose to limit the sample to only undergraduate courses and argue that only statistics related to undergraduate teaching are meaningful to prospective students. In that case the fraction is 6 out of the 8 undergraduate courses, or 75%. But how many undergraduate students have a full-time instructor? Of the 245

Table 2.1: Hypothetical course offerings for an academic department at a college. The course number, title, credit hours and enrollments are listed. The last column indicates whether the instructor is full or part time.

Course offerings

Course	Level	Credits	Enrollment	Instructor
101.01	Introductory Studies	4	50	Full-time
101.02	Introductory Studies	4	50	Full-time
150.01	Laboratory Experience	1	50	Part-time
150.02	Laboratory Experience	1	50	Part-time
240	Sophomore Studies I	4	15	Full-time
280	Sophomore Studies II	4	15	Full-time
350	Junior Studies	4	10	Full-time
420	Senior Project	4	5	Full-time
501	Graduate Studies I	3	10	Part-time
650	Graduate Research	3	2	Full-time

Observation: Most students take 100-level courses but most courses are at the 200-level or above.

students enrolled in undergraduate courses, only 145 (59%) have full-time instructors. For how many undergraduate credit hours are full-time instructors responsible? In this case 24 out of 26 (92%) of the credits offered are from full-time teachers.

So the answer to the question posed is heavily dependent on the both sample and the weighting factor chosen. If the sample is restricted to undergraduate courses, the answer is 59% if the students are weighted equally, 75% if the courses are weighted equally, and 91% if the credits are weighted equally.

The Numerical Outcome Principle

So what is the correct formula for calculating full-time teaching coverage? There is actually no absolutely "correct" method for doing this calculation. But if for some reason the issue of full-time teaching coverage becomes newsworthy, you can be assured that two events will happen. (1) Some policy-making group—either the administration, a campus committee, the board of trustees, or an accrediting body—will decide on an exact quantitative formula for determining the answer. (2) Thereafter, department chairs will arrange course schedules to make the number determined by the formula as high as possible.

If it is decided that students should be given equal weighting in calculating full-time teaching, part-time instructors will only teach thinly populated advanced courses. The heavily populated introductory courses and laboratories will always have full-time instructors. Is it a desirable outcome to have part-time instructors teach the most advanced courses? Some years it might be, some years it may not be, but the desirability of the outcome will no longer be an issue. What will matter is the number.

So far, a relatively obscure issue in academia—full-time teaching coverage—has been used to illustrate the multiple options for computing averages and the choices that must be made. While the example might be obscure, the behavior it illustrates is universal. I will now state a general principle on behavior and give some not-so-obscure examples.

The Numerical Outcome Principle

Once *a number* is used to judge *outcomes*, people will adjust their behavior to *maximize that particular number*. The *actual* outcome no longer matters.

Examples of the "Numerical Outcome Principle"

Standardized admission tests (SATs, MCATs, etc.)

Numerical outcome desired: Colleges and professional schools admit students with the highest test scores.

Goal: Standardized tests are intended to provide all students with an equal opportunity for admission to college or professional school. The makers and marketers of standardized tests claim to provide an objective measure of student ability. In theory, a student from a poor inner city school district and a student from an expensive private prep school, who have identical SAT scores, should have equal abilities to succeed in college.

Desired outcome: A level playing field for admission to college. Standardized tests identify the most able students for admission, who are most likely to succeed, without regard to social and economic background.

Actual outcome: An industry appears that profits through the sale of test preparation services to students. Kaplan, a company that specializes in test preparation courses, offers a full range of preparation services for every test that the ETS (Educational Testing Services) administers. Tuition for Kaplan's SAT preparation courses start at $349 for an online course. Instruction in a classroom for 16 two-and-a-half-hour classes is $899, and the lowest cost package for private home tutoring is $2199 for 10 two-hour classes. Kaplan "guarantees" that a student's score will improve if he or she completes the entire course and all the course materials, although the degree of improvement is not specified. Princeton Review, a competing company for test preparation courses, "guarantees" a minimum 100-point improvement in a student's combined SAT score after completing their $899 course. Both companies (Kaplan and Princeton Review) boast that the combined SAT scores for their students increase more than 100 points as a result of their services.

ETS, the maker of the SAT, admits that test preparation services improve student scores but argues that the effect is small. A document titled "SAT Highlights" available in March 2004 for download from their Website—http://www.ets.org—has the following bizarre statement downplaying the effectiveness of test preparation services:

> *"**Coaching**. Studies that have been carried out in accordance with standard academic procedures indicate that the average effect of coaching on SAT scores is modest. One recent study estimated the effect of coaching on verbal and math scores at 26 points beyond the expected gain of about 30 points. The average gains were greater on the math section (18 points) than on the verbal on (8 points)."*

It would be interesting to know the precise mathematical definition of the phrase "beyond the expected gain" in a statement that claims that gains are "modest." However, the "studies" that were in "accordance with standard academic procedures" are not actually cited.

What the number fails to communicate: There is no way to know from a raw SAT score if the number represents innate ability or intensive prep work.

Question to ask: Is it desirable to have students devoting time, expense, and effort, to beating a test rather than saving for college and completing their current course of studies? Actual success in college depends not only on ability, but many other intangibles such as desire, focus, motivation and maturity. These intangibles defy quantification, but a competent admissions officer is usually able to make an accurate judgment.

Tests of students to evaluate teaching

Numerical outcome: School-wide student test scores in basic subjects should meet agreed upon standards.

Goal: Hold teachers and school administrators accountable for their students' learning outcomes.

Desired outcome: Identify the best teachers for pay raises and promotions. Identify poor teachers for attrition. Determine the best teaching methods. Identify schools that fail to adequately educate their students and work to improve the school.

Actual outcome: The stakes in standardized tests have increased considerably because of the Elementary and Secondary Education Act passed in 2002. Commonly known as the "No Child Left Behind" law, this Federal legislation mandates that *all* schools meet test score targets or face sanctions. Schools can actually have their funding *cut* if test scores and test participation do not meet mandated targets. Widespread differences in student backgrounds, income levels, and geographic locations are not recognized. It is a "one size fits all" test.

The result is that teachers "teach the test" rather than the subject manner. Instead of reading and discussing classic literature, hours are spent practicing word analogies. Math class emphasizes strategies for quickly answering multiple-choice questions rather than learning the reasoning and methods for tackling complex real-world problems. Because standardized tests are by definition "standard," natural differences in talents, interests and abilities that exist among children — differences that should be embraced and celebrated — are instead considered a problem that must be solved.

An article in *The Baltimore Sun* on November 26, 2003 profiled the early retirement of a longtime Anne Arundel County school principal. She retired because of the increasing emphasis on the improvement of test scores, which resulted in the mandated use of identical textbooks and programs in every single school.

In reference to test scores, Diane Lenzi was quoted as saying, "That's the only goal. It just saddens me. I understand you have to have [academic] standards, but children are not widgets. There are some children who blossom with art and music and sports."

Within two years after passage of the Elementary and Secondary Education Act, many states have looked for ways to opt out. While everyone agrees with the goals, the unintended consequences—punishing teachers and schools that fail to meet unrealistic test score targets—does more harm than good. Allowing poor performing students to transfer out of "failing" schools into schools that meet the standards tends to move the low-test score problem somewhere else rather than fix it.

What the number fails to communicate: Natural variations in time and geography of student abilities. The United States is a large and diverse county that includes students with a wide variety of backgrounds and abilities. Year-to-year fluctuations in student performances are also normal and to be expected, no matter how hard the teacher works to improve his or her teaching. All teachers know that the ability of the random 25-50 students assigned to them varies every year. Students are all unique, and good teachers approach students at their unique level. Fluctuations are normal, but long-term trends that result in improvement or a reduction in average test scores will not be noticed if everyone focuses on the target.

Question to ask: Is it desirable to micromanage teaching? A good teacher knows the unique abilities, talents, and weaknesses of each of his or her students. Isn't it better to let teachers teach rather than to have them enforce cookie-cutter curriculum goals dictated by state and federal bureaucrats?

An additional question: Is a test even necessary to identify problem schools? Everyone knows that many large urban school districts have schools that fail to educate their students. Threats of sanctions or actual sanctions are not going to fix problems overnight that have persisted for decades.

Corporate quarterly earnings per share (EPS)

Numerical outcome: Maximize the ratio of the total company earnings divided by the total number of outstanding shares of stock.

Goal: Determine if the company is prosperous and growing and if the share price of the corporation's stock has a fair market value.

Desired outcome: Rational investment decisions. Investors pour money into successful companies that earn money and abandon money-losing companies.

Actual outcome: Because accounting practices are open to interpretation and judgment, pressure is brought to bear to make sure the EPS ratio is always positive, on target, and growing. All kinds of accounting tricks are used—witness Enron, WorldCom, Global Crossing, Waste Management, and Sunbeam. As a result, a whole new phrase has entered the national lexicon—"aggressive accounting."

In his book, *The Number: How the Drive for Quarterly Earnings Corrupted Wall Street and Corporate America,* Alex Berenson, describes the "cult of the number." "The number" is Wall Street parlance for the earnings per share figure that corporations must report to their investors on a quarterly basis. Rather than focus on sound business practices, the "cult of the number" drove investor and corporate decision-making through the 1990s. Because they were focused only on this one number, executives found it in their interest to employ whatever accounting tricks they could find to meet and grow reported quarterly earnings, regardless of whether those earnings were real. Berenson interweaves a history of stock market booms and busts and accounting practices over the last century, to show the origins of the accounting scandals that brought down many well-known corporations in the early 2000s.

What the number fails to communicate: A single number rarely reflects the true health of a company. The integrity of the top executives has a big impact on long-term success, but it is not quantifiable. When a single number is relied upon, investors have no way of knowing if it is real or fake unless they know many other intangibles.

Question to ask: How *objective* is the accounting? In principle, accounting practices should not be "aggressive" or "passive." Accountants should provide an objective, unbiased report on company finances. But often accounting firms are paid by the companies to which they report and have cozy consulting contracts with these same companies. Imagine a judge that allows the assistant district attorney's boss to serve on a jury while he or she argues a case. The Securities and Exchange Commission tolerates the equivalent of that practice for publicly traded companies. Conflicts of interest involving hundreds of millions of dollars are rarely questioned.

Home appraisals

Numerical outcome: The amount of the mortgage should not be more than the market value of the home.

Goal: Insure that lenders and ultimately taxpayers, because many lenders issue government-backed loans, will recover their money if the borrower defaults on the loan.

Desired outcome: All participants in a real estate transaction— buyer, lender and insurer—know the exact amount of risk. If the buyer defaults on the loan or must move and sell the property, the funds raised through the sale should pay off the mortgage.

Actual outcome: Because "appraised values" determine mortgage eligibility, it is possible for colluding realtors, lenders, and appraisers to create deceptive appraisals that hide the true value of the property. One method is through "flip" transactions, where a home is bought and quickly resold to an unsuspecting buyer at a price substantially above market value. A Baltimore realtor, Otto Schmidbauer, who pleaded guilty to charges stemming from his real estate transactions, bought and resold at least 58 single-family homes that involved more than $5 million in fraudulent FHA-backed loans. Schmidbauer colluded with pre-selected lenders, loan officers and appraisers to complete the transactions. One loan officer also entered a guilty plea.

Kenneth M. Donohue, Inspector General for the Department of Housing and Urban Development, in a July 2003 report to Congress, stated that nationwide, 148 Assistant U.S. States Attorneys were investigating 1400 subjects on suspicion of fraud. They had originated more than $1 billion in loans involving 36,000 FHA-insured properties.

An irony of the home-appraisal deception is that often the appraiser does not need to deviate from the accepted methods used to provide honest home appraisals. Standard practice for providing home appraisals is to use "comparables." Appraisers determine the value of the property from the sale prices of similar properties or comparables in the neighborhood that have been recently sold. According to Donohue, the concentration of flipped properties in some neighborhoods became so great that appraisers used the values of inflated properties as comparables for appraising other properties. That means a realtor can initiate a home appraisal scam by purchasing a few properties at inflated prices and asking that the home appraiser use them for comparables. Neither the realtor nor the appraiser has to tell an outright lie.

What the number fails to communicate: Whether the buyer was informed or not. The value of a house is not what an appraiser says, but what someone is willing to pay for it. However, if the buyer has been misled, the amount paid could be much higher than an informed buyer would pay.

Question to ask: What are the realtor's and lender's interests in the proposed deal? Obviously they profit from immediate sales, not the long-term financial health of the buyer. Remember, that if the government backs the loan, the lender is at no risk. Before agreeing to buy real estate, do your own appraisal by going to the county courthouse to search property records on your own. Many counties now have property records online.

Executive salaries

Numerical outcome: Companies strive to be in the 75th percentile for executive compensation.

Goal: Attract the best management by paying top tier salaries to CEOs and top-level executives.

Desired outcome: Because a company pays the best, only the best people will be hired.

Actual outcome: Rapidly escalating salaries for top executives. Because every company moves their compensation package to the top quartile for the previous year, each year the amount of compensation required to be in the top quartile increases substantially. In 1980 the CEO made 40 times what an average worker made. By 2000 the CEO made about 400-550 times what an average worker made. CEO pay has increased so rapidly, there is no longer a connection between pay and performance. Some particularly outrageous examples are as follows:

In 1996, The Disney Company fired Michael Ovitz after just 14 months as company president. His failed tenure triggered a $140 million severance package. Shareholders in Disney filed a lawsuit to recover the money. As of this writing, eight years later, the lawsuit is still pending.

In 2003, John Grasso, head of the New York Stock Exchange, had to resign when the details of his $140 million compensation became public. Grasso was hailed as a hero after he oversaw the reopening of the stock exchanges only six days after the

September 11 attacks devastated New York's financial district. It then became public that in addition to his $140 million regular pay, he received a $5 million *bonus* for restarting the stock exchange in just six days. Tough work I'm sure, but thousands of people who earn much less, put in long hours after September 11 performing heroic, sometimes life-threatening work, for no extra compensation. New York State Attorney General Elliot Spitzer has filed a lawsuit to recover the money. Grasso is unapologetic, has no plans to return the money, and intends to fight the lawsuit.

The above examples are just two of many outrageous executive compensation packages I could mention. An entire chapter is devoted to other examples of excessive executive compensation in David Cay Johnston's book *Perfectly Legal: The Secret Campaign to Rig Our Tax System to Benefit the Super Rich — and Cheat Everybody Else*. The creativity of some of the compensation packages he describes is as impressive as the chutzpah.

What the number fails to communicate: Performance. Executives are paid high salaries for the sole purpose of staying competitive with other executive's high salaries. The quality of management and performance of the company becomes a minor factor in determining executive compensation.

Question to ask: Is any one person's performance worth tens of millions of dollars to a company? No one has divine powers. In 2004, William McDonough, former president of the Federal Reserve Bank of New York, called rising CEO pay "grotesquely immoral" in a speech he gave in Washington, D.C. before the Committee for Economic Development.

Academic Publishing

Numerical outcome: Faculty performance judged based on the number of their publications.

Goal: Hire and promote only the most productive scholars.

Desired outcome: Only scholars with the greatest impact on their field of expertise will receive tenure and financial support for their research.

Actual outcome: A deluge of journal articles that no one has time to read but must at great cost be printed, indexed, and stored. As of 2002, *Ulrich's International Periodical Directory* listed 169,000 periodicals published worldwide. In an article in the March 2004 issue of *Physics Today*, physicist Mohammad Gad-el-Hak questions why his field of research — fluid mechanics — has 250 dedicated English language journals. He asks the rhetorical question: "Not considering the multitude of other languages for a moment, who can keep up with 250 journals?" Gad-el-Hak blames this explosion of paper on the practice of evaluating a person by counting the number of their publications.

As ridiculous as counting papers might appear, that is exactly how many scientists are judged. Jokes about "LPUs" (which stands for "least publishable units") and "publions" (a play on the word photon) are routine. Scientists have learned that maximizing the number of published papers is achieved by minimizing the information content of each one.

What the number fails to communicate: The impact of a person's published work. Simply having a long list of published works is meaningless if no one ever reads the publications, gains further insight from them, changes their own work because of their reading, and/or cites the publications in future published works.

Question to ask: Is churning out reams of published papers doing anything more than filling up library shelf space and padding the length of a resume? To answer that question requires that those doing the evaluating make the effort to actually understand the work. Counting is much easier.

Summary

An insidious trend in our society is the avoidance of responsibility by hiding behind the pseudo-respectability of meaningless averages. This trend has become particularly corrupting in the fields of business and education. A number that represents an average—test score, home price, earnings report—is intended to provide "accountability." More often than not, relying on numbers does the exact opposite. The number either becomes a crutch for people who do not want to be accountable for exercising good judgment or a smokescreen to hide poor judgment or even dishonesty.

Are averages completely meaningless? Should you never look at a number when making a decision? That is not intent of my argument. My argument is that numbers must be placed in context and their origin understood.

When acting as a student, investor, or homebuyer, if you place your faith in a single number provided with no context or explanation, you are setting yourself up to be fooled. When large groups of people make decisions based on a single number, it distorts the market place. Money is wasted that could be spent on something useful. Witness the millions of investors taken in by phony accounting practices in the 1990s. Witness thousands of homebuyers stuck with mortgages they can't pay on property worth far less than they paid. In all cases the numbers looked good on paper. When a person's performance, a company's future, or a product's value is judged solely by a number, it invites mathematically deceptive behavior on the part of the providers of that number.

Numbers are not useless.

A publicly traded corporation should make money and be able to account for how much is made. An in-bound college student with a combined SAT score of 650 is probably not going on to medical school. A teacher who has students who consistently under-perform year after year should have his or her teaching practices closely examined. If a house you are considering for purchase sells for either substantially more or substantially less than other homes in the neighborhood, you should find out why.

It is blind obedience to numbers that is a problem because the real world is dynamic and desired outcomes must adjust to conditions. People are highly adaptable to changing conditions, which means that desired outcomes must have a time dependence. Formulas are static and do not adjust for changing conditions. Instead people adjust their behavior to the formula.

Why I Would Fail Third Grade Math

During American Education Week one year, I visited my daughter's third grade math class. Five minutes into the class I realized that if I were a student, I would have a tough time passing.

The teacher went over problems on a test she had just given. She read a problem out loud.

"If Johnny has $88 and spends $32 on clothes, write a number sentence that shows how much money Johnny has left."

She then wrote on the board the following: $88 - $32 = $56

Then she turned to the class and asked, "Is that a number sentence?"

At this point I realized that I would be in trouble in this class. I had no idea how to answer her question. In my line of work, this kind of expression is called an "equation."

The class came through. In unison they yelled, "Yes."

The teacher wrote a second equation on the board:

$$\begin{array}{r} \$88 \\ - \ \underline{\$32} \\ = \$56 \end{array}$$

"Is this a number sentence?"

Again I had no idea, but the class in unison yelled, "No."

"All of you know what a number sentence is. The directions

on the test were to write a number sentence. But I just looked at the papers, and 10 out of 28 of you wrote this." She pointed to the second, the column method of subtraction on the board. "That is not a number sentence so I had to mark all of those papers wrong."

A child raised his hand. "But I got the right answer."

"I know you got the right answer, but you didn't follow directions. The directions were to write a number sentence."

A second child raised her hand. "But I got the right answer."

"I know you can do the problem. But when we take the state exam in the spring, they won't know that you can do the problem. The graders will want to see a number sentence. It's important that you follow directions because we want to show them what smart students we have at our school."

A third child raised her hand. "But I got the right answer."

"But, I just explained. You didn't write a number sentence. If I mark that correct now, you will do that again in the spring. The people grading the state exam want to see a number sentence. They won't know that you know how to do the problem."

None of the children looked convinced. More hands went up. Exasperated, she cut off further discussion with an old parental standby.

"It's for your own good."

Chapter 2 Resources

Alex Berenson, *The Number: How the Drive for Quarterly Earnings Corrupted Wall Street and Corporate America* (New York, NY: Random House, 2003). Berenson, a financial investigative reporter for the *New York Times*, examines the systemic failures in the accounting practices that brought down Enron and Worldcom and tarnished many other companies in the late 1990s. "The number" is Wall Street parlance for earnings per share, a key ratio that investors have come to base their buy and sell decisions on. His belief is that "as long as investors remain too focused on the number, companies will find ways to manipulate it."

David Cay Johnston, *Perfectly Legal: The Secret Campaign to Rig Our Tax System to Benefit the Super Rich—and Cheat Everybody Else* (New York, NY: Penguin Group, 2003). In Chapter 4 "Big Payday," Johnston provides examples of how executives amass fortunes through investment opportunities that ordinary people can only dream about. Imagine having a your retirement money safely invested in Treasury notes, but when you retire if it turns out that in hindsight, company stock would have been a better investment you are entitled to the higher amount you would have made from investing in company stock. That is one feature of the compensation package the CEO of Westinghouse received.

Darrell Huff, with illustrations by Irving Geis, *How to Lie with Statistics* (New York, NY: W. W. Norton, 1954) is a classic that is still in print. The numbers in the examples are dated, but the techniques for the mathematical deceptions he exposes are still in use today. Chapter 2 "The Well-Chosen Average" has further examples to show how easy it is to manipulate averages.

CHAPTER THREE

Financial Planning

Is it reasonable?

"How many piano tuners are there in Chicago?"

—Enrico Fermi
1938 Nobel Prize winner for physics
Question put to his physics students

In 1994, my wife and I were returning from an entire day spent with our realtor shopping for our first house.

"How many homes do you think he sells in a year?" my wife asked.

"We could calculate that," I replied.

My response intrigued my wife. "How can you arrive at personal information about someone through a calculation?"

I thought out loud as I figured it out. "What do we know about our realtor? He is approximately 25 years old and recently received a bachelors degree from a local state college. He is intelligent, works full time selling homes, and appears reasonably competent although inexperienced. What would someone with those attributes make in one year? Certainly more than $20,000, because if he didn't make at least that much he could find something more profitable to do with his time. Does he make over $40,000? No, because if he did, lots of people with new college degrees would flock to real estate sales. That's not happening, so he must make around $30,000 a year, enough to make it worthwhile but not so much that he would be overwhelmed with competitors."

"How much does he make on a home sale? A typical house costs about $100,000. The buying agent gets one quarter of the 5% commission, about $1250. Therefore, my guess is that he sells about 25 homes a year, about one every two weeks."

The next week we met with our agent for another round of shopping.

"How many homes do you sell a year?" my wife asked.

"I sold 27 homes last year."

A Different Way of Planning

Your first thought might be what does financial planning have to do with estimating the number of homes my real estate agent sells? But, the essence of planning is the projection of future outcomes. If you plan to become a real estate agent you must project the number of homes that you will need to sell to produce an acceptable income. In that case most people would do the calculation I just described in the reverse order. They would figure out how much income each sale would generate and then divide that number into their yearly income goal. The result would be the number of homes they need to sell. Then they would plan their efforts—number of: contacts to make, hours spent per client, closings to attend, etc.—to achieve that sales goal.

However, in this Chapter, I will challenge you to think about financial planning in a different way. Rather than asking what do you need to achieve your goal, first ask yourself, what is the most reasonable outcome to expect for your investment and/or efforts? I do not know my real estate agent's sales goal, but it turns out I do know his actual sales just by thinking about the most reasonable income for a person in his position. Suppose I plan to be a realtor. Rather than decide on my sales goal, I should first estimate a reasonable outcome and then compare that estimate to the actual results of an active realtor. If my estimate turns out wrong there would be an opportunity. For example,

I estimated my realtor sold one home every two weeks. But, suppose he sold a home every week (50 per year). If that were true, then most likely he is an exceptional salesman and I should try to learn more about his sales techniques. If he sells a home every month (12 per year) I should also try to learn more about what he does. If he makes that little money I should plan ways of being a much better realtor or abandon my plans altogether.

In this instance, my estimate of homes sold by my realtor is accurate. That accuracy is not a surprise because most outcomes are not exceptionally good or bad. The most reasonable outcome is usually what happens. The purpose of this chapter is to teach how to estimate reasonable outcomes by applying arithmetic to common life experiences. Whether the plan is for a new job, a new business or a new investment, the most likely outcome can be estimated from the beginning by using "reasonability tests." These reasonability tests are founded on what I call the "mediocrity assumption"—which is the assumption that your life experiences and observations are typical. For many people financial planning is based on positive thinking that borders on wishful thinking. My assertion is that financial planning should begin by considering the mundane. I do not mean to say that greater success is not possible, or should not be sought. My point is that rising above the mediocre requires being different, but before you can be different you need to know what is typical.

"Fermi Problems"

People like me, who have advanced training in physics, will recognize the reasoning I used to estimate the number of homes the real estate agent sells, as an example of a "Fermi Problem." The term refers to the Nobel prize-winning Italian physicist, Enrico Fermi, who habitually posed these kinds of questions for his students. The most well-known estimation problem Fermi asked his students is the following: How many piano tuners are there in Chicago?

Your first reaction to the piano tuner problem might be like my wife's with the real estate agent—how would you have any idea? But the point of Fermi's question was that you know much more than you think you do. If you make some reasonable assumptions based on what you do know and apply some simple arithmetic, you can make surprisingly accurate estimates.

One approach to the piano tuner problem would be to start with the number of people in the city. Fermi lived in Chicago, but the reasoning required to estimate the number of piano tuners in Chicago can be adapted to any city of any size. I will do the problem for my location, metropolitan Baltimore, which has about 2,500,000 people. Let us figure on roughly four people per household or about 600,000 households. Notice that I am not doing exact arithmetic because this is only an estimate. How many households have pianos? Think about all the people you know. More than half would be a high estimate, but certainly at least 10% would have pianos. That means there are roughly 60,000 pianos in metropolitan Baltimore. If each piano is tuned about once a year, the yearly demand is 60,000 piano tunings.

How many piano tuners does it take to meet this demand? The piano tuner must go to the piano and spend about an hour. It is difficult to imagine a tuner servicing more than four pianos a day. That would correspond to twenty per week, multiply by 50 weeks, and it appears a tuner could service 1000 pianos per year. There needs to be about 60 piano tuners to meet this demand.

At the time of this writing the Baltimore *Yellow Pages* showed listings for 45 piano tuning services, a number not far from the rough estimate outlined above. It is possible to argue all the details surrounding all the assumptions that went into that estimate. Many pianos are not tuned every year, church and school pianos are not counted, 10% is just a guess, and so on. However, the details are not important. By making reasonable guesses and performing simple arithmetic, it is easy to understand that the market in Baltimore would not support hundreds of piano tuners, but fewer than ten piano tuners would not be able to meet the demand.

Investing in a Business or Job

If you plan to be a real estate agent or a piano tuner, or open a store or run a restaurant or sell cars or own or invest in any kind of business, you need to know from the beginning the size of the market, the current market price of the product, and the performance required for success. It doesn't matter whether you own a single-person business or bought stock in a large company, the same mathematical constraints apply. You should always ask what is the most reasonable outcome. I will state this as a general rule.

The Reasonability Test

Any sales, business, investment, or employment proposal should pass a simple mathematical examination for reasonability.

To examine reasonability, there are general sets of questions to consider:

Performance questions

- Why would a customer choose the business's product rather than a competitor's product?
- How much of the product can the business supply?

Market questions

- How large is the market for the product?
- What fraction of the market does the largest supplier serve?
- What fraction of the market does the smallest supplier serve?

Cost questions

- •What is the current market price for the product?
- •What does it cost to supply the product?
- •What does it cost to run the business? (This is known as the overhead.)
- •What does it cost to open the business? (The start-up costs.)

Outcome questions

- •What is the most the business can lose?
- •How many sales are required to break even? (This means cover the overhead and start up.)
- •How many sales are required for the business to be worth running?
- •What is the most the business can make?

All but one of the above questions has a mathematical answer. The first question in the performance category is not mathematical, but if it doesn't have a good answer, don't bother doing any math.

If you plan to start a business or invest in one, it is essential to ask these questions.

If you plan to purchase a product or service, asking these questions will tell you if the price and performance claims are reasonable. Everyone wants "a deal" when making a purchase, but no one works for free or gives away merchandise.

Even if you are an employee, it is worthwhile to ask these questions about the business you work for and to consider the implications of the answers. Here are some examples:

Opening a store

You plan to open a clothing store.

First consider the performance issues—the kinds of clothes sold and the reasons customers buy them. Suppose your store will sell children's clothes that are above average cost but unique and high quality. You will stock the store with clothes from manufacturers who are too small to sell to the major discount chains.

Next consider the market questions. A similar store in your area has 200 shoppers per day of which 10 make purchases that average $60 each. The store is open 25 days per month. That is a cash flow of $15,000 per month. The wholesale discount on the clothes is 50%, which means it costs $7500 for the goods sold. Your store will cost $2000 per month for the rent, utilities, phone and other costs. A single employee will cost $2500 per month for wages and benefits. Therefore your overhead to run the store will be $4500 per month. Now consider your start-up costs. You will need to pay the first month's rent and deposit (about $1500) before you open the store and have at least one month of stock on hand. It will cost a minimum of $7500 for stock. Therefore it costs $1500 + $7500, or $9000 just to open for business.

If you can generate a similar $15,000 per month cash flow to the other store, subtracting the $12,000 monthly costs will leave you $3000 per month profit. It will take about three months to recoup your initial investment if you reach this level of sales. If you make no sales, your store will lose the $4500 per month in overhead costs each month it remains open. To break even you will need to make $9000 in sales each month because it will cost you $4500 for those goods and the resulting $4500 difference between the sales and the cost of goods will pay for the overhead.

Hiring a contractor

You plan for a new deck built on your house. A contractor says he will do it for $900. You ask how long it will take. He tells you he and an assistant will do it in one day. To you $900 seems like a lot for a one-day project, and you wonder how much he would come down.

Think about the reasonability questions from the contractor's point of view. The lumber and hardware for the deck you plan costs $400. That is a fixed cost that neither of you can do anything about. If he splits the remaining $500 with his assistant, that is $250 each for a day's work. Is any skilled carpenter going to work an entire day for much less? If you estimate the job yourself, it becomes clear that $900 is a reasonable price, given the materials and labor involved.

Acting as an employee

Consider the retail clothing store example from the point of view of the hourly employee. If the store is open 10 hours per day and has 200 shoppers, that amounts to 20 per hour, or about one every three minutes. If you work alone in the store, you might ring up one sale per hour, but you must greet and assist a new customer every three minutes. What will be happening if the one sale takes 15 minutes to ring up? If the owner is unwilling to work with you, the job might be unreasonable for you to handle by yourself. It is also clear from the cash flow generated by the store that the owner cannot afford to hire a second employee. If the owner expresses an unwillingness to work in the store but plans to hire additional help in the future, you might be better off refusing this job. The store will never generate the cash flow to justify a second employee if you are the sole salesperson.

Limits and Saturation

Note that all of the reasonability questions have most likely outcomes and upper and lower limits. The limits can be thought of as best and worst-case scenarios. In the contractor example, even if you convince someone to work for free, it will still cost $400 in materials. In the store example, no matter how many customers want to buy, you can never sell more than you can stock. It is not possible to stock more than you have money to invest and space in which to put the stock.

It is also important to know about the phenomenon of "saturation" that will be explained further in Chapter 5. Saturation has to do with the upper limit on the amount of income that can be generated from a particular economic activity. Everyone has heard the economic adage that "supply meets demand," but few stop to ponder that demand is always finite and that puts an upper limit on supply. In the piano tuner example, there are a finite number of people who own a finite number of pianos. The supply of piano tuners is limited by the availability of pianos to tune. Once the number of piano tuners is sufficient to meet demand, the market has reached a level of saturation. It is not possible to substantially increase the number of piano tuners beyond the saturation point. If more people abandon acoustic pianos for electronic keyboards that require no tuning, then the saturation level must decrease. Fewer people will be in the piano tuning business.

Markets tend towards saturation. Supply meets demand, but both are finite. Whenever a new idea or product emerges that receives unexpectedly high demand, competitors immediately appear until the saturation level is reached. Some examples are as follows:

•The ABC television network's quiz show: *Who Wants to be a Millionaire?* became so popular when it was introduced that it was shown three nights a week. Expressions such as "Is that your final answer?" and "Can I use a lifeline?" became clichés in a matter of months. Also within months imitation shows appeared. Soon viewers could watch quiz shows almost every night of the week on multiple channels. The market became so saturated with quiz shows that *Who Wants to be a Millionaire?* was cancelled.

•The booming stock market of the late 1990s appeared to be a fix for all of America's financial problems. The doubling in the S&P 500 index that occurred between 1996 and 2000 led some to project that even 10 to 15 years in the future there would be plenty of wealth for all. Politicians talked openly of investing social security funds in the market in order to solve the crisis expected to occur when the baby boom generation retires. But

Social Security taxes form such an enormous pot of money that the federal government would become the single largest player in the stock market. No one asked the obvious question: What happens to our free-market capitalism when the federal government becomes the single largest stockholder in American corporations? Wouldn't that amount to a nationalization of American private industry? The normal greed and fear that propel the markets would be replaced by threats from Congressmen attempting to score political points. No politician ever had to answer these questions. By the time politicians began promoting the stock market to fix Social Security, the demand for stocks had gone far beyond saturation to form one of the biggest market bubbles in history. After the resulting implosion, political talk of the government investing Social Security funds in the stock market quieted. By 2005 political talk about Social Security had evolved into proposals for "private accounts." The individuals would assume the risk.

Investing in Stocks

The same reasonability questions that apply to individuals and small businesses also apply to investing in the stock market. The actual numbers are much bigger, and stocks have a jargon of their own that must be penetrated. But the concepts of performance, market share, costs, limits and saturation all apply nonetheless. If your financial plans depend on investing in stocks you should learn to apply reasonability tests to the companies that you invest in.

For example, in late 1999 when stocks in technology companies were soaring, my father asked me if I would consider buying stock in Microsoft. His broker heavily pushed Microsoft, touting it as a safe bet that should continue to increase dramatically in value. My response? "There are four billion shares of Microsoft currently outstanding that sell for about $120 per share. That makes it a $500 billion company. For Microsoft to double in value it would have to become a one trillion-dollar company. Can there be such a thing as a one trillion-dollar company?

Where would all that wealth come from? And where would Microsoft go from there? Maybe decades from now the market can support multi-trillion dollar companies, but the total market capitalization of the entire NASDAQ stock index is about five trillion dollars. Is the market capitalization of Microsoft going to swallow up the entire NASDAQ?"

My father said, "Now that you put it that way, I won't buy Microsoft."

He clearly had not thought through the implications of the numbers. However, like the examples of estimating the market conditions that support small businesses and individuals, there is much information to be gained by simply asking how the broader market supports large companies.

Myths about stocks

Watching the stock market has almost replaced baseball as our national pastime. The frenzy is fed by 24-hour television and Internet coverage of talking "experts," combined with real-time price information that reacts instantly to world events. The result has led to unreasonable expectations, both good and bad, and little critical examination of the mathematical implications of commonly held beliefs.

It has been said that the stock market is a place where people "plant acorns and expect tall oaks *the next day*." Suppose the stock market did return 20% per year. That is a doubling time of 3.5 years. In a generation of 35 years, there would be 10 doublings or a 1000-fold increase in wealth. The five trillion-dollar NASDAQ becomes five thousand-trillion-dollars, enough wealth that if distributed equally among Americans would give every man, woman, and child ten million dollars each. That rate of return is impossible because growth must saturate. Over the time period of one generation, the increase in resources—capital, natural, and people—cannot possibly be great enough to support that much additional wealth.

Similar tests of mathematical reasonability can be applied to aspects of investing. Consider some common misconceptions people have when making a stock purchase.

Myths on Stocks

- Potential appreciation of a stock is related to its share price. A company with a stock price of $20 per share is a better investment than one with a stock price of $100 per share.

- Stocks that make the most actively traded list on a given day are "in play" and should be checked out.

- Stocks in mature established companies are "safer" investments.

- Companies with cheap stocks (less than $5 per share) offer the best growth potential.

Each of these myths can be debunked using purely mathematical arguments related to reasonability.

Share Price: Growth potential has little to do with share price. The value of a company is its share price multiplied by the number of outstanding shares, what analysts refer to as the *market capitalization*. While most publicly traded stocks listed on the major exchanges have share prices between $2 and $200 per share, the number of outstanding shares varies dramatically. Large companies like Microsoft, General Electric, and EMC have outstanding shares that number in the billions while small start-up companies might have only a few hundred thousand shares. The greater the supply of outstanding shares, the more difficult it is for demand to drive up price. *An investor interested in growth potential should ask first about the market capitalization, not the share price.*

Active Trading: Most newspapers publish in their business section a list of the most actively traded stocks the day before. Active trading is defined as stocks with the greatest number of shares changing ownership. The number of shares traded on a given day is referred to as the stock's *volume*. Active trade lists provide little information of value because if you read these lists of high volume stocks day after day, the same companies continually appear—Microsoft, General Electric, and EMC etc. The newspapers could save themselves the trouble of checking the markets each day and instead simply list the companies with the greatest number of shares outstanding. If 1% of Microsoft's four billion shares trade on a given day, that amounts to 40 million shares. There are hundreds of companies that would have to trade in excess of 100% of their shares to take a place alongside Microsoft on the most active list.* There is nothing newsworthy about Microsoft being on the most active list; its sheer size guarantees that it will be a daily event. However, a small company that experiences a sudden doubling or tripling in its daily volume is newsworthy. That event will not make the most active trade list, but the underlying reason could be worth investigating. *An investor interested in finding a stock "in play" should look for a volume change on a stock that is unusual for that particular stock. In general, the most active lists published in daily newspapers provide information on stocks with the most shares outstanding, not on unusual trading activity.*

Mature Companies: Large established companies have less volatile stock prices but are not necessarily "safer" investments. Market professionals talk about two broad categories of stocks—*growth* stocks and *cyclical* stocks. When a product is new, it is possible to have exponential growth in the sales of that

---

* This is not a mathematical impossibility. During the Internet bubble of the late 1990s some new issues did have trading volume in excess of 100% of their shares on a single day. There is nothing that forbids all the shares in a company to be bought and resold repeatedly in a single day. However, for large public companies, trading volume in excess of 100% of the outstanding shares is a highly unusual event.

product. There was a time when products such as automobiles, telephones, photocopiers, did not exist. Successful companies that sold these products could double their sales repeatedly over short periods of time as more people adopted the new technology. Stocks in the Ford Motor Company, ATT, and Xerox experienced tremendous price increases as their products gained widespread use. But all exponential growth processes eventually stop. This is the phenomenon of saturation that will explained in Chapter 5. When everyone owns an automobile, a telephone, and/or a photocopier, there are no more new customers to capture. Businesses that supply these products focus on competing for market share and keeping products current. Exponential growth ends when everyone owns the product. The total number of available paying customers might be large, but it is always finite.

Companies with new products are usually in the category of growth stocks. It is possible for their value to increase exponentially *if* the product gains widespread use. The risk is that the new product could fail because people may not adopt the new product. Companies with products that are in universal use are usually cyclical stocks. It is already known that people will buy automobiles, telephones, and photocopiers. However overall demand for these products rises and falls in cycles. The risk with cyclical stocks isn't so much that the product will fail but that the investor will make the common mistake of purchasing at the top of the cycle when the product is most in demand. No one wants to be left out when newspapers report on a great increase in demand for a product. However, when demand and news coverage for a *cyclical product is greatest, that is usually the time to sell a cyclical stock*. Also be aware that some established products "cycle" out of demand permanently. Few people buy typewriters any more. Soon demand for traditional silver halide photographic film may disappear as digital cameras gain widespread use. *An investor seeking the safety of an established company should know where in the cycle of demand that company's product lies.*

Cheap Stocks: Stocks that sell for less than $5 per share are generally not ones to purchase. If a stock sells for under $5 per share it is usually either in a highly speculative company or in a large company with many that outstanding shares that is in trouble (Lucent for example). Cheap shares have a number of drawbacks associated with them. If a stock's price falls below $1 per share for more than 30 days it will be de-listed from the major stock exchanges. Also, trading rules forbid buying on *margin* with shares that sell for less than $5. When an investor buys on margin, shares already owned are used as collateral to borrow money for the purchase. Shares used to buy on margin must sell for more than $5 and the borrowed funds cannot exceed 50% of the stock's value. If either condition is no longer met, the broker will issue a "margin call" which is a demand that the borrowed funds be paid or the margined shares will be liquidated to pay the debt. Because of these drawbacks, large mutual fund companies that drive demand in the stock market generally avoid cheap stocks.

But many people avoid buying stocks if the share price is too high. To attract individual investors, most publicly traded companies prefer to keep their stock price less than $200 per share. As their market capitalization rises, a company will reduce the price per share of their stock by increasing the number of outstanding shares. The share price reduction is accomplished by issuing stock *splits*. An investor who owns 50 shares of a $100 per share stock that splits "two for one" will own 100 shares at $50 per share. Notice that the share price multiplied by the number of shares—the market capitalization—is the same before and after a split. That means a split does not change the value of the company or the value any stockholder's investment. Companies do not have to issue stock splits; but if growth continues, share price becomes prohibitively expensive for the average investor. Class A shares in Warren Buffet's company, Berkshire Hathaway, have not been split and a single share costs over $80,000.* Needless to say, not many people own the Class

---

* Class A shares in Berkshire Hathaway can be exchanged for 30 Class B shares, which consequently trade for 1/30 of the value of the Class A shares.

A shares in his company, not many are traded, and not many are outstanding.

It is understandable that most publicly traded companies do not want to have share prices in the thousands or tens of thousands of dollars because they want average investors to purchase their stock. But, many companies constantly issue meaningless stock splits (such as 3 for 2, or 5 for 4) as a way of generating excitement and publicity. Stock splits make investors feel good, but the fact is splits are not necessarily a good thing. If a stock is split too frequently, a market downturn could land it in the under $5 per share category and it would have all the drawbacks associated with low-priced stocks. Actually investors never benefit as much from splits as the traders do, because many traders assess their fees based on the number of shares traded, not the share price.

Investors should generally look at stocks selling over $10 per share. Also be aware that stock charts of past winners are highly deceptive because historical charts are always "split adjusted." It might appear on a chart that a big price movement began when the stock sold for $5 per share, but if the stock split two-for-one twice during the history the chart covers, it means that in the beginning the stock sold for $20 per share. A historical chart can cover up the fact that a stock may never in its history have sold for less than $10 per share. A large company such as Microsoft has split so many times that any historical chart would show it selling for pennies in the past. However, Microsoft in its entire history has never been a penny stock. More on stock charts will be discussed in Chapter 4.

The Mediocrity Assumption

The discussion of mathematics as it applies to investments raises a question: Is there a mathematical formula for success in the stock market? The answer is of course not, and it is instructive to consider the reason. Formulas are by definition static. Once a formula is known, it remains the same forever. If a formula for beating the market were discovered, it would immediately become useless. Everyone would apply the formula to achieve instant wealth; but in the short run, wealth is finite: it is not possible for everyone to suddenly have more. A formula would mean everyone behaves exactly the same, and nothing changes if everyone behaves according to the same formula. Markets are by nature ever-changing reflections of human activities and progress. Historically, wealth and living standards increase in time; and by investing in diversified funds that follow the general market, it is possible to have a share in an expanding economy and accumulate money over time. Beating the market is difficult and requires behaving in some manner that is different from the other investors. There are people who do beat the market, but obviously they must be a minority and they cannot be following a widely known formula.

Of course everyone wants to be the person who is different, and it is easy to convince ourselves or allow someone else to convince us that we are. But the most reasonable assumption is that investment opportunities are not all that different. It is also most reasonable to assume that people are not all that different. There are many thousands of people trying to beat the stock market. They cannot all do it. And this reasoning applies beyond just the stock market to any "new" idea or proposal. There are many thousands of people who received an invitation to the "invitation only" sale. A salesperson's job is to sell at a profitable price to as many people as possible, not just give special deals to a select few. Unless you have a compelling reason, always assume that there is nothing special about present opportunities.

NON SEQUITUR © 2006 Wiley Miller. Dist. By UNIVERSAL PRESS SYNDICATE.

The entire idea behind "Fermi problems", that opened this chapter on reasonability, is that *you can arrive at accurate numerical estimates for many outcomes because your experiences and viewpoints are typical.* There is no reason to believe my real estate agent makes substantially more or less money than any other 25-year-old college graduate that I know. There is no reason to believe that people in the entire city of Baltimore own substantially more or fewer pianos per household than other people I know. There is no reason to believe that I, or my broker, know any more or less about a stock than thousands of other stock traders. There is no reason to believe that any business can grow revenue beyond the availability and financial abilities of the customers. I will summarize this as a general principle:

The Mediocrity Assumption

A first assumption should always be that any idea or proposal is mediocre. You should have a compelling reason to believe in uniqueness.

Yes, special and unique opportunities do occur, but there must be a *compelling* reason. You should always ask why an event, idea, product, or investment is unique. Often a little research uncovers many possibilities you never thought about but others have. Obvious questions that need to have answers are the following: Why haven't others thought of this idea? Why aren't others profiting from this idea? What are the reasons for current practices? What is special about my position? If these questions do not have answers, you could be deluding yourself about the actual potential for success.

Summary

"Plurality is not to be assumed without necessity."
—William of Ockham, *Quodlibeta*, Book V (ca. 1324)

The above quote by a fourteenth-century English theologian has today become known as "Occam's Razor" (Occam is the Latin spelling of his name). To a modern scientist, Occam's Razor is a reminder that the simplest explanation for a phenomenon is usually the more correct explanation. If a scientist, attempting to explain an event, must choose between an improbable chain of events or a single cause and effect, the single cause is almost always what actually happened. Fermi problems, which are methods to arrive at plausible estimates of economic activity, are a quantitative use of Occam's Razor. The simplest method for numerically estimating economic outcomes is to assume that your experiences are typical, that the people involved are typical, and that the most likely outcome will be typical. Whether you are investing in a house, a new business, a career, or the stock market, you must consider the most likely outcome of your endeavor, not the outcome you wish. This is not to say that a business or investment might be much more successful than previously imagined. But the possibility of greater success must be present at the beginning. There must be a compelling answer to the question: What is it about this business or investment that is different?

The Tale of the Quarter Without a Tail

At a family gathering my wife sorted through some quarters my sister had brought with her from a trip to Seattle. She searched for ones needed to complete her collection of state quarters, in particular those with the "D" stamp from the mint in Denver that circulate mostly in the West. In the East, our quarters usually carry the "P" stamp from the mint in Philadelphia.

"Did you know that you have a two headed quarter?" my wife

said to my sister.

"What?"

"Both sides of this quarter have heads."

We all examined the quarter carefully using a magnifying glass. A strange object, indeed. It appeared to be a real quarter, but each side had the familiar head of George Washington, the word "Liberty" and the motto "In God We Trust." Each side also had a date stamped, but to compound the mystery one side had 1996 and the other 1986.

The obvious question we all asked: Is this a one-of-a-kind coin that would be of great value to coin collectors?

My sister's husband, who had some coin collecting experience, said that depended on how many got into circulation. Are there tens of thousands of such mistakes or just a few? But if there are many thousands of such coins in circulation, wouldn't we know about it? The mint takes extraordinary care to make sure mistakes are not circulated. And how could the dates be a decade off? Could an unfinished quarter from 1986 be stamped again in 1996? We talked for over half an hour about the coin, trying to imagine how it could have been made, and most importantly, what it might be worth. Where could we get it appraised? My sister began fantasizing about having a down payment for a house.

Finally, I suggested that we go on the Internet and search for information on two-headed quarters. I went to the search engine Google at http://www.google.com (an extremely powerful search engine that everyone should know about) and entered the words—two headed quarter. Within seconds the computer screen filled with links to dozens of sites about two-headed quarters. A few mouse clicks later, an explanation for our find appeared on the screen. Alas, a reasonable, mundane explanation, that made perfect sense, but one that I never would have imagined.

Two-headed quarters are for sale on the Internet from online stores that specialize in equipment for magicians. For $7.49 plus shipping and handling, anyone can own one. According to the online catalog, the quarter is made by the precision cutting of two genuine quarters in half to obtain two heads. The two heads are then carefully bonded together.

The catalog didn't go into magician tricks, but I could immediately imagine some. Rub a coin with your hand and change the date by a decade. Or act out for real the opening scene from *Rosencrantz and Guildenstern are Dead*, where one of the characters flips a coin over and over and always gets heads.

Internet sites devoted to coin collecting explained that two-headed quarters are almost always magician props that have accidentally been put in circulation. In the words of one coin collecting site, "the odds against finding a genuine two-headed coin are greater than the odds against winning the lottery." There are a few documented cases, but they are extremely rare. The site stated that a test to determine whether the coin is genuine would be to drop it and compare the sound it makes to that of a real quarter.

To be absolutely sure, we gathered around and dropped a real quarter on the kitchen counter and heard a distinctive ring. I raised the two-headed quarter to the same height and let go. It landed with a dull thud.

Chapter 3 Resources:

The Ewing Marion Kauffman Foundation of Kansas City (http://www. kauffman.org) offers a course for entrepreneurs called Fasttrac™. The course teaches people with ideas for businesses how to ask and answer the key questions needed to determine feasibility. The course is available nationwide through participating local agencies. Learn about the course and locations where it is offered at http://www.fasttrac.org .

Investor's Business Daily is a newspaper published five times a week with extensive technical information on the stock market (http://www.investors. com). The paper and its companion Website provide a screen for stocks with unusual trading volume in relation to the stock's normal volume. Their data tables also rank groups of stocks so that investors can see quickly the industries that are both in and out of favor for the current cycle of demand.

Gregory Derry, *What Science is and How it Works* (Princeton, NJ: Princeton University Press, 1999) discusses the criteria used by scientists for evaluating the reasonability of scientific theories and results.

CHAPTER FOUR

Charting

Pictures Worth More Than a Thousand Words

"Let's look at the next chart now. This chart gives you an idea of which spending categories are headed in which direction. Average annual real growth—now, I want to tell you what this means. I haven't lived in Washington very long so I still use ordinary meanings for words. When you see real on a government chart, that means adjusted for inflation. You'll never find that in a dictionary, but that is what it means."

—Bill Clinton
Remarks to the Future of Entitlements Conference
Bryn Mawr, Pennsylvania
December 13, 1993

You must decide between four possible career paths. One consideration in your decision is future salaries. Each career path has a "typical" starting salary and annual raise. While doing research you encounter charts that show anticipated salary increases for each career path. The four charts (Figures 4.1a, 4.1b, 4.1c, and 4.1d), shown on the next two pages, each provide salary information over a 20-year time span. Which of these career paths would you prefer? At first glance the answer seems obvious. Clearly the picture in Figure 4.1a of rapidly rising earnings is the career to choose. But study the details of the charts closely. Note on each chart how the vertical axes are labeled and scaled. Examine which vertical axes are labeled in dollars and which are labeled in percentages. If you can move

Figure 4.1: Charts depicting typical salary increases at the end of each year for a 20-year time period. Four possible careers are shown.

(a) Career track one

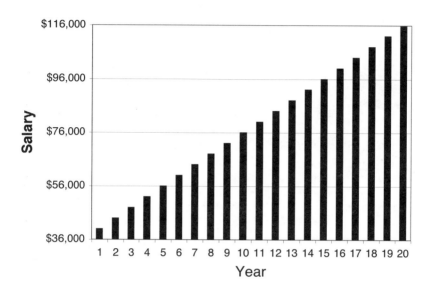

(b) Career track two

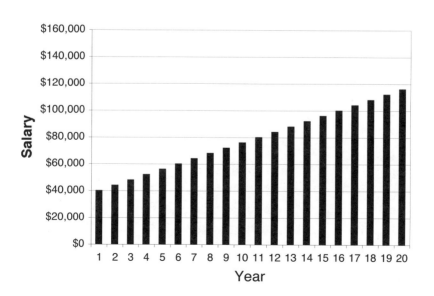

Observation: In contrast to Figures 4.1a and 4.1b, it is not possible to know the actual salaries in Figures 4.1c and 4.1 d because only the salary increases are shown.

(c) Career track three

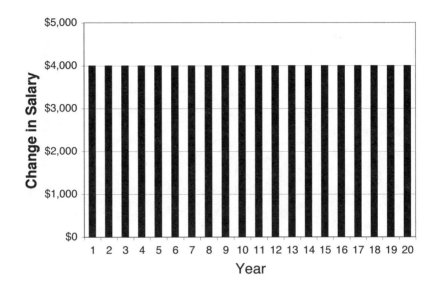

(d) Career track four

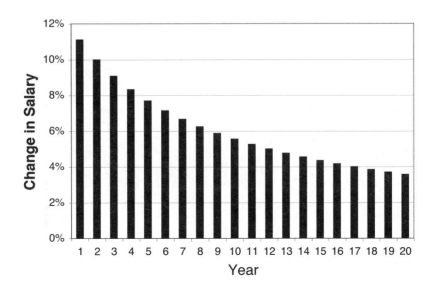

beyond the visual experience to consider the mathematical details, you might discover the trick answer to this question. Each chart depicts the same set of salary data. The choice is an illusion.

Different Pictures of the Same Data

The charts shown in Figures 4.1a-d, all depict a hypothetical career with a starting salary of $36,000 followed by annual $4000 raises at the end of each year. But each chart shows the same data differently.

Figure 4.1a shows salaries on the vertical axis at the end of each year. Therefore the salary at the end of year 1 is $36,000 + $4000, or $40,000. Each successive year the salary increases by $4,000 until it finally reaches $116,000 at the end of year 20. The years are shown on the horizontal axis. The resulting picture shows a yearly increase in salary that follows a straight line. But the increase appears particularly dramatic because the lower limit on the vertical axis is $36,000 rather than $0. A person making a quick glance at the chart sees a rapid rise from "nothing," but a bar with zero height in on this chart represents $36,000.

Figure 4.1b is constructed with exactly the same set of numbers as Figure 4.1a. The only difference is that the range of the vertical axis is widened. Instead of encompassing only the range of numbers needed ($36,000 to $116,000) the axis range is set from $0 to $160,000. Widening the range of the vertical axis has the visual effect of making the $4,000 annual increases appear less dramatic. On this chart a bar with zero height really means zero salary.

Figure 4.1c shows only the annual *increases* in salary. Because the increase is always the same $4,000, Figure 4.1c shows a flat line. The visual impact of a flat line is one of stasis. There appears to be no change over time. But the change itself is what is shown. Figure 4.1c is flat because the yearly salary increase does not change. Also, because only the yearly change is shown, it is not possible to know from Figure 4.1c the actual salary each year. The $4000 increase could be on top of a $1,000,000 starting salary or a $10,000 starting salary. The chart in Figure 4.1c does not communicate the starting salary or any of the future salaries.

Figure 4.1d is closely related to Figure 4.1c because it only shows annual increases. But the annual increases are shown in percent changes from the year before, not in actual dollar amounts. As total salary increases, $4,000 becomes a progressively smaller percent change each successive year. When the total salary is $40,000, a $4000 increase is a 10% percent increase. But at the $80,000 level, a $4,000 increase is only a 5% change. The annual raise is the same dollar amount, but the percent change has dropped by a factor of two. In contrast to the unbounded rise of Figure 4.1a, the picture in Figure 4.1d is one of gloom. By itself, Figure 4.1d communicates even less information on the actual salary than Figure 4.1c. Not only is the starting salary unknown, the actual dollar amounts of the annual raises are also unknown.

Which chart would I use to depict this set of salary data? It would depend on my audience and my motives. If I were an executive at a corporation, I would use Figure 4.1a when talking to workers to show that their salaries steadily improve. I would use Figure 4.1d when talking to my own boss to show that I am holding the line on salary increases. I would use Figure 4.1c when talking to the Board of Directors to show stability. Each chart presents a different picture, but there is no dishonesty because each chart shows the same set of data plotted with the same mathematical precision.

Charts and graphs are important because we interpret the world primarily though our eyes. As a result, charts and graphs are extremely useful tools for making sense out of complex tables of data. However, a question that enters my mind any time someone shows me a chart is: could the same numerical data be charted in different formats to produce different visual impressions? The answer is always yes and this Chapter will show how to present different pictures of the same data. The techniques used in Figures 4.1a-d, work on any data set. I will apply these techniques to charts showing government spending and charts of stock price performance. I use these examples because politicians and corporate executives routinely confront us with charts when asking us to make a choice. The problem is that these people often have strong motivations for wanting us to "see" the data their way.

Your Tax Dollars

We usually do not think of taxes as a personal financial decision because payment is compulsory. But in principle, tax money is supposed to be spent for the common good and that includes many essential services that we depend on each day. Taxes are one of the largest items in a household budget. The sum total of: federal, state, Social Security, Medicare, property, sales, and local income taxes, usually consumes a minimum of 25% of a typical income and often 35% or more depending on an individual's job, location, and assets. The fact is when we vote or petition elected officials we are influencing how the use of a substantial portion of our money in the form of taxes will affect us personally in the kinds of services that government provides. Our political actions or lack of action are often personal financial decisions.

Politicians seeking our votes like to support their positions with charts because audiences remember visual impressions long after spoken details are forgotten. Those who remember Ross Perot's half-hour long television rants on federal spending during the 1992 presidential election can recall his use of charts throughout his monologue to emphasize major points. And when positions conflict and the charts convey conflicting visual impressions, does this mean proponents on each side of an issue have their own completely different set of numbers? Surprisingly the same data source is often used because it is easy to construct charts from the same data set that produce alternative visual impressions. The same techniques used in Figures 4.1a-d can be employed on any data set.

As an example, consider the debate over federal spending and debt where we frequently encounter charts that convey conflicting visual impressions. In January 2004 President Bush provoked a vigorous election year debate with his $2.4 trillion proposed budget and a projected $524 billion deficit. Democrats charged that federal spending was "out of control." Republicans countered that deficit spending combined with tax cuts would "stimulate the economy." Each side produced charts to provide visual emphasis for their arguments. From the charts alone, it might appear each side is working with completely different sets of data, but actually all of the data came from one source —the Congressional Budget Office. In January 2004, I visited the Congressional Budget Office Website (http://www.cbo.gov) and downloaded a document with the federal government's own numbers for federal spending and debt. I then reproduced charts similar to ones shown on editorial pages across the country that argued both sides of the issue. My charts shown in Figures 4.2a-d, present four different pictures of federal debt. These four charts are constructed with the same techniques used in Figures 4.1a-d.

Democratic-leaning newspapers published charts similar to Figure 4.1a that show a projection of total federal debt in billions of dollars held by the public for the years 2003 to 2014. To finance deficit spending the federal government borrows money from others and issues bonds and notes in return that are promises to pay back the money at a later date with interest. Securities in the form of U.S. savings bonds, and treasury notes are examples of debt held by the public. Because the government plans to run a deficit each year until about 2011, Figure 4.1a shows that the total amount owed to the public increases each year until then. If deficit spending stops, the total debt levels off but will not decrease. The only way that Figure 4.1a could show a decrease would be for the government to have a surplus, which is an event not projected to happen until 2014. Even then, the projected surplus is so small that the resulting decrease in debt is barely perceptible in Figure 4.1a. The visual impact of Figure 4.1a is of a government with out-of-control spending, sinking ever deeper

Figure 4.2: Four different pictures of federal deficit spending. Each chart depicts the same budget projections published by the Congressional Budget Office on January 26, 2004.

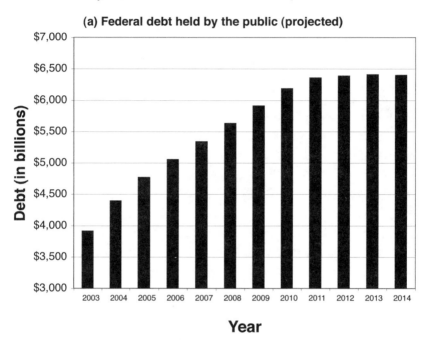

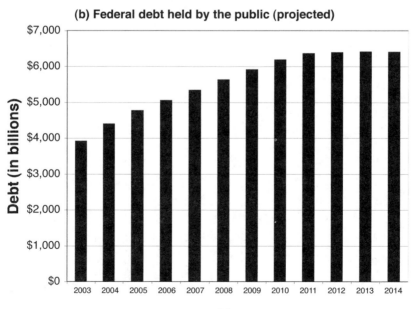

Observation: Even when the deficit declines (Figures 4.2c and 4.2d) debt still accumulates (Figures 4.2a and 4.2b).

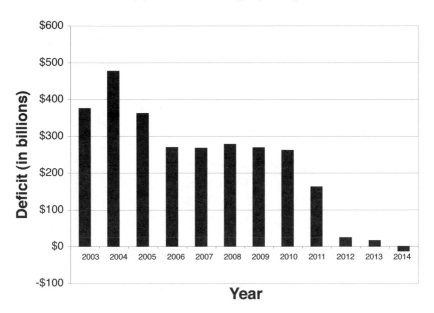

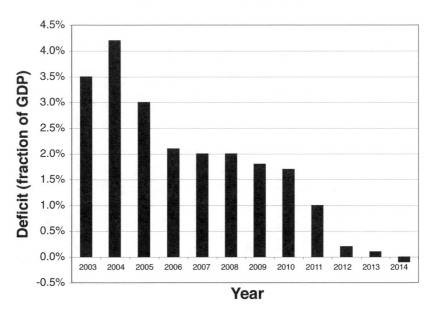

into debt. The debt increase looks especially bad because like in Figure 4.1a, the lower limit on the vertical axis Figure 4.1a is not zero. A bar with zero height in Figure 4.1a represents a total government debt of $3 trillion.

More moderate publications would publish the same data but use a chart similar to the one in Figure 4.2b. For this chart the lower limit on the vertical axis is set to zero. Just as in Figure 4.1b, where the starting salary is not close to zero, Figure 4.2b shows that the total government debt in 2003 is already substantial. The projected increase from nearly $4 trillion to just over $6 trillion does not look as bad as it does in Figure 4.2a because the vertical axis now includes zero.

Is there an even more positive way to present these debt projections? Republican-leaning newspapers published charts similar to Figure 4.2c that shows a dramatic improvement in projected federal deficits for the same 2003 to 2014 time period. Figure 4.2c leads you to believe that the government is on its way to eliminating the its spending problem. The visual impact of Figure 4.2c is completely different from Figure 4.2b, but both charts are constructed with the same set of numbers taken from the same Congressional Budget Office document. Both figures show the same debt projections for the same years. But because Figure 4.2c shows the yearly deficit rather than the debt it shows a decrease for the future. The yearly deficit (or surplus) is the *change* in the total debt each year. It is not the total debt itself. Figure 4.2c is similar to Figure 4.1c that showed the *change* in salary each year rather than the actual salary. It is not possible from to know from looking at Figure 4.1c the total salary and similarly, by just looking at Figure 4.2c, it is not possible to know the total government debt. The change in debt is not cumulative like the total debt shown in Figure 4.2b. Even when the deficit is declining, Figure 4.2b shows an increase because the total debt increases for any size deficit.

But Figure 4.2c still shows steady deficit spending projected for years 2006-2010. Figure 4.2d shows an even brighter picture of future government spending that appeared in some Republican oriented newspapers because it depicts a decline in deficit spending for the 2006-2010 period. In Figure 4.2d the deficits are not shown in dollars, but rather as a percentage of the U.S. Gross Domestic Product (GDP in the jargon of economists). The GDP is the total value of all goods and services produced within the United States during the year and is a measure of the country's economic activity. The Congressional Budget Office document provides projected deficits expressed both in billions of dollars and as a fraction of the GDP. When expressed as a fraction of the GDP, the actual numbers for the deficit are small, around 3 to 4 percent and declining.

Figure 4.2d shows a decline in the deficit for the 2006-2010 time period because the GDP is projected to increase. Total dollars borrowed will remain about the same, but that amount will become a progressively smaller fraction of an increasing GDP. Figure 4.2d shows a decline in the deficit for the same reason that Figure 4.1d shows a decline in annual raises. The actual raise in Figure 4.1d is the same every year, but because salary increases each year the raise expressed as a percentage of total salary becomes progressively smaller. This is why Figure 4.2d shows improvement in the deficit from 2006 to 2010 while Figure 4.2a shows debt continuing to accumulate for this time period. The government plans to continue borrowing about the same amount of money each year but expects the economy to keep growing.

Charts Not Seen

So is federal debt bad? Are deficits less problematic if they are small compared to the GDP? I will let economists debate those questions. My interest is in the techniques for creating charts and graphs that deliver specific messages to targeted audiences. The Congressional Budget Office document I downloaded from their Website is actually eleven pages of facts and figures. When it comes to making charts, there is no reason to stop with just Figures 4.2a-d. I decided to chart some of the other financial data from the document. What follows are charts that I did not find in any newspaper. Actually, I saw no mention of any of the following data in the news, but all of these numbers came from the same Congressional Budget Office document as the charts and numbers that I did find in the newspapers.

Figure 4.3 projects the GDP for the 2003 to 2014 time period. You will be comforted to know that the federal government expects continued economic growth and prosperity for that decade. No economic slow-downs or recessions that might cause a leveling off in GDP or even dips in the GDP are forecast. At this point you might wonder what the government is projecting will happen in 2010 to dramatically reduce the deficit and then eliminate it entirely in by 2014, especially because no sudden surge in the GDP is forecast for those years. In fact the GDP forecast is based primarily on historical averages for GDP growth. The government does not have a method for calculating the GDP a decade in the future beyond assuming that the economy will continue to grow at the same rate it has in the past, about 4.4 percent each year.

Figure 4.3: Projection of the United States Gross Domestic Product (GDP) published by the Congressional Budget Office on January 26, 2004.

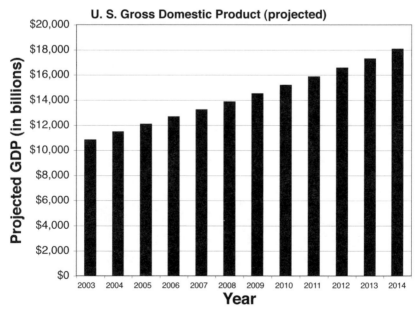

Observation: Government budget projections assume a steady uninterrupted growth of the U. S. economy.

The Congressional Budget Office document does contain a financial forecast that explains the sudden deficit elimination, but it takes some careful reading to understand the reason. In the middle of the document is a table of data titled, "The Budgetary Effects of Policy Alternatives Not Included in CBO's Baseline." At the top of this table is a line titled "Extend Expiring Tax Provisions, Effect on the Deficit or Surplus" and a list of figures follows the abbreviations EGTRRA and JGTRRA. A footnote explains that these abbreviations stand for the Economic Growth and Tax Relief Reconciliation Act of 2001 and the Jobs and Growth Tax Relief Reconciliation Act of 2003. Figure 4.4 is a chart of the additional deficits that result if this "policy alternative" is chosen. The figure shows an abrupt surge in the deficit in the year 2010 and this continues on into the future.

What exactly is this policy alternative that would substantially increase the deficit starting in 2010? In the media the EGTRRA

Figure 4.4: Projection of the additional deficit if the tax cuts do not expire published by the Congressional Budget Office on January 26, 2004.

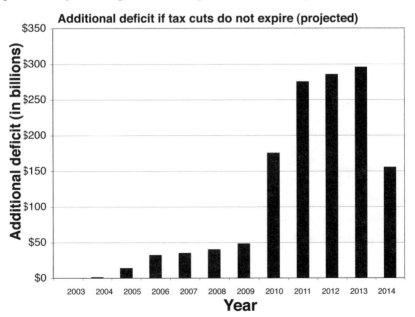

Observation: If tax cuts do not expire the projected decrease in the deficit for years 2011–2014 shown in Figure 4.2c will not occur.

and JGTRRA laws are commonly referred to as the "Bush tax cuts," and these tax cuts have an expiration date of 2010. The Congressional Budget Office projections shown in Figure 4.4 are based on that law and assume that the tax cuts will expire in 2010. The "event" in 2010 that suddenly reduces the deficit is the expiration of the tax cuts. If the tax cuts do not expire, the Congressional Budget Office document projects that deficits will continue at the same level as before the year 2010. This policy alternative creates a humorous situation. President Bush argued that the tax cuts should be made permanent because the budget will be in balance by 2010. But the projected balanced budget is based on a law that states that the tax cuts will expire that year.

Defining the "Deficit"

"And so the budget I set up says the payroll taxes are only going to be spent on one thing, and that's Social Security—that the Congress won't be using the payroll taxes for other programs."

—George W. Bush
Remarks to the National Newspaper Association
40th Annual Government Affairs Conference
March 22, 2001

Another question arises when examining the Congressional Budget Office figures: How does the government define the deficit? The answer is simple and at the same time mathematically deceptive. The deficit is the total amount of money borrowed from sources outside the government. That means the federal government is free to "borrow" from itself and not label that obligation part of the deficit. Because the government controls several large trust funds that are supposedly set-aside for future needs, opportunities to "borrow" are always present.

Figure 4.5 shows the projected borrowing from the Social Security Trust Fund for the 2003 to 2014 time period. The government has no plans to stop borrowing from Social Security for the foreseeable future and no plan to pay the money back. Each year the government collects more in Social Security taxes than is needed to pay current retirees. In principle that money is saved in a trust fund to be used in the future when an aging population results in Social Security taxes that fall short of what is needed to pay benefits. In practice, the excess Social Security revenues are used to pay for the current operations of the government. To do this, the government "borrows" from the trust fund but because the government owns these funds none of this "borrowing" is considered part of the deficit shown in Figures 4.2c and 4.2d.

The situation with the Social Security trust fund is equivalent to an individual who contributes regularly to a retirement account and then immediately borrows against the account. As time goes by, the contributions add up, and the amount "saved" for retirement appears to be substantial. However, the amount "borrowed" is close to the amount "saved," and there is no plan to pay back the "borrowed" funds. Strictly speaking, the

Figure 4.5: Projection of the total debt owed by the federal government to the Social Security Trust Fund published by the Congressional Budget Office on January 26, 2004.

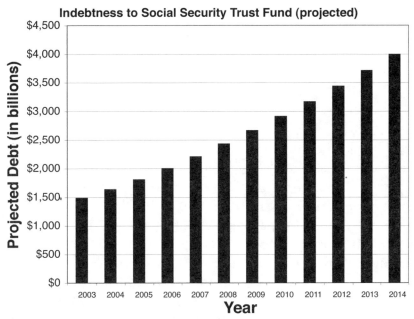

Observation: The federal government has no plans to discontinue the use of Social Security tax revenues to pay for its other programs.

individual is not in debt because no money is owed to an outside creditor. But is this individual "saving" for retirement?

A practice that I call "re-labeling" is examined in various places in this book. Re-labeling is the use of deceptive descriptions for a practice such as "save and borrow" in place of a more accurate description, such as "spend." The chapters in this book on loans examine the ways finance charges can be re-labeled with other terms like "service fees." The question in this section is the following: what is an accurate label for Social Security? Here are some possible labels to choose from:

- •Social Security is equivalent to a retirement fund that has "invested" its assets in U.S. treasury notes. As the notes mature, the "investment" will realize a gain from interest paid by the U.S. government.

- •Social Security is equivalent to a savings account in a bank that the U.S. government has "borrowed" from. The "loan" will be repaid in the future with interest.

- •Social Security is equivalent to a "tax." The IRS forcibly collects Social Security taxes, and the U.S. government uses the money to pay for its day-to-day operations that include payment of Social Security benefits to current retirees.

Politicians usually use one of the first two labels but only the last label is accurate. Saying that Social Security funds have been "invested" or "loaned" makes no sense because U.S. taxpayers, the supposed beneficiaries of this "investment" are the ones responsible for paying back the loan and the interest. The bottom line is that Social Security is a multi-trillion dollar re-labeling scam. It functions as a tax, but the government refuses to call it a tax. President Bush has argued that citizens would be better off investing their Social Security contributions in private retirement accounts. But that dodges the question: what would the government do to operate on a daily basis if Social

Security taxes ended? The government would still have to levy a tax to collect all the revenue that it would no longer be able to "borrow." But once Social Security is labeled a "tax," people might then question its regressive features.* On a percentage basis, Social Security affects low-income workers more than high-income workers because in 2005, the tax was only levied on the first $90,000 earned in wages. Wages earned in excess of $90,000, and income derived from investments were not subject to Social Security taxes.**

*A "regressive" tax is one that takes a greater percentage of income from those on the low end of the income scale than those on the high-income end. In contrast a "progressive" tax, like the income tax, takes a greater percentage of income from high-income earners and a smaller percentage from low-income earners. A "flat" tax would take the same percentage of income from all earners.

**Social Security and Medicare taxes in 2005 were levied on the first $90,000 of wages that an individual earned. The cap in wages subject to these taxes is indexed so that it automatically increases each year to keep up with rising wages. In 2004 the cap was $87,900. Individuals must pay 7.65% of their earnings for Social Security and Medicare, and their employer must match that amount. If the individual is self-employed, he or she becomes responsible for both the employer and employee contributions. That means a total of 15.30 percent of self-employed earnings must go to Social Security and Medicare taxes. But wages earned in excess of $90,000 are not subject to Social Security taxes. That means as more income is earned above $90,000, the fraction of total income that goes to Social Security is smaller. Consider the table below that shows income levels and the fraction of income paid for Social Security and Medicare taxes in 2005.

Income	Employee Tax	Employee Fraction (%)	Self-employed Tax	Self-employed Fraction (%)
$50,000	$3825	7.65	$7650	15.30
$100,000	$6885	6.88	$13,770	13.77
$150,000	$6885	4.59	$13,770	9.18
$200,000	$6885	3.44	$13,770	6.88

Consequences of this method of taxation include the following:

- The tax system is much "flatter" than the government admits. Those in higher tax brackets are getting a large break on Social Security taxes so their overall tax rate is not that much greater than low-income earners.
- It costs employers more than the stated hourly wage to employ someone. It costs an employer $10.76 per hour to pay an employee $10 per hour. A person seeking self-employed work must charge $10.76 per hour to earn the equivalent wage of an employee paid $10 per hour.
- People who derive all of their income from investments get a huge tax break because they do not pay Social Security and Medicare tax. Only income derived from labor is subject to these taxes.

To close this discussion on federal spending, I present one last chart that uses numbers from the same Congressional Budget Office document. Figure 4.6 shows a projection of "gross federal debt" for the years 2003 to 2014. Gross federal debt is the total amount owed to the public plus the Social Security trust fund, plus all the other government funds that are borrowed against, which include the Civil Service Retirement, Military Retirement, Medicare, Unemployment insurance and the Airport and Airway Trust Funds. Figure 4.6 shows that the gross federal debt is projected to almost double over the 2004-2014 decade. It is projected to increase from $6.7 trillion to $12.9 trillion and remain between 35 to 40 percent of the U.S. economy's GDP the entire time. Even with expiring tax cuts included in this projection, there are no plans to end federal "borrowing" in the foreseeable future.

"Think of the federal government as a gigantic insurance company (with a side line business in national defense and homeland security) which only does its accounting on a cash basis–only counting premiums and payouts as they go in and out the door. An insurance company with cash accounting is not really an insurance company at all. It is an accident waiting to happen."

–Peter R. Fisher
Under Secretary of the Treasury
Remarks to the Columbus Council on World Affairs
Columbus, Ohio
November 14, 2002

Figure 4.6: Projection of gross federal debt published by the Congressional Budget Office on January 26, 2004.

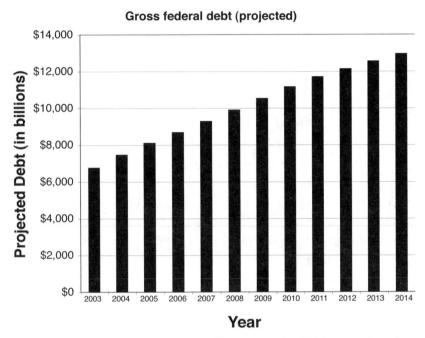

Gross federal debt (projected)

Observation: Gross federal debt will increase in 2014 even though a "surplus" is projected for that year — see Figure 4.2c.

Stock Charts

Financial reports, newspapers and advertisements for financial services frequently use charts. Many times these charts are not intentionally misleading, but readers deceive themselves by not understanding the context of the chart. Often the providers of these charts know that readers deceive themselves and do nothing to help correct the misconceptions. As in the previous examples, the reader should look beyond the immediate visual impression and understand the scale of the chart, its time frame and the reason for the chart. For examples, we will examine charts of prices on stocks and discuss how people become fooled by visual impressions.

Comparisons of price movement

Compare Figure 4.7a that shows the price per share of stock in
General Electric (GE) over a one-year period with Figure 4.7b
that shows the price per share of stock in Occidental Petroleum
(OXY) over a one-year period. The initial visual impression is
that these stocks performed equally well. But closer inspection
of the scales reveals substantial differences. The scale for the
chart showing GE stock has a $14 range ($25 - $39) while the
price scale for the OXY chart covers a $60 range ($20 - $80).
That means the price scales on the left side of these charts differ
by more than a factor of four. Because the scales are so different,
comparisons of price movement based on visual impressions
alone are deceptive. Look carefully at the numbers. GE stock
rises from about $30 per share to $36 per share over the one
year time period shown, a gain of 20 percent. Stock in OXY is
more expensive at the beginning—about $50 per share—but the
rise to nearly $75 per share amounts to a 50 percent gain over
one year. Although the gains "look" similar, when the scales
are considered, it becomes clear that OXY would have been the
better investment.

The time frame should also be examined. The charts in Figures
4.7a and 4.7b each show a one-year time frame around years
2004 and 2005. However, the time frames are offset by two
months. The price of GE stock is shown from April 2004 to April
2005 while the time frame of OXY is shown from June 2004 to
June 2005. When I constructed Figures 4.7a and 4.7b I wanted to
show two different stocks over a one-year period but have their
charts convey similar visual impressions. But I did not need to
choose the exact same year for each stock to achieve that goal.
I looked at charts of these stocks over three-year time frames
and then selected one-year segments of each that looked similar.
Selective choice of time frames is a technique to keep in mind
when reading advertisements for mutual funds. The creators of
the chart obviously pick a time frame for the fund that leaves a
favorable visual impression. Embarrassing dips and periods of
lagging the market might lie just outside the chosen time frame.

Figure 4.7: Comparison of the price movement for two stocks for a one-year time period. (a) Occidental Petroleum from June 15, 2004 to June 14, 2005. (b) General Electric from April 12, 2004 to April 8, 2005.

(a) Occidental Petroleum stock (OXY)

(b) General Electric stock (GE)

Observation: The magnified vertical scale for Figure 4.7b makes the price movement for GE look greater than for OXY. In fact the reverse is true.

The scaling difference between Figures 4.7a and 4.7b also results in deceptive visual impressions of the price fluctuations. It appears that GE stock fluctuates more in price, but that appearance is false. The small range of the price scale for the GE charts magnifies the price swings. During the time frame shown, GE stock never decreases by more than $2 per share in price, a downward fall of about 6 to 7 percent. The OXY stock in comparison undergoes several reversals of $6 to $7 per share that amount to about 10 percent of its overall price. The OXY stock only looks more stable than the GE stock because of the much larger range of its price scale.

General Electric not only has the more stable stock, it also has a much larger market capitalization than Occidental Petroleum. Market capitalization, explained in Chapter 3, is the stock's price *multiplied* by the total number of outstanding shares and it is the true measure of the market value of a company. A chart that only shows the share price tells no information on market capitalization. Even though GE shares are about half the price of OXY, the 10.6 billion outstanding shares of GE give it a market capitalization of about $370 billion when it sells for $35 per share. There are roughly 400 million outstanding shares of OXY which means that at $75 per share its market capitalization is $30 billion, less than one tenth that of GE's. Even though GE stock has lower price per share than OXY, the market value of GE is substantially greater.

Split-adjusted charts

Many people who invest in stocks become fixated on owning a certain number of shares, usually multiples of 100. A "round lot" in market jargon is 100 shares and round lots are the preferred quantity to buy. As a result small investors, who have limited funds, gravitate toward lower priced stocks. A small investor with $3000 to invest might buy 100 shares of GE based on the $30 per share price, rather than 60 shares of OXY at $50 per share because 60 seems like an odd number of shares to own. Companies feed this psychological need by constantly "splitting" their stock as it rises. But as explained in Chapter 3, a stock split always leaves the market capitalization unchanged. That means the value of an individual's investment is the same before and after a split. For example, when a stock is split two for one, the number of outstanding shares is doubled, but the price per share is halved: that means the product of these two numbers has not changed. But stock splits result in highly deceptive historical charts and feed the common misconception that the biggest winners have low per share prices.

Consider Figure 4.8a that shows a historical chart of stock in Dell Computer over the two and one half years from January 2, 1997, to June 30, 1999. The chart shows an almost 16-fold increase starting at about $3 per share in January 1997 to a peak about two years later of nearly $50 per share. If you had invested $3000 in Dell in January 1997, you would have had about $50,000 worth of stock at its peak. Does that mean that your search for winning stocks should include trolling the lists for $3 per share companies and reading your spam on the penny stocks that are "projected" to rise to hundreds of dollars per share?

Actually if you had purchased stock in Dell computer in January 1997, you would have had to pay $60 per share. A $3000 investment would have only bought 50 shares. A few months later with Dell stock selling at $150 per share, $3000 would have only bought 20 shares, but that would have still been a great investment. The fact that historical charts on stocks are always "split adjusted" hides all that information. A historical chart that you never see in financial pages is shown in Figure 4.8b. It shows the actual listed price of Dell Computer shares over the same January 1997 to June 1999 time period. The chart in Figure 4.8b has four price gaps that correspond to the *four* 2-for-1 splits that took place during that two and one half years. Because of the splits, the number of shares of Dell increased 16-fold, from 153 million to 2.44 billion during that time. That meant that 50 shares of Dell in January 1997 purchased for $3000 would became 800 shares worth about $50,000 at its peak. Even 20 shares purchased just before the first split would have become 320 shares. If you invested $3000 for just 20 shares of Dell at $150 per share, the

Figure 4.8: (a) Split-adjusted price of Dell Computer stock compared with (b) listed price for the same time period—January 2, 1997 to June 30, 1999.

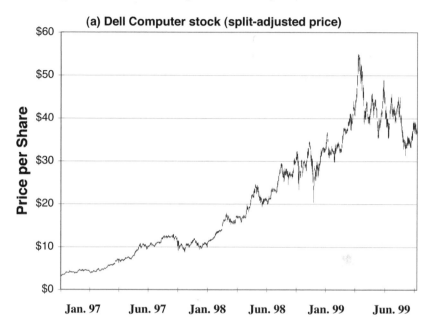

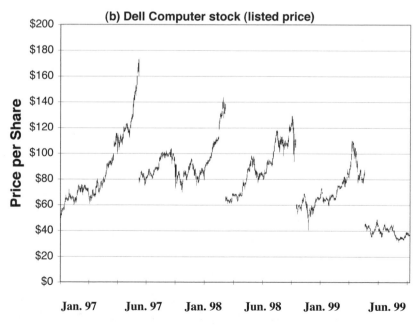

Observation: The lowest listed price is at the *end* of the big price increase.

investment would have grown to $16,000. Notice that before its stock began its big move, Dell was not a small company. In January 1997 it already had a market capitalization of $9 billion and that would grow to more than $120 billion.

Because historical charts of any big winner from the past are always split-adjusted, you should not think too much about share price and affording round lots when you purchase stocks. Instead, think in terms of the percent gain or loss of your investment. If you have a fixed amount to invest, it is better to own 20 high-priced shares of a great company than 100 low-priced shares of a mediocre company. Ignore spam pushing low-priced stocks of unknown companies. Big winners are usually established companies with stock prices already higher than $10 per share. Do not be fooled by "split-adjusted" historical charts.

Summary

In mathematics a careful distinction is made between a quantity that varies over time and the *change* in that quantity over time. For example, if the total debt owed by the federal government at the end of each year is the quantity, then the yearly deficit is the change in that quantity. It is possible to have a decreasing change while the quantity itself increases. Again using federal spending as an example, a decreasing change—the deficit—still means that the quantity—debt—is increasing.

Often when a person making an argument or presentation confuses a quantity with its change, the misdirection is intentional. If someone shows a chart that pictures a budget, benefit, deficit, salary or expense being "cut," you should examine the chart carefully and determine whether the chart shows the actual quantity or the change in that quantity. Often a downward trending chart that shows a "cut" actually means that the yearly increase is less than it was in previous years. For example, anytime the federal budget deficit is less than expected, politicians will hail that as great news, all the while ignoring the fact that a deficit still means an increase in debt.

There are some other facts of arithmetic to keep in mind when looking at a chart. Examine the chart to see if the change shown is in actual dollars, or is a percent change from the value before. The choice made by the person making the chart could be used to hide his or her motives.

Changes shown in actual dollars have nothing to do with the total value of the quantity. In Figure 4.1c the same $4000 salary increase is shown each year, but that information alone tells us nothing about the base salary at the beginning. Likewise, if the government runs a $524 billion deficit in a given year, that information says nothing about the total debt accumulated. And knowing that a stock rose one point in share value tells us nothing about the percentage gain unless we know the price of the stock. A chart that shows only change in actual dollars might be used to hide the actual value of the quantity. For example, politicians who only talk of yearly deficits but never mention the total debt accumulated hide the long-term consequences of deficit spending.

Changes shown in terms of a percentage depend critically on the total value of the quantity. It is a fact of arithmetic that, as numbers become larger, the repeated addition of a fixed amount represents a progressively smaller percent change. A one-point gain in a stock that sells for $10 per share is big news. A one-point gain for a $200 per share stock is not news. But, again it is not possible to know the total value of the quantity if the only information given is the percent change. Knowing that a stock rose 10 percent provides no information about the share price. In Figure 4.1d it is not possible to know that the decreasing values represent the same annual salary increase unless you know the base salary. A chart that shows change in terms of a percentage might be used to disguise a large increase in a quantity as a small percentage change.

A recurring theme throughout this book is that the context of numbers must be understood and the motivation of the person providing the numbers must be examined. The same is true for charts. An illustration, such as a chart, is always created to emphasize a point. Pay attention to the context of the chart and the motivation for its use. A chart provides a pretty picture for a presentation, but it may not be any more than that—a pretty picture.

Medical Malpractice: A Two-Headed Quarter?

The rising cost of malpractice insurance is a problem for medical doctors. Many doctors complain that if the trend continues, it will become impossible to practice medicine. Threats by doctors to close medical practices have prompted states to consider legislation to address the problem. The governor of Maryland called back the entire state legislature for a special session during the 2004-05-holiday recess just to deal with the "crisis" in malpractice insurance. Even Congress has considered intervening. Bills introduced in 2003 before the House and Senate would restrict certain kinds of malpractice awards.

But where is the source of the problem? Is it with the juries that make the awards, the insurance companies trying to make profits, or a health care system with spiraling costs? Each party can produce charts that blame the other parties, and all the charts are accurate.

A report from the Congressional Budget Office issued on January 8, 2004, and titled "Limiting Tort Liability for Medical Malpractice" has a chart that could be used to blame juries. It shows the "Average Insurance Payment for Closed Malpractice Claims, 1986–2002," and it is a chart that shows a steady increase from $95,000 in 1986 to $320,000 in 2002. This chart, based on data attributed to the Physician Insurers Association of America, is shown in Figure 4.9a. According to the Congressional Budget Office document, the increase in malpractice awards "represents an annual growth rate of nearly 8 percent—more than twice the general rate of inflation."

But a report from a lobbying group—Public Citizen's Congress Watch—issued a year earlier and titled "Medical Misdiagnosis: Challenging the Malpractice Claims of the Doctors' Lobby," provides a different picture of data on rising malpractice awards. This report argues that the appropriate comparison of the growth rate in malpractice awards is not with the general inflation rate, but with the healthcare inflation rate because the bulk of malpractice awards go to pay medical bills. A chart in the report compares the growth in health insurance costs with the growth in malpractice awards. A chart similar to the one in the report that uses their data is shown in Figure 4.9b. It shows a rise in malpractice awards that roughly tracks the rise in health insurance premiums. The change in malpractice awards even shows a decline in 2001 that leaves it slightly lagging behind the change in health insurance premiums.

Figures 4.9a and 4.9b show different pictures of the same phenomenon, but both present the same mathematical truth. There are several points to consider when comparing these figures before you recognize the agreement between them. Note that Figure 4.9b shows a much smaller time frame (1998–2001) than Figure 4.9a (1986–2002). Discerning long-term trends based on short time frames is difficult. If Figure 4.9b showed one fewer year (1998–2000), the reader would reach the opposite conclusion—that malpractice awards are rising much faster than health insurance premiums. Also note that Figure 4.9b shows the percent change in malpractice payments from the year before, not the actual payments. That means the decrease from years 2000 to 2001 shown in Figure 4.9a still represents an increase in the actual value of malpractice payments. It is also not possible to determine the value of malpractice payments from Figure 4.9b because only the change has been shown.*

*The CBO figure shows that the average malpractice payment in 2001 was about $300,000. The data, published in the Public Citizen's Congress Watch report that was used to construct Figure 4.9b states that the median for malpractice payments in 2001 was $135,000. Despite the large difference in these two numbers there is no contradiction because in statistical jargon the *average* or *mean* of a series of numbers is not the same as the *median*. As an example consider a series of five dollar amounts: $100,000, $120,000, $135,000, $500,000, and $800,000. The *mean* or average of these five values is $331,000 but the *median* is $135,000. That is because the median is simply the value in the list that has as many values greater than it as less than it. In a data set that includes many "typical" values and a small number of extremely large values, the median will always be significantly less than the mean. Malpractice awards, and for that matter home prices, usually present those kinds of data sets because there will always be some very large values, but never values less than zero that would bring a computation of the average down to the value of the median.

Figure 4.9: Two different pictures of the growth in malpractice awards.

(a) Average insurance payment for closed malpractice claims, 1986-2002. Figure is from a Congressional Budget Office (CBO) Economic and Budget Issue Brief published on January 8, 2004 titled: "Limiting Tort Liability for Medical Malpractice."

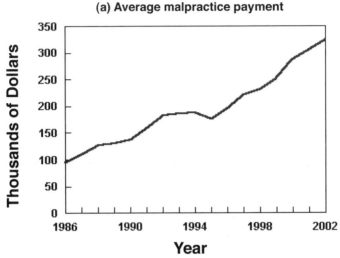

(b) Comparison of the growth in both health insurance costs and malpractice awards. Data is from a report by Public Citizen's Congress Watch titled "Medical Misdiagnosis: Challenging the Malpractice Claims of the Doctors' Lobby," published in January 2003. A figure similar to the one below is published in the report.

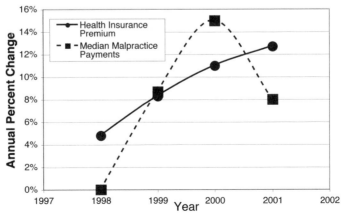

Observation: Sixteen years of data is shown in Figure 4.9a while just four years of data is shown in Figure 4.9b.

So doctors cannot afford to practice medicine because of rising malpractice awards. Malpractice awards rise because medical costs rise. Which side of the coin is the head really on? The Congressional Budget Office document provides us with a perspective if we look at the size of the numbers involved.

"Malpractice costs amounted to an estimated $24 billion in 2002, but that figure represents less than 2 percent of overall healthcare spending. Thus, even a reduction of 25 percent to 30 percent in malpractice costs would lower health care costs by only about 0.4 percent to 0.5 percent, and the likely effect on health insurance premiums would be comparably small."

The rise in the cost of malpractice insurance might be driving your doctor out of business, but it is not driving up the cost of your healthcare insurance.

Chapter 4 Resources:

Peter G. Peterson, *Running on Empty: How the Democratic and Republican Parties Are Bankrupting Our Future and What Americans Can Do About It* (New York, NY: Farrar, Straus and Giroux, 2004) provides a frightening look into the future of federal entitlement programs. The mathematical fact that Social Security and Medicare are unsustainable in their current form could have catastrophic economic consequences unless the politicians in Washington abandon their partisan bickering and take responsibility for the fiscal mess they have created. Peterson explains how demographic trends—an aging population—will cause the current method for financing Social Security to unravel in the near future.

The Congressional Budget Office provides analyses of budget and economic policies on a wide variety of topics. Reports are available for free at http://www.cbo.gov.

Part II

Income

CHAPTER FIVE

Earning and Saving

The Deceptive Math of Income Growth

"Over time, money compounds. Over a lot of time, money compounds dramatically!"

—David Bach
The Automatic Millionaire
(New York, NY: Broadway Books, 2004) p. 96

A nightmare for the math phobic—you are at the pearly gates and St. Peter is explaining the compensation plans in heaven. There are two choices:

Plan A: Starting salary 1000 Talents, pay increases 10% per year.

Plan B: Starting salary 10,000 Talents, pay increases 1000 Talents per year.

You are asked to choose one of the plans. The choice seems obvious. Plan B pays ten times more initially, and the raise after the first year is also ten times more so you choose B. St. Peter frowns and says, "If you're not planning on spending an eternity in heaven, you will not be let in at all." The gate is slammed shut in your face. It was a trick question.

What is wrong with Plan B? Initially you will make more money with Plan B, but over the long run Plan B cannot come close to competing with the earnings of Plan A. Think about what 10% per year means. In the first year, the 10% raise under Plan A is only 100 Talents, but each year the raise increases. The second year it is 110, the third year 121, and so on. There will be a year when the raise is 1000 Talents, and in all years after that the raise will be larger than 1000 Talents. At some point, your salary will be 100,000 Talents, and your next year's raise becomes 10,000 Talents. At this point your raises are 10 times those you would receive with Plan B and your raises will grow larger still.

The comparison between Plans A and B is easier to see graphically. Figure 5.1 compares the two plans. It takes 40 years for Plan A to catch up with plan B, but when it does, earnings under Plan A grow extraordinarily fast. By year 80 your salary under Plan A will be so large that there will be no point to making a comparison to Plan B.

Figure 5.1: Comparison of two salary plans. Plan A increases by a fixed percentage each year while Plan B increases by a fixed amount each year.

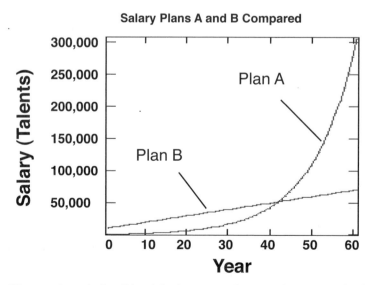

Observation: At first Plan A is slow to catch up to Plan B, but after it does its increase becomes rapid in comparison.

Plan A is much better in the long run because of a mathematical effect that finance books refer to as "compounding." Just as in this example, compounding can lead to counter-intuitive results. The best choice is not always obvious. Choice is always about judging future outcomes. In this chapter, I will show how the mathematics of compounding applies to earning and saving money and how to use that math to project financial outcomes. In the discussion that follows, a variety of specific numerical examples will be given. The examples relate to common financial choices that most people will face at some point in their life, only for each individual situation the numbers will be different. To assist you in making your own decisions with your specific numbers, I have designed worksheets that are included in Appendix I (make photocopies for repeated use) and are available online at http://www.TheTwoHeadedQuarter.com. Each example given in the text has a notation at the end indicating the worksheet used, the table used, and the specific quantities used in filling out the worksheet. By using the worksheets and tables in this book, you should be able to adapt any of the examples to your own situations and make choices that are best for you.

Lines versus Exponentials

In mathematics a rule that describes the dependence of one quantity on another — salary on time in the previous example — is referred to as a *function*. A function is a rule that given an input quantity, such as a specific time, allows you to determine an output quantity — the salary at that specific time. A function that takes time as the input quantity is referred to as "a function of time," and its rule is applied to the time quantity. A particular function can have its rule described in words, shown pictorially with a graph, tabulated in a table, or expressed with a mathematical formula. All would be equivalent representations of the same function. Many functional relationships that occur repeatedly have special names. Mathematicians have a large vocabulary of names for commonly occurring functions.

In the language of mathematics, the rule for salary Plan B and the equivalent graph is a function of time known as a *line*. A line is a function that *describes a quantity that changes by a fixed amount per unit of time*. The rule for salary Plan A approximates a function of time known as an exponential. An *exponential function describes a quantity that changes by a fixed percentage per unit of time*.

Strictly speaking, a true exponential function requires that the change happen continuously rather than at fixed time intervals. An annual raise that is a percentage of the previous year's salary results in growth that is "close" to exponential. The approximation to exponential growth becomes better when the time intervals at which raises are awarded are small compared to the complete timeline. An exponential function is a good approximation to Salary Plan A because if you're going to be in heaven forever, a year is a small time. While Figure 5.1 shows a time line of 60 years, (rather than forever) because the adjustment interval is one year (a number much smaller than the 60), the curve shown for Plan A is difficult to distinguish from a true exponential. But, if the overall timeline is five years, the exponential growth of Plan A would not be easily distinguishable from the linear growth of Plan B.

Exponentials are deceiving because while their initial growth is close to linear, over the long run a line can never keep up with an exponential. Linear growth is characterized by a *starting point* and a *fixed rate of change*. For Plan B, the starting point is 10,000 Talents and the rate of change is 1000 Talents per year. Because the rate of change remains fixed for linear growth, the annual raise is the same forever. An exponential is characterized by a *starting point* and a *fixed growth rate*. For Plan A the starting point is 1000 Talents and the growth rate is 10 percent per year. Notice that a *growth rate* is *not* the same thing as a *rate of change*. In the example of Salary Plan A where the starting point is 1000 Talents and the growth rate is fixed at 10%, the change after one year is 100 Talents, after two years 110 Talents, after three years 121 Talents and so on. In other words, if the growth rate is fixed the rate of change continually increases. It is for this reason, that exponential functions become so much larger than functions described by lines.

Money that increases at a fixed growth rate is said to "compound" because the more money there is, the faster it grows and the process feeds on itself. The resulting growth approximates an exponential function.

The Doubling Rule

When negotiating salaries or investing in the stock market, many people think in terms of fixed dollar amounts, not fixed growth rates. But this is a mistake. Suppose you invest $1000 in a stock and a year later the stock is worth $1100. In absolute dollars, your gain is not very much. After all, $100 won't even pay the monthly grocery bill for a family of four or a typical monthly car payment. It hardly seems worth the effort of saving the $1000 to begin with. However, the percentage gain in your investment is 10%, a large gain for one year. If you continue to save and find equally successful investments, over time your gains will add up to large sums of money. If your $1000 investment continued to earn 10% for the next 20 years and no additional money were added or subtracted, it would become more than $8,000.

To understand why a 10% rate of return would become so large, you need to know about a fascinating feature of exponential functions. For a given rate of growth the "doubling time" is always the same. In the example with the Talents illustrated in Figure 5.1, the salary under Plan A that has a 10% growth rate doubles approximately every seven years starting from *any* salary level. Pick any point on the graph of Plan A, say at year eight when the salary is 1900 Talents; and seven years later, in year 15, it will have doubled to 3800 Talents. If you pick year 11 when your salary is 2500 Talents, again seven years later, in year 18, the salary will have doubled to 5000 Talents. It does not matter what point you pick on an exponential curve: the growth rate determines a doubling time that is fixed for all eternity. In contrast, the doubling time for a line gets progressively longer. Under Plan B, it takes 10 years to double the salary the first time,

20 years to double it again, 40 years to double a third time.

Doubling times for exponentials are very sensitive to the growth rate. There is a simple formula that gives a good approximation of the doubling time for annual growth rates of less than 50%.

The Doubling Rule

The doubling time in years, T_d, is:

$$T_d = (72) / R$$

where R is the annual growth rate in percent.

For example a 6% growth rate has a 72 divided by 6, or 12-year doubling time, but a 10% growth rate has a 72 divided by 10, or a 7.2-year doubling time. Shortening the doubling time makes dramatic differences in the end result. Invest your money at 4%, and it doubles twice over a 36-year period because the doubling time is 72 divided by 4, or 18 years. That means $1000 invested at 4% will double once to $2000 and again to $4000 in 36 years time. A mathematician would call this an increase by a factor of 4. Invest your money at 10%, and it doubles 5 times over the same 36-year period. That means an initial $1000 invested at 10% would double to $2000, double again to $4000, double a third time to $8000, double a fourth time to $16,000, and double a fifth time to $32,000 over the same 36 years (a factor of 32 total increase). But the 10% investment earns 75% of its money in the final 14.4 years of the 36-year period. You have to wait 21 years before a dramatic difference between the two investments becomes apparent. Just like the difference between salary Plans A and B, if you are only looking at the total amount earned, you might be deceived by the slow initial growth of the exponential. Successful investments are often unremarkable at first. It takes time to see the difference between linear and exponential growth, and most people are not that patient.

One way to quickly estimate the future value of a fixed-rate investment is to know the "multiplying factor" associated with the number of times it will double over the time period that the investment is owned. In the previous examples, it is apparent that the multiplying factor associated with doubling an investment two times is 4 and the factor associated with four doublings is 16. The multiplying factor for any arbitrary number of doublings can be computed and tabulated. Table 5.1 lists the multiplying factors for any number of doublings between 1 and 20. In mathematical jargon these are known as the "powers of 2."

Table 5.1: Multipliers for the first 20 powers of 2.

Powers of 2	
Power	**Multiplier**
1	2
2	4
3	8
4	16
5	32
6	64
7	128
8	256
9	512
10	1024
11	2048
12	4096
13	8192
14	16,384
15	32,768
16	65,536
17	131,072
18	262,144
19	524,288
20	1,048,576

Observation: Every 10 doublings of a quantity is an increase by roughly a factor of 1000. That means for 30 doublings the multiplier is about 1 billion, 40 doublings is about 1 trillion, etc.

Because the multiplying factors in Table 5.1 increase so rapidly, the future value of a long-term investment is extremely sensitive to the annual growth rate. Imagine investing $1000 at a fixed rate of 7% for 30 years. The doubling time according to our formula is 72 divided by 7, or about 10 years. The number of doubling times over 30 years is 30 divided by 10, or three times. From Table 5.1, you can see that the multiplying factor for three doublings is 8. The $1000 investment becomes 8 x $1000 or $8000. Consider the same $1000 invested for 30 years at 12%. Now the doubling time is 72 divided by 12, which is 6 years. The number of doubling times is 30 divided by 6, or 5 times. From Table 5.1 the multiplier for 5 is 32. The original investment is now worth 32 x $1000 or $32,000. While 12% annual growth is less than twice the 7% annual growth, over 30 years it makes a 400% difference in the final value of the investment.

Another useful pattern to note in Table 5.1 is that every 10 doublings is equivalent to multiplying by about 1000. The first 10 powers of 2 show that 10 doublings is 1024, and 20 doublings is 1,048,576 (about 1 million). If Table 5.1 were continued beyond 20 doublings, the pattern would continue: 30 doublings would be about 1 billion, 40 doublings about 1 trillion, and so on.

© 2005 Creators Syndicate, Inc. Reprinted by permission of John L. Hart FLP, and Creators Syndicate, Inc.

Fixed Growth Rates

There are many situations—salary negotiations, investment planning, saving for college, budget planning—where choices must be made that require knowing a future value or cost. In most cases the value or cost is not static, but undergoes a "typical" percent increase each year. The "Doubling Rule" can be used to estimate future values, but a more precise summary of growth at a fixed annual percentage rate is shown in the Fixed-rate Growth Table (Table 5.2). The future value of *any* quantity that grows at a fixed percentage rate each year can be projected using Table 5.2. The rows are annual percentage rates and the columns are time periods in years. The values in Table 5.2 are compounded annually. This means that at the end of each year, the value for the previous year is increased by the percentage shown in the row.

The doubling property of exponential growth can be seen in Table 5.2. Consider growth at a 15% annual rate that, according to the doubling rule, should have a doubling time of 72 divided by 15, or 4.8, which is approximately five years. In the 15% row, the amounts at five-year intervals are $2.011, $4.046, $8.137, $16.37, $32.92, and $66.21, which is an approximate doubling every five years. For growth at a 7% annual rate, the doubling time is 72 divided by 7, or about 10 years. The values in the 7% row at 10-year intervals are $1.967, $3.870, and $7.612, which is a doubling every 10 years. Table 5.2 can also be used to determine past rates of growth. Examples for use of the Fixed-rate Growth Table follow. Use Worksheets A1.a–c in Appendix I to do projections that are similar to those in the examples.

Table 5.2: Future value of $1 invested at a fixed rate of return for the number of years in the column heading. The rate is an annual percentage rate; returns are compounded yearly.

Fixed-rate growth

Rate (%)	Years into the Future					
	2	3	4	5	6	8
0.0	$1.000	$1.000	$1.000	$1.000	$1.000	$1.000
0.5	$1.010	$1.015	$1.020	$1.025	$1.030	$1.041
1.0	$1.020	$1.030	$1.041	$1.051	$1.062	$1.083
1.5	$1.030	$1.046	$1.061	$1.077	$1.093	$1.126
2.0	$1.040	$1.061	$1.082	$1.104	$1.126	$1.172
2.5	$1.051	$1.077	$1.104	$1.131	$1.160	$1.218
3.0	$1.061	$1.093	$1.126	$1.159	$1.194	$1.267
3.5	$1.071	$1.109	$1.148	$1.188	$1.229	$1.317
4.0	$1.082	$1.125	$1.170	$1.217	$1.265	$1.369
4.5	$1.092	$1.141	$1.193	$1.246	$1.302	$1.422
5.0	$1.103	$1.158	$1.216	$1.276	$1.340	$1.477
5.5	$1.113	$1.174	$1.239	$1.307	$1.379	$1.535
6.0	$1.124	$1.191	$1.262	$1.338	$1.419	$1.594
6.5	$1.134	$1.208	$1.286	$1.370	$1.459	$1.655
7.0	$1.145	$1.225	$1.311	$1.403	$1.501	$1.718
7.5	$1.156	$1.242	$1.335	$1.436	$1.543	$1.783
8.0	$1.166	$1.260	$1.360	$1.469	$1.587	$1.851
8.5	$1.177	$1.277	$1.386	$1.504	$1.631	$1.921
9.0	$1.188	$1.295	$1.412	$1.539	$1.677	$1.993
9.5	$1.199	$1.313	$1.438	$1.574	$1.724	$2.067
10.0	$1.210	$1.331	$1.464	$1.611	$1.772	$2.144
11.0	$1.232	$1.368	$1.518	$1.685	$1.870	$2.305
12.0	$1.254	$1.405	$1.574	$1.762	$1.974	$2.476
13.0	$1.277	$1.443	$1.630	$1.842	$2.082	$2.658
14.0	$1.300	$1.482	$1.689	$1.925	$2.195	$2.853
15.0	$1.323	$1.521	$1.749	$2.011	$2.313	$3.059
16.0	$1.346	$1.561	$1.811	$2.100	$2.436	$3.278
17.0	$1.369	$1.602	$1.874	$2.192	$2.565	$3.511
18.0	$1.392	$1.643	$1.939	$2.288	$2.700	$3.759
19.0	$1.416	$1.685	$2.005	$2.386	$2.840	$4.021
20.0	$1.440	$1.728	$2.074	$2.488	$2.986	$4.300
21.0	$1.464	$1.772	$2.144	$2.594	$3.138	$4.595
22.0	$1.488	$1.816	$2.215	$2.703	$3.297	$4.908
23.0	$1.513	$1.861	$2.289	$2.815	$3.463	$5.239
24.0	$1.538	$1.907	$2.364	$2.932	$3.635	$5.590
25.0	$1.563	$1.953	$2.441	$3.052	$3.815	$5.960
26.0	$1.588	$2.000	$2.520	$3.176	$4.002	$6.353
27.0	$1.613	$2.048	$2.601	$3.304	$4.196	$6.768
28.0	$1.638	$2.097	$2.684	$3.436	$4.398	$7.206

Observation: The combination of high growth rates and long time periods produces dramatic increases in future values.

Fixed-rate growth

Rate (%)	Years into the Future					
	10	12	15	20	25	30
0.0	$1.000	$1.000	$1.000	$1.000	$1.000	$1.000
0.5	$1.051	$1.062	$1.078	$1.105	$1.133	$1.161
1.0	$1.105	$1.127	$1.161	$1.220	$1.282	$1.348
1.5	$1.161	$1.196	$1.250	$1.347	$1.451	$1.563
2.0	$1.219	$1.268	$1.346	$1.486	$1.641	$1.811
2.5	$1.280	$1.345	$1.448	$1.639	$1.854	$2.098
3.0	$1.344	$1.426	$1.558	$1.806	$2.094	$2.427
3.5	$1.411	$1.511	$1.675	$1.990	$2.363	$2.807
4.0	$1.480	$1.601	$1.801	$2.191	$2.666	$3.243
4.5	$1.553	$1.696	$1.935	$2.412	$3.005	$3.745
5.0	$1.629	$1.796	$2.079	$2.653	$3.386	$4.322
5.5	$1.708	$1.901	$2.232	$2.918	$3.813	$4.984
6.0	$1.791	$2.012	$2.397	$3.207	$4.292	$5.743
6.5	$1.877	$2.129	$2.572	$3.524	$4.828	$6.614
7.0	$1.967	$2.252	$2.759	$3.870	$5.427	$7.612
7.5	$2.061	$2.382	$2.959	$4.248	$6.098	$8.755
8.0	$2.159	$2.518	$3.172	$4.661	$6.848	$10.06
8.5	$2.261	$2.662	$3.400	$5.112	$7.687	$11.56
9.0	$2.367	$2.813	$3.642	$5.604	$8.623	$13.27
9.5	$2.478	$2.971	$3.901	$6.142	$9.668	$15.22
10.0	$2.594	$3.138	$4.177	$6.727	$10.83	$17.45
11.0	$2.839	$3.498	$4.785	$8.062	$13.59	$22.89
12.0	$3.106	$3.896	$5.474	$9.646	$17.00	$29.96
13.0	$3.395	$4.335	$6.254	$11.52	$21.23	$39.12
14.0	$3.707	$4.818	$7.138	$13.74	$26.46	$50.95
15.0	$4.046	$5.350	$8.137	$16.37	$32.92	$66.21
16.0	$4.411	$5.936	$9.266	$19.46	$40.87	$85.85
17.0	$4.807	$6.580	$10.54	$23.11	$50.66	$111
18.0	$5.234	$7.288	$11.97	$27.39	$62.67	$143
19.0	$5.695	$8.064	$13.59	$32.43	$77.39	$185
20.0	$6.192	$8.916	$15.41	$38.34	$95.40	$237
21.0	$6.727	$9.850	$17.45	$45.26	$117	$304
22.0	$7.305	$10.87	$19.74	$53.36	$144	$390
23.0	$7.926	$11.99	$22.31	$62.82	$177	$498
24.0	$8.594	$13.21	$25.20	$73.86	$217	$635
25.0	$9.313	$14.55	$28.42	$86.74	$265	$808
26.0	$10.09	$16.01	$32.03	$102	$323	$1,026
27.0	$10.92	$17.61	$36.06	$119	$394	$1,301
28.0	$11.81	$19.34	$40.56	$139	$479	$1,646

Example 5.1

Project a future salary

You begin a career with a starting salary of $25,000. If each year your raise is 5%, what will be your salary 10 years in the future?

In Table 5.2, at the intersection of the 5% row with the 10-year column is $1.629. If your salary follows that trend, in 10 years you will earn $1.629 x 25,000 = $40,725.

[Worksheet A1.a, Table 5.2: Rate = 5%, Duration = 10 years, Initial Value = $25,000; Result is Final Value = $40,725]

Example 5.2

Differences in investment returns for short time periods

If you invest $1000 for eight years, what is the difference in the final values between a 4% annual rate of return compared to an 8% annual rate of return?

According to Table 5.2 you will earn $1.369 for each dollar invested at 4% compared to $1.851 for each dollar invested at 8%. For a $1000 investment, the difference at the end is $1851, compared to $1369. The 8% investment finishes with 35% more money than the 4%.

[Worksheet A1.a, Table 5.2: Rate = 4%, Duration = 8 years, Initial Value = $1,000; Result is Final Value = $1369]
[Worksheet A1.a, Table 5.2: Rate = 8%, Duration = 8 years, Initial Value = $1,000; Result is Final Value = $1851]

Example 5.3

Differences in investment returns for long time periods

If you invest $1000 for 30 years, what is the difference in the final values between a 4% and an 8% annual rate of return?

You will earn $3.243 for each dollar invested at 4% compared to $10.06 invested at 8%. Over the 30-year time period your $1000 investment at 8% grows to $10,060 compared to $3243 at 4%. The 8% investment finishes with 310% more money than the 4%.

[Worksheet A1.a, Table 5.2: Rate = 4%, Duration = 30 years, Initial Value = $1,000; Result is Final Value = $3243]
[Worksheet A1.a, Table 5.2: Rate = 8%, Duration = 30 years, Initial Value = $1,000; Result is Final Value = $10,060]

Example 5.4

Past increases in college costs

In 1975 annual tuition at a private college was $3000. In 2005, annual tuition at the same college is $25,000. What is the average annual increase in tuition at this school?

Tuition has increased by a factor of $25,000 divided by $3000, or 8.33. It costs $8.33 for every dollar spent 30 years ago. Look down the 30-year column in Table 5.2 to find where $8.33 would fall. It is between $7.612 and $8.755, which are the values in the 7.0% and 7.5% rows. Tuition raises at this college have averaged 7.0 to 7.5% per year over this time period.

[Worksheet A1.b, Table 5.2: Final Value = $25,000, Initial Value = $3,000, Duration = 30 years,; Result is Rate between 7.0 to 7.5%]

Example 5.5

Project college tuition in the future

If the annual tuition at a private college is $25,000 in 2005, and tuition increases an average of 5% per year. In what year will annual tuition reach $40,000?

In that particular year, tuition will have increased by a factor of $40,000 divided by $25,000, or 1.6 compared to year 2005. Look in the 5% row in Table 5.2. At a 5% annual rate of return a dollar becomes $1.629 in 10 years. That means if 5% growth continues, in year 2015 tuition will cost close to $40,000.

[Worksheet A1.c, Table 5.2: Final Value = $40,000, Initial Value = $25,000, Rate = 5%,; Result is Duration = 10 years]

Growth Not Measured in Dollars

Because I have focused this book on financial decision-making, the values in Table 5.2 are expressed in dollars and my examples are financial. But the numbers do not have to represent dollars. *The doubling rule and the more precise values in Table 5.2 apply to any fixed-rate growth process.* The projection could refer to population, market share, product adoption, spread of disease, or any other quantity that is undergoing growth at a fixed percentage per year. Of course not all growth processes proceed at a fixed percentage per year and those that do cannot maintain that growth forever. The limitations of exponential growth will be examined later in this chapter. Here are some examples for projecting growth in quantities that are not monetary. Ignore the dollar signs in Table 5.2 when doing these problems.

Example 5.6

Population growth (short-term)

During the decade of the 1990's, world population increased from 5.28 billion people to 6.00 billion people. What is the average annual rate of growth during this time period?

Over 10 years the total number of people increased by a factor of 6.00 divided by 5.28, or 1.14. In the 10-year column of Table 5.2, the number 1.14 falls between the numbers 1.105 and 1.161. Annual population growth averaged between 1.0 and 1.5%.

[Worksheet A1.b, Table 5.2: Final Value = 6.00 billion, Initial Value = 5.28 billion, Duration = 10 years,; Result is Rate between 1.0 to 1.5%]

Example 5.7

Population growth (long-term)

At the beginning of the year 2000 there were 6.00 billion people in the world. If population growth averages 1% for the next century, what will world population be in the year 2100?

For this estimate use the doubling rule because one century is beyond any of the time periods that Table 5.2 provides. A 1% growth rate has a doubling time of 72 divided by 1, or 72 years. That means the population will double to 12 billion by the year 2072 and be about halfway to doubling again 36 years from that time. Expect a world population of just under 18 billion people in the year 2100 if the 1% annual population growth continues.

Integrated Fixed-rate Growth

Often it is useful to know the *total* amount of money spent over a period of time. If there is no change from year to year in the expenditure, the addition is simple. For example, if tuition at a college is $15,000 per year and does not change, a four-year degree costs $60,000. But if growth in the expenditure occurs each year, the problem is more complicated. If tuition rises 7% per year, the cost of a four-year degree is obviously more than $60,000. The question becomes how much more than $60,000 should you budget? Mathematicians call the process of adding a quantity that continuously changes *integration*.

Table 5.3 shows the results of "integrated" growth that is at a fixed percentage rate. This table is useful for calculating total expenditures over the period of years listed in the column heading. To see how this works, imagine that this year you must spend a dollar on a candy bar, the next year 10% more or $1.10, the next year an additional 10% or $1.21, and the fourth year an additional 10% or $1.33. Over four years, you have spent $1 + $1.10 + $1.21 + $1.33 or $4.64 on candy bars. In Table 5.3 under the 4-year column in the 10% row is $4.64, the total amount per dollar spent in the first year when the expenditure increases 10% each year. Here are some examples for using Table 5.3.

Example 5.8

Saving for college

Your child will begin a four-year college six years from now. Today expenses at that college average $25,000 per year for tuition, room, and board. If college costs continue to rise at an average of 7% per year, what is the total projected cost of your child's education?

Determine the first-year cost six years from now using Table 5.2. From the 7% row in the six-year column, you find the multiplier is $1.501. Expect to pay $1.501 x 25,000 or $37,525 for the first year of college. From Table 5.3, if 7% growth continues for the four years of college, total costs will be $4.44 x 37,525 or $166,611.

[Worksheet A1.a, Table 5.2: Rate = 7%, Duration = 6 years, Initial Value = $25,000; Result is Final Value = $37,525]
[Worksheet A1.a, Table 5.3: Rate = 7%, Duration = 4 years, Initial Value = $37,525; Result is Final Value = $166,611]

Example 5.9

Multiple year budgeting

You are the owner of a small company and must produce a budget for total expenditures on health benefits for your employees for the next three years. If healthcare costs are projected to rise 12% per year and this year you will spend $25,000, what will total healthcare costs be over the next three years?

The 12% row, three-year column has $3.37. Over three years, plan on spending $3.37 x 25,000 or $84,250.

[Worksheet A1.a, Table 5.3: Rate = 12%, Duration = 3 years, Initial Value = $25,000; Result is Final Value = $84,250]

Table 5.3: Total earnings per initial $1 at a fixed rate of return for the number of years in the column heading. Each year an additional $1 is added. Rate is an annual percentage rate; returns are compounded yearly.

Integrated fixed-rate growth

	Years into the Future					
Rate (%)	2	3	4	5	6	8
0.0	$2.00	$3.00	$4.00	$5.00	$6.00	$8.00
0.5	$2.00	$3.02	$4.03	$5.05	$6.08	$8.14
1.0	$2.01	$3.03	$4.06	$5.10	$6.15	$8.29
1.5	$2.01	$3.05	$4.09	$5.15	$6.23	$8.43
2.0	$2.02	$3.06	$4.12	$5.20	$6.31	$8.58
2.5	$2.03	$3.08	$4.15	$5.26	$6.39	$8.74
3.0	$2.03	$3.09	$4.18	$5.31	$6.47	$8.89
3.5	$2.04	$3.11	$4.21	$5.36	$6.55	$9.05
4.0	$2.04	$3.12	$4.25	$5.42	$6.63	$9.21
4.5	$2.05	$3.14	$4.28	$5.47	$6.72	$9.38
5.0	$2.05	$3.15	$4.31	$5.53	$6.80	$9.55
5.5	$2.06	$3.17	$4.34	$5.58	$6.89	$9.72
6.0	$2.06	$3.18	$4.37	$5.64	$6.98	$9.90
6.5	$2.07	$3.20	$4.41	$5.69	$7.06	$10.08
7.0	$2.07	$3.21	$4.44	$5.75	$7.15	$10.26
7.5	$2.08	$3.23	$4.47	$5.81	$7.24	$10.45
8.0	$2.08	$3.25	$4.51	$5.87	$7.34	$10.64
8.5	$2.09	$3.26	$4.54	$5.93	$7.43	$10.83
9.0	$2.09	$3.28	$4.57	$5.98	$7.52	$11.03
9.5	$2.10	$3.29	$4.61	$6.04	$7.62	$11.23
10.0	$2.10	$3.31	$4.64	$6.11	$7.72	$11.44
11.0	$2.11	$3.34	$4.71	$6.23	$7.91	$11.86
12.0	$2.12	$3.37	$4.78	$6.35	$8.12	$12.30
13.0	$2.13	$3.41	$4.85	$6.48	$8.32	$12.76
14.0	$2.14	$3.44	$4.92	$6.61	$8.54	$13.23
15.0	$2.15	$3.47	$4.99	$6.74	$8.75	$13.73
16.0	$2.16	$3.51	$5.07	$6.88	$8.98	$14.24
17.0	$2.17	$3.54	$5.14	$7.01	$9.21	$14.77
18.0	$2.18	$3.57	$5.22	$7.15	$9.44	$15.33
19.0	$2.19	$3.61	$5.29	$7.30	$9.68	$15.90
20.0	$2.20	$3.64	$5.37	$7.44	$9.93	$16.50
21.0	$2.21	$3.67	$5.45	$7.59	$10.18	$17.12
22.0	$2.22	$3.71	$5.52	$7.74	$10.44	$17.76
23.0	$2.23	$3.74	$5.60	$7.89	$10.71	$18.43
24.0	$2.24	$3.78	$5.68	$8.05	$10.98	$19.12
25.0	$2.25	$3.81	$5.77	$8.21	$11.26	$19.84
26.0	$2.26	$3.85	$5.85	$8.37	$11.54	$20.59
27.0	$2.27	$3.88	$5.93	$8.53	$11.84	$21.36
28.0	$2.28	$3.92	$6.02	$8.70	$12.14	$22.16

Observation: Small annual increases in expenditures add up to large amounts of money when compounded over decades of time.

Integrated fixed-rate growth

Rate (%)	Years into the Future					
	10	12	15	20	25	30
0.0	$10.00	$12.00	$15.00	$20.00	$25.00	$30.00
0.5	$10.23	$12.34	$15.54	$20.98	$26.56	$32.28
1.0	$10.46	$12.68	$16.10	$22.02	$28.24	$34.78
1.5	$10.70	$13.04	$16.68	$23.12	$30.06	$37.54
2.0	$10.95	$13.41	$17.29	$24.30	$32.03	$40.57
2.5	$11.20	$13.80	$17.93	$25.54	$34.16	$43.90
3.0	$11.46	$14.19	$18.60	$26.87	$36.46	$47.58
3.5	$11.73	$14.60	$19.30	$28.28	$38.95	$51.62
4.0	$12.01	$15.03	$20.02	$29.78	$41.65	$56.08
4.5	$12.29	$15.46	$20.78	$31.37	$44.57	$61.01
5.0	$12.58	$15.92	$21.58	$33.07	$47.73	$66.44
5.5	$12.88	$16.39	$22.41	$34.87	$51.15	$72.44
6.0	$13.18	$16.87	$23.28	$36.79	$54.86	$79.06
6.5	$13.49	$17.37	$24.18	$38.83	$58.89	$86.37
7.0	$13.82	$17.89	$25.13	$41.00	$63.25	$94.46
7.5	$14.15	$18.42	$26.12	$43.30	$67.98	$103
8.0	$14.49	$18.98	$27.15	$45.76	$73.11	$113
8.5	$14.84	$19.55	$28.23	$48.38	$78.67	$124
9.0	$15.19	$20.14	$29.36	$51.16	$84.70	$136
9.5	$15.56	$20.75	$30.54	$54.12	$91.25	$150
10.0	$15.94	$21.38	$31.77	$57.27	$98.35	$164
11.0	$16.72	$22.71	$34.41	$64.20	$114	$199
12.0	$17.55	$24.13	$37.28	$72.05	$133	$241
13.0	$18.42	$25.65	$40.42	$80.95	$156	$293
14.0	$19.34	$27.27	$43.84	$91.02	$182	$357
15.0	$20.30	$29.00	$47.58	$102	$213	$435
16.0	$21.32	$30.85	$51.66	$115	$249	$530
17.0	$22.39	$32.82	$56.11	$130	$292	$647
18.0	$23.52	$34.93	$60.97	$147	$343	$791
19.0	$24.71	$37.18	$66.26	$165	$402	$967
20.0	$25.96	$39.58	$72.04	$187	$472	$1,182
21.0	$27.27	$42.14	$78.33	$211	$554	$1,445
22.0	$28.66	$44.87	$85.19	$238	$651	$1,767
23.0	$30.11	$47.79	$92.67	$269	$765	$2,160
24.0	$31.64	$50.89	$101	$304	$898	$2,641
25.0	$33.25	$54.21	$110	$343	$1,055	$3,227
26.0	$34.94	$57.74	$119	$387	$1,239	$3,942
27.0	$36.72	$61.50	$130	$438	$1,454	$4,813
28.0	$38.59	$65.51	$141	$494	$1,707	$5,873

Example 5.10

Comparing careers

A career at Widget Incorporated has a starting salary of $35,000 per year and a pay scale that averages 4% annual increases in salary. A career at Think Tank Incorporated has a starting salary of $30,000 per year and a pay scale that averages 6% annual increases in salary. How do total earnings over a 30-year time period compare?

Expect to make a total of $56.08 x 35,000 or $1.96 million with Widget while Think Tank pays $79.06 x 30,000 or $2.37 million.

[Worksheet A1.a, Table 5.3: Rate = 4%, Duration = 30 years, Initial Value = $35,000; Result is Final Value = $1.96 million]
[Worksheet A1.a, Table 5.3: Rate = 6%, Duration = 30 years, Initial Value = $30,000; Result is Final Value = $2.37 million]

Example 5.10 is a more realistic version of the problem posed at the beginning of this chapter. Do you choose the higher starting salary or the faster growth rate? The crossover point, when the higher-earning career pays the higher salary can be read from Table 5.2. Widget initially pays $35,000 divided by $30,000, or 1.17 more than Think Tank. Take the numbers in the 4% row of Table 5.2, multiply them by 1.17, and compare them to corresponding numbers in the 6% row. For time periods less than 15 years the salary from Think Tank will be less, but after 15 years Think Tank will pay more and that difference will grow. People beginning professional careers often choose jobs that provide opportunities for further professional development but have lower salaries. The financial payoff comes later on in the career when the additional experience gives them the leverage to grow their income at a faster rate.

Example 5.11

Deciding on further education

Joe graduates from college at age 22 and takes a job starting at $40,000 per year with a 5% annual increase. Karen is the same age and declines a similar job offer. Instead she goes to business school for two years at a cost of $75,000 for tuition and board plus the two years of lost wages. She will graduate at age 24 and go to a job starting at $60,000 that increases 6% annually. Is it worth it for Karen to go to school?

Consider the total earnings for Joe and Karen after each has worked 30 years. Joe will earn $66.44 x 40,000 or $2.66 million. Karen will have earned $79.06 x 60,000 or $4.74 million. Now subtract Karen's expenses from her 30-year earnings. Karen's lost salary can also be computed using Table 5.3 by taking the value in the two-year column and 5% row which is $2.05 and multiplying by the $40,000 offer she declined which amounts to $82,000. The total cost of Karen's education is $75,000 + $82,000, or $157,000. After subtracting this from $4.74 million the result is $4.58 million, an amount that is $1.9 million ahead of Joe. Even though the 30-year mark for career earnings will occur two years earlier for Joe than for Karen, Joe's earnings can never catch up. Over the long run, Karen's investment in more education is well worth it.

[Worksheet A1.a, Table 5.3: Rate = 5%, Duration = 30 years, Initial Value = $40,000; Result is Final Value = $2.66 million]
[Worksheet A1.a, Table 5.3: Rate = 6%, Duration = 30 years, Initial Value = $60,000; Result is Final Value = $4.74 million]
[Worksheet A1.a, Table 5.3: Rate = 5%, Duration = 2 years, Initial Value = $40,000; Result is Final Value = $82,000]

Example 5.12

Effect of delayed entry into a career

*Bob begins a career at age 25 with a starting salary of
$30,000 per year. Pay increases average 3% per year for the
next 30 years. Sue, who is the same age as Bob, begins the
same career five years later at age 30 with a starting salary
of $33,000 and pay increases that also average 3% per year.
At the same age of 55 how do the total lifetime earnings of
Bob and Sue compare?*

Bob will have worked 30 years and earned $47.58 x 30,000
or $1.43 million. Sue will have worked 25 years and earned
$36.46 x $33,000 or $1.20 million. The difference is $230,000,
which is more than the five years of lost work, because Sue
cannot catch up with Bob's salary. Although both are age 55,
use of Table 5.2 shows that Bob earns $72,810 per year while
Sue earns $69,100. If average yearly raises are greater than
3%, the discrepancy between total earnings grows further.
For example, if raises average 5% per year, Bob will have
earned $2.00 million compared to $1.58 million for Sue,
and their salaries at age 55 will be $130,000 and $111,700
respectively.

[Worksheet A1.a, Table 5.3: Rate = 3%, Duration = 30 years, Initial Value =
$30,000; Result is Final Value = $1.43 million]
[Worksheet A1.a, Table 5.3: Rate = 3%, Duration = 25 years, Initial Value =
$33,000; Result is Final Value = $1.20 million]
[Worksheet A1.a, Table 5.2: Rate = 3%, Duration = 30 years, Initial Value =
$30,000; Result is Final Value = $72,810]
[Worksheet A1.a, Table 5.2: Rate = 3%, Duration = 25 years, Initial Value =
$33,000; Result is Final Value = $69,100]
[Worksheet A1.a, Table 5.3: Rate = 5%, Duration = 30 years, Initial Value =
$30,000; Result is Final Value = $2.00 million]
[Worksheet A1.a, Table 5.3: Rate = 5%, Duration = 25 years, Initial Value =
$33,000; Result is Final Value = $1.58 million]
[Worksheet A1.a, Table 5.2: Rate = 5%, Duration = 30 years, Initial Value =
$30,000; Result is Final Value = $130,000]
[Worksheet A1.a, Table 5.2: Rate = 5%, Duration = 25 years, Initial Value =
$33,000; Result is Final Value = $111,700]

Example 5.13

Cumulative effect of a higher starting salary

Ted is offered a starting salary of $34,000 per year but asks for and receives $2,000 more for a total starting salary of $36,000. Jane is offered $34,000 for the same job and accepts. Pay increases average 3% per year for the next 20 years for both Ted and Jane. How do the total earnings of Ted and Jane over this 20-year time period compare?

In Table 5.3 look under the 20-year column in the 3% row and you'll find $26.87. Ted will earn $26.87 x 36,000 or $967,320 while Jane will earn $26.87 x 34,000 or $913,580, a difference of about $54,000. Their salaries after 20 years can be determined from Table 5.2. Ted will be making $65,000, and Jane $61,400, which is a greater difference than the original $2000. If the trend continues for another 10 years, the difference will continue to grow. After 30 years Ted makes $87,370 and Jane $82,520.

[Worksheet A1.a, Table 5.3: Rate = 3%, Duration = 20 years, Initial Value = $36,000; Result is Final Value = $967,320]
[Worksheet A1.a, Table 5.3: Rate = 3%, Duration = 20 years, Initial Value = $34,000; Result is Final Value = $913,580]
[Worksheet A1.a, Table 5.2: Rate = 3%, Duration = 20 years, Initial Value = $36,000; Result is Final Value = $65,000]
 [Worksheet A1.a, Table 5.2: Rate = 3%, Duration = 20 years, Initial Value = $34,000; Result is Final Value = $61,400]
[Worksheet A1.a, Table 5.2: Rate = 3%, Duration = 30 years, Initial Value = $36,000; Result is Final Value = $87,370]
 [Worksheet A1.a, Table 5.2: Rate = 3%, Duration = 30 years, Initial Value = $34,000; Result is Final Value = $82,520]

These last two examples, 5.12 and 5.13, illustrate potential sources of gender inequities in career earnings. Women often delay or interrupt careers and often are not as aggressive as men in salary negotiations. Employers do not have to openly discriminate to end up with vast differences between male and female earnings. All employers have to do is adhere to the following practices in determining pay, which in some fields, like education, are common.

- •The employer bases starting offers either on what the employee earned in his or her last job or on total years of experience.
- •The employer offers slightly less than he or she is willing to pay and only goes higher if the employee asks for more.
- •The employer determines the next year's salary by increasing the current salary for *everyone by the same percentage*.

Even if the percentage used to calculate the raise varies from year to year—5% in the first year, 7% in the second, 2% in the third, etc.—as long as it is applied equally to everyone on the payroll, discrepancies in initial starting salaries will grow over time. Those at the lower end of the payroll will complain that they are falling further and further behind while the employer will argue that everyone is receiving equal treatment. Mathematically, both of these statements will be true. Everyone is receiving the same percentage increase in pay, but that means that in absolute dollars, those who make more receive more and that causes even small differences to grow large over time.

According to Linda Babcock and Sara Laschever, in *Women Don't Ask: Negotiation and the Gender Divide*, an individual who does not negotiate their first salary loses more than $500,000 by age 60. Their research finds that men initiate negotiations about four times more often than women and that women who do negotiate salaries earn about $1 million more during their careers than women who don't. They suggest that the gender gap in career earnings might be closed if women negotiated their first salary because in one study, men who negotiated were able to increase their starting salaries by an average of 7.4%.*

* Linda Babcock and Sara Laschever, http://www.womendontask.com/stats.html.

Dilbert: © Scott Adams/Dist. by United Feature Syndicate, Inc.

Changing the Compounding Interval

The tables for fixed-rate growth (Table 5.2) and fixed-rate integrated growth (Table 5.3) use an annual percentage rate and compounding of growth on an annual basis. For all the examples given so far, change is an annual event and Tables 5.2 and 5.3 apply. But there are instances when growth is compounded on shorter time scales. For example, a savings account or certificate of deposit might specify an annual interest rate, but accrue interest on a daily or monthly or even quarterly basis. It is interesting to examine the effect of changing the compounding interval on fixed-rate growth. Tables 5.4a–d compare the difference between daily, monthly, quarterly, and yearly compounding for annual growth rates of 4% (5.4a), 8% (5.4b), 12% (5.4c), and 16% (5.4d) over selected time periods.

Surprisingly the difference between daily compounding and yearly compounding often does not produce that great a difference in the end result. For low annual percentage rates over short time periods, the difference between compounding intervals is barely discernable. For example over five years, one dollar invested at 4% annual interest becomes $1.217 if the interest is compounded yearly or $1.221 if interest is compounded daily. That means a $1000 investment at 4% will earn four dollars more over five years when daily compounding is allowed.

The effect of shorter compounding intervals does make a difference for long-term high-rate-of-return investments. Compounded daily over 30 years, an 8% rate of return turns that dollar into $11.02, which is 10% more than the $10.06 that results from yearly compounding. At much higher rates of return, daily compounding for long time periods significantly enhances the future value of an investment. At 16% annual interest for 30 years, one dollar becomes $121 when compounded daily, but only $86 when compounded yearly. The daily compounding produces 40% more money in the end, a fact not lost on banks that compound daily high-interest credit card debt owed by their customers. Banks profit greatly from daily compounding because of the high interest rates they charge. Customers with savings accounts receive little benefit from daily compounding because of the low interest rates (usually less than 4%) that the banks pay. Here are some examples for using Table 5.4. No worksheet is provided for Table 5.4. Use of this table should be straightforward.

Example 5.14

Value of a certificate of deposit (CD) at maturity

What is the future value of $5,000 invested in a five-year CD with 4% annual interest compounded quarterly?

According to Table 5.4a each dollar becomes $1.22 for this investment. The final value will be $1.22 x 5000 or $6100.

Example 5.15

Choosing between retirement investments

You plan to put $10,000 saved towards retirement in a long-term investment. Uptown Bank credits gains to your account on a monthly basis while Downtown Bank credits gains on a quarterly basis. Assuming each investment returns 8% per year, by how much will the future values of your investment differ 30 years from now?

Table 5.4: Comparison of daily, monthly, quarterly and yearly compounding intervals for different interest rates. Future value for $1 invested at a fixed rate of return is shown for the number of years in the column heading.

Fixed-rate growth for different compounding periods

(a) 4% Annual Interest Rate

			Term (years)			
	1	2	5	10	15	30
Daily	$1.041	$1.083	$1.221	$1.492	$1.822	$3.320
Monthly	$1.041	$1.083	$1.221	$1.491	$1.820	$3.313
Quarterly	$1.041	$1.083	$1.220	$1.489	$1.817	$3.300
Yearly	$1.040	$1.082	$1.217	$1.480	$1.801	$3.243

(b) 8% Annual Interest Rate

			Term (years)			
	1	2	5	10	15	30
Daily	$1.083	$1.173	$1.492	$2.225	$3.320	$11.02
Monthly	$1.083	$1.173	$1.490	$2.220	$3.307	$10.94
Quarterly	$1.082	$1.172	$1.486	$2.208	$3.281	$10.77
Yearly	$1.080	$1.166	$1.469	$2.159	$3.172	$10.06

(c) 12% Annual Interest Rate

			Term (years)			
	1	2	5	10	15	30
Daily	$1.127	$1.271	$1.822	$3.319	$6.048	$36.58
Monthly	$1.127	$1.270	$1.817	$3.300	$5.996	$35.95
Quarterly	$1.126	$1.267	$1.806	$3.262	$5.892	$34.71
Yearly	$1.120	$1.254	$1.762	$3.106	$5.474	$29.96

(d) 16% Annual Interest Rate

			Term (years)			
	1	2	5	10	15	30
Daily	$1.173	$1.377	$2.225	$4.951	$11.02	$121
Monthly	$1.172	$1.374	$2.214	$4.901	$10.85	$118
Quarterly	$1.170	$1.369	$2.191	$4.801	$10.52	$111
Yearly	$1.160	$1.346	$2.100	$4.411	$9.266	$86

Observation: The difference between daily and yearly compounding is only noticeable for high interest rates compounded over long periods of time.

Compare the monthly and quarterly rows in Table 5.4b. Over 30 years the quarterly compounding will result in $10.77 x 10,000 or $107,700 while the monthly compounding will result in $10.94 x 10,000 or $109,400. The difference is $1700.

Saturation

"It's the velocity of growth that you need to measure now: two new stores opening and $1 billion worth of U. S. real estate bought up every week; almost 600,000 American employees churned through in a year (that's a 44 percent turnover rate). My thumbnail calculation suggests that by the year 4004, every square inch of the United States will be covered by supercenters, so that the only place for new supercenters will be on top of existing ones.

Wal-Mart will be in trouble long before that, of course, because with everyone on the planet working for the company or its suppliers, hardly anyone will be able to shop there."

—Barbara Ehrenreich
New York Times columnist
Baltimore Sun, July 27, 2004

Projecting the future value of investments, salaries, or costs by assuming growth at a fixed percentage per year over a long period of time often leads to numbers that are hard to believe. In fact the numbers should not be believed because the projected outcome will not happen. As Barbara Ehrenreich points out in the quote above, if the growth of Wal-Mart continues indefinitely at its current rate, eventually all the real estate in the United States will be owned by Wal-Mart. Obviously this will not happen. The United States is a finite landmass with a finite number of people. Eventually the growth of Wal-Mart will stop because the availability of new customers to sustain further growth will end.

St. Peter might be able to offer a 10% raise every year for eternity, but Earth is not heaven. All exponential growth processes eventually run into the limit of finite resources. The problem with using the past to project the future is that indefinite exponential growth, especially at high rates, is unsustainable. Eventually growth processes reach a point of *saturation*, which means that there is no longer any available money, customers, resources, or whatever else that feeds the growth process for it to continue.

More realistic mathematical models to project the future must account for saturation. In fact most growth processes are described by "S-shaped" graphs known as *S-curves* or *logistic curves*. In his book *A Mathematician Reads the Newspaper*, John Allen Paulos points out that S-curves have been used to describe processes as "disparate as Mozart symphony production, the rise of airline traffic, new mainframe computer installations, and the building of Gothic cathedrals."*

Figure 5.2 shows a typical S-curve. There are four distinct time periods on an S-curve. At the beginning there is exponential growth just like Plan A in Figure 5.1, but the growth rate becomes linear, then slows continuously, and then finally becomes a flat

Figure 5.2: S-shaped or "logistic" curve that describes growth over time. The curve has four distinct time periods: (1) initial exponential growth, (2) linear growth, (3) slowing growth, (4) zero growth (steady-state).

Features of an S-curve

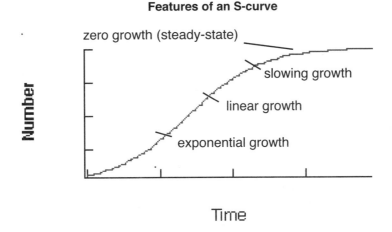

Observation: For a process described by an S-curve, exponential growth only occurs for a short time in the beginning.

* John Allen Paulos, *A Mathematician Reads the Newspaper* (New York, NY: Anchor Books, 1995) p. 91

line, which means no growth at all. The flat line does not mean the process described by the curve has ended; it means that a condition of "steady-state" has been reached. For example the S-curve might describe demand for a certain new drug in the years following its introduction. The beginning of the S-curve shows growth in the number of prescriptions as the drug enters the market. The flat line at the end of the S-curve shows the number of prescriptions filled each year once all doctors know about the drug and its appropriate use. Obviously growth must end and demand level off because the number of prescriptions cannot exceed the finite number of people with the medical condition that the drug treats.

To use Tables 5.2 and 5.3 for projecting the future, you must know where on the S-curve the growth process falls. It is that judgment or lack thereof that leads to all sorts of mathematically deceptive arguments and projections. It is important to know when a condition of saturation is approaching or you might be deceived into believing in a future outcome that is dramatically different from what is actually possible. Consider saving and investing to secure your financial future.

Ordinary individuals who save and invest can compound the value of their investments over long periods of time. For example, it is possible to grow your retirement savings exponentially over the course of your career because your individual wealth will always be a small fraction of the total wealth available. Saturation is not possible. In saving for retirement, it pays to diversify and be patient. Using Tables 5.2 and 5.3 along with knowledge of the historical rates of return for various investments will help plan for your financial future. This topic and some examples will be explored in the next chapter.

But, if you invest in an individual company be careful. Large companies that already control a major share of the market for their product or service cannot maintain a fixed rate of growth forever. Under these circumstances, Tables 5.2 and 5.3 will not project the future. During the 1990s numerous high profile accounting scandals shook U.S. financial markets. Major corporations including Waste Management, Rite Aid, Enron, WorldCom, and Global Crossing falsified their accounting to report profits that were actually losses. Stockholders lost enormous sums of money when the fraud became exposed. A common thread in the management of these companies was an insistence that earnings grow quarter after quarter in order to maintain the value of the stock. Stock purchasers paid a premium for their shares because of promises of even greater earnings in the future. Simple math would have told everyone involved that the projected growth in earnings would soon exceed the financial resources of the available customer base. Rather than publicly acknowledge that fact, executives made up numbers to represent earnings that did not exist.

Often the word "crisis" is used to describe exponential growth that is reaching saturation. Currently, industries as varied as healthcare, colleges, baseball, and malpractice insurance companies warn of impending disaster if costs are not controlled. It is not costs that are the problem in these industries, but the high rate of *growth* in the costs. Over the past 30 years each of these industries has experienced growth in the cost of providing service that has averaged more than 7% per year. College tuitions at four-year private schools have risen from around $4000 per year in the mid-1970s to more than $40,000 per year in the mid-2000s. Average salaries for major league baseball players have soared from about $50,000 per year in the mid-1970s to more than $2.5 million per year in 2003. Does this mean that 30 years from now colleges will be charging $400,000 per year and baseball players will each be paid an average of $100 million every year? Unless there is massive inflation in the next 30 years, these scenarios are highly unlikely. The looming "crisis" is that the exponential growth in budgets that the providers of these services have depended on is reaching a point that is unsustainable. Saturation will be reached soon, and the providers of these services will be forced to re-create their business models to operate within a framework that in terms of inflation-adjusted dollars is steady state.

Summary

The use of mathematical models to project the future is tricky. It is important to understand the difference between fixed-percentage rate growth, linear growth, and zero growth (steady-state) because future results differ dramatically depending on which of these conditions is present. A discussion of fixed percentage rate loss will be in the next chapter when the subject of inflation is addressed.

Tables 5.2 and 5.3 apply only to fixed-percentage rate growth. For an investor, fixed-percentage rate growth is an ideal condition because it means that your money "compounds" over time. To realize that benefit requires patience because in the beginning it is difficult to discern the difference between fixed-percentage rate growth and much slower linear growth.

The "doubling time" for fixed percentage rate growth is extremely sensitive to the growth rate. Because of this sensitivity, apparently small differences in growth rates and starting investments can result in dramatic differences in future results. But no quantity that represents a fraction of a finite resource can double forever. Eventually a condition of "saturation" is reached, and growth ends because there are no more resources to feed the growth process. Be skeptical of growth projections that lead to unbelievable results in the future. Often the providers of such projections have either neglected or conveniently forgotten to account for saturation. Be aware that a mathematical model to project the future is only as good as the assumptions that go into it. Always examine the assumptions and the motives of the people providing them.

Mixing Water and Oil

On a radio talk show, I heard an economist discuss the issue of government management of natural resources. The economist argued that the government should have minimal involvement in regulating the sale and distribution of natural resources. He stated that consumers benefit the most when private enterprises are allowed to harvest and sell natural resources in a free unregulated market.

To support his argument, he compared the markets for water and crude oil. Water resources are publicly owned and usually managed by local and state governments. Oil exploration, drilling, refinement, and distribution are usually undertaken by private industries. The result, in the economist's words, *"is that as time has gone by water has become more scarce and oil more plentiful."*

While the issue of government involvement in natural resource management is outside the scope of this book, it is worth noting that this particular argument is complete nonsense. As mentioned before, the concepts in this chapter apply to other types of resources, not just capital. Both water and oil are finite resources and the concepts of growth, limits, and saturation apply. But, the limits on water and oil production arise for different reasons.

The chemical composition of water is not altered by its normal use. Water is constantly recycled in the environment. The amount of water on the planet is fixed, although most of it is in an unusable condition, and human activity threatens to render more of it unusable. Water has become economically scarce because human population growth means increasing numbers of people must compete for their fraction of a fixed quantity. As populations grow, the fractions must get smaller because there is no practical method for manufacturing water.

Oil is also not manufactured. It must be taken from the environment. But, in contrast to water, the chemical composition of oil is irreparably altered by its use. No recycling is possible. Even though the production of petroleum products has increased exponentially over the past century, it is not correct to conclude that because of its greater availability, oil is becoming more plentiful. Because oil is underground, it is not possible to know exactly how much exists, but as methods for obtaining oil from the ground improve, more of the resource has become accessible. However, eventually oil production will be constrained by the fact that it is a finite resource and exponential growth will end. Will the time when the oil supply dries up be measured in decades or centuries is the issue behind the debate.

I have no expertise in the geology of oil supplies, but with my knowledge of math I can put an absolute upper limit on the time when growth in the demand for oil will end. To do this, first calculate the volume of the Earth that is accessible to oil exploration. The deepest oil wells drilled go about five miles down. The volume of the top five miles of the Earth's crust expressed in barrels of oil (1 barrel = 42 gallons = 159 liters) is about 25 million trillion barrels. Obviously the amount of oil present in the ground cannot exceed this number.

Current worldwide consumption of oil amounts to 30 billion barrels per year. Assume a modest 2.5% annual growth in the consumption of oil, and Table 5.3 can be used to calculate total barrels of oil consumed over the next 30 years. The intersection of the 30-year column and 2.5%-row in Table 5.3 shows 43.90, so the total number of consumed barrels of oil would be 43.90 x 30 billion or 1.32 trillion barrels. Using the rule that the doubling time for a 2.5% growth rate is 70 divided by 2.5, or 28 years, we find that 30 years from now consumption of oil will be in excess of 60 billion barrels per year and in the following 30 years 2 x 1.32 trillion or 2.64 trillion barrels will be consumed. All told, 1.32 + 2.64 trillion or nearly 4 trillion barrels will have been consumed in 60 years. But because of the 2.5% growth rate, consumption has doubled again over this 30-year time period. It is now necessary to multiply 1.32 trillion by 4 to get the total for the next 30 years. If this sequence is continued 30 years at a time using the power of 2 multipliers from Table 5.1 and adding each 30-year projected consumption of oil to the previous total, the result is that the total oil consumed after 700 years is equal to the volume of the top five miles of the Earth's crust.

Obviously even a modest 2.5% growth rate in oil consumption is unsustainable for even a few centuries, no matter who manages the oil resources. At some point, growth in the production of oil will stop, and the best that can be hoped for is a steady-state consumption level that can be maintained for a longer period of time. However, even steady-state use will eventually deplete the resource. Steady-state still means that oil is being consumed and the Earth still has a finite volume. We also know that the top five miles of the Earth's crust are not completely filled with oil.

Chapter 5 Resources

Linda Babcock and Sara Laschever, *Women Don't Ask: Negotiation and the Gender* (Princeton, NJ: Princeton University Press, 2003) provide research on the financial impact of failing to negotiate salaries early in a career. The authors show that fear of negotiation affects women more than men and that small differences in starting salaries obtained by negotiation add up over the course of a lifetime to significant amounts of money.

Michael K. Evans, in *Practical Business Forecasting* (Malden, MA: Blackwell Publishers, 2002) gives a technical description of S-curves.

CHAPTER SIX

Investing

Wealth for the Future

"I have a problem with too much money. I can't reinvest it fast enough, and because I reinvest it, more money comes in. Yes, the rich do get richer."

—Robert Kiyosaki
Author of *Rich Dad, Poor Dad*

Most people save for the future by investing money incrementally over an extended period of time. For example, if saving for retirement consisted of using a lump sum early in life to buy a fixed-rate certificate of deposit that would mature the year you retire, the fixed-rate growth table in Chapter 5 (Table 5.2) would tell you the exact value of the investment in that year. But this strategy is not effective because most people do not have a large lump sum of money to put aside early in life. Realistically, wealth is built by setting aside money each year to add to previous investments that have appreciated in value and will continue to appreciate over time.

The difficulty is deciding how to invest money as it is accumulated. There exists a dizzying array of financial instruments—money market accounts, stocks, bonds, mutual funds etc.—and countless choices for each type of instrument. Annual rates of return on investments are rarely fixed for long periods of time and every investment entails risks of loss that are difficult to quantify. To further complicate matters inflation is an ever-present effect that historically exhibits great variability. Even if you could predict the actual value of a future investment, the real value—meaning what it would purchase—is hard to know.

The purpose of this chapter is to examine the mathematics of investing and discover some of the counter-intuitive results from that math. I will explain how money appreciates over time and how inflation erodes the real value of money over time. The combined effects of appreciation and inflation result in an "effective rate of return," that should be considered when deciding how to invest. Learning to think in terms of an "effective rate of return" exposes what I call the "investment paradox"—that "safe" investments entail substantial risk. We will also learn that the phenomenon of "the rich getting richer" is real and is a direct result of the math.

Just as in the previous chapter, examples with specific numbers are given. By using the tables and worksheets provided you should be able to adapt the examples to your own situation.

The Math of Investing

To see how the process of saving each year works, imagine that at the end of this year you save one dollar and find an investment for that one dollar that returns 10% per year. Over the second year, you save another dollar and at the end of the year add it to your original investment that is now worth $1.10. Your total investment is now worth $2.10, and by the end of the third year it earns 10% more or $0.21. At this time you add another dollar and have a total of $3.31. At the end of the fourth year, your investment has earned another 10%, giving you $3.64. With the savings of an additional dollar, you now have a total of $4.64.

You might recognize the pattern in this sequence of numbers —$1.00, $2.10, $3.31, and $4.64. In Chapter 5, when the integrated growth tables were introduced, these same numbers appeared when discussing total expenditures on candy bars over a 4-year period when the cost goes up by 10% each year. In that example our thought process was different because continually increasing expenditures were added up. The candy bar cost $1.00 in the first year; a second bar cost $1.10 in the next year for a total of $2.10 spent on 2 bars; and a third bar cost $1.21 in the third year for a total of $3.31, until the fourth year is reached and the $1.33 candy bar brings the total to $4.64. The two problems—computing total expenditures for a quantity that increases by a fixed percentage each year and computing total savings at a fixed rate of return over a period of time—might appear to be different, but the underlying mathematics is the same.

The observation that the solutions to both problems produce the same numbers leads to an additional use for the integrated growth table. Table 5.3 can be used to project the future value of savings that are built up over time and appreciate at a fixed annual growth rate. Here are some examples for using Table 5.3 to project the future value of savings and investments.

Example 6.1

Short-term savings

You decide each month to set aside $100 to invest. If your investments return 6% annually, how much will you have after five years?

At this rate you invest 12 x $100 or $1200 each year for five years. At the intersection of the 6% row and the five-year column of Table 5.3 is $5.64. This means each dollar per year invested at 6% adds up to $5.64 over five years. You will have 1200 x $5.64 or $6768, which is $768 more than the $6000 total you have invested.

[Worksheet A1.a, Table 5.3: Rate = 6%, Duration = 5 years, Initial Value = $1200; Result is Final Value = $6768]

Example 6.2

Long-term savings

You decide each month to set aside $50 to invest. If your investments return 6% annually, how much will you have after 25 years?

At this rate you invest 12 x $50 or $600 each year for 25 years. At the intersection of the 6% row and the 25-year column of Table 5.3 is $54.86. This means that a dollar per year invested with a 6% annual return will add up to $54.86 over 25 years. You will have 600 x $54.86 or $32,916, which is $17,916 more than the $15,000 total you have invested.

[Worksheet A1.a, Table 5.3: Rate = 6%, Duration = 25 years, Initial Value = $600; Result is Final Value = $32,916]

Example 6.3

Retirement planning with a fixed rate of return

You decide that you need $500,000 to retire 20 years from now. If your investments return 8% per year, how much do you need to save each month?

At the intersection of the 8% row and the 20-year column of Table 5.3 is $45.76. Divide $500,000 by $45.76 to get $10,926, which is the amount per year that needs to be saved. Divide this by 12 to get the monthly amounts, which are $910.

[Worksheet A1.d, Table 5.3: Rate = 8%, Duration = 20 years, Final Value = $500,000; Result is Initial Value = $10,926]

Example 6.4

Retirement planning with fixed savings

You decide that you need $500,000 to retire 20 years from now. If you save $600 per month, what annual rate of return on your investment do you need to achieve your goal?

A savings of $600 per month is 12 x $600 or $7200 per year. Divide $500,000 by $7200 to get $69.44. Look down the 20-year column in Table 5.3 to find the number closest to $69.44, which is $72.05 and found in the 12% row. Your investments need to return an average of 12% per year each year for the next 20 years to achieve this goal. You should rethink the amount invested each month because averaging a return of 12% per year for 20 consecutive years would be an extraordinary success. Such a streak is unlikely to happen.

[Worksheet A1.b, Table 5.3: Final Value = 500,000, Initial Value = $7200, Duration = 20 years; Result is Rate = 12%]

Example 6.5

Benefit of time

Wendy contributes $100 per month for 30 years to an IRA (Individual Retirement Account) that averages a 7% annual rate of return. Charlie is the same age but starts saving for retirement much later. Charlie contributes $200 per month for 15 years to an IRA that has the same 7% rate of return. At the end of this time period Wendy and Charlie both retire. How do their total savings compare?

Wendy invests 12 x $100 or $1200 per year. According to Table 5.3 at 7%, each dollar per year adds up to $94.46 over 30 years. Wendy will have $94.46 x 1200 or $113,352. Charlie invests 12 x $200 or $2400 per year. According to

Table 5.3 at 7% each dollar per year adds to $25.13 over 15 years. Charlie will have $25.13 x 2400 or $60,312. Wendy and Charlie have invested the same amount—$36,000—each and earned the same annual rate of return, but because Wendy spread out her investments over a longer period of time, she has nearly twice as much money in the end as Charlie.

[Worksheet A1.a, Table 5.3: Rate = 7%, Duration = 30 years, Initial Value = $1200; Result is Final Value = $113,352]
[Worksheet A1.a, Table 5.3: Rate = 7%, Duration = 15 years, Initial Value = $2400; Result is Final Value = $60,312]

Example 6.6

Effect of deferred taxes

You currently pay 15% of your adjusted gross income for federal taxes and 5% in state taxes. If you reduce your take-home pay by $16 per week by investing in a tax-deferred IRA, how much will you have after 25 years if the investment returns average 8% per year?

After state and federal taxes, you only keep 80% or 0.8 of your pay. A $16 after-tax reduction in pay means that the $16 divided by 0.8, or $20, is there before taxes. If $20 is invested each week, $20 x 52 or $1040 is invested per year. According to Table 5.3, every dollar per year invested at 8% becomes $73.11 over 25 years. You will have $1040 x 73.11 or $76,034 if your investments return 8% per year. All that results from reducing your take-home pay by just $2.28 each day. Learn to live on $5 per day less and that $76,000 amount is more than doubled.

[Worksheet A1.a, Table 5.3: Rate = 8%, Duration = 25 years, Initial Value = $1040; Result is Final Value = $76,034]

Inflation

A fact of economic life is that as time passes, costs increase and a given amount of money buys fewer goods and services. Perusing advertised prices in magazines that are decades old is both nostalgic and amusing. Forty years ago a car that cost $5,000 really was an expensive car, even though the dollar amount is absurdly low by today's standards. As we plan for the financial future, inflation distorts the true meaning of the results. Simply knowing that your savings will be valued at $100,000 in 15 years, doesn't mean anything if you do not know what $100,000 will buy 15 years from now. Knowing the inflation rate is as important as knowing the rate of return on your investments. The effects of inflation also compound over time. Apparently modest rates of inflation (2-3% per year) when compounded over decades can seriously erode the value of a pile of cash stuffed under a mattress.

While inflation might be a common gripe as people age, it is an economic effect with real winners and losers. In fact inflation is an insidiously deceptive form of wealth transfer. Even the word "inflation" that conjures an image of growth is deceptive because what is actually happening is that assets in the form of cash or accounts receivable are losing value. Inflation produces these winners and losers.

Losers to inflation

Savers: Setting aside money to use in the future is a poor strategy if the value of the money erodes over time. In countries with hyperinflation, this statement is particularly obvious. A 15% annual inflation rate over 30 years renders saved money completely worthless. In countries like the United States, where inflation rates are small, simply saving money is still not an effective method for building wealth. Even small inflation rates accumulate over time to devalue money. Some form of investment, even in a modest interest-bearing savings account, must be made to help counteract the effect of inflation.

Renters: Rents are market-driven and rise with inflation. If their earnings do not keep pace with inflation, renters can be forced out of their apartment or house. Renters never build any equity in the property in which they live. Because rents rise with inflation, landlords gain both equity in their property and a greater source of income. Renters stay only if they can afford the rent. If they can not they must incur the expense of moving to a cheaper place.

People on fixed pensions: Inflation causes people who live on a fixed pension or annuity to lose buying power over time. If your retirement plan depends on a fixed annuity, you should be aware that you will probably need other sources of income. With modern life expectancies reaching the 80s and 90s, retirements can last 20 to 30 years, a long enough time for inflation to de-value an apparently comfortable pension.

People who depend on the minimum wage to maintain an income floor are effectively on a fixed income because the minimum wage increases slowly and does not keep pace with inflation. Ironically one of the arguments businesses make against raising the minimum wage is that to do so would be "inflationary," because prices on their goods and services would be raised to pay for increased wages. For some reason, businesses do not consider rising stock prices and executive compensation inflationary but rather a sign of prosperity.

Winners from Inflation

Debtors: People who owe money always benefit from inflation because the dollars they pay back have less value than the dollars they borrowed. In his book, *Credit Card Nation*, Robert Manning profiles a fundamental shift in the nation's attitude towards debt and attributes this change in part to the double-digit inflation of the late 1970s and early 1980s. When high inflation erased savings and debts, the moral approbation that came with debt diminished.

Homeowners: Owning your home is the best protection an individual can have against inflation. The value of the home will rise with inflation, but fixed mortgage payments stay fixed and become a progressively smaller fraction of inflated income. However, home ownership does not completely shield your housing budget from the effects of inflation. Many seniors on fixed incomes struggle to afford rising costs for property taxes and homeowners' insurance. When my parents finished paying off their mortgage, they discovered that payments for taxes and insurance had become greater than the amount going towards principal and interest. Their monthly housing budget was only slightly reduced because taxes and insurance must be paid forever.

Government: From the government's point of view, inflation is mathematically equivalent to a tax. If the government needs money to pay off debts, it could use its power of taxation to forcibly take money from its citizens or it could just print additional money. When the government puts money into circulation at a rate faster than the real growth of the economy, it de-values the money already in use and that produces inflation. By making both the money people have and the government's debts worth less than before, inflation accomplishes exactly what taxation would, but without the need for coercion.

At the time of this writing (early 2005), the U.S. government has not chosen inflation as a fix for its increasing debt. However, since 2000, the value of the U.S. dollar has fallen sharply relative to other currencies. In late 2000, it cost about $0.90 to purchase one Euro; in late 2004 it cost about $1.30 to purchase one Euro. This drop in the value of the dollar of more than 30% relative to the Euro in just four years coincided with the largest increase in federal debt in U.S. history. What that means is that many currency investors are betting that the U.S. government will have to de-value the dollar to solve its mounting problems with debt. Whether that will actually happen is still a matter of debate.

Effect of Inflation

The effect of inflation over time on the value of money is shown in Table 6.1. The table projects future values of one dollar for the given inflation rates and time periods. The rows represent annual inflation rates, and the columns are years into the future. Notice that for high inflation rates (greater than 10%) and long time periods (decades) a dollar today can become completely worthless in the future. Even low inflation rates compounded over long time periods can erode the present value of the dollar by a significant amount. Here are some examples for using Table 6.1.

Example 6.7

Inflation adjusted retirement planning

Your retirement planner informs you that your current rate of savings and return on investments should, 20 years from now, result in a retirement nest egg of $750,000. If the inflation rate over the next 20 years averages 2.5%, how much buying power in current dollars will you have?

The intersection of the 2.5% row in Table 6.1 with the 20-year column shows that each dollar today will be worth $0.61. Your nest egg will buy $0.61 x $750,000 or $457,500 of goods and services.

[Worksheet A1.a, Table 6.1: Rate = 2.5%, Duration = 20 years, Initial Value = $750,000; Result is Final Value = $457,500]

Example 6.8

The effect of high inflation

If a 12% inflation rate continues for six consecutive years, what is the value of one dollar at the end of this time period? What would be the value in another six years (12 years later) if this trend continues?

The intersection in Table 6.1 between the 12% row and the six-year column shows $0.507. For this inflation rate, money will lose half its value in just six years. Allow this inflation rate to continue for another six years, and it will lose half its value again. The intersection of the 12% row with the 12-year column shows $0.257.

[Worksheet A1.a, Table 6.1: Rate = 12%, Duration = 6 years, Initial Value = $1; Result is Final Value = $0.507]
[Worksheet A1.a, Table 6.1: Rate = 12%, Duration = 12 years, Initial Value = $1; Result is Final Value = $0.257]

Example 6.8 shows that high, "double-digit" annual rates of inflation can render money worthless in relatively short periods of time. The inflation rates of the late 1970s that exceeded 10% annually caused great economic disruption because of this fact. People had no incentive to save and invest, and lenders had to charge usurious interest rates just to break even.

Table 6.1: The future value of $1 for a fixed inflation rate after the number of years in the column heading. Rate is an annual percentage rate that compounds yearly.

Fixed-rate inflation

Rate (%)	Years into the Future					
	2	3	4	5	6	8
0.0	$1.000	$1.000	$1.000	$1.000	$1.000	$1.000
0.5	$0.990	$0.985	$0.980	$0.975	$0.971	$0.961
1.0	$0.980	$0.971	$0.961	$0.951	$0.942	$0.923
1.5	$0.971	$0.956	$0.942	$0.928	$0.915	$0.888
2.0	$0.961	$0.942	$0.924	$0.906	$0.888	$0.853
2.5	$0.952	$0.929	$0.906	$0.884	$0.862	$0.821
3.0	$0.943	$0.915	$0.888	$0.863	$0.837	$0.789
3.5	$0.934	$0.902	$0.871	$0.842	$0.814	$0.759
4.0	$0.925	$0.889	$0.855	$0.822	$0.790	$0.731
4.5	$0.916	$0.876	$0.839	$0.802	$0.768	$0.703
5.0	$0.907	$0.864	$0.823	$0.784	$0.746	$0.677
5.5	$0.898	$0.852	$0.807	$0.765	$0.725	$0.652
6.0	$0.890	$0.840	$0.792	$0.747	$0.705	$0.627
6.5	$0.882	$0.828	$0.777	$0.730	$0.685	$0.604
7.0	$0.873	$0.816	$0.763	$0.713	$0.666	$0.582
7.5	$0.865	$0.805	$0.749	$0.697	$0.648	$0.561
8.0	$0.857	$0.794	$0.735	$0.681	$0.630	$0.540
8.5	$0.849	$0.783	$0.722	$0.665	$0.613	$0.521
9.0	$0.842	$0.772	$0.708	$0.650	$0.596	$0.502
9.5	$0.834	$0.762	$0.696	$0.635	$0.580	$0.484
10.0	$0.826	$0.751	$0.683	$0.621	$0.564	$0.467
11.0	$0.812	$0.731	$0.659	$0.593	$0.535	$0.434
12.0	$0.797	$0.712	$0.636	$0.567	$0.507	$0.404
13.0	$0.783	$0.693	$0.613	$0.543	$0.480	$0.376
14.0	$0.769	$0.675	$0.592	$0.519	$0.456	$0.351
15.0	$0.756	$0.658	$0.572	$0.497	$0.432	$0.327
16.0	$0.743	$0.641	$0.552	$0.476	$0.410	$0.305
17.0	$0.731	$0.624	$0.534	$0.456	$0.390	$0.285
18.0	$0.718	$0.609	$0.516	$0.437	$0.370	$0.266
19.0	$0.706	$0.593	$0.499	$0.419	$0.352	$0.249
20.0	$0.694	$0.579	$0.482	$0.402	$0.335	$0.233
21.0	$0.683	$0.564	$0.467	$0.386	$0.319	$0.218
22.0	$0.672	$0.551	$0.451	$0.370	$0.303	$0.204
23.0	$0.661	$0.537	$0.437	$0.355	$0.289	$0.191
24.0	$0.650	$0.524	$0.423	$0.341	$0.275	$0.179
25.0	$0.640	$0.512	$0.410	$0.328	$0.262	$0.168
26.0	$0.630	$0.500	$0.397	$0.315	$0.250	$0.157
27.0	$0.620	$0.488	$0.384	$0.303	$0.238	$0.148
28.0	$0.610	$0.477	$0.373	$0.291	$0.227	$0.139

Observation: Over long periods of time, even small rates of inflation result in a substantial reduction in the real value of saved money.

Fixed-rate inflation

Rate (%)	Years into the Future					
	10	12	15	20	25	30
0.0	$1.000	$1.000	$1.000	$1.000	$1.000	$1.000
0.5	$0.951	$0.942	$0.928	$0.905	$0.883	$0.861
1.0	$0.905	$0.887	$0.861	$0.820	$0.780	$0.742
1.5	$0.862	$0.836	$0.800	$0.742	$0.689	$0.640
2.0	$0.820	$0.788	$0.743	$0.673	$0.610	$0.552
2.5	$0.781	$0.744	$0.690	$0.610	$0.539	$0.477
3.0	$0.744	$0.701	$0.642	$0.554	$0.478	$0.412
3.5	$0.709	$0.662	$0.597	$0.503	$0.423	$0.356
4.0	$0.676	$0.625	$0.555	$0.456	$0.375	$0.308
4.5	$0.644	$0.590	$0.517	$0.415	$0.333	$0.267
5.0	$0.614	$0.557	$0.481	$0.377	$0.295	$0.231
5.5	$0.585	$0.526	$0.448	$0.343	$0.262	$0.201
6.0	$0.558	$0.497	$0.417	$0.312	$0.233	$0.174
6.5	$0.533	$0.470	$0.389	$0.284	$0.207	$0.151
7.0	$0.508	$0.444	$0.362	$0.258	$0.184	$0.131
7.5	$0.485	$0.420	$0.338	$0.235	$0.164	$0.114
8.0	$0.463	$0.397	$0.315	$0.215	$0.146	$0.099
8.5	$0.442	$0.376	$0.294	$0.196	$0.130	$0.087
9.0	$0.422	$0.356	$0.275	$0.178	$0.116	$0.075
9.5	$0.404	$0.337	$0.256	$0.163	$0.103	$0.066
10.0	$0.386	$0.319	$0.239	$0.149	$0.092	$0.057
11.0	$0.352	$0.286	$0.209	$0.124	$0.074	$0.044
12.0	$0.322	$0.257	$0.183	$0.104	$0.059	$0.033
13.0	$0.295	$0.231	$0.160	$0.087	$0.047	$0.026
14.0	$0.270	$0.208	$0.140	$0.073	$0.038	$0.020
15.0	$0.247	$0.187	$0.123	$0.061	$0.030	$0.015
16.0	$0.227	$0.168	$0.108	$0.051	$0.024	$0.012
17.0	$0.208	$0.152	$0.095	$0.043	$0.020	$0.009
18.0	$0.191	$0.137	$0.084	$0.037	$0.016	$0.007
19.0	$0.176	$0.124	$0.074	$0.031	$0.013	$0.005
20.0	$0.162	$0.112	$0.065	$0.026	$0.010	$0.004
21.0	$0.149	$0.102	$0.057	$0.022	$0.009	$0.003
22.0	$0.137	$0.092	$0.051	$0.019	$0.007	$0.003
23.0	$0.126	$0.083	$0.045	$0.016	$0.006	$0.002
24.0	$0.116	$0.076	$0.040	$0.014	$0.005	$0.002
25.0	$0.107	$0.069	$0.035	$0.012	$0.004	$0.001
26.0	$0.099	$0.062	$0.031	$0.010	$0.003	$0.001
27.0	$0.092	$0.057	$0.028	$0.008	$0.003	$0.001
28.0	$0.085	$0.052	$0.025	$0.007	$0.002	$0.001

The Halving Rule

Actually, just as investment returns lead to a "doubling time" when a given annual rate of return stays fixed, inflation rates result in a "halving time" when a given annual inflation rate stays fixed. The formula that approximates "halving times" is the same as the one in Chapter 5 for doubling times. The only change that needs to be made is to substitute an inflation rate.

The Halving Rule

The halving time in years, T_h, is:

$$T_h = (72) / I$$

where I is the annual inflation rate in percent.

Notice how this formula agrees with the last example because 72 divided by 12 is equal to six. That means each six years at a 12% inflation rate should reduce the present value of money by about one half, which was the result obtained from Table 6.1. If the inflation rate is 14%, the halving time is 72 divided by 14, or about five years. Look at the values rounded to the nearest penny in the 14% row in Table 6.1 as they appear in the columns that are multiples of five years — $0.52 at five years, $0.27 at 10 years, $0.14 at 15 years, $0.07 at 20 years, $0.04 at 25 years, and $0.020 at 30 years. Each value in the sequence is approximately half the value preceding it. The final value at 30 years, that for a 14% inflation rate is six halving times, is close to one dollar divided by 64, or $0.016, which rounds to $0.02

The above analysis can be applied to any inflation rate. For example, for a 5% annual inflation rate, saved money will be worth 1/64 of its present value in 84 years. How do we know? For a 5% annual inflation rate the halving time is 72 divided by five, or about 14 years. Therefore six halving times would be 6 x 14 or

84 years. An important realization coming from this analysis is that after six halving times, saved money is essentially worthless. Therefore thinking beyond six halving times is pointless because money can never be less than worthless. Unlike the doubling of investment returns, which can go on forever, the halving of money due to inflation has a lower boundary of zero.

The Effective Rate of Return

Because of inflation, financial planning requires thinking in terms of an "effective rate of return." Figures 6.1a-d are three-dimensional graphs that illustrate the effective change in the value of money resulting from the combined effects of investment return and inflation. The two horizontal axes are the annual inflation rates (in percent) and annual returns on investment (in percent). The vertical axis is the *change* in the value of one dollar. Because change is plotted vertically, the zero line means no change, or that the future value of one dollar is still equal to the present value of one dollar. Positive change happens when the investment return is greater than the inflation rate. Negative change happens when an investment return fails to keep up with inflation. Therefore a diagonal line can be drawn on each graph that represents inflation rates equal to investment returns, and that line will separate the areas of positive and negative change. Each graph shows the change for a given period of time. Figure 6.1a is for five years; 6.1b is for 10 years; 6.1c is for 20 years; and 6.1d is for 30 years.

An important feature of these graphs is the asymmetry that develops as time progresses. The graph of change that occurs after five years is symmetrical. The positive change that results when investment returns beat the inflation rate is about the same as the negative change that occurs when the rate difference is reversed. But the 30-year graph is not symmetrical because it needs a large vertical axis to display the positive change that results from high-interest rate, low-inflation returns, while the negative changes are barely perceptible on the vertical scale. The reason for this asymmetry is that negative change is bounded.

Figure 6.1: The change in the value of $1 arising from the combined effects of inflation and investment return over four different time periods.

Effective return on investment

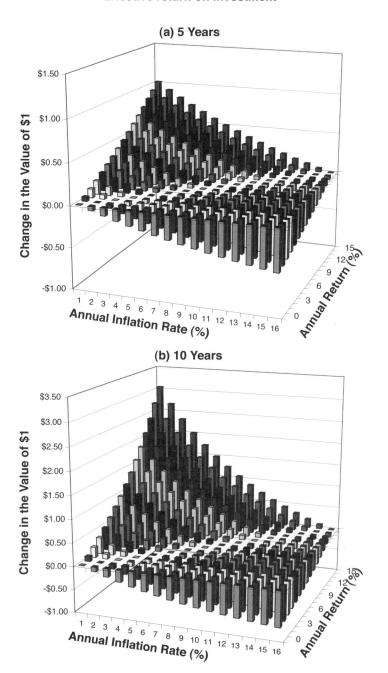

Observation: The asymmetry that develops as the time periods lengthen is because losses are bounded but gains are not.

Effective return on investment

(c) 20 Years

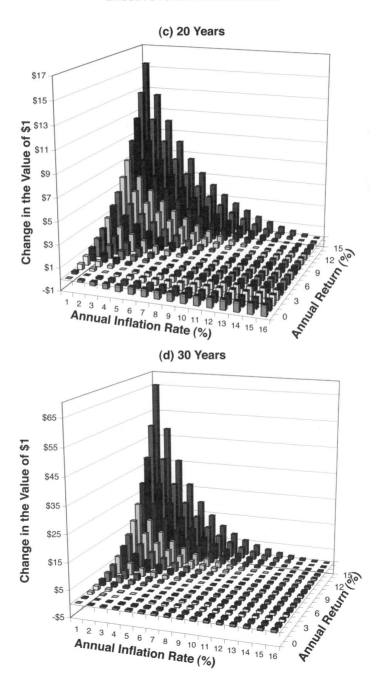

(d) 30 Years

As we observed in the previous section, inflation can never render money less than worthless, but positive change has no upper boundary. As long as investment returns beat the inflation rate by any amount, no matter how small, investments will continue to grow ever larger over time. The lesson from these graphs is the following paradox—so-called "conservative" investments are in fact risky.

The Investment Paradox

Playing it safe can be risky

When you keep all your assets in the form of cash or savings accounts or you buy into fixed annuities, you risk losing to inflation. Buying into a diversified stock fund gives you a solid stake in an economy that historically tends to expand. Buying real estate gives you a tangible asset with a market-driven price that will rise with inflation. What deceives people is that when stock prices or real estate prices fall, the numbers that express the value of the asset decrease. Panic sets in when the stock tables are read and the numbers are less than the day before. When the value of cash falls, the numbers written on the bills remain the same. Because the numbers do not change, people feel safer and ignore the fact that the economic value a dollar bill represents does change.

Short-Selling

A "short sale" is a method for profiting from falling stock prices. When you consider the investment strategy of "short-selling," remember that a value of zero limits how far a stock can fall but stock appreciation has no limit. A short-seller does the exact opposite of what most people do when they invest in stocks. Most investors take what are called "long positions"—that is, purchasing a stock with the hope that it will appreciate in value and be sold at a later date for more than the purchase price. An investor who takes a "short position" sells the stock first with the hope of buying the shares back at a later date for an amount less than the sale price. The short-seller is responsible for the difference between the initial sale price and the later purchase price. If the stock falls in price and can be repurchased at a later date for less money, the short-seller profits. The risk arises because the shares to be sold have to come from somewhere. Usually the short-seller borrows the shares from his or her broker and becomes obligated to replace them at a later time. If the shares rise in value instead, they still must be repurchased, but now the purchase price is higher than the sale price. When share prices rise, the short-seller loses money.

Short-selling is a high-risk, low-reward investment strategy because gains from short positions are bounded but losses are not. A short-seller can never make more money than the original sale price. Whether the stock is sold short for $10 or $50 or $100 per share, the original sale price is an upper limit on the most a short-seller can make. However, if the stock is sold short and then starts to rise, there is no upper limit on the loss. If a stock is sold short for $20 per share and then rises to $60 per share, the short-seller is facing losses of $40 per share. If the losses from a short position approach wiping out the value of a brokerage account, the broker will liquidate the account to purchase the shares needed to cover the short position, an action known as a "buy in." In contrast, an investor with a long position can never lose more than the original investment and therefore has the option of keeping the shares when the market falls in hopes the market will come back. A short-seller may not have the option of riding out a rising market in hopes that the market will fall later on if the broker must buy him in. The unlimited exposure to loss makes keeping a short position in a rising market untenable. Short-sellers also risk getting caught in a "short squeeze." If too many shares of the same stock are sold short, a slight rise in the stock could trigger all the short-sellers to cover their short positions. The sudden demand for shares that action generates can accelerate the rise in price.

The best-case scenario for a short position would be for an Enron-type fiasco, where a high-priced stock is sold short and then its value drops suddenly to near zero in a matter of weeks. In this case, the short position could be "covered" for pennies on the dollar. But timing is everything when taking a short position. If you shorted Enron on the way up, say at $30 per share, you might be forced to cover the short position well before the peak near $80 per share. You might have been correct in guessing that Enron was on its way to bankruptcy, but profiting from that hunch would have required exquisite timing.

The Rich Really Do Get Richer

Most investment income arises from assets that appreciate in value and the appreciation compounds over time. Because of compounding, small discrepancies in rates of return result in large discrepancies in the value of an investment at later times. These discrepancies will continue to grow as time passes. The maxim that "the rich getting richer" is true and is a direct result of the mathematics of investing.

Consider two hypothetical co-workers, Alice and Bob, who work the same job and are paid the same amount. Each manages to save and invest $100 every month. Alice finds a safe investment with a guaranteed 5% annual rate of return. Bob invests more aggressively and manages a 12% rate of return. After one year Bob owns 51% of their combined $2500 wealth. But after 10 years Bob owns 60% of their combined $38,500 wealth; and when they retire 30 years later, Bob will own 80% of their combined $430,000 wealth. Allow this process to continue over time and the disparity between Alice's and Bob's wealth will continue to grow. Bob will control a continually increasing fraction of their combined wealth even if both Alice and Bob earn and save the same amount.

Figure 6.2 shows what happens to Alice's and Bob's wealth if the disparity between their investment returns continues for 50 years. The light bars represent the total savings of Alice and the dark bars represent the total savings of Bob at five-year intervals. The graph shows that the fraction of total savings that belongs to Bob increases from 54% after five years to 94% after 50 years. Notice that both Alice's and Bob's savings increase as time passes while at the same time the disparity between their two savings grows too.

There are no investments with a guaranteed 12% annual rate of return. The difference between the return on Bob's investments compared to those of Alice might be luck. It is unlikely that two investors would find two different investments that yield identical returns. But the mathematical fact is that when the combined assets of Alice and Bob are considered, Bob who receives a higher rate of return on his investments acquires a progressively greater fraction of the total wealth, *even though both are successful investors.*

Replace Alice and Bob with Alice's family and Bob's family and the origin of "rich become richer" phenomena is apparent.

Figure 6.2: Comparison over a 50-year time period of Alice's investments that return 5% annually with Bob's investments that earn 12% annually.

Comparison of investments with two different returns

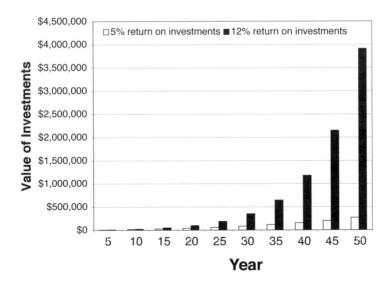

Observation: Investments that earn 5% and 12% respectively both grow over time, but the disparity between the values of the investments also grows.

There is no guaranteed formula for becoming rich. But those who are rich or have more money than most – whether by talent, skill, luck, or a combination—have opportunities to leverage their money to obtain even more wealth. For example, people who own assets either in the form of homes, businesses, stocks, or specialized skills have the opportunity to invest more in those assets to further increase their value. Business owners who reinvest money to grow their businesses might easily get an annual rate of return of 20% to 30% on that money. In contrast, low-skilled wage earners with no assets have limited opportunities for high-yield investments. Or consider homeowners who build equity as the mortgage is paid down and have the opportunity to invest in home improvements to increase the value of their property. Homeowners are also able to borrow money against the home equity at reduced interest rates to fund a business or obtain more education. In contrast, apartment dwellers receive a place to live in exchange for rent.

If 30 years elapse and Alice and Bob pass their wealth to their children and the investments compound for an additional 30 years, Bob's family will control more than 99% of the combined wealth. The heirs of both Alice and Bob will be better off than their parents, but Bob's will be substantially better off. Allow this process to continue for several more generations and the fraction of wealth controlled by Alice's family becomes an insignificant part of the combined wealth owned by the families of Alice and Bob.

The compounding of successful investments over generations is a mathematical problem that societies throughout history have had to face. In the Old Testament the problem was solved by commandment. The ancient Hebrews were required to declare a "Jubilee" year every 50 years and effectively reset the financial clock. The book of Leviticus commands:

> *"You shall thus consecrate the fiftieth year and proclaim a release through the land to all its inhabitants. It shall be a jubilee for you, and each of you shall return to his own property, and each of you shall return to his family."*

—Leviticus 25:10

The Jubilee Year meant each of the tribes of Israel received back their original land, even if it had been sold earlier. As a result, no tribe could become permanently landless, no matter what transactions had taken place during the intervening 50 years.

In modern times we have estate taxes. Estate taxes, first instituted in 1916, are intended to break up and redistribute the fortunes of the super-wealthy by government appropriation using the tax system. The estate tax functions much like the Hebrews' Jubilee Year because it prevents more successful families from permanently acquiring all the wealth.

The estate tax strikes many people as unfair. There is never a reason to apologize for success through talent and hard work, or even success through luck. All of us want our families and heirs to enjoy the fruits of our success. It appears natural that children and grandchildren of successful people should benefit. President George W. Bush fought hard for the repeal of the estate tax, calling it the "death tax" and arguing that wealth taxed during a person's lifetime should not be taxed again upon death.

Bush's argument against the estate tax makes sense to many people, but surprisingly, some very wealthy people have argued that not having an estate tax is worse. William H. Gates Sr., the father of Microsoft founder Bill Gates, co-authored a book with Chuck Collins entitled *Wealth and Our Commonwealth: Why America Should Tax Accumulated Fortunes*. They argue that allowing untaxed fortunes to pass from one generation to the next will result in the creation of a permanent aristocracy. If a small number of individuals control the majority of the wealth, American democracy will be weakened and equal opportunity for its citizens denied.

"It was understood a century ago that the estate tax was an attempt to balance conflicting American values: on the one hand, our respect for private enterprise and personal wealth, and on the other, our concern for democracy and equality of opportunity."

—William H. Gates Sr.
Madison Capital Times
June 4, 2001

Estate taxes might be construed as punishing those who worked hard to succeed financially. Why work hard to succeed if in the end the government comes and takes the money? Is this an example the government should set for future generations? But the mathematics of long-term compounding is irrefutable. Paradoxically, not having an estate tax makes it more difficult for hard workers and innovators in the future to obtain a significant economic stake because those who were successful in the past will control most of the wealth.

Realistic Models for Investing

Wealth may increase over time because of opportunities to reinvest earnings, but the increase rarely happens in a predictable or uniform manner. Realistic projections of the future are more difficult than most people realize. Many financial planners project the future by assuming fixed rates of return on investments that are based on historical averages. For example, each year the company that manages my retirement accounts provides a summary of the projected value of my investments when I reach age 65. An impressive dollar amount is stated along with a bunch of footnotes. The footnotes state the assumptions that went into the calculation. The basic assumptions are that my contributions will continue until I am age 65, that stocks will return 8% annually and bonds 5%. The figures for the annual returns for these types of investments are based on historical averages. Using these rates of return, I can make the same projection using Table 5.3 and arrive at the same dollar amount on my statement. This projection is useful because it tells me whether my rate of savings and investment allocations make any sense. If the projected value of my investments when I retire is intolerably low, I need to save and invest more. But I still do not know how much I will have when I retire; nor will I know until the day I actually retire.

Anyone who invests knows that projecting the future is not that simple. The historical averages are just that—averages. Stocks do not return 8% per year every single year. Even "safe" money market accounts have interest rates that fluctuate. As of this writing, money market rates are at historic lows (less than 1%). If you shop for a mutual fund, all the advertisements will boast impressive rates of return because the advertisement will describe a successful time period in the fund's history. But all mutual fund advertisements contain in the fine print a disclaimer —"past performance is no guarantee of future returns." While the ad sets readers up to believe the high positive rate of return will continue, that fine print states one simple fact—*no one knows the future*. The rate of return on an investment for any *specific* period of time will never be exactly equal to the average. In fact if you have been investing regularly you can use Table 5.3 to see how your results compare to the historical averages. Here is an example for determining past performance.

Example 6.9

Past performance analysis

For the past eight years you have invested $200 per month in a stock fund. Currently your investment in that fund is worth $22,000. What has been your average annual rate of return?

You have invested 12 x $200 or $2400 each year and now have $22,000. That means that each dollar per year invested over eight years has resulted in $22,000 divided by $2400, or $9.16. Look down the eight-year column of Table 5.3 to find the number closest to $9.16. That value, which is $9.21, is found in the 4% row. Your annual rate of return is slightly under 4%.

[Worksheet A1.b, Table 5.3: Final Value = 22,000, Initial Value = $2400, Duration = 8 years; Result is Rate = 4%]

Because investing is not predictable, it helps to consider some strategies that fit more closely with what actually happens. Next I will discuss two approaches—dollar-cost averaging and Monte Carlo simulators.

Dollar cost averaging

One particularly simple and effective approach to long-term investing is to invest a fixed amount of money in an "indexed" stock fund every month. This approach is known as "dollar cost averaging." An "indexed" fund is one that has shares in companies that make up one of the major stock indices. For example, the Standard and Poors 500 index is based on the share prices of 500 established companies selected from a broad range of market sectors. The "S&P 500," as it is called, is a benchmark that many mutual fund managers use to judge their performance. A mutual fund that is "indexed" to the S&P 500, by definition, has the performance of this benchmark. Such a fund would never lag or lead the S&P 500, because it owns shares in the companies that are in the S&P 500. The proportions of shares owned for each of the 500 companies are set so that the fund performance exactly matches the index. While it might sound boring to own a fund that by definition can never "beat the market," there is the security of never lagging the market. The fact is that most actively managed mutual funds over the long haul under perform the S&P 500. It is rare to find a mutual fund manager who can consistently do as well as the S&P 500, let alone find a manager who consistently beats the index.

When dollar cost averaging is used, the investor never considers whether the market is up or down, or even which direction it is going. The same dollar amount is invested each month and in months where the market is up, that amount buys fewer shares. In months when the market is down, the investor receives more shares. The investor actually benefits from dips in the market because the lower prices offer greater ownership.

To see how investors can benefit from a dip, consider Table 5.2 that shows how dollar cost averaging would have worked for the 24-month time period from January 1, 2002, to January 1, 2004. This was an uncertain period of time for investors because it included a market bottom that followed the Internet bubble collapse in 2000. Of course the "bottom" is only observable in hindsight. No one knew at that time when or even if the market would bottom and how low the bottom would be. Table 5.2 shows shares in a hypothetical fund where each share is priced in dollars equal to the value of the S&P 500 index. An investor with $24,000 to invest on January 1, 2002, could purchase 20.9045 shares at a cost of $1148 each. On January 1, 2004, when the S&P 500 closed at 1112, those same shares would be worth $23,244, a loss of 3.15%. But if the investor took the $24,000 and invested $1000 in the fund on the first of every month for 24 months starting on January 1, 2002, a total of 24.6737 shares would be owned. On January 1, 2004, those shares would be worth $27,435, which is a cumulative gain of 14.3% over the same two-year period. The gain happens even though during this time period the S&P 500 never gets back to the January 1, 2002, level. The gain arises because of the dip that the S&P 500 took during that two-year period. The averaging method allows the investor to take advantage of the lower prices during that time and accumulate more shares.

Dollar cost averaging will show a loss for a market that only goes down. It will also show a loss for a time period where the market goes up and then comes down—like the late 1990s market bubble. But over long periods of time (decades or more), the general trend of the market has been up. Bubbles and dips both get averaged away over a time period of decades. People who used dollar cost averaging to accumulate wealth over the past 50 to 60 years have done extremely well. The beauty of the method is that it works well with a regular budget, and most people rarely have a lump sum to invest even if they want to. The main advantage of dollar cost averaging is that it requires no thought. Simply invest a fixed part of your pay each month and ignore the daily noise in the markets. Even better, invest a fixed percentage of your pay, rather than a fixed dollar amount, and then your contributions will rise as your earnings rise.

Table 6.2: Example of dollar-cost averaging into a hypothetical fund indexed to the Standard & Poors 500. Each share of the fund is priced in dollars equal to the S&P 500 index. The table shows what would have happened to an investor who purchased $1000 worth of shares on the 1st of each month for 24 consecutive months starting on January 1, 2002 and continuing through December 1, 2004.

Dollar Cost Averaging into the Standard & Poors 500

Date purchased	S&P 500 close	%change since 1/2/02	Amount invested	Shares purchased	Total shares owned	Value of total investment	Total gain (%)
1-Jan-02	1148	0.0	$1000	0.871	0.871	$1,000	0.0
1-Feb-02	1122	−2.2	$1000	0.891	1.762	$1,977	−1.1
1-Mar-02	1132	−1.4	$1000	0.884	2.646	$2,994	−0.2
1-Apr-02	1147	−0.1	$1000	0.872	3.518	$4,033	+0.8
1-May-02	1086	−5.4	$1000	0.920	4.438	$4,822	−3.6
1-Jun-02	1067	−7.0	$1000	0.937	5.375	$5,736	−4.4
1-Jul-02	969	−15.6	$1000	1.032	6.408	$6,207	−11.3
1-Aug-02	885	−22.9	$1000	1.130	7.538	$6,669	−16.6
1-Sep-02	916	−20.2	$1000	1.092	8.630	$7,905	−12.2
1-Oct-02	848	−26.1	$1000	1.179	9.809	$8,317	−16.8
1-Nov-02	901	−21.5	$1000	1.110	10.919	$9,838	−10.6
1-Dec-02	936	−18.4	$1000	1.068	11.987	$11,224	−6.5
1-Jan-03	880	−23.4	$1000	1.137	13.124	$11,546	−11.2
1-Feb-03	856	−25.5	$1000	1.169	14.292	$12,230	−12.6
1-Mar-03	841	−26.7	$1000	1.189	15.481	$13,022	−13.2
1-Apr-03	858	−25.2	$1000	1.165	16.646	$14,290	−10.7
1-May-03	916	−20.2	$1000	1.091	17.737	$16,253	−4.4
1-Jun-03	964	−16.1	$1000	1.038	18.775	$18,092	+0.5
1-Jul-03	982	−14.4	$1000	1.018	19.793	$19,443	+2.3
1-Aug-03	980	−14.6	$1000	1.020	20.813	$20,400	+2.0
1-Sep-02	1008	−12.2	$1000	0.992	21.805	$21,980	+4.7
1-Oct-03	1018	−11.3	$1000	0.982	22.788	$23,203	+5.5
1-Nov-03	1051	−8.5	$1000	0.952	23.739	$24,943	+8.4
1-Dec-03	1070	−6.8	$1000	0.934	24.674	$26,404	+10.0
Totals on							
1-Jan-04	**1,112**	**−3.1**	**$24,000**		**24.674**	**$27,435**	**+14.3**

Observation: Even though during this time period, the S&P 500 never returns to the January 1, 2002 close, the investor shows a net gain of 14.3% on January 1, 2004.

Monte Carlo simulators

Of course there are many times when investors cannot ignore the gyrations in the financial markets. The year 2000, like every year, had a crop of new retirees who saw a significant portion of their wealth wiped out by the ensuing downturn in the market. Unplanned adjustments in living standards had to be made. While market professionals always say reassuringly, "the market always comes back," that is a historical trend with no guarantee for the future. No one gets to live through an "average" period of history. Each of us, by accident of birth, is stuck in a specific period of time and forced to cope with the historic events that by chance happen to coincide with our lifetime.

One method to build indeterminacy into investment planning is to use a "Monte Carlo" simulator. A Monte Carlo simulator is a computer program that analyzes events that have multiple outcomes and calculates the probability associated with each outcome. Physicists have used the technique for years to solve complex problems in quantum mechanics and statistical physics. Many complex physical systems do not evolve towards a single determined outcome but can yield multiple outcomes with each outcome having an associated probability. Multiple outcomes are possible because the sequences of events that determine the outcomes are random in nature.

To understand Monte Carlo simulation it helps to think about the origin of its name. Monte Carlo is a principality on the Mediterranean Sea famed for its casinos. Imagine you are planning a trip to Monte Carlo and have a $1000 budget for blackjack and time to play 500 hands. Before going, you decide to test out different strategies for playing the game. With a computer programmed with a Monte Carlo simulator for blackjack, the computer can run through your planned 500 hand, $1000 budget scenario thousands of times. The outcome of each scenario would be different because the individual hands have random outcomes. The computer would use a random number generator to simulate shuffling the deck. But after the computer runs the same scenario a few thousand times, patterns would emerge. Suppose using your planned bet size and playing strategy, the simulation showed that you run out of money by the 400th hand 100 times in 5000 simulations. Your probability of going broke after 400 hands is 100 divided 5000 or 0.02, which is 2%. Suppose the same 5000 simulations produced a doubling of your money after 500 hands 250 times. Then your probability of doubling your money is 250 divided by 5000 or 0.05 which is 5%.

After running the Monte Carlo simulation thousands of times, you still do not know what will happen on your actual trip. But you will have a good idea of the range of possible outcomes and the relative likelihood of each one. For example, if after 5000 simulations not one resulted in a tripling of your money, you can be confident that that outcome is highly unlikely. A tripling of your money could happen, and you might wish for it, but the probability is remote.

For investment planning, a Monte Carlo simulator tests an investment strategy by running the proposed scenario thousands of times and tabulating the different outcomes. Suppose part of your investment strategy is to invest $10,000 per year for the next 20 years in a fund indexed to one of the market's benchmark indices. The Monte Carlo simulator would run through this scenario thousands of times with different yearly investment returns used each time for the calculation. The yearly returns would be randomly chosen based on historical precedents. Suppose historical analysis showed that on average, the benchmark used to index the fund you want to invest in, loses 20% once out of every 15 years. A probability of 1 out of 15 would be assigned to a year with a 20% loss, and each time the Monte Carlo simulation ran, 20% losses would happen randomly with this frequency. A 12% gain might occur one year out of every 10 years, therefore a probability of 1 in 10 would be assigned to 12% gains. Each time the Monte Carlo simulation runs, a different outcome results; but after thousands of trials, patterns will emerge. From these patterns the probabilities of meeting, exceeding, or failing to meet your investment goal can be computed.

A Monte Carlo analysis of an investment strategy provides probabilities for varying degrees of success or failure. The analysis might show that you have an 80% chance of meeting your goal, a 10% chance of falling 50% short of your goal, a 1% chance of going broke, and so on. Some investment firms like T. Rowe Price (http://www.troweprice.com) offer Monte Carlo analyses as part of their financial advising services. These analyses helps investors better understand the varying degrees of risk associated with investing and to better understand the relationship between risk and reward. But just remember, an actual trip to Monte Carlo happens once, not 10,000 times in a simulator. So it will be with the next 20 years in the markets: the trip will only happen once. History is a sequence of one-time events.

History's Lessons

History is of course the problem when it comes to investment planning. Monte Carlo simulators still rely on the past to predict the future. The probabilities assigned to future market returns are determined by analyzing events in the past. While the past is the only possible source of data to analyze, the real lesson from history is that the unexpected is to be expected. No one predicted the collapse of the Soviet Union in the 1980s, the rise of the Internet, the NASDAQ stock market bubble in the 1990s, or the attacks of September 11, 2001. All these events have had a profound economic impact.

Financial planners advise us to stay in stocks for the long run because of their historically superior rates of return. Indeed, the traumatic events of the last decade are no more traumatic than events of the past century. The United States suffered massive economic upheaval during the Great Depression of the 1930s, fought a horrific world war in the 1940s, coped with massive social changes brought on by the Civil Rights Movement that started in the 1950s, endured assassinations of key national leaders in the 1960s, lost the Vietnam War, and adjusted to the Arab oil embargo in the 1970s. Through all these decades the

U.S. economy has remained remarkably resilient, and stocks have maintained a general trend upward.

History will certainly continue and dramatic life-altering events will always occur. There is no reason to believe the U.S. economy will not continue to adjust and that stocks will not continue a general upward trend. But there is also no reason to believe that the market will continue to rise. Stock markets are not predestined to always go up. The Japanese stock market has been in a downturn for over 20 years.

The real danger in planning for the future is the tendency for people to assume that the economic conditions of the moment will continue indefinitely. I remember an annuity salesman in 1979 showing me a projection of the hundreds of thousands of dollars I would have when I retire by investing just $50 per month in his annuity. He explained that there was no risk, but his projection assumed that interest rates on simple money market accounts would remain at the then current 12% annual rate for the next four decades. Looking back, I see that this is a laughable calculation given that at the time of this writing (2005), money market funds return less than 1% annually. In the mid-1990s, investors with stock funds that returned less than 20% annually felt left out of the boom. The market was rising so fast that many people made plans to retire as millionaires in less than 10 years. Somehow all that anticipated cash fail to materialize out of the cyberspace that investors bet so heavily on. When the bubble burst, more people lost money than gained. As I write this paragraph in 2006, interest rates charged on mortgage debts are at historic lows. As a result, housing prices have been bid up to extraordinarily high levels because buyers are able to take on much more debt than in the past. The danger today is that if mortgage rates rise all that debt could become crushing and housing prices could fall as rapidly as they rose. No one knows whether that will happen, but change has always occurred in the past, and it will always occur in the future. This is a trite statement, but one many people easily forget when making financial plans.

THE WIZARD OF ID   PARKER & HART

© 1997 Creators Syndicate, Inc. Reprinted by permission of John L. Hart FLP, and Creators Syndicate, Inc.

Summary

If you desire a secure financial future, be aware that apparently small decisions made early in life can have a great impact later on. That is because when it comes to building wealth, the most important factor is time. Given sufficient time, the exponential character of investment growth usually takes shape. Market bubbles and market crashes that distort short-term results cancel out, and the actual rate of investment return approaches the historical averages. I use the word "market" in the broadest possible sense here, to include all forms of assets and liabilities —stocks, bonds, real estate, cash, and even debts. Each of these investment classes has a market-driven price that fluctuates depending on the prevailing economic conditions. Even the value of cash varies in time. It is a mistake to believe that the values of the bills in your wallet are "safe" from market gyrations.

Because market fluctuations tend to average out over long time periods, an investor who starts saving and investing early in life is exposed to less risk and that allows the investor to take advantage of investments such as indexed stock funds, that historically have higher rewards but greater fluctuations. Investors who start late in life can easily go broke trying to make up for lost time by chasing "hot" investments. Investors who start early but always "play it safe," risk having inflation consume their small but steady returns.

It is a simple mathematical fact that wealth builds wealth, and that fact causes small disparities in savings and investments to grow large over time. You can argue about the fairness of the rich getting richer, but the technique of leveraging existing capital to acquire more capital works for anyone. Understand the math and make it work for you.

Following the Money Trail

The beauty of investing is that seemingly inconsequential sums of money can have an enormous impact on many people and businesses. It is interesting to follow what became of an investment of a small amount of money I made as a teenager doing yard work for neighbors. In March 1975, at the age of 15, I followed a recommendation of my father's and purchased 50 shares of Sanders Associates at 5 1/4 per share. The total cost with commission was $299.56 (I still have the receipt). During the next 11 years that I held the stock, it split twice. In 1986 Lockheed Martin acquired Sanders. I sold my now 200 shares for $50 per share, a total proceeds of $10,000. At that time, I was living the austere life of a graduate student and didn't need the money. CD rates were just over 9%, so I parked the money for two years in a CD and it became $12,000.

In 1988 my father was stretched thin for working capital to operate his construction business. He needed a bid deposit for a large job he had estimated and he was short on cash. I redeemed the CD and sent him the $12,000. A year later when the job was complete, he sent me back the money with the interest the bank would have charged had he borrowed the money from the bank. I now had $13,500. At the end of 1988 my first child was born. My wife quit her job to spend her full time with our child. In 1989 I finished my Ph.D. in physics, moved out of state at my own expense, and began three years of low-paid postdoctoral training. The $13,500 helped pay for the move and was used to make ends meet for the next three years, until I finished my training and could begin a higher paid job. My wife was able to stay home full time with our child. The few hundred dollars I made mowing lawns as a teenager had gone a long way before it was finally spent.

Chapter 6 Resources

For some useful and practical guides on financial planning over an entire lifetime see:

Jane Bryant Quinn, *Smart and Simple Financial Strategies for Busy People* (New York, NY: Simon and Schuster, 2006)

Elizabeth Warren and Amelia Warren Tyagi, *All Your Worth: The Ultimate Lifetime Money Plan* (New York, NY: Free Press, 2005)

David Bach, *Automatic Millionaire* (New York: NY, Broadway Books, 2004)

Lee Eisenberg, *The Number: A Completely Different Way to Think About the Rest of Your Life* (New York, NY: Free Press, 2006)

For a discussion on the growing disparities of accumulated wealth in the United States and the detrimental impact this will have in the future on American society see:

William H. Gates Sr. and Chuck Collins, *Wealth and Our Commonwealth: Why America Should Tax Accumulated Fortunes* (Boston, MA: Beacon Press, 2004)

CHAPTER SEVEN

Gambling

The Probability Paradox

"How dare we speak of the laws of chance? Is not chance the antithesis of all law?"

—Joseph Bertrand
Calcul des probabilités
(original publication: 1888)

For fifteen consecutive Sundays, beginning on September 26, 1937, and ending on January 2, 1938, the Zenith Radio Corporation used its nationwide radio network to conduct a series of experiments on telepathy. Over one million people participated, and after tabulating all the data, the Zenith Foundation that conducted the study, announced a stunning conclusion—the odds against pure chance accounting for the number of correct responses to the tests were 10,000,000,000,000,000 to 1, which is ten thousand trillion to 1. Telepathy appeared to have been scientifically proved. Later in 1938, a Northwestern University psychologist Louis D. Goodfellow analyzed the Zenith radio data and concluded that indeed chance was not at work, but neither was telepathy.* Goodfellow provided a psychological

---

*Louis D. Goodfellow, "A Psychological Interpretation of the Results of the Zenith Radio Experiments in Telepathy," *Journal of Experimental Psychology*, vol. 23 (1938) pp. 601-632

interpretation of the data that required no need to invoke psychic phenomena.

Although interpretations differed, the Zenith Radio experiments themselves were straightforward and easy to understand. A roulette wheel was used to generate a sequence of five binary outcomes. A binary outcome is one with only two possibilities. Images, such as heads or tails, white or black, circle or cross, were assigned to each outcome in the sequence. Ten "senders" in a small room next to the studio "concentrated" on each image in the sequence one at a time in an attempt to telepath the image to the audience. A narrator prompted listeners to write down the images one at a time on a postcard to send in the mail. An audible bell alerted the audience when the "senders" switched their concentration to the next image in the sequence. For example, on October 10, 1937, the binary sequence was black, white, white, black, white; and on December 12, 1937, it was tail, tail, head, head, head.

In essence, the audience members were asked to guess the outcome of a random sequence of events. Gamblers who bet on roulette and other games of chance attempt essentially the same thing. The twist in the Zenith Radio experiments is that the events had already happened and the "senders" knew the outcome. The premise behind these experiments was that if the audience performed better than chance at guessing the outcomes, then the "senders" must have been successful in the telepathic transmission of their knowledge. But this premise was deeply flawed because of psychological effects within the audience that are shared by almost everyone. These same psychological effects influence the decisions many people make when they gamble. As we examine the mass delusion of the Zenith Radio experiments we will uncover the psychology behind many of the fallacious beliefs on gambling. It is a psychology of denial rooted in the fact that many results from the mathematics of probabilities are so counter-intuitive that people refuse to believe them. Because this psychological denial is so deep-rooted many people are inherently prone to making disastrous decisions when it comes to gambling.

Probabilities for Random Sequences

"Misunderstanding of probability may be the greatest of all impediments to scientific literacy."

—Stephen Jay Gould
Biologist and author

To understand why both Goodfellow and the Zenith Foundation agreed that the results of the telepathy experiments could not be explained by chance, it is necessary to understand what would happen if chance alone operated. For the purposes of this discussion, I will use 1's and 0's to represent the binary images. Depending on the week, 1 would equal head and 0 would equal tail, or 1 would equal cross and 0, circle. For five binary events there are 32 possible sequences that can result. Among these are 11111, and 10110, and 11000. If the sequences are generated randomly *then each sequence is equally likely.* This last assertion troubles most people, but it is at the heart of Goodfellow's psychological explanation. It is difficult to convince most people that the sequence 11111 is just as likely as 10110. The reason is that people correctly understand that a randomly generated 5-member binary sequence that is all 1's is much less likely than a sequence with three 1's. But the equal probability assertion does not apply to all sequences with three 1's. The assertion is that the *exact* sequence 10110 has an equal probability of occurrence as the sequence 11111.

To understand the distinction between exact sequences and sequences with a specific number of ones, imagine writing each possible binary sequence on 32 separate index cards and throwing them into a hat. The sequence 11111 appears on only one card so the chance of picking it out of the hat is 1 in 32. But the sequence 10110 also appears on just one card and has the same 1 in 32 chance of being picked. The confusion arises because only one card has five 1's but ten cards have three 1's. The ten sequences 10011, 10110, 11100, 01011, 01101, 00111, 11001, 10101, 01110, and 11010 all have three 1's and appear on separate cards. The chance of picking a card with three 1's is 10 in 32, which is much higher than picking the single card with five 1's. As a result, people tend to incorrectly believe that an exact sequence containing three 1's, such as 10110, is more likely than 11111.

To avoid this common confusion, I will borrow some language from statistical physics that makes clear what the equal probability assertion for exact sequences means. Each of the 32 possible binary sequences has anywhere from zero to five 1's. I can write down each sequence on a separate index card, and I can sort my 32 index cards into six separate bins labeled with the number of 1's in the sequence. For example, bin 1 has one card with the sequence 00000, while bin 2 contains the five cards with the sequences 10000, 01000, 00100, 00010, and 00001. I refer to each bin as a *macro-state* and characterize each of the six possible macro-states by the number of 1's on each card in that bin. Each card in a bin has an exact sequence and is referred to as a *micro-state*. After sorting all 32 cards (micro-states) we see that some of the bins (macro-states) contain more cards (micro-states) than others. The number of micro-states associated with each macro-state is referred to as the *multiplicity*. The results of the sorting process are shown in Table 7.1.

In the language I have just introduced, my equal probability assertion applies only to the micro-states. The probability of picking the card with 10000 is equal to the probability of picking 01100. But because the micro-states are all equally likely, each macro-state has a different probability of occurrence. It is apparent from this list that macro-state 2 (a sequence with a single 1) is less likely than macro-state 3 (a sequence with two 1's) because it has half as many micro-states (5 as opposed to 10). The probability of each macro-state depends on its multiplicity. The higher the multiplicity, the more frequently the macro-state occurs. A five-member binary sequence with two 1's is twice as likely to occur as a five-member binary sequence with a single 1. Note that this is a different statement from my previous assertion that 10000 and 01100 are equally likely occurrences. The micro-states are all equally likely, but the macro-states are not.

Table 7.1: Results of sorting the 32 possible five-member binary sequences into bins that contain a specific number of 1's.

Five-member binary sequences

Bin	Number of 1's on cards (macro-state)	Index cards contained (micro-states)	Number of cards (Multiplicity)	Fraction of Total (%)
1	0	00000	1	3.125
2	1	10000, 01000, 00100, 00010, 00001	5	15.625
3	2	01100, 01001, 11000, 10100, 10010, 00011, 00110, 01010, 10001, 00101	10	31.250
4	3	10011, 10110, 11100, 01011, 01101, 00111, 11001, 10101, 01110, 11010	10	31.250
5	4	11110, 11101, 11011, 10111, 01111	5	15.625
6	5	11111	1	3.125

Observation: Each of the 32 possible sequences is equally likely but 20 out of the 32 contain two or three 1's.

The Game of Poker

Before examining the Zenith radio data, consider the above language applied to a game that is more familiar to most people—poker. In poker, five cards are randomly assigned to each player from a standard 52-card deck. Because there are 52 distinct cards in the deck, there are many more possibilities for 5-card poker hands (2,598,960 to be exact) than for 5-member binary sequences. Each of the 2,598,960 possible five-card poker hands is a distinct micro-state. The equal probability assertion means that every possible hand is equally likely. In other words, the probability of receiving Ace-diamonds, Ace-hearts, Ace-spades, Ace-clubs, 5-diamonds is exactly equal to the probability of receiving 2-spades, 5-clubs, Jack-clubs, 9-hearts, King-diamonds. But most people do not believe this assertion because four Aces is a rare and valuable hand that most poker players would be willing to wager a large sum of money on. The other hand is worthless, and most good poker players would quickly fold it.

The reason for the confusion is that in poker, specific hands (micro-states) are not ranked, rather it is groups of hands with common characteristics (macro-states) that are ranked. The rules of poker recognize, name, and rank eight distinct macro-states (straight-flush, four-of-a-kind, full-house, flush, straight, three-of-a-kind, two-pair, pair). Table 7.2 summarizes the eight kinds of poker hands and their multiplicities. But within each macro-state, the possible hands are equally likely. The probability of being dealt an Ace-high straight-flush in spades: Ace-spades, King-spades, Queen-spades, Jack-spades, 10-spades (royal flush in poker jargon) is equal to the probability of being dealt a 10-high straight flush in hearts. To rank hands within a macro-state a convention has been adopted that the macro-state containing the highest card wins. By convention a royal flush beats any other kind of straight flush because it contains an Ace, not because it is more likely than any other straight flush. Similarly, even though the probability of receiving four Jacks is the same has receiving four 2s, the Jacks win because of the high card convention.

Table 7.2: Definitions of poker hands and their multiplicities (number possible) in order of rank from highest to lowest.

Five-card poker hands

Kind of hand	Definition	Number Possible	Example
Straight-flush	Five sequential cards of the same suit.	40	9, 8, 7, 6, 5, all in diamonds.
Four-of-a-Kind	Four cards of the same rank.	624	5, 5, 5, 5, 9.
Full House	Three cards of one rank and two of another rank.	3744	8, 8, 8, Jack, Jack.
Flush	Five cards of the same suit. The order does not matter.	5108	Ace, Jack, 7, 3, 2, all in spades.
Straight	Five sequential cards. The suits do not matter.	10,200	Jack, 10, 9, 8, 7, in different suits.
Three-of-a-Kind	Three cards of the same rank.	54,912	6, 6, 6, 10, 2.
Two Pair	Two cards of the same rank. and two of another rank.	123,552	4, 4, 2, 2, 9.
One Pair	Two cards of the same rank.	1,098,240	9, 9, Ace, 10, 2.

Observation: The fewer possible ways for a kind of hand to occur the higher it is ranked.

But any kind of straight-flush will win against four 2s because the macro-states are ranked in order of their multiplicities with the lowest multiplicity hands (least likely) assigned the highest ranks. There are only 40 five-card combinations out of the 2,598,960 that meet the definition of a straight flush (five sequential cards in the same suit). Because of this low multiplicity, straight flushes are extremely improbable and are given the highest rank. There are 624 five-card hands that contain four-of-a-kind, which makes these hands 15 times more likely than a straight-flush but still very rare given the total number of possible hands.*

Most of 2,598,960 possible five-card combinations (1,302,540 to be exact) do not fit into any of the eight macro-states recognized by the rules of poker and are usually discarded by the players because they would have little value in a showdown. But, each *exact* combination of cards is *equally* likely. The hand 3-clubs, 5-diamonds, 10-clubs, 9-hearts, Queen-diamonds is just as likely as an Ace-high straight-flush in spades. It is the pre-defined macro-state known as a royal flush that is so rare. Many poker players can go a lifetime and never have a royal flush, but that is just an example of the improbability of receiving any one of the 2,598,960 possible hands, not just the four possible royal flushes. If you did a survey at a poker game and asked before the deal for the players to use their "psychic abilities" to predict their next five-card hand, I am willing to bet that no one would predict a royal flush for themselves. Everyone would consider that outcome too improbable. I'm also willing to bet that no one's exact prediction for his or her next five cards would be correct either.

*Many people stop me here and say: "Wait a minute, there are only 13 ranks in a card deck so how can there be 624 ways to be dealt four-of-kind?" The reason is that standard poker is a five-card game. If you receive four Aces there are 48 remaining possibilities for the fifth card so that means there are 48 ways to be dealt four Aces. The same statement is true for all 13 ranks. Therefore there are 48 x 13, or 624 ways to be dealt four-of-kind. This assertion seems counterintuitive and both four-of-kind and straight flushes are very rare poker hands. But if you play poker long enough to start seeing some of these rare hands you will discover that hands with four-of-kind occur much more frequently than straight flushes. As we will learn in Chapter 12 on number size, the frequencies of different kinds of "infrequent" events can vary greatly.

The Zenith Radio Data

When the Zenith Foundation tabulated the postcards listeners sent in and concluded that "chance" could not account for the results, the foundation meant "chance" as understood by the formal structure of probability theory, not "chance" as understood by the average radio listener. Remember the radio listeners know that these are random sequences. The listeners are not trying to guess sequences of letters that make up words or phrases; they are trying to guess a sequence that they expect follows the outcome of a random process. If everyone had their own roulette wheel, spun it five times, and honestly recorded and mailed whatever sequence of reds and blacks resulted, the postcards would reflect "chance" as understood by probability theory. A chart showing the frequency of all 32 possible 5-event outcomes would show no preference for one outcome over another. Just as many postcards would have 11111 as 00000 as 11010. But people were asked to mail in what they *think* is a random sequence of 5-events, and very few people think that 11111 or 00000 is a random outcome.

Figure 7.1 shows the Zenith radio data, compiled over the entire 15 weeks that the experiments ran. Each bar on the chart represents a binary sequence and the height of the bar is the percentage of people who responded with either that exact binary sequence or its exact complement. By complement I mean two sequences that have alterations that form the same pattern. An alteration is an event that differs from the one preceding it. The sequences 11111 and 00000 are complements because they have same pattern—no alteration takes place in the sequence. Likewise 11010 and 00101 are complements because they share the same pattern—alterations take place on the third, fourth, and fifth events. The reason that complements are grouped together is that the Zenith radio data shows that the responders prefer certain patterns.

The preference for certain patterns is immediately obvious from the chart. Had a truly random process been used to generate the contents of the postcards, the bars in the chart in Figure 7.1 would all be the same height. Each bar would show that 6.25 percent of the postcards had either the sequence or its complement. But the chart is far from flat. For example, the first bar on the left labeled "11111" shows that a total of only 0.84 percent of the postcards received had either 11111 or its complement 00000. The peak of the chart is the sixth bar from the left that shows that 14.32 percent of the postcards received had either 11010 or its complement 00101.

Figure 7.1 shows that "chance" is not at work when people are asked to write down what they think are random sequences. There is a clear preference for sequences with frequent alterations. More people respond with 10010, a sequence with three alterations than a sequence such as 11000 that alternates only once. That meant that on October 24, 1937, when the images were circle, cross, cross, circle, cross, far more people sent in correct responses than chance alone would predict. The Zenith

Figure 7.1: Zenith radio data. The frequency of use for each of the sixteen possible five-sequence patterns is shown.

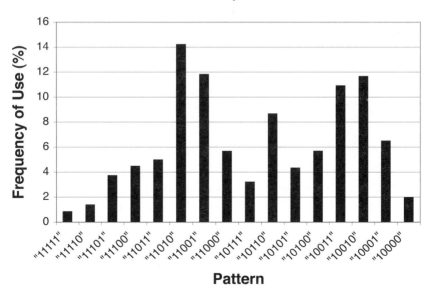

Observation: The audience showed a clear preference for certain patterns even though all patterns were equally likely.

Foundation interpreted the result as evidence of telepathy, but Goodfellow's explanation is that more people believe that the sequence 10010 is the result of a random process than 11000. If Goodfellow's explanation is correct then on December 12, 1937, when the images were tail, tail, head, head, head, far *fewer* people should get the correct sequence than chance alone would predict. That is exactly what happened. On that Sunday the "senders" were anti-telepathic. Clearly, chance is not at work in these experiments, but neither is telepathy. What the Zenith radio data shows is that people share widespread faulty beliefs on what constitutes randomness.

The Frequency of Improbable Events

The Zenith Radio data shows that people do not understand that all possible five-member sequences (micro-states) are equally likely. But do people correctly estimate how often a sequence contains macro-states (three 1's as opposed to five 1's)? In other words, if I sort all the listener response cards into six bins corresponding to the six possible macro-states will the results match the percentages in Table 7.1? Additional psychological insight is available if a chart is made that compares the macro-states from the Zenith radio data to the macro-states expected by chance. Figure 7.2 compares the percentage of listener responses that contained a specific number of 1's to the percentages listed in Table 7.1 that are computed under the assumption that chance alone operates. Each of the six categories in the chart corresponds to the number of 1's present. The first category is zero 1's while the next category includes all responses with a single 1. That means the five sequences 10000, 01000, 00100, 00010, and 00001would all be grouped in the single 1 category. Figure 7.2 shows that as a group, people have a striking misunderstanding of the mathematics of probabilities. In general people tend to *overestimate the frequency of the most likely macro-states and underestimate the frequency of the least likely macro-states.*

Sequences that contain two or three 1's should occur more frequently than the other sequences, but people believe that these sequences occur much more frequently than chance alone would predict. On the other hand, people believe that sequences such as 11111 and 00000 occur far less frequently than chance would predict. People tend to believe that more likely events happen more often than they should, and less likely events happen less often than they should. If the probability of an event is much less than the probability of a competing event, then the less likely event should not happen. In other words, the most likely events are mentally assigned a probability of "almost always occurs," and the least likely events are mentally assigned a probability

Figure 7.2: Comparison of the use of the six possible macro-states in the Zenith radio data with their predicted use from chance alone.

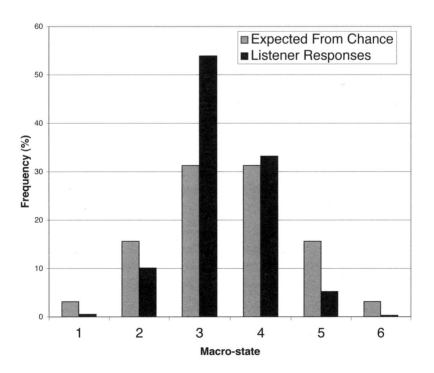

Observation: The audience believed that infrequent events happen even less often than probability theory predicts.

of "hardly ever occurs." These mental judgments are similar to the beliefs that will be discussed in Chapter 12—that all large numbers are equally large and all small numbers are equally insignificant.

Psychologists have studied the ability of people to judge randomness and found that we are poor judges. Consider flipping coins repeatedly. To most of us, the sequence of coin-flips HTHTTHHT appears more random than HHHTTT and therefore more likely to occur. A sequence such as TTTTHT is thought not be random at all. The psychologists who conducted many of these experiments, Tversky and Kahneman, have dubbed this fallacious thinking—"belief in the law of small numbers."* People mistakenly believe that a small sample, picked at random from a much larger sample, should reflect the larger sample as a whole. That means that in a series of 100 coin flips, that are roughly half heads and half tails, people believe that a small subset of the sequence, say six coin flips, should contain about three heads and three tails. People might allow for four occurrences of one possibility but certainly not five or six. Asked to judge the randomness of a sequence of coin flips, people invariably select sequences where H and T alternate frequently and long streaks such as HHHHHH or TTTT are absent. But the laws of probability theory dictate that long streaks *must* occur. Pick small samples from a long sequence of coin flips, and streaks such as HHHHHH or TTTT will be found. Small samples do not represent the fairness of the coin.

Interestingly, people do not believe that sequences such as HTHTH and THTHT are random either. If the two possible outcomes alternate, that is perceived as a pattern and therefore not random. The Zenith Radio data also shows this effect. The chart in Figure 7.1 shows a dip in the number of responses with the 10101 pattern and its complement. Apparently the psychological phenomenon of "anchoring," discussed in the Chapter 1 on shopping, plays a role in judging randomness.

*Amos Tversky and Daniel Kahneman, "Belief in the law of small numbers," *Psychological Bulletin*, vol. 2 (1971) pp. 105-110

Asked to write down a random sequence of binary events, people begin by imagining an alternating sequence because it satisfies the "law of small numbers." Then the sequence is "adjusted" in an attempt remove the pattern that consists of 100% alterations of the outcomes. But because people tend to believe a truly random sequence must be devoid of long streaks the sequence remains biased towards too many alterations. The crux of what I call the probability paradox is that *unless the sequence actually contains some long streaks, the number of times on average that outcomes alternate will exceed 50%.*

If a binary event such as a coin flip is truly random, then on average the fraction of the events where the outcome alternates should only be 50%. A head should follow a tail only half the time. That means that if a very long sequence of coin flips were to occur, say 100 or more events and streaks of heads longer than three events were absent, you would have to conclude that the outcomes were not random. It would mean that tails follow heads more than 50% of the time.

The Probability Paradox

Improbable streaks *must* happen or the probabilities
would be completely wrong.

The fact is there is big difference between the concepts of "never" and "infrequent." But many people confuse the two ideas and assume that infrequent events should never happen.

How long is long enough?

This discussion raises the question: Is it possible to ever determine from observation the actual probabilities associated with a sequence of random events? How do we know when a deviation from the results expected by chance is a normal fluctuation or a real effect? The psychologists Tversky and Kahneman who coined the phrase "belief in the law of small numbers" actually made a play on words. The expression they played on is an important and real theorem in statistics known as "the law of large numbers." The law of large numbers states that as the number of repetitions becomes large the observed frequencies of the different events will converge to the frequencies expected from probability theory.

This statement appears sensible, but the difficulty with its application is that "large" is a relative term. The number of repetitions that qualifies as "large" depends on the number of outcomes possible—or the "variability" in outcomes to use a statistical term. In mathematics, to say that one number is large compared to another usually means that the larger number is at a minimum 10 times greater than the smaller number—a 100 times greater or more would be preferable. So for the Zenith radio experiments where there are 32 possible 5-sequence outcomes, if we observed in excess of 320 sequences the results would begin to converge to the predictions of probability theory (Table 7.1). Another factor of 10 (about 3000 patterns) would help to make sure that the observed frequency of each pattern does coincide with its expected frequency.

But what about for a game like poker, where the number of possible outcomes is greater than 2.5 million? Do we need to be dealt more than 25 million hands to know if the shuffle is "fair?" Do we need to see tens of millions of hands to know for certain that we received our fair share of straight-flushes (Table 7.2)? The answer to these last two questions is yes and that is the problem people encounter when they try to generalize their personal experiences with gambling. Most games of chance have highly variable outcomes so the law of large numbers rarely applies to the average gambler. Instead many gamblers draw erroneous conclusions about their successes and failures because their experiences are limited to a number of repetitions that is small in comparison to all the possible outcomes.

The "Gambler's Fallacy"

Belief in the law of *small* numbers is a variation of a belief known as "the gambler's fallacy." Many gamblers incorrectly believe that when streaks occur, the probability that the streak will end increases. This fallacious thinking leads gamblers to believe that if they increase the size of their bets on events that are "overdue" they can make up for past losses and turn a profit. If a series of repeated coin-flips results in a streak of five tails, believers in the gambler's fallacy will bet heavily that the next flip will be a head because heads are now "overdue." Even though each coin-flip is an independent random event, gamblers often believe that somehow the coin's past history affects the future. I tease people who believe this with questions on how well do they know the coin's history. Is the coin newly minted and without any past? Did the past owner ever flip the coin? Did the coin's past ever include long streaks of heads? If you put the coin away and don't flip it for a month, will a head still be "overdue?" These are all obviously silly questions, but if the coin's past affects the future they should all have relevant answers.

Interestingly many gamblers who believe in the "overdue concept" also believe in its logical contradiction—that one should bet on streaks or look for other repetitive patterns in the past and bet on the patterns continuing. Of course the belief in streaks and repetitive patterns shares the same underlying fallacy as the overdue concept, the fallacious idea that a past sequence of independent random events affects future random events. The idea that a past sequence of random coin flips has no effect on future random coin flips is difficult for most people to accept. When I continue to ask people why they believe past coin-flips affect future ones, I find behind their reasoning two underlying beliefs. It is my observation that these beliefs are universal to the human condition. They are as follows:

- All events happen for a reason.
- Observed patterns found in a past history of events can be used to predict future events.

For events that are random, the above two statements are false. In fact, the negation of the above two statements is a good definition of randomness. In other words, if we go back to random coin-flips:

- There is no reason for the outcome of the next coin-flip.
- Patterns found in a past sequence of coin-flips have no predictive value.

Probability is one of the hardest areas of mathematics to learn because it goes against these core human beliefs. Random events affect our lives in many ways, but no person wants to believe that a great many of the important events that define their life happened for no reason, unless of course the event was bad. Misfortune is always attributed to bad luck while success is always attributed to hard work, skill, insight, fortitude, and I could go on with a long list of positive character adjectives. Few people attribute their successes to good luck.

Probability and Gambling

Probability theory, when correctly understood, is applicable to evaluating the profit potential from gambling. Because gambling is such a popular activity and probability theory so poorly understood, there is a prodigious quantity of mathematically deceptive advice on gambling. Entire books have been published on various gambling topics with mathematically deceptive premises. In fact, I could fill an entire bookshelf with books on gambling that make elaborate claims and describe sophisticated betting systems, but do not provide any advice that would *improve* your chances of winning. I emphasize the word "improve" because any gambling system will win some of the time. You can always find people who won following a particular system, just as you can always find people who won by not following the system. The question is this: are there more people who won and fewer people who lost? This is a question that most sellers of gambling systems never accurately test. But before examining some of the common mathematical deceptions on gambling, first we need to know how profits are realized from gambling.

Land-based casinos, state governments, and online gaming sites reap enormous profits from gambling, while the average person who gambles rarely realizes any financial benefit. The difference lies in the *expected value* of the bets. The expected value is how much the bet will win or loose on average if placed repeatedly. Bets that are expected to produce winnings over the long run have positive expected values, while bets that lose over the long run have negative expected values. Break-even bets have an expected value of zero. Repetition is important for understanding expected value. A bet with a positive expected value will not win every time and a bet with a negative expected value will not lose every time. Expected values reflected the sum total of wins and losses after many repetitions.

The expected value of a bet depends two quantities: the odds against success and the payoff on the amount wagered. The odds against a bet succeeding are expressed as a ratio that compares the average number of failures for every success. The odds against success for a coin-flip are 1 to 1. That means that, on average, for each success calling heads or tails, there is one failure. If the odds against a particular bet are 3 to 1, that means that on average there are three failures for each success. The payoff is also expressed as a ratio. It is the number of dollars paid for each dollar wagered. If you risk $1 on a bet that pays 1 to 1, you receive an additional $1 if you win, and you lose your $1 if you do not. If you risk $1 on a bet that pays 3 to 1, you receive an additional $3 if you win and lose your $1 if you do not. With these definitions we can summarize the golden rule on betting:

The Golden Rule for Betting

For a bet to have a positive expected value, the payoff on the wager must be greater than the odds against success.

Note that the payoff is the critical ratio for determining the expected value of a bet. If the payoff is equal to the odds against success, the expected value is zero. For payoffs less than the odds against success, the expected value is negative. To see how this works, imagine a bet where the odds against success are 3 to 1. If you place $1 bets repeatedly and the payoff is 4 to 1, you will win $4 for each success while losing $3 for the three failures. On average, for every $4 bet you will be left with $5 in your pocket—the $4 won on the one success plus the $1 not lost. The ratio of 5 to 4 is 1.25 so the expected value is $1.25 minus $1 or $0.25. But if you play the same game with the same 3 to 1 odds against success and the payoff is 2 to 1, you will lose money. Again imagine making repeated $1 bets. Under these circumstances, you win $2 for each success while losing $3 on the three failures. On average, for every $4 bet you will be left with $3 in your pocket—the $2 won on the one success plus the $1 not lost. The ratio of 3 to 4 is 0.75 so the expected value is $0.75 minus $1 or –$0.25. With a negative expected value, this becomes a money-losing game. If the payoff is 3 to 1, it is a break-even game. On average, for every $4 bet you will be left with $4 in your pocket—the $3 won on that one success plus the $1 not lost. Note that the odds against success are the same in all three of these cases, it is the payoff that determines whether the expected value is positive, negative or zero.

FOXTROT © 2004 Bill Amend. Reprinted with permission of UNIVERSAL PRESS SYNDICATE. All rights reserved.

I qualify all these statements with the words "on average" because as we just learned in the discussion of the Zenith radio data—small samples are not representative of the long-term averages. If the odds against a bet succeeding are 3 to 1, that does not mean that every four bets placed will include one success. If gambling were that predictable, no one would gamble. A long sequence of bets will include both winning and losing streaks, and it is the streaks that keep people coming back. The "average" will only become apparent after enough trials have occurred to satisfy the "law of large numbers" and that depends on the variability of outcomes. In fact the expected value of a bet is independent of its variability. A high-expected value bet might also have high variability, which means that many repetitions would be required to be certain of realizing a profit from that particular bet. The key concept if you gamble is repetition. To profit over the long-term from gambling, the following three conditions must be present.

Profitable Gambling

• You must place bets with *positive* expected values.

• You must place many, many bets so that the long-term results do approach the averages.

• You must have a bankroll sufficiently large in relation to the size of the bets placed so that normally occurring losing streaks do not wipe it out.

Casinos realize large profits because their gambling activities meet all three of these conditions. All casino games have a negative expected value for the player and a positive one for the house.* The average person cannot profit from gambling because it is usually illegal to place a bet with a positive expected value. In the state of Maryland where I live, I can play the heavily promoted state-run lotteries and keno games, but I cannot run my own lottery or keno game. There is nothing to stop me from wagering money at an online casino, but I cannot turn my own computer into an online casino. As of this writing, the governor wants to legalize slot machines, but if that happened it would only be at certain select locations and run by certain select companies. I would be able to play those slot machines, but I still could not open up my own slot parlor and solicit customers to play my slot machines. The average person in the state of Maryland has many legal bets with negative expected values available to him or her, but I cannot think of any bets with positive expected values that can be legally placed.**

*A blanket statement such as this invariably raises questions about the games of blackjack and poker. There is an extensive literature on the mathematics of blackjack and how under certain, very specific conditions, it can be beaten. Blackjack played with a standard deck is a game with a negative expected value for the player. Beating the game requires knowing when the deck's composition favors the player. Knowledge of a favorable deck composition is gained by process of elimination. A skilled blackjack player will keep track of the cards that are played and then know the cards that remain, a method known as "card counting." This gets into the subject of *conditional* probability that will be covered in Chapter 13.

   Poker is an altogether different game from any other offered in a casino because the players compete against each other and not the house. The house profits from poker in the same way a stock or real estate broker profits, by taking a cut of each transaction, known as the rake. The expected values associated with bets in poker cover a wide range and include both negative and positive values. A skilled poker player learns to judge the expected values of the different betting opportunities and to bet when the value is positive and fold when it is negative.

**This statement refers to casino style gambling where the expected values for the bets are known in advance. People might ask whether bets on horse races or for that matter the stock market can have positive expectations. In the case of horse races the expected values of the bets are estimates that can never be known with as much certainty as casino games. The reason is that horse races are one-time events. The same race under the exact same conditions can never be run multiple times to determine an average outcome. Your bet on a horse race might have a positive expected value but you will never know for certain because even if you win that does not mean it had a positive expected value. In casinos bets with negative expected values win frequently, just observe any slot machine. The stock market is a similar situation because exact conditions can never be duplicated. Unlike most casino games, it is not possible to compute the exact odds against success in the stock market or even know the exact payoffs.

The unavailability of bets with positive expected values has not stopped people from believing they can profit from gambling, and it has not stopped sellers of gambling advice from claiming that profits are possible. But before examining deceptive advice on gambling, there is an important fact about expected values to know.

The Size Rule for Betting

The expected value of a bet is independent of its size.

That means that you cannot profit by varying the size of your bets in response to streaks or patterns, if the bets placed have a negative expected value. Despite what many books will tell you, *there exists no system for varying bet sizes that can profit over the long run if the expected values of the bets are negative.*

Books on Gambling

Gambling books tend to fall into two categories: honest books and mathematically deceptive books. It is rare to find a book with outright falsehoods, although some of the mathematical deceptions I have encountered come close. Honest books will teach you the rules of the various games and the best way to play. The phrase "best play" usually means the strategies available that will keep losses to a minimum. Deceptive advice on gambling usually falls into two categories—(1) betting systems that claim you can profit by observing past trends and events, (2) betting systems that claim you can profit by playing for the "short-run."

(1) Claims that the past affects the future are fallacious, but these claims are often dressed up in elaborate mathematical language to give a false aura of scientific validity. Consider the book *The Basics of Winning Lottery/Lotto*, by Professor Jones (New York, NY: Cardoza Publishing, 1997) Much of the

book consists of explaining "frequency analysis" and "position analysis" to identify "hot numbers" and "overdue" numbers. The author claims that both strategies, betting on "hot" numbers and "overdue" numbers are good strategies. His advice, if read literally, appears to have a logical contradiction. Is a number that has appeared frequently "hot" and should be bet, or does that mean that other numbers that haven't appeared recently are now overdue? Don't worry he also describes how to identify "hot numbers that are overdue." A blurb on the cover states "#1 Best Selling Gambling Series Over 3,000,000 sold." Now that's what I call winning the lottery.

The use of frequency analysis is not unique to lottery players. Books on roulette advise players to look for "biased" wheels. How do you know when a wheel is biased? Again by looking for frequently occurring numbers. What the books do not say is that you would have to observe frequently occurring numbers for a long time—most likely days—to determine if a roulette wheel is genuinely biased. Numbers that occur frequently over just an hour or two would most likely be randomly occurring streaks.

Baccarat players are so wedded to a belief in streaks that casinos provide scorecards for them so that they can keep track of the streaks and bet accordingly. In *Secrets of Winning Baccarat* by Brian D. Kayser (New York, NY: Cardoza Publishing, 2003), readers are taught to keep score and advised to "bet the trend."

Some books are based on premises that are just outright silly. R. D. Ellison in *Gamble to Win: Advanced Craps* (New York, NY: Kensington, 2005) argues that the "output of random numerical events at a table is a cause and effect situation" and that "dice and wheel do possess the equivalent of memory." He writes, "My position is that some force has to be causing those numbers to behave in line with their inherent probabilities." His position is just a dressed-up version of the fallacious belief in "overdue" numbers for which he has made up an impressive mathematical label: "The Theory of Statistical Propensity." His "theory" contains a logical contradiction because random events are by definition not caused. But most of his book is not so much about looking for overdue numbers, as it is looking for patterns and trends. Among the trends he identifies are "hot tables," "choppy tables," and "repeating tables."

(2) The other common advice given in gambling books is to play for the "short run." These books argue correctly that if you stay at a table for an extended period of time, your results will approach the long-term averages, and you will lose. Therefore you should move from table to table. If you start losing, quit; and if you start winning, bet heavily. This kind of play is often referred to as "hit and run." Advice of this kind often resonates because people who gamble can remember numerous times where they were ahead but gave the money all back and then some. In fact, advice to play for the short run is extremely deceptive because half the time it does work. Of course it is easy to forget about the other half of the time when it does not work.

Take baccarat, for example. For every $1 bet, the casino wins on average $1.0136 if the bet is on the player and $1.0117 if the bet is on the banker. That means the house edge in this game is so small that the outcome of any single hand is very close to that of a coin-flip. Half the time if you quit after the first hand, you will walk away a winner. But that does not mean you can profit from baccarat if you walk away the moment you are ahead. There will be just as many times that you fall behind on the first hand and never catch up. A series of "first" bets at a lot of tables has the same expected value as a continuing series of bets at the same table. It is easy for gamblers to convince themselves the situations are different because the average recreational gambler is never going to play long enough on a weekend outing to a casino to have results that approach the averages. In games where the expected value of the bets are only slightly in favor of the house, a significant fraction of the time a recreational gambler will leave ahead. That does not mean that he or she has a profitable betting system.

Actually, there is nothing wrong with following any of the betting systems that any of these books describe because applying them is just as profitable as not applying them. No matter what betting system you use, what patterns you observe, *the expected values of the bets do not change*. What all of these books mentioned have in common are elaborate charting, scoring, and mathematical analyses to identify *past* patterns. The deception is this: sequences of random events will *always* have identifiable patterns, but those patterns are *not* predictive of future events. Prediction is the key concept because unless you can predict the future, your chances of winning remain the same.

Summary

In this chapter I have touched on just a small part of the large body of psychological research that has been directed towards understanding how people judge uncertain events. What all the research shows is that the intuitions and preferences people have and the predictions people make, do *not* conform to the mathematical laws of probability theory. As a result, under uncertain circumstances where random effects influence the outcomes, people tend to make irrational decisions. When the irrational decisions are of an economic nature, those actions undermine the fundamental tenet behind a market economy— the assumption that the market is efficient because it results from everyone acting in their own interests.

Gambling is just one example of an economic activity where people do not act in their own self-interest. People should be aware that the marketers of gambling activities are knowledgeable of both the math and the psychology. State-run lotteries are a particularly egregious example, where government-sponsored promotions are intended to induce people into playing a game that is stacked heavily in favor of the government. All of this is done under the guise of "free choice."

Many people regard gambling and investing as similar activities. In both cases money is risked on an uncertain future outcome. But there is a key mathematical difference between the two activities. Gambling is always a zero-sum activity because each loss is someone else's gain. The idea of investing is to create value where it did not exist before. In this way gambling differs from investing. Risk money to start a new company, or bring a new product to market, and success benefits many others. People who spend large sums of money on lottery tickets every week should read Chapter 6 of this book on investing. Over time, the money spent weekly on lottery tickets could add up to a substantial amount if it were invested and the odds of success would more likely be in their favor.

The beliefs that gambling can be profitable, that telepathy and other psychic phenomena are real, that hidden causes are behind all events, all arise because people are extraordinarily good at finding and recognizing patterns. If you search for patterns in *any* past sequence of events, even events that result entirely from chance, you will find patterns. The ability to discern patterns is a powerful learning tool and in fact makes science and mathematics possible. A scientist usually begins an investigation by noticing a pattern. But a scientist is concerned with far more than just finding a pattern. The scientist needs to discover if the pattern allows for prediction of the future. Essential to predicting the future is identifying a plausible cause for the pattern. Knowing when a pattern is predictive is actually difficult and will be addressed in Chapter 13. However, for random events the answer is always no. Patterns in past sequences of random events have no cause and are not predictive of the future.

Music or Noise?

The book *The Bible Code*, written by Michael Drosnin and published in 1997, occupied *The New York Times* bestseller list for a number of months. It was such a success that he followed it up with *Bible Code II: The Countdown* published in 2002. Drosnin claimed to have discovered a code that hid secret messages in the first five books of the Bible. The messages were "predictions" of future events such as the 1995 assassination of Israeli Prime Minister Yitshak Rabin. Drosnin claimed he discovered the prediction of Rabin's before it happened and tried unsuccessfully to warn him what would happen a year ahead of time. (I suspect Drosnin was not the only one giving Rabin warnings at that time.)

Drosnin discovered the "code" by using the letters of the original Hebrew text with all spaces and punctuation removed. He programmed a computer to generate different sequences of letters by choosing a starting letter and a step size. For example, with a step size of four, the computer would generate a sequence by choosing every fourth letter from the starting point. These equidistant letter sequences would next be arranged in a huge matrix to form a kind of crossword puzzle. The computer would look for names of people that intersected with Hebrew words. Using this method Drosnin claimed the names of President Kennedy, Egyptian President Anwar Sadat as well as Prime Minister Rabin were linked to the word for assassin. Because of these linkages he concluded that predictions of their assassinations were encoded in the Bible.

Some religious groups seized upon the "code" as a proof of God's existence because only God could know of events thousands of years in the future and have the ability to secretly encode these messages in the Bible. Drosnin himself believed that space aliens put the messages in the Bible, which should tell you something about the believability of his entire work.

Despite all the hype, the fact is Drosnin's "code" is nothing more than an elaborate charade for rearranging characters and any text the size of the Bible can be rearranged to spell anything. There are 304,805 Hebrew letters in the first five books of the Bible. To "predict" Rabin's assassination, Drosnin parsed the text with a step size of 4772. Obviously there are an enormous number of letter rearrangements possible if different choices of starting letters and step sizes are tried on a sequence of characters this long. Certainly if a high-speed computer is used to start rearranging characters in a multitude of different ways, it will spell out at least some of the myriad events that have happened in the past 5000 years.

Actually Drosnin's methods can be applied to any text of sufficiently large size. Skeptics began applying the methods to other works of literature that competed with the Bible for sheer size. *War and Peace* and *Moby Dick* were analyzed and found to contain all sorts of "predictions." "Encoded" in *Moby Dick* were the assassinations of Robert Kennedy and Martin Luther King. Of course it is easy to "predict" something that has already happened, or might happen soon as in the case of Rabin's assassination, because you know what to look for. If you don't know what to look for these kinds of "codes" will not be of much help.

The fascinating part of Drosnin's logic is that if his dire predictions of the future do not come true, he can say that his warnings were heeded and prevented the disasters. Like calling heads on the flip of a two-headed quarter, he can claim success no matter which side the coin lands on. Therefore his beliefs are unassailable. This same kind of reasoning is why the majority of books that "predict" events in the future are usually apocalyptic. If the events happen, the book is true. If the events do not happen, the warning was heeded and therefore the book is still true. If books like the *Bible Code* predicted a coming utopia it would be much harder to sell the book. People would know immediately that the book is false.

Chapter 7 Resources

Deborah J. Bennett, *Randomness* (Cambridge, MA: Harvard University Press, 1998) examines the history of statistics, games of chance, and sources for random numbers. She writes: "Every day we can see evidence that the human species does not yet have a very highly developed probabilistic sense."

Sam Braids, *The Intelligent Guide to Texas Hold'em Poker* (Towson, MD: Intelligent Games Publishing, 2003) has a discussion of the mathematics of poker and the conditions necessary for successful gambling.

CHAPTER EIGHT

Risk-Taking

Going Broke to Get Even

"When it comes to buying or selling a stock, don't tell me where you bought it; tell me where it's going. That is all that matters when it comes to buying or selling a stock."

—James J. Cramer
Real Money: Sane Investing in an Insane World
(New York, NY: Simon and Shuster, 2005) p. 44

One year, I purchased a stock for $80 per share and watched it rise to $90. Then conditions for the general market, industry sector, and the company went bad. The stock fell to $70 but rallied and leveled off near $80. My judgment was that the stock should be sold, but on the day I came to that conclusion the stock price was $78. I thought if I waited a few more days I could get my $80 back. I might even get a few dollars above $80, and then I would have at least a small gain to show for my efforts. Overnight a bad earnings report came out for the company. The next morning the stock opened at $60. I eventually sold the stock a few months later for $50 per share, nearly 40% off what I paid, although still at a higher price than it would sell for the following year.

That same year I also purchased a stock for $10 per share in a beaten down but improving industry sector. Within a few months the stock price rose to $15, a 50% increase. When the price started to correct, I panicked at the thought of losing my profit and sold it for $12, locking in a 20% gain. In less than a year that stock went on to sell for over $30 per share.

No one ever went broke taking 20% gains to the bank, but locking in 20% gains while allowing losses of a few percent to swell to 40% will lead to disaster. Unfortunately my decision-making processes in regards to these stock sales are not uncommon. I believe many investors have similar stories to tell. Many people are quick to take profits but slow to sell for a loss. From a mathematical point of view, this behavior makes no sense. To maximize investment return, it would make more sense to sell the losers fast, even at a small loss, and let the winners ride so that small gains have a chance to become large gains. But from a psychological point of view, selling for any kind of loss, even a small one, is an admission of error. Most people are reluctant to admit error, even to themselves. In contrast, selling for any kind of a gain means the buyer was right, and even if the stock tanks afterwards the buyer was still right and never again has to worry again about being wrong.

Clearly when it comes to decisions having uncertain outcomes, psychological needs for self-esteem and certainty conflict with the mathematical requirements for success. In this chapter we will examine both the math and the psychology of taking risks. Any time you make a financial decision that has an uncertain outcome, you are taking a risk. That uncertainty creates a set of psychological needs that can be both detrimental and beneficial to the decision-making process. The point of this chapter is to learn when those needs cause us to act in our best interest and when they do not. We will also learn that these same psychological factors influence many kinds of decisions, including financial decisions that do not involve risk.

Risk

Many readers might assume that the previous chapter on gambling has no relevance to them because they don't gamble.

They might also wonder why I have this separate chapter titled "Risk-taking," because to many people gambling and risk-taking are synonymous. Many people believe playing the stock market is the same as going to a casino and avoid it altogether. Others who play the stock market act as though they are in a casino and have predictably disastrous outcomes as a result. But I am going to discuss financial risks in this chapter in a far broader context than just playing the stock market. I am also going to draw a distinction between "gambling" and "risk-taking."

Gambling involves betting money on a game or contest for the purpose of winning more money. Some attractions of gambling include the thrill, the entertainment value, and the possibility of gaining wealth without work. Risk-taking involves using money to achieve broader goals that have an uncertain outcome. Anyone who pays for an education, buys a house, relocates for a new job, or starts a business is taking a risk. Money will be spent with the expectation of a better future, but without certain knowledge of what that future will bring.

You can live your entire life and never gamble, but risk-taking is unavoidable. You *must* make decisions concerning your health, education, living quarters, job, driving habits and so on, and all these decisions involve financial risk. A key difference is that your money becomes a tool—specifically a lever—when it is risked in such decisions. You leverage your money to achieve personal and professional goals that go beyond merely having more money. These risks are unavoidable because as we learned in Chapter 6, perpetual risk-avoidance is itself a risky behavior.

But risk is by definition probabilistic in nature; and, as a result, the mathematical principles on gambling, learned in Chapter 7, are still relevant. For example, if you decide to buy insurance (or not buy insurance) you are taking a financial risk where the outcome is uncertain, not determined. That means even if you are not "gambling," you still need to know something about the math and psychology of gambling. Also the same psychology that causes problems for gamblers can cause poor decision-making when it comes to financial risk.

Behavioral Finance

Behavioral finance is the study of the way people make financial decisions. It combines both economics and psychology in order to develop models that predict the financial choices people will make under different circumstances. Of particular interest is the way to predict how people make decisions that involve risk. An apparently logical first assumption is to assume that people faced with financial choices will act "rationally" in the mathematical sense of the word, meaning that the goal of their choices will be to maximize monetary gains and minimize losses. Therefore, if two presentations of a choice are mathematically equivalent there should be no effect on behavior. For example, the offers "buy one and get one free" and "buy two and get 50% off" are two different, yet mathematically equivalent presentations. If people are rational in the mathematical sense, their decision to buy should not depend on which of these phrases is used. The model for behavior that results from this assumption of rationality is known as the "Expected Utility Theory." If people make decisions that "utilize" their money in the most effective way, those decisions can be predicted by determining through calculation which set of choices will maximize their income and minimize their expense.

Of course, for decisions that involve risk, outcomes are probabilistic in nature. A calculation to determine exactly how to maximize income and minimize expense is not possible. For scenarios that involve risk, the Expected Utility Theory assumes that the choices people make will have the highest "expected value." Here "expected value" means exactly what it did in Chapter 7—how much the risk (bet) will win or lose on average if placed repeatedly. If a person always makes the choice with the highest expected value, his or her financial results on average will be the best that could possibly be predicted. Of course the outcome of each individual choice might be far better or far worse than the expected value. But, if all the players in the personal finance game make the choice with the highest expected value, the group as a whole will have optimal results, although individual results will vary considerably. That is because the choices an individual makes will always make up a small sample and as we learned in the previous chapter, small samples often do not represent the whole. One person might pick five stocks that all go down 20% while a different person might pick five stocks that all rise 50%. Together their combined results might be about average even though the individual outcomes differed.

Prospect Theory

The rationality assumption behind the Expected Utility Theory is a good starting point for understanding financial decisions, but it does not explain the way people actually behave. My claim is not that people are "irrational," just that rationality in the behavioral sense has more than mathematical dimensions. In 1979 two psychologists, Kahneman and Tversky, challenged the Expected Utility Theory, with an alternative explanation for how people make choices under conditions of uncertainty. They called their model "Prospect Theory."* Through the use of survey questions, they showed examples of situations where the majority of respondents chose the alternative with the lower expected value, a clear violation of the Expected Utility Theory. For example, consider having to decide between the following two choices (or "prospects," to use their wording).**

Prospect 1: An 80% chance to gain $4000 and a 20% chance to gain nothing.
Prospect 2: A certain gain of $3000.

---

* Daniel Kahneman and Amos Tversky, "Prospect Theory: An Analysis of Decision Under Risk," *Econometrica* vol. 47, no. 2 (1979) pp. 263-291

**There are no currency symbols in the original paper by Kahneman and Tversky. They note that the amounts in their questionnaire referred to Israeli currency and that the median net monthly income at this time was about 3000 Israeli pounds. I have taken the liberty of adding U.S. currency symbols to make this relevant to my intended readership. The main point is that these amounts were significant, although not astronomical, to the people answering the questionnaire.

Most (80%) of the people surveyed in this study chose the certain $3000. But, notice that Prospect 1 is the "better" bet because it has the higher expected value ($3200). Now consider these two choices:

Prospect 1: An 80% chance to lose $4000 and a 20% chance to lose nothing.
Prospect 2: A certain loss of $3000.

Now the gamble has the lower expected value (–$3200). However, in this survey 92% of the respondents would take the gamble rather than the sure loss of $3000.

Through a series of similar questions with different variations of certainty and chance in the choices, Kahneman and Tversky discovered the following pattern: *people are more willing to gamble to avoid losses, but are less willing to gamble with gains.* The aversion to loss is so strong that many people prefer the prospect with the lower expected value if it provides some chance of loss avoidance. But when gains are the issue, people become risk-averse. Most people prefer a small certain gain rather than a risk for a larger gain, even if the expected value associated with the risk is greater than the certain gain. The conclusion is that people will not always act in a manner consistent with maximizing the use of their money over the long term.

Prospect Theory explains my behavior in regards to the stock purchases I described. I held a stock I knew should be sold in hopes of recovering a small loss. But when holding a stock that was doing well, I would not risk losing a small gain. Many investors share this behavior, and as a result, average investors tend to do so much worse than market averages. DALBAR Inc., a financial services market research firm, issued a report in July 2003 that analyzed investor behavior over the prior 19 years (1984-2003). Their Quantitative Analysis of Investor Behavior (QAIB) study found that the average investor earned 2.57% annually over that time period compared to 12.22% annually for the Standard and Poors 500 index.* The results of the average investor did not even keep pace with inflation that averaged 3.14% annually during this same 19-year period. Factors that DALBAR cited for the poor results included loss aversion. Investors tend to cut their gains short and let their losses run.

A further consequence of Prospect Theory is that behavior will change if the perception of gains and losses is changed. A person must have a reference point in order to know whether he or she is experiencing a gain or loss. For the survey questions used in the Prospect Theory paper, that reference point was the status quo. But if the reference point shifts, the perception of whether a financial outcome is a gain or loss can shift, and risk-averse behavior can become risk-seeking. For example during the stock market bubble of the late 1990s, investors in funds that only made 10% annually experienced their gain as a loss because the market indices returned more than 20% during some of those years. Many investors took risks they ordinarily would not have in an effort to keep up with others who they perceived as doing better. Conversely in the market crash that followed, investors with modest losses perceived their results as gains when compared to others. Taking risks to overcome modest losses became less likely.

However, truly rational buying and selling decisions should not be dependent on prices in the past. The future performance of a stock does not depend on the exact price an individual paid for a security on a particular day in the past. In his book *Real Money: Sane Investing in an Insane World,* Jim Cramer describes how the performance of his portfolio improved dramatically after his wife took a bottle of Wite-Out® and painted over the prices that he originally paid for all the stocks he owned. Up until then he wrote, "My judgment was stymied by the stigma of unrealized loss that each negative position carried." After blotting out the prices paid, she said, "There, now you can think clearly."**

*DALBAR Inc., "Market chasing mutual fund investors earn less than inflation," http://www.dalbarinc.com.

**James J. Cramer, *Real Money: Sane Investing in an Insane World* (New York, NY: Simon and Shuster, 2005) p. 43

When Bad Bets Are Good

Risking large losses in attempts to recover small losses is financially self-destructive behavior. But if we go back to the two example questions given, I would still vote with the majority of the respondents. In the first case, I would avoid the gamble and take the certain gain; and in the second case, I would gamble to avoid the certain loss. The situations presented are contrived so that the expected values of the choices most people prefer are worse for them than the expected values of the choices most people avoid. I suspect that if the payoffs in some of the questions had been tinkered with slightly, such as changing the gambles to a "70% chance of a $4000 gain" or a "70% chance of a $4000 loss," the responses to the questions would not change although this new wording would mean respondents would then favor the better bet. The real point of Prospect Theory is that the expected value of the bet is not the determining factor in the choice. Under certain circumstances most people willingly choose the prospect that is worse mathematically—the "bad bet"—a violation of Expected Utility Theory. In the mathematical sense of comparing expected values, people behave in a manner counter to their self-interest. But I will argue that under certain circumstances "bad bets" are desirable, rational, and even necessary. What you need to know is when circumstances call for a bad bet and when bad bets should be avoided.

The problem with the questions presented is that the other two conditions for successful gambling mentioned in Chapter 7, are not present. Gambling successfully requires more than just placing bets with positive expectations—"good bets." You must also have a sufficiently large bankroll so that normally occurring losses do not wipe you out. In other words, do not gamble with money that you cannot afford to lose. With the exception of a minority of people who are pathological gamblers, most people wisely avoid bets that could lead to financial ruin, no matter how favorable the odds. For example, consider a rephrasing of the first question, but with dollar amounts that to most people would be astronomical.

Prospect 1: An 80% chance to gain $4,000,000 and a 20% chance to gain nothing.
Prospect 2: A certain gain of $3,000,000.

Anyone of modest means would be a fool not to take the second choice. Gambling with a certain $3,000,000 for an 80% chance at $4,000,000 makes no sense unless your net worth is so high that losing the $3,000,000 would not matter too much. Now let us rephrase the second set of choices.

Prospect 1: An 80% chance to lose $4,000,000 and a 20% chance to lose nothing.
Prospect 2: A certain loss of $3,000,000.

In this circumstance, if you do not have $3,000,000 to lose, you probably do not have $4,000,000 to lose so you might as well take the gamble and hope for the best. Even though Prospect 1 is has the lower expected value, there is nothing irrational about preferring Prospect 1 over Prospect 2.

The third condition for successful gambling is that you must place bets repeatedly so that the overall results do approach the averages. That means that another problem with these questions is that they are presented as one-time events. Consider the effect of repetition on the same questions.

Prospect 1: 1000 opportunities for an 80% chance to gain $4,000 and a 20% chance to gain nothing.
Prospect 2: 1000 opportunities for a certain gain of $3,000.

With the introduction of repetition, anyone can safely take the gamble (Prospect 1) because it would be nearly impossible to gamble under these conditions and walk away with significantly less than the certain 1000 x $3000 or $3,000,000 gained in Prospect 2. The gamble with the higher expectation would be preferred because with so many repetitions, it is a safe choice. And if the second question on losses is re-worded to allow for 1000 repetitions, it is now better to take the certain loss. Gambling in an attempt to avoid a loss will clearly not succeed.

The investment advice associated with this third condition for gambling is to diversify. Owning many different kinds of investments is equivalent to taking many risks that hopefully all have a positive expectation, but if any particular risk fails it represents just one of many trials. On average, the successes should more than compensate for the failures.

The problem is that many people have resources and opportunities that are too limited to meet the mathematical conditions for successful gambling. Many people must take the certain gain rather than the higher-expectation gamble because of simple self-preservation. Choosing the safe steady job over the potentially lucrative but high-risk business venture is not irrational even if the expected value for the business opportunity is greater. A person might be risking more than he or she can afford to lose on that one chance for success. But, the combined effect of many individuals making safe, low-expected value choices means that the group of individuals as a whole is not achieving the best possible use of their resources. A paradox is at work. I call this the risk paradox.

The Risk Paradox

Individual behavior that is rational in response to risk
becomes irrational for the entire group.

Groups have different criteria and priorities for judging risk than individuals. The group as a whole would be better off if each individual chose the option with the highest expected value. But individuals need to consider how all three conditions for successful gambling apply to them when taking a risk; and as a result, it is often reasonable to choose the option with the lower expected value. The risk paradox will be encountered again in Chapter 12 when risks associated with medical advice are discussed.

Insurance

The "risk paradox" is of particular importance when it comes to decisions on insurance because individuals who purchase insurance are usually choosing the risk with the lower expected value. The purchase of insurance is usually a "bad bet" because the expected value is negative by design. It must be negative or insurance companies would not be in business. No insurance company could sell policies with positive expected values because that would mean that more money is paid in claims than collected in premiums—a recipe for bankruptcy. Insurance is by definition a gamble where the odds favor the insurance company, not the policyholder. But under certain circumstances, you should purchase insurance, despite the negative expected value, because many times you are forced to gamble with more than you can afford to lose. Any time you purchase a home, drive a car, have financial dependents, you are gambling with more than you can afford to lose. For example, the odds are in my favor that over the next year my house will not be destroyed by a fire or storm, but I still buy insurance because a large fraction of my net worth is the house I own. I cannot afford to lose my house even if the probability of loss is small.

The decision to purchase insurance should rest on the question: Can you afford the loss? If the answer is no, you need insurance, even if the probability of loss is extremely small. But if the answer is yes, you do not need insurance, even if the probability of loss is high. With this criterion it is easy to separate insurance into those types that you need and those types that you do not.

Insurance that you need

Home: For many homeowners, the home represents more than 50% of their net worth, and for some homeowners it might be all of their net worth. If the home is destroyed or significantly damaged, the homeowner could lose far more than his or her equity. If the home is mortgaged, the lender still expects payment and that means it will be impossible to buy a new home.

Auto: A single error or lapse in judgment by a driver can result in an accident costing tens or even hundreds of thousands of dollars in damages. Anyone who drives is exposing him or herself to almost unlimited financial risk. That is why many states require drivers to have insurance.

Life: It is only necessary to have life insurance if you have financial dependents. You need life insurance to protect your spouse and children from the potential loss of decades of your earnings in the event of your unexpected death. But if no one depends on you financially, there is no reason to have life insurance. If your "financial dependents" are just creditors, let them worry about making claims against your estate.

Health: Healthcare in the United States has evolved into one of the most bizarre economic universes ever constructed. Health insurers have coalesced into groups large and powerful enough to actually control the price of the services that they insure. Think about how counter to normal market forces this system is. Insurers of homes and automobiles do not control the price for these products: the market does. Your auto insurer does not negotiate the price of cars; it simply insures cars at their market price. But health insurers negotiate prices and have the ability to get services at a small fraction of the price charged to the uninsured. You need healthcare insurance not only to protect from catastrophic losses, but to be able to afford normal healthcare. People without health insurance lack the protection of the group and can be charged highly inflated amounts for the simplest of items and procedures.

Disability: For most people, almost all of their income comes from their job. Unless you have multiple sources of income and can absorb the loss of income from your job, you need disability insurance.

Insurance that you do not need

Loan payoff insurance: It is common for lenders to try to add more to a monthly payment in order to pay for insurance on the loan balance in case the borrower dies before the loan is paid. This kind of insurance is always over-priced. If you have dependents, just make sure you have enough life insurance to cover your outstanding debts. If you do not have dependents, you have nothing to worry about. Lenders like this insurance because they do not have to make claims against your estate. The first time I purchased a car, the salesman gave me a hard sell on loan payoff insurance. Being single and childless at the time, I told him that if I died, the finance company was welcome to repossess the car.

Extended warranties: It has become impossible to purchase any object without getting a high-pressure sales pitch for an "extended warranty," or "service contract." Once in an electronics store, I put a television in my shopping cart and on the trip to the cash register was approached by three different salespeople offering to sell me a service contract. Not one had offered to help me earlier when I had to decide which television to purchase. I have since found out that in some appliance and electronic stores the sales people *must* sell a certain number of these contracts as a condition for continuing employment. That is not surprising because money spent on these contracts is pure profit for the store. Almost all electronic devices and appliances become obsolete before they break down.

The sale pitches for extended warranties and service contracts are carefully scripted to feed on the natural aversion to loss documented by the behavioral finance studies cited. I find it amusing to be sold on how great a product is, only to be told all the things that can go wrong once I make a decision to buy. If you make it a rule to always decline offers for extended warranties, you will save more than enough money in the long run to pay for the few repairs that are actually needed.

Accidental death insurance: It is more economical to purchase a single life insurance policy than to purchase separate policies for different causes of death. Accidental death insurance is particularly deceptive because while accidental deaths generate the most press coverage, the vast majority of deaths in the United States are caused by illnesses (see Table 12.3g in Chapter 12 on estimating). I find offers for accidental death insurance that state, "no health screening required" or "no age limit" particularly amusing. From the insurance company's point of view, the ideal policyholder would be an elderly person in poor health who never goes out. It is unlikely a person in those circumstances will die in an accident.

Features to avoid in insurance that you need

Many people pay extra for high-priced insurance features they do not need. Insurance companies push many of these features by appealing to loss-aversion. But it would be better financially to avoid insuring against small losses and use the saved money to pay out of pocket for life's normal mishaps. Again the question that should be asked is: "Can you afford the loss?" If the answer is "yes," do not buy the insurance. Some examples follow:

Low deductibles: When you purchase automobile or homeowners insurance, you should have the highest deductible that you can reasonably afford. Policies with low deductibles are significantly more expensive because it is costly to process small claims. Insurance companies are also quick to drop policyholders who make many small claims. The irony about low deductibles is that many people pay extra for this feature and then are reluctant to use it. If your car has $350 worth of damage and the deductible is $250, do you (a) make a claim for $100 and risk having your rates raised or (b) pay the entire cost and not involve the insurance company. If you chose option (b), then your deductible is too low. See how much you can save by having it raised.

Numerous small policies: Many clubs, organizations, and financial institutions sell small insurance policies—often types of life insurance—to the members. Most of these policies have small benefits, are overpriced, and contain numerous exclusions. It is unlikely that many of the policyholders ever collect benefits. Rather than waste time keeping track of all these policies, the cost of each, and the various exclusions, it is more economical to buy a single policy with the features and benefits that you actually need.

Mental Accounting

> *"A friend of mine was once shopping for a quilted bedspread. She went to a department store and was pleased to find a model she liked on sale. The spreads came in three sizes: double, queen and king. The usual prices for these quilts were $200, $250 and $300 respectively, but during the sale, they were all priced at only $150. My friend bought the king-size quilt and was quite pleased with her purchase, though the quilt did hang a bit over the sides of her double bed."*

—Richard H. Thaler
"Mental Accounting Matters"
Journal of Behavioral Decision Making
vol. 12 (1999) pp. 183-206

The lesson from Prospect Theory is that from a cognitive point of view, not all dollars are created equal. Financial decisions depend on the dollar amounts involved and on how the choice is presented—or "framed," the term used by psychologists. The psychological effects of framing affect many kinds of financial decisions, not just those that involve risk.

Consider another study by Kahneman and Tversky.* People were asked whether they would be willing to drive 20 minutes to another branch of a store to get the sale price for an item. In one scenario, the item was a $15 calculator on sale for $10 at the other location, and the majority of respondents said they

*A. Tversky and D. Kahneman, "The Framing of Decisions and the Psychology of Choice," *Science* vol. 211 (1981) pp. 453-458

would make the trip. But when the item was a $125 jacket on sale for $120, most respondents answered that they would not make the trip. Of course a mathematically equivalent frame for each of these questions would be: "Are you willing to drive 20 minutes to save $5 on a purchase?" Presumably, if all dollars are viewed as equal in value, the answer to that question should be independent of the item being purchased.

Richard Thaler extended the idea of decisions being dependent on framing further with his theory of "mental accounting." He proposed that just as companies perform accounting by putting money into different categories, people have their own "mental" categories for tracking income and expenses. Each mental account has its own set of rules. Framing affects choice because it determines the mental account for the expense or income. Prospect Theory is one example of this cognitive effect because gains and losses apparently go into different mental accounts. The fact that people are strongly averse to losses means that buying decisions can be influenced if expenses are somehow framed as a gain.

Framing matters, and marketers know this. The popularity of "sales pricing" means that buyers feel as if they are gaining something even though they are the ones parting with the money. In the story of the quilt, even though all the quilts are equally priced, the woman buys the one she doesn't need because it is "marked down" the most. Likewise any time a sale price can be "framed" as a greater gain, buyers are more likely to respond. The "buy one and get one free" offer will entice more buyers

Dilbert: © Scott Adams/Dist. by United Feature Syndicate, Inc.

than "buy two and get 50% off." Mathematically these two offers are equivalent, but the first presentation makes it appear that the buyer gets something for nothing. Another technique that relies on mathematical equivalence is to frame the actual numbers. A salesperson pushing $1000 per year memberships to a gym would frame it as $2.74 per day or about the cost of a large coffee with whipped cream at Starbucks. But a person selling a $1500 exercise machine would compare the cost of the machine to the $1000 per year gym memberships and say that the machine will "pay for itself" in less than two years.

Mental accounting is not always bad. In fact, mental accounting can be useful if it operates in a way to achieve goals. Many people have change jars to save for vacations and special outings. Rationally, it would be easier to write out a single check to pay for a vacation. But having the cash on hand to write a large check is difficult. Emptying loose change and one-dollar bills each day into a jar can be a painless approach to accumulating enough money for a vacation or other special purchase. In fact, saving small amounts of loose change can be an effective way to accumulate wealth. In Example 6.6 I framed the accumulation of $76,000 over 25 years in terms of living on $2.28 per day less of after-tax income. David Bach in his book *Automatic Millionaire* frames his program for wealth accumulation in terms of "The Latte Factor."* He shows that by giving up a latte each day, or a pack of cigarettes, or some other equivalent but small purchase, anyone can accumulate significant wealth by simply investing the money saved. He frames wealth accumulation in terms of foregoing small daily purchases. Bach's program is essentially a mental accounting procedure, but one designed to achieve a worthwhile goal.

---

*David Bach, "The Latte Factor: Becoming an Automatic Millionaire on Just a Few Dollars a Day," *Automatic Millionaire* (New York, NY: Broadway Books, 2004)

Summary

"I see no useful purpose in worrying about whether or not mental accounting is 'rational.' Mental accounting procedures have evolved to economize on time and thinking costs and also to deal with self-control problems. As is to be expected, the procedures do not work perfectly. People pay attention to sunk costs. They buy things they don't need because the deal is too good to pass up. They quit early on a good day. They put their retirement money in a money market account."

—Richard H. Thaler
"Mental Accounting Matters"
Journal of Behavioral Decision Making vol. 12 (1999) pp. 183-206

Mental accounting might not be "rational" in the mathematical sense of the word, but I believe it is necessary for money management. It is not possible from a mental health standpoint to determine the optimum use of money for every single financial decision. People must separate money into categories and develop efficient procedures that do not require considering the entire financial picture for every decision. After listing the problems mental accounting causes, Thaler goes on to say that rather than working to eliminate mental accounting, people should learn to modify their mental accounting to achieve certain goals. I agree with Thaler on this point. I believe that a person's mental accounting rules should be evaluated for effectiveness and modified when he or she finds that goals are not being achieved.

To do this requires being aware of your own mental accounting and periodically examining the big picture. My recommendations are as follows:

•For buying decisions, practice being in the marketer's role and mentally reframe the choices. See if your mind changes if the $2.75 coffee you buy each day is reframed as $1000 per year or one-fortieth of a $40,000 per year salary. Would you change your mind if the one-time expense of $1500 on new windows saved $30 per month on utilities for the next 10 years—$3600 total?

•For budgeting, ask if the big picture makes sense? Are you failing to save and invest for retirement while at the same time frittering away money on small purchases? If so, start making some of those "small purchases" contributions to a retirement account. As we saw in Chapter 6, small amounts can accumulate over time to become large savings. Are you regularly saving in a retirement account while at the same time accumulating a large amount of credit card debt? If so, check to see if your net worth is increasing. Saving for the future while your net worth plummets in the present is not an accomplishment. If that is the case, you need to focus on controlling debt. Get a software package like *Quicken* and track *all* of your assets and liabilities. Looking at the big picture will tell if your mental accounting is working for or against you.

•For risk-taking, ask what are you afraid of? If the answer is financial ruin, the risk is too big to take. But if the answer is a small loss, or being wrong, or not getting all of your original investment back, you should consider taking the risk if the expectation of success is reasonable. And if you are putting your long-term retirement savings in a money-market account to avoid the risk of stocks, ask yourself what would happen if stocks did go down for the next couple of decades. Do really believe that having a relatively small amount of cash would completely shield you from the consequences of a prolonged economic downturn? Cash is not risk-free holding. It is only worth what it can buy.

You also need to examine your motivations when taking a risk. If the motivation is to "get even," it is time to accept the loss and move on. Do not become fixated on trying to justify a decision made in the past when conditions differed. If the conditions that justified the original decision are no longer present, then there is no reason to stay committed to the investment. It is easy to go broke trying to get even.

When is a vice a virtue?

The morality of a financial decision can also be affected by framing. Consider the issue of gambling.

In many states and jurisdictions, gambling is regarded as a vice. Concerns that the authorities have include the following: pathological gamblers can self destruct financially if gambling is easily available, the work ethic is undermined if too many people aspire to the lure of money obtained without work, and it is difficult to tax and regulate an activity that only involves money passing back and forth between individuals without any accompanying goods and services. Many people support laws against gambling because money lost gambling comes from the mental account for lost money, something most people are naturally averse to.

In some states and jurisdictions, gambling is major part of the economy and heavily advertised and promoted. That requires re-framing the decision to gamble. Instead of a "vice," gambling becomes a form of "entertainment." People routinely spend hundreds of dollars for a night out that includes dinner and a movie, or a show, or a ballgame, so why not advertise casino gambling as a night out having fun. Then gambling losses are not deducted from the mental account for lost money, but instead the mental account for entertainment.

But some states and jurisdictions want to have it both ways when it comes to gambling. These jurisdictions want to profit from gambling while at the same time labeling it a vice that needs to be outlawed. Pulling this trick off requires a completely different framing of the decision to gamble. The frame now is that gambling is a vice unless the lost money goes to a good cause and then it becomes a virtue. For example, in the state of Maryland, state-run lotteries, keno games and proposed slot machines are for "education." No politician in Maryland has ever proposed a lottery to raise funds for his or her salary, legislature salaries, or state bureaucrats' salaries. Lottery commercials never mention controversial or unpopular state programs as a use for the money.

Just try to imagine a lottery promoted as a way to help pay the expenses of the state income tax auditors. By appealing to one of the government's loftier goals—education—people who lose money gambling deduct the loss from their mental account for charitable contributions and feel virtuous. Never mind that the intention of all gamblers is to win money, not to lose.

Of course, all money that goes to the state is spent by the state. Once money is deposited in the general fund, it does not matter where it came from. And it is also possible to use a libertarian frame for gambling—that what people do with their money is their own business.

Chapter 8 Resources

Richard Thaler, *The Winner's Curse* (Princeton, NJ: Princeton University Press, 1994) provides in depth study of behavior finance by one its founders.

For discussions on the role of chance in the market place see:

Nassim Nicholas Taleb, *Fooled By Randomness: The Hidden Role of Chance in the Markets and in Life* (New York, NY: Texere, 2001)

John Allen Paulos, *A Mathematician Plays the Stock Market* (New York, NY: Basic Books, 2003)

Part III

Loans

CHAPTER NINE

Borrowing

A Numerical Black Box

"We miscalculated."

—Tony
A car salesman
Explaining to me three days after the sale why my loan payments would
be greater than the amount specified in our agreement.

I received my first consumer loan three months after I graduated from college. I needed to commute to my first job, so I purchased a used Chevrolet Chevette from a local car dealership. The year was 1981, and because of double-digit inflation, interest rates had climbed to historically high levels. Mortgages ran about 13%, and consumer loans started at 18%. After agreeing on the price of the car, we negotiated the loan. The car dealership offered a 21% interest rate, but I refused to consider anything higher than 18%. I knew my bank would finance the car for 18% so I held firm and the salesman backed down. I signed a contract for a three-year loan at 18% that specified the exact monthly payments, received the keys and drove away.

Three days later the dealership called back. In their words, a "miscalculation" had occurred on the monthly payments. They would have to send me a new contract to sign, but not to worry. The new monthly payments would only be a "few dollars" higher per month. I asked how much, and they told me. It was not a large amount, but it raised my curiosity.

I decided to calculate the loan payments myself. I soon discovered the "miscalculation." In order to reproduce the new monthly payment, I needed to use a 21% annual interest rate. Sure enough, when the new contract arrived in the mail, buried in the fine print was a 21% rate, not the 18% we agreed on.

I called back and told them that I would not sign the new contract. When caught in the act, con artists often accuse their intended victim of dishonesty. The dealer's response followed that script. They accused me of stealing the car and threatened legal action if I did not pay them immediately. I went to my bank, borrowed the money at 18%, and took them a check. Their greed cost them the chance to make any money on the financing.*

A Black Box

"An informed borrower is simply less vulnerable to fraud and abuse."

—Alan Greenspan
Former Federal Reserve Chairman

Physicists use the expression "a black box," when referring to a device or process that they do not understand. A black box can be a piece of equipment, a computer program, a manufacturing process, or anything else that when given inputs produces an output. For a physicist all black boxes are objects of suspicion because the process that transforms inputs to output is not known. Physicists are trained not to depend on any unknown processes.

---

* I have since learned that car dealers use this tactic of changing the financing terms after the sale so often that it has a special name—"yo-yo financing." Often buyers are hit up for extra cash towards the down payment on top of higher interest rates. For many buyers going to the bank as I did and getting the cash is not so simple. Dealerships will threaten repossession if the cash isn't produced and if the buyer wants to negate the deal that is not possible because his or her trade-in vehicle has already been sold. More on this practice will be covered at the end of this chapter.

For most consumers, loan calculations are black boxes. In go the purchase price, interest rate and duration; out comes a monthly payment. Exactly how the monthly payment depends on the input factors is not known. The loan calculation is a "numerical black box," and the consumer often has no choice other than to trust the sales person. Doing the calculation as I did is often not an option because many consumers would not know how. But consumers would be wise to develop the physicist's skepticism of black boxes. Sales people, loan officers, banks, and finance companies have their own agendas and legal protections are not as strong as many believe.**

In this Chapter I will open up the "numerical black box" of consumer financing. I will explain how loans work and how the inputs lead to the outputs. This chapter is filled with tables that relate to loan payments and financing costs. The tables apply to any kind of purchase made on credit (mortgages, car loans, credit cards, payday loans). I will use many examples to show how to make common financial decisions by using the tables. Keep these tables and examples on hand when deciding on credit purchases. Just as in Chapters 5 and 6 on income and investments, to aid in using the tables in Chapters 9 and 10 on loans, worksheets are provided in Appendix I and at http://www. TheTwoHeadedQuarter.com.

Few people pay cash for everything and never take on debt. In fact, most of us begin our adult lives by taking on debt. We borrow to go to school or undergo job training; we need a car to commute to work, clothes appropriate for our job. We go into debt because these purchases must be made before we can earn money. Properly understood and managed, school and consumer loans can be among the best investments you will make. How else could you transform your teenage earning power—minimum wages for nearby service jobs—into professional level wages and salaries? However, failing to understand the loans you sign can set you in debt for years longer than necessary. The financial rewards of your work go to your creditors instead of you.

** See the essay "Yo-yo Financing" at the end of this chapter for an example of a legal case.

Monthly Payments on a Loan

Fixed monthly loan payments depend on three factors: the amount borrowed (principal), the periodic interest rate, and the loan's duration (term). Monthly payments per $1000 borrowed are shown in Table 9.1. The column on the left lists annual interest rates in percents, and the top row of the table lists various loan durations. You can use Table 9.1 to determine the fixed monthly payments required to completely pay off a loan no matter whether you are shopping for a house, a car, or any other purchase on credit.

Example 9.1

Determining monthly car payments

You decide to purchase a $15,000 car. What is the cost per month if the finance rate is 9% annually and you pay it back over five years?

The amount at the intersection of the 9% row and 5-year column is $20.76. To determine the monthly payment, divide the financed amount by $1000. In this example, $15,000 divided by $1000 is 15. Your monthly payment would be 15 x $20.76, or $311.40.

[Worksheet A2.a, Table 9.1: Rate = 9%, Duration = 5 years, Principal = $15,000; Result is Monthly Payment = $311.40]

Example 9.2

Determining how much to spend on a car

You decide that the most you can afford on monthly car payments is $350 per month. Current finance rates are 4% for a 5-year loan. How much can you afford to spend on a car?

At the intersection of the 4% row and 5-year column is $18.42. Divide this number into your planned monthly payment of $350 and the result is 19. You can borrow up to 19 x $1000, or $19,000 to purchase a car.

[Worksheet A2.d, Table 9.1: Rate = 4%, Duration = 5 years, Monthly Payment = $350; Result is Principal = $19,000]

Example 9.3

Shopping for an interest rate

You decide to switch your high-interest $5000 credit card balance to a low-interest home equity loan. Your goal is to pay $100 each month and have the balance paid in 5 years. What interest rate do you need for a home equity loan to achieve that goal?

Divide $5000 by 1000 and the result is 5. That means each month you will pay $100 divided by 5, or $20 per month for every $1000 you owe. Look in the 5-year column of Table 9.1 and find the number closest to $20. That number, $20.04, is in the row corresponding to a 7.5% interest rate. You need a 5-year home equity loan at a 7.5% annual rate of interest to achieve your goal.

[Worksheet A2.b, Table 9.1: Principal = $5000, Duration = 5 years, Monthly Payment = $100; Result is Rate = 7.5%]

Table 9.1: Monthly loan payments per $1000 borrowed. Rate is an annual percentage; interest is compounded monthly.

Monthly loan payments

Rate(%)	Loan Duration (years)					
	2	3	4	5	6	8
0.0	$41.67	$27.78	$20.83	$16.67	$13.89	$10.42
0.5	$41.88	$27.99	$21.05	$16.88	$14.10	$10.63
1.0	$42.10	$28.21	$21.26	$17.09	$14.32	$10.84
1.5	$42.32	$28.42	$21.48	$17.31	$14.53	$11.06
2.0	$42.54	$28.64	$21.70	$17.53	$14.75	$11.28
2.5	$42.76	$28.86	$21.91	$17.75	$14.97	$11.50
3.0	$42.98	$29.08	$22.13	$17.97	$15.19	$11.73
3.5	$43.20	$29.30	$22.36	$18.19	$15.42	$11.96
4.0	$43.42	$29.52	$22.58	$18.42	$15.65	$12.19
4.5	$43.65	$29.75	$22.80	$18.64	$15.87	$12.42
5.0	$43.87	$29.97	$23.03	$18.87	$16.10	$12.66
5.5	$44.10	$30.20	$23.26	$19.10	$16.34	$12.90
6.0	$44.32	$30.42	$23.49	$19.33	$16.57	$13.14
6.5	$44.55	$30.65	$23.71	$19.57	$16.81	$13.39
7.0	$44.77	$30.88	$23.95	$19.80	$17.05	$13.63
7.5	$45.00	$31.11	$24.18	$20.04	$17.29	$13.88
8.0	$45.23	$31.34	$24.41	$20.28	$17.53	$14.14
8.5	$45.46	$31.57	$24.65	$20.52	$17.78	$14.39
9.0	$45.68	$31.80	$24.89	$20.76	$18.03	$14.65
9.5	$45.91	$32.03	$25.12	$21.00	$18.27	$14.91
10.0	$46.14	$32.27	$25.36	$21.25	$18.53	$15.17
11.0	$46.61	$32.74	$25.85	$21.74	$19.03	$15.71
12.0	$47.07	$33.21	$26.33	$22.24	$19.55	$16.25
13.0	$47.54	$33.69	$26.83	$22.75	$20.07	$16.81
14.0	$48.01	$34.18	$27.33	$23.27	$20.61	$17.37
15.0	$48.49	$34.67	$27.83	$23.79	$21.15	$17.95
16.0	$48.96	$35.16	$28.34	$24.32	$21.69	$18.53
17.0	$49.44	$35.65	$28.86	$24.85	$22.25	$19.12
18.0	$49.92	$36.15	$29.37	$25.39	$22.81	$19.72
19.0	$50.41	$36.66	$29.90	$25.94	$23.38	$20.33
20.0	$50.90	$37.16	$30.43	$26.49	$23.95	$20.95
21.0	$51.39	$37.68	$30.97	$27.05	$24.54	$21.58
22.0	$51.88	$38.19	$31.51	$27.62	$25.13	$22.22
23.0	$52.37	$38.71	$32.05	$28.19	$25.72	$22.86
24.0	$52.87	$39.23	$32.60	$28.77	$26.33	$23.51
25.0	$53.37	$39.76	$33.16	$29.35	$26.94	$24.17
26.0	$53.87	$40.29	$33.72	$29.94	$27.55	$24.84
27.0	$54.38	$40.83	$34.28	$30.54	$28.18	$25.51
28.0	$54.89	$41.36	$34.85	$31.14	$28.81	$26.19

Observation: As the interest rate increases, lengthening the duration of a loan has a diminishing effect on reducing monthly payments.

Monthly loan payments

Rate(%)	Loan Duration (years)					
	10	12	15	20	25	30
0.0	$8.33	$6.94	$5.56	$4.17	$3.33	$2.78
0.5	$8.55	$7.16	$5.77	$4.38	$3.55	$2.99
1.0	$8.76	$7.37	$5.98	$4.60	$3.77	$3.22
1.5	$8.98	$7.59	$6.21	$4.83	$4.00	$3.45
2.0	$9.20	$7.82	$6.44	$5.06	$4.24	$3.70
2.5	$9.43	$8.05	$6.67	$5.30	$4.49	$3.95
3.0	$9.66	$8.28	$6.91	$5.55	$4.74	$4.22
3.5	$9.89	$8.51	$7.15	$5.80	$5.01	$4.49
4.0	$10.12	$8.76	$7.40	$6.06	$5.28	$4.77
4.5	$10.36	$9.00	$7.65	$6.33	$5.56	$5.07
5.0	$10.61	$9.25	$7.91	$6.60	$5.85	$5.37
5.5	$10.85	$9.50	$8.17	$6.88	$6.14	$5.68
6.0	$11.10	$9.76	$8.44	$7.16	$6.44	$6.00
6.5	$11.35	$10.02	$8.71	$7.46	$6.75	$6.32
7.0	$11.61	$10.28	$8.99	$7.75	$7.07	$6.65
7.5	$11.87	$10.55	$9.27	$8.06	$7.39	$6.99
8.0	$12.13	$10.82	$9.56	$8.36	$7.72	$7.34
8.5	$12.40	$11.10	$9.85	$8.68	$8.05	$7.69
9.0	$12.67	$11.38	$10.14	$9.00	$8.39	$8.05
9.5	$12.94	$11.66	$10.44	$9.32	$8.74	$8.41
10.0	$13.22	$11.95	$10.75	$9.65	$9.09	$8.78
11.0	$13.78	$12.54	$11.37	$10.32	$9.80	$9.52
12.0	$14.35	$13.13	$12.00	$11.01	$10.53	$10.29
13.0	$14.93	$13.75	$12.65	$11.72	$11.28	$11.06
14.0	$15.53	$14.37	$13.32	$12.44	$12.04	$11.85
15.0	$16.13	$15.01	$14.00	$13.17	$12.81	$12.64
16.0	$16.75	$15.66	$14.69	$13.91	$13.59	$13.45
17.0	$17.38	$16.32	$15.39	$14.67	$14.38	$14.26
18.0	$18.02	$16.99	$16.10	$15.43	$15.17	$15.07
19.0	$18.67	$17.67	$16.83	$16.21	$15.98	$15.89
20.0	$19.33	$18.37	$17.56	$16.99	$16.78	$16.71
21.0	$19.99	$19.07	$18.31	$17.78	$17.60	$17.53
22.0	$20.67	$19.78	$19.06	$18.57	$18.41	$18.36
23.0	$21.35	$20.50	$19.82	$19.37	$19.23	$19.19
24.0	$22.05	$21.23	$20.58	$20.17	$20.05	$20.02
25.0	$22.75	$21.96	$21.36	$20.98	$20.88	$20.85
26.0	$23.46	$22.70	$22.13	$21.79	$21.70	$21.68
27.0	$24.17	$23.45	$22.92	$22.61	$22.53	$22.51
28.0	$24.90	$24.21	$23.71	$23.43	$23.36	$23.34

Example 9.4

Paying off a credit card with a fixed monthly payment

If you make the minimum monthly payment of $66 on your $3000 credit card bill, how long will it take to pay off the balance?

The number of $1000 amounts owed is $3000 divided by $1000, or 3. A payment of $66 per month on $3000 is the equivalent of $66 divided 3, or $22 per month on each $1000. Look at the interest rate on your credit card. If the rate is 18%, find the column in the 18% row that is closest to $22. In this example that is the six-year column. If you make a $66 payment every month for the next six years, you would pay off the balance.

[Worksheet A2.c, Table 9.1: Principal = 3000, Rate = 18%, Monthly Payment = $66; Result is Duration = 6 years]

Example 9.5

Minimum credit card payments

If you always make the minimum payment on a credit card bill that is initially $3000, how long will it take to pay off the balance?

The short answer to this question is "not in your lifetime." Why is this question so different from the previous question? *Table 9.1 does not apply because minimum credit card payments are not fixed.* The duration of the loans in the Table 9.1, assumes that the same fixed amount is paid every month. Credit card issuers reduce the minimum monthly payment as the balance is reduced. Usually there is a floor of $10 that the minimum payment cannot fall below no matter how low the total balance drops. That floor means that the loan will eventually be paid off, but it takes a long time.

For example, a credit card agreement from one of my banks stated that "the minimum payment will be approximately 2.2% of the new balance or $10.00, whichever is greater." Following this formula for minimum payments and assuming a fixed 18% interest rate (their actual rate varies monthly with the market), a calculation shows that it would take 346 months (two months short of 29 years) to completely pay off a $3000 initial balance. During that time a total of $8,773 will have been paid (nearly three times the initial balance).

Loans to which Table 9.1 does not apply

As the last example showed, not all loans conform to the conditions assumed when calculating the payments in Table 9.1. For Table 9.1 to apply the loan agreement must meet the following conditions:

- The interest rate stays fixed over the life of the loan.
- The interest rate is a monthly rate, determined by dividing the annual rate by 12.
- Interest on the remaining principal accumulates every month.
- The loan payments are the same every month.

Here are some examples of loans that do not meet these conditions:

Variable payment loans: Credit cards, like the one just mentioned, do not require that a fixed monthly payment be made. As a credit card balance is reduced, so is the required monthly payment.

Variable rate loans: Most credit cards and some mortgages are not fixed rate. Credit card companies usually reserve the right to change the interest rate at any time. Some mortgages, called adjustable rate mortgages or ARMs, have a variable interest rate that is usually adjusted on a yearly basis according to strict rules laid out in the original loan agreement. Whenever the interest rate changes during the life of a loan, the monthly payments must be adjusted if the term is to remain the same.

Loans with daily interest rates: Most credit cards, some mortgages, and some car loans charge a daily interest rate, determined by dividing the annual rate by 365. Interest on the remaining principal accumulates on a daily basis. If this is the case, the monthly payments determined using Table 9.1 are close but not exact. More interest accumulates because of the daily compounding; and because the number of days in each month is not the same, monthly interest charges vary. The exact date a payment is posted will also determine interest charges.

Loans with retroactive interest: Many "free" financing offers— "90 days same as cash," "no interest or payments for six months," and even credit cards that charge no interest if paid within 30 days—have retroactive interest computations built into the agreement. That means if interest is ever charged to the loan it accrues from the date of purchase. For example, if you do not pay the *entire* balance on your new dining room table within 90 days from the date of purchase then 90 days of interest are *retroactively* charged to your account. If you are one day late with your credit card payment then you owe interest for the entire month plus a late fee.

Periodic Finance Rates

When evaluating loans, be aware that lenders use different periodic interest rates to compute finance charges. Table 9.1 and the next two tables (9.2 and 9.3) assume a monthly periodic interest rate and a monthly finance charge. At the end of each month, the interest accrued during the month becomes money owed that the lender charges interest on for the next month. A payment at the end of the month reduces the total amount owed to the lender—the loan balance when the month began plus the amount of interest accrued during that month. If payment toward the loan is not at least equal to the interest accrued during the previous month, the balance on the loan will grow rather than shrink. No matter how long you take to pay the loan off, if the loan is eventually to be paid, monthly payments cannot be reduced below the monthly finance charges.

Loans with a daily period interest rate have interest added each day to the loan balance and the next day interest is charged on the interest posted the day before. As dramatic as charging daily interest sounds, the cost difference for someone making regular monthly payments on a loan with daily finance charges is small compared to making regular monthly payments on loan with monthly finance charges. For example, with a monthly periodic rate, $1000 borrowed at a 5% annual rate becomes a debt of $1004.16 after one month. If the interest is compounded daily, the same $1000 with the same 5% annual rate becomes a debt of $1004.25 after 31 days. Because daily compounding does not add significantly more interest, the monthly payments listed in Table 9.1, are close to those needed to pay off a loan with daily finance charges.

Lenders use the following terminology when specifying finance charges:

Annual Percentage Rate: usually abbreviated APR. The "APR" is usually the advertised interest rate, but it is not the rate actually charged. Lenders almost never assess interest charges on an annual basis.

Monthly periodic rate: defined as the APR divided by 12. For loans with monthly interest charges, lenders use the monthly periodic rate to compute interest. For example a loan with a 9.9% APR has a monthly periodic rate of 0.825%. At the end of each month, the interest charge for that month is determined by multiplying the loan balance by 0.0825. That interest is then added to the loan balance. The calculations for Tables 9.1, 9.2 and 9.3 were based on a monthly periodic rate.

Daily periodic rate: defined as the APR divided by 365. For loans with daily interest charges, the daily periodic rate is used to compute interest. For example, a loan with a 9.9% APR has a daily periodic rate of 0.02712329%. At the end of each day, the interest charge for the day is determined by multiplying the loan balance by 0.0002712329. That interest is then added to the loan balance and becomes money owed for the next day when the interest is again computed.

Although the differences in the various periodic finance rates are small, they are real. Consider a credit card that advertises a 9.9% APR, but in the fine print uses a daily period rate. Compounded daily, every $1000 that is not paid back to the lender during the course of a year, becomes $1104. From the lender's point of view, that is an annual rate of return on their investment of 10.4%. However, advertising a "9.9% APR" is more eye catching than a brochure that has a 10.4% annual finance charge. In fact the "APR" qualifier appears next to all advertised interest rates to cover up the deception that the annual rate that interest accrues is greater than the annual percentage rate specified in the loan agreement.

Total Cost of a Loan

Consider the first example for use of Table 9.1 where the monthly payments for a $15,000 car financed at 9% annual interest for five years are determined to be $311.40. The total amount of money paid out over five years is the number of months (12 x 5 or 60 months) times the monthly payment of $311.40, which is 60 x $311.40 or $18,684. When it is financed according to these terms, the $15,000 car actually costs $18,684.

When financing a purchase you should think about the total cost of the purchase rather than the monthly payments. Total loan costs are summarized in Table 9.2, which uses the same layout as Table 9.1 with interest rates listed in the rows and loan durations for the columns. The amounts tabulated are the total dollars paid back to the lender for each $1000 initially borrowed. Note that the cost of borrowed money increases as *both* the interest rate and the duration increase.

Here are some examples of the use of Table 9.2:

Example 9.6

Difference between 15-year and 30-year mortgages

You need to decide between a 15-year and a 30-year mortgage. If you purchase a house for $140,000, how does the total cost of a 15-year mortgage at a 7% rate, compare to a 30-year mortgage at the same 7% rate?

Look across the 7% row to find that over 15 years $1618 is paid back for every $1000 borrowed; over 30 years the amount is $2395 for every $1000 borrowed. The number of $1000 borrowed is $140,000 divided by $1000 or 140. For the 15-year mortgage, multiply 140 by $1618 to determine that the total cost is $226,520. The 30-year mortgage costs 140 x $2395 or $335,300. The difference is $108,780 in extra finance charges for the 30-year loan, compared to the 15-year loan. For a 30-year mortgage, more money is paid in finance charges over the life of the loan than for the house itself.

[Worksheet A3.a, Table 9.2: Rate = 7%, Duration = 15 years, Cash Price = $140,000; Result is Total Cost = $226,520]
[Worksheet A3.a, Table 9.2: Rate = 7%, Duration = 30 years, Cash Price = $140,000; Result is Total Cost = $335,300]

Table 9.2: Total cost per $1000 borrowed. Rate is an annual percentage; interest is compounded monthly.

Total cost of a loan

Rate (%)	Loan Duration (years)					
	2	3	4	5	6	8
0.0	$1,000	$1,000	$1,000	$1,000	$1,000	$1,000
0.5	$1,005	$1,008	$1,010	$1,013	$1,015	$1,020
1.0	$1,010	$1,015	$1,021	$1,026	$1,031	$1,041
1.5	$1,016	$1,023	$1,031	$1,039	$1,046	$1,062
2.0	$1,021	$1,031	$1,041	$1,052	$1,062	$1,083
2.5	$1,026	$1,039	$1,052	$1,065	$1,078	$1,104
3.0	$1,032	$1,047	$1,062	$1,078	$1,094	$1,126
3.5	$1,037	$1,055	$1,073	$1,092	$1,110	$1,148
4.0	$1,042	$1,063	$1,084	$1,105	$1,126	$1,170
4.5	$1,048	$1,071	$1,095	$1,119	$1,143	$1,193
5.0	$1,053	$1,079	$1,105	$1,132	$1,160	$1,215
5.5	$1,058	$1,087	$1,116	$1,146	$1,176	$1,238
6.0	$1,064	$1,095	$1,127	$1,160	$1,193	$1,262
6.5	$1,069	$1,103	$1,138	$1,174	$1,210	$1,285
7.0	$1,075	$1,112	$1,149	$1,188	$1,228	$1,309
7.5	$1,080	$1,120	$1,161	$1,202	$1,245	$1,333
8.0	$1,085	$1,128	$1,172	$1,217	$1,262	$1,357
8.5	$1,091	$1,136	$1,183	$1,231	$1,280	$1,382
9.0	$1,096	$1,145	$1,194	$1,246	$1,298	$1,406
9.5	$1,102	$1,153	$1,206	$1,260	$1,316	$1,431
10.0	$1,107	$1,162	$1,217	$1,275	$1,334	$1,457
11.0	$1,119	$1,179	$1,241	$1,305	$1,370	$1,508
12.0	$1,130	$1,196	$1,264	$1,335	$1,408	$1,560
13.0	$1,141	$1,213	$1,288	$1,365	$1,445	$1,613
14.0	$1,152	$1,230	$1,312	$1,396	$1,484	$1,668
15.0	$1,164	$1,248	$1,336	$1,427	$1,522	$1,723
16.0	$1,175	$1,266	$1,360	$1,459	$1,562	$1,779
17.0	$1,187	$1,283	$1,385	$1,491	$1,602	$1,836
18.0	$1,198	$1,301	$1,410	$1,524	$1,642	$1,893
19.0	$1,210	$1,320	$1,435	$1,556	$1,683	$1,952
20.0	$1,221	$1,338	$1,461	$1,590	$1,725	$2,012
21.0	$1,233	$1,356	$1,486	$1,623	$1,767	$2,072
22.0	$1,245	$1,375	$1,512	$1,657	$1,809	$2,133
23.0	$1,257	$1,394	$1,538	$1,691	$1,852	$2,195
24.0	$1,269	$1,412	$1,565	$1,726	$1,896	$2,257
25.0	$1,281	$1,431	$1,592	$1,761	$1,939	$2,321
26.0	$1,293	$1,450	$1,618	$1,796	$1,984	$2,385
27.0	$1,305	$1,470	$1,646	$1,832	$2,029	$2,449
28.0	$1,317	$1,489	$1,673	$1,868	$2,074	$2,515

Observation: For high interest rate, long duration loans, more is paid in finance charges than in principal.

Total cost of a loan

Rate (%)	Loan Duration (years)					
	10	12	15	20	25	30
0.0	$1,000	$1,000	$1,000	$1,000	$1,000	$1,000
0.5	$1,025	$1,031	$1,038	$1,051	$1,064	$1,077
1.0	$1,051	$1,062	$1,077	$1,104	$1,131	$1,158
1.5	$1,077	$1,093	$1,117	$1,158	$1,200	$1,242
2.0	$1,104	$1,126	$1,158	$1,214	$1,272	$1,331
2.5	$1,131	$1,159	$1,200	$1,272	$1,346	$1,422
3.0	$1,159	$1,192	$1,243	$1,331	$1,423	$1,518
3.5	$1,187	$1,226	$1,287	$1,392	$1,502	$1,617
4.0	$1,215	$1,261	$1,331	$1,454	$1,584	$1,719
4.5	$1,244	$1,296	$1,377	$1,518	$1,667	$1,824
5.0	$1,273	$1,332	$1,423	$1,584	$1,754	$1,933
5.5	$1,302	$1,368	$1,471	$1,651	$1,842	$2,044
6.0	$1,332	$1,405	$1,519	$1,719	$1,933	$2,158
6.5	$1,363	$1,443	$1,568	$1,789	$2,026	$2,275
7.0	$1,393	$1,481	$1,618	$1,861	$2,120	$2,395
7.5	$1,424	$1,520	$1,669	$1,933	$2,217	$2,517
8.0	$1,456	$1,559	$1,720	$2,007	$2,315	$2,642
8.5	$1,488	$1,598	$1,773	$2,083	$2,416	$2,768
9.0	$1,520	$1,639	$1,826	$2,159	$2,518	$2,897
9.5	$1,553	$1,680	$1,880	$2,237	$2,621	$3,027
10.0	$1,586	$1,721	$1,934	$2,316	$2,726	$3,159
11.0	$1,653	$1,805	$2,046	$2,477	$2,940	$3,428
12.0	$1,722	$1,891	$2,160	$2,643	$3,160	$3,703
13.0	$1,792	$1,979	$2,277	$2,812	$3,384	$3,982
14.0	$1,863	$2,069	$2,397	$2,984	$3,611	$4,266
15.0	$1,936	$2,161	$2,519	$3,160	$3,842	$4,552
16.0	$2,010	$2,255	$2,644	$3,339	$4,077	$4,841
17.0	$2,086	$2,350	$2,770	$3,520	$4,313	$5,132
18.0	$2,162	$2,447	$2,899	$3,704	$4,552	$5,426
19.0	$2,240	$2,545	$3,029	$3,890	$4,793	$5,720
20.0	$2,319	$2,645	$3,161	$4,077	$5,035	$6,016
21.0	$2,399	$2,746	$3,295	$4,266	$5,279	$6,312
22.0	$2,480	$2,848	$3,430	$4,457	$5,524	$6,610
23.0	$2,563	$2,952	$3,567	$4,649	$5,769	$6,907
24.0	$2,646	$3,057	$3,705	$4,842	$6,016	$7,206
25.0	$2,730	$3,162	$3,844	$5,036	$6,263	$7,504
26.0	$2,815	$3,269	$3,984	$5,231	$6,510	$7,803
27.0	$2,901	$3,377	$4,125	$5,426	$6,759	$8,103
28.0	$2,988	$3,486	$4,267	$5,622	$7,007	$8,402

Example 9.7

Cash price of an automobile

An advertisement for an automobile sale states that monthly payments are $395. The fine print indicates that the financing terms are for five years at with an 8% annual rate of interest. Nowhere in the advertisement is a cash price given for the model so that you can compare it to other dealers' prices. What cash price is the dealer basing the monthly payments on?

The total cost for this automobile is $395 x 5 years x 12 months, or $23,700. At the intersection of the 5-year column, 8% row in Table 9.2 is $1217. That means you pay $1217 back for every $1000 financed or $1.217 for each $1. The cash price for the car is $23,700 divided by $1.217, or $19,474.

[Worksheet A3.d, Table 9.2: Rate = 8%, Duration = 5 years, Total Cost = $23,700; Result is Cash Price = $19,474]

Example 9.8

Automobile negotiations

You are negotiating the purchase of an automobile. The salesman is offering $16,000, and you insist $15,000 is your best offer. The manager is brought out, and he is willing to agree to your price, provided you accept a slightly higher interest rate of 5.5%, instead of the going 5%, on a four-year loan. What should you do?

The salesman's offer that requires borrowing $16,000 for four years at 5% will cost 16 x $1105 or $17,680. The total cost of your offer of $15,000 and a 5% rate is 15 x $1105 or $16,575. The manager's offer, that requires borrowing $15,000 at the higher 5.5% rate will cost 15 x $1116 or $16,740. You might as well take the manager's offer. It is only $165 more than yours, and it is $940 less than the salesman's offer.

[Worksheet A3.a, Table 9.2: Rate = 5%, Duration = 4 years, Cash Price = $16,000; Result is Total Cost = $17,680]
[Worksheet A3.a, Table 9.2: Rate = 5%, Duration = 4 years, Cash Price = $15,000; Result is Total Cost = $16,575]
[Worksheet A3.a, Table 9.2: Rate = 5.5%, Duration = 4 years, Cash Price = $15,000; Result is Total Cost = $16,740]

Example 9.9

Comparing sale prices to special financing offers

The "Mega Blowout Sale" at the local furniture store is offering 20% off. That means the $3000 living room set you want will only cost $2400. You have no cash so the furniture store agrees to finance your purchase for three years at a 15% annual rate. Across the street, a competing furniture store is having its "Once in a Lifetime Sale." They offer an equivalent living room set for $2995 and 0% financing for three years. Which is the better deal?

For the three-year 15% loan, you will pay $1248 for every $1000 borrowed. The number of $1000's borrowed is $2400 divided by $1000, or 2.4. The total cost of the furniture will be 2.4 x $1248 or $2995. Across the street you will pay the same amount $2995 in the same equal monthly payments over three years. The cost to you of either offer is the same.

Which deal should you take? All things being equal you should choose the sale price and the 15% loan. Usually loans can be paid off early, and that saves money on future finance charges. Do check the fine print on the loan to make sure there is no early payoff penalty. (Avoid loans that have penalties for early payoffs.) If during the next three years, you can afford to pay off the entire loan, your total cost will be less than $2995. However, if you choose the full price and 0% loan, you are committed to paying $2995. Early payoff of a loan will not change the principal. More on the topic of 0% financing will be discussed in Chapter 10 when we examine car loans.

[**Worksheet A3.a, Table 9.2: Rate = 15%, Duration = 3 years, Cash Price = $2400; Result is Total Cost = $2995**]

Equity Accrual

Equity is the difference between the cash value of an asset and the amount of debt needed to finance that asset. For example, if you owe $110,000 on a mortgage and the market price of your house is $125,000, your equity is $125,000 minus $110,000 or $15,000. Expressed as a percent your equity in the house is $15,000 divided by $125,000 times 100, or 12%. Your equity in an asset can also be negative. You might own a car that still has $6000 remaining to be paid on a loan, but the cash value of the car is $4000. In this case your equity is –$2000.

If you finance the purchase of an asset without making a down payment, you begin with zero equity. As time passes your equity will change as the loan is paid down and the cash value of the asset changes. If the asset either appreciates or stays the same (usually the case with houses) you will accrue positive equity as the principal on the loan is paid down. If the asset depreciates (usually the case with cars) you risk accruing negative equity if the depreciation is faster than the decrease of the principal on the loan.

The rate that the principal on a loan decreases depends on the interest rate and the term of the loan. When a loan payment is made, the interest is paid first and the amount paid above the interest charges goes towards the principal. Because interest is paid first, unless you have a loan with a 0% interest rate, the time to pay off 50% of the principal will always be longer than half the loan's duration. Tables 9.3 and 9.4, show how principal decreases over time. Table 9.3 shows the time it will take, in years, to pay 20% of the principal. Table 9.4 shows the time, in years, to pay 50% of the principal. Notice that for long-term loans, especially at high interest rates, a significant decrease in the principal takes a long time.

The most important pattern to observe in the Tables 9.3 and 9.4 *is that the higher the interest rate, the longer it takes to pay down the principal.* This result is counterintuitive because as Table 9.1 shows, higher interest rates require higher monthly payments. But, while monthly payments rise with increasing interest rates, the fraction of the payment that goes towards the principal in the early stages of a loan, actually decreases. A feature of the mathematical formula that determines monthly loan payments is that as the interest rate rises, more of the principal payment is shifted towards the end of the loan term. This mathematical property of the loan payment formula explains why it is so difficult to get rid of debt. People with significant debts are judged to be greater credit risks and as a result charged higher interest rates. As the interest rate increases, more of the monthly payment goes to interest and less to principal reduction. The debt accumulation process reinforces itself. Financial math leads directly to what I call the "debt trap."

The Debt Trap

High debts are used to justify high interest rates.
As interest rates rise, significant debt reduction shifts
further into the future.

To avoid the "debt trap" use Tables 9.3 and 9.4 for planning purchases. Here are some examples for using Table 9.3:

Example 9.10

Automobile settlements

At what point for a six-year car loan with 8% annual interest, do you have 20% of the loan paid?

The intersection of the six-year column with the 8% row in Table 9.3 gives 1.45 years. In other words, it takes 18 months to reduce the loan balance by 20%. Your brand new car probably lost 20% of its value the moment you drove it off the lot. If that car is totaled during the first year of ownership, it will be difficult to receive enough from the insurance company to pay off the loan.

[Worksheet A4.a, Table 9.3: Rate = 8%, Duration = 6 years; Result is Time = 1.45 years]

Example 9.11

Use of home equity loans to purchase automobiles

At what point have you paid 20% of a car loan financed with a 15-year home equity loan at 8% annual interest?

Table 9.3 shows the intersection of the 15-year column and 8% row, to be 4.76 years. This example shows one danger of using long-term home equity loans to pay for cars. Even though there are tax advantages, the car will have no resale value long before the loan balance is significantly reduced. If you buy a new car with a home equity loan, make sure you pay it off on a five-year schedule. Use Table 9.1 to determine the payments on a five-year loan with equivalent interest and principal and apply that amount each month to your home equity loan.

[Worksheet A4.a, Table 9.3: Rate = 8%, Duration = 15 years; Result is Time = 4.76 years]

Example 9.12

Dropping private mortgage insurance

At what point, in a 30-year 7.5% mortgage, do you have a 20% stake in the house and can drop private mortgage insurance (PMI)?

It takes 13.2 years, nearly half the life of the loan, to pay 20% of the principal on this mortgage. Often a house will appreciate more than 20% in less than 13 years. If the value of your house has increased enough to give you 20% equity, get an appraisal and ask the lender to drop the PMI.

[Worksheet A4.a, Table 9.3: Rate = 7.5%, Duration = 30 years; Result is Time = 13.2 years]

Private mortgage insurance (PMI) is usually required when the homebuyer lacks the cash to make a down payment equal to 20% of the purchase price. If the buyer has less than 20% equity in the home, the lender will not be able to recover all of his or her money if the home goes into foreclosure. The lender would have to pay for the cost of legal fees, real estate commissions, and additional settlement charges. Buyers must purchase an insurance policy from a private company to insure that the lender recovers all of his or her costs should a foreclosure occur. The PMI becomes part of the monthly payment and for a typical home is usually about $50 to $100 per month extra. Because of this extra expense it is in the homeowner's interest to drop the PMI as soon as possible. You should contact your mortgage holder to drop PMI as soon as 20% equity is achieved in your home, either by appreciation of the property or reduction of the loan balance. Remember you pay to insure the lender's investment, not your own. PMI is not the same as hazard insurance that covers the actual loss of the home and its contents. Hazard insurance protects your investment and should always be paid. PMI will be discussed further in Chapter 10 in the section on real estate loans.

Table 9.3: Time in years to pay 20% of a loan balance. Rate is an annual percentage; interest is compounded monthly.

Time required to pay 20% of the principal

Rate (%)	Loan Duration (years)					
	2	3	4	5	6	8
0.0	0.40	0.60	0.80	1.00	1.20	1.60
0.5	0.40	0.60	0.81	1.01	1.21	1.63
1.0	0.40	0.61	0.81	1.02	1.23	1.65
1.5	0.40	0.61	0.82	1.03	1.24	1.68
2.0	0.41	0.61	0.83	1.04	1.26	1.71
2.5	0.41	0.62	0.83	1.05	1.27	1.73
3.0	0.41	0.62	0.84	1.06	1.29	1.76
3.5	0.41	0.63	0.85	1.07	1.30	1.79
4.0	0.41	0.63	0.85	1.08	1.32	1.82
4.5	0.41	0.63	0.86	1.09	1.34	1.85
5.0	0.42	0.64	0.87	1.10	1.35	1.88
5.5	0.42	0.64	0.87	1.12	1.37	1.91
6.0	0.42	0.64	0.88	1.13	1.38	1.94
6.5	0.42	0.65	0.89	1.14	1.40	1.97
7.0	0.42	0.65	0.89	1.15	1.42	2.00
7.5	0.42	0.66	0.90	1.16	1.43	2.03
8.0	0.43	0.66	0.91	1.17	1.45	2.06
8.5	0.43	0.66	0.92	1.18	1.47	2.09
9.0	0.43	0.67	0.92	1.20	1.49	2.12
9.5	0.43	0.67	0.93	1.21	1.50	2.16
10.0	0.43	0.68	0.94	1.22	1.52	2.19
11.0	0.44	0.68	0.95	1.24	1.56	2.26
12.0	0.44	0.69	0.97	1.27	1.59	2.32
13.0	0.44	0.70	0.98	1.29	1.63	2.39
14.0	0.45	0.71	1.00	1.32	1.67	2.46
15.0	0.45	0.72	1.01	1.34	1.70	2.53
16.0	0.45	0.73	1.03	1.37	1.74	2.61
17.0	0.46	0.73	1.04	1.39	1.78	2.68
18.0	0.46	0.74	1.06	1.42	1.82	2.75
19.0	0.46	0.75	1.08	1.45	1.86	2.83
20.0	0.47	0.76	1.09	1.47	1.90	2.90
21.0	0.47	0.77	1.11	1.50	1.94	2.97
22.0	0.48	0.78	1.13	1.53	1.98	3.05
23.0	0.48	0.79	1.14	1.55	2.02	3.12
24.0	0.48	0.80	1.16	1.58	2.06	3.20
25.0	0.49	0.80	1.18	1.61	2.10	3.27
26.0	0.49	0.81	1.19	1.64	2.14	3.35
27.0	0.49	0.82	1.21	1.67	2.19	3.42
28.0	0.50	0.83	1.23	1.69	2.23	3.49

Observation: For high interest rate, long duration loans, paying 20% of the principal takes more than half the duration of the loan.

Time required to pay 20% of the principal

Rate (%)	Loan Duration (years)					
	10	12	15	20	25	30
0.0	2.00	2.40	3.00	4.00	5.00	6.00
0.5	2.04	2.46	3.09	4.16	5.26	6.37
1.0	2.08	2.52	3.19	4.33	5.52	6.76
1.5	2.12	2.58	3.28	4.51	5.81	7.18
2.0	2.17	2.64	3.38	4.69	6.10	7.61
2.5	2.21	2.70	3.48	4.88	6.40	8.06
3.0	2.25	2.77	3.59	5.07	6.72	8.53
3.5	2.30	2.84	3.69	5.27	7.04	9.02
4.0	2.34	2.90	3.80	5.48	7.38	9.52
4.5	2.39	2.97	3.92	5.69	7.72	10.0
5.0	2.44	3.04	4.03	5.90	8.08	10.6
5.5	2.49	3.11	4.15	6.12	8.43	11.1
6.0	2.54	3.19	4.27	6.35	8.80	11.6
6.5	2.59	3.26	4.39	6.57	9.16	12.2
7.0	2.64	3.34	4.51	6.80	9.53	12.7
7.5	2.69	3.41	4.63	7.04	9.90	13.2
8.0	2.74	3.49	4.76	7.27	10.3	13.7
8.5	2.79	3.57	4.89	7.50	10.6	14.2
9.0	2.84	3.65	5.01	7.74	11.0	14.7
9.5	2.90	3.72	5.14	7.98	11.4	15.2
10.0	2.95	3.81	5.27	8.21	11.7	15.7
11.0	3.06	3.97	5.54	8.68	12.4	16.6
12.0	3.17	4.13	5.80	9.14	13.1	17.4
13.0	3.28	4.30	6.07	9.59	13.7	18.2
14.0	3.40	4.47	6.33	10.0	14.3	18.9
15.0	3.51	4.64	6.59	10.4	14.8	19.5
16.0	3.63	4.81	6.85	10.8	15.3	20.1
17.0	3.75	4.98	7.10	11.2	15.8	20.6
18.0	3.86	5.14	7.35	11.6	16.2	21.1
19.0	3.98	5.31	7.59	11.9	16.7	21.5
20.0	4.10	5.47	7.82	12.3	17.0	21.9
21.0	4.21	5.64	8.05	12.6	17.4	22.3
22.0	4.33	5.79	8.27	12.8	17.7	22.6
23.0	4.44	5.95	8.48	13.1	18.0	22.9
24.0	4.56	6.10	8.68	13.4	18.3	23.2
25.0	4.67	6.25	8.87	13.6	18.5	23.5
26.0	4.78	6.40	9.06	13.8	18.8	23.8
27.0	4.89	6.54	9.24	14.0	19.0	24.0
28.0	4.99	6.67	9.41	14.2	19.2	24.1

Table 9.4: Time in years to pay 50% of a loan balance. Rate is an annual percentage; interest is compounded monthly.

Time required to pay 50% of the principal

Rate (%)	Loan Duration (years)					
	2	3	4	5	6	8
0.0	1.00	1.50	2.00	2.50	3.00	4.00
0.5	1.00	1.51	2.01	2.52	3.02	4.04
1.0	1.00	1.51	2.02	2.53	3.04	4.08
1.5	1.01	1.52	2.03	2.55	3.07	4.12
2.0	1.01	1.52	2.04	2.56	3.09	4.16
2.5	1.01	1.53	2.05	2.58	3.11	4.20
3.0	1.01	1.53	2.06	2.59	3.13	4.24
3.5	1.02	1.54	2.07	2.61	3.16	4.28
4.0	1.02	1.54	2.08	2.62	3.18	4.32
4.5	1.02	1.55	2.09	2.64	3.20	4.36
5.0	1.02	1.56	2.10	2.66	3.22	4.40
5.5	1.03	1.56	2.11	2.67	3.25	4.44
6.0	1.03	1.57	2.12	2.69	3.27	4.47
6.5	1.03	1.57	2.13	2.70	3.29	4.51
7.0	1.03	1.58	2.14	2.72	3.31	4.55
7.5	1.04	1.58	2.15	2.73	3.33	4.59
8.0	1.04	1.59	2.16	2.75	3.36	4.63
8.5	1.04	1.60	2.17	2.76	3.38	4.67
9.0	1.04	1.60	2.18	2.78	3.40	4.70
9.5	1.05	1.61	2.19	2.79	3.42	4.74
10.0	1.05	1.61	2.20	2.81	3.44	4.78
11.0	1.05	1.62	2.22	2.84	3.48	4.85
12.0	1.06	1.63	2.24	2.87	3.53	4.92
13.0	1.06	1.64	2.26	2.90	3.57	4.99
14.0	1.07	1.66	2.27	2.93	3.61	5.06
15.0	1.07	1.67	2.29	2.96	3.65	5.13
16.0	1.08	1.68	2.31	2.98	3.69	5.19
17.0	1.08	1.69	2.33	3.01	3.73	5.26
18.0	1.09	1.70	2.35	3.04	3.77	5.32
19.0	1.09	1.71	2.37	3.07	3.81	5.38
20.0	1.10	1.72	2.39	3.10	3.84	5.44
21.0	1.10	1.73	2.40	3.12	3.88	5.50
22.0	1.11	1.74	2.42	3.15	3.92	5.56
23.0	1.11	1.75	2.44	3.18	3.95	5.62
24.0	1.12	1.76	2.46	3.20	3.99	5.67
25.0	1.12	1.77	2.48	3.23	4.02	5.72
26.0	1.13	1.78	2.49	3.25	4.06	5.77
27.0	1.13	1.79	2.51	3.28	4.09	5.82
28.0	1.14	1.80	2.53	3.30	4.12	5.87

Observation: Unless the finance rate is 0% it always takes more than half the duration of the loan to pay back 50% of the principal.

Time required to pay 50% of the principal

Rate (%)	Loan Duration (years)					
	10	12	15	20	25	30
0.0	5.00	6.00	7.50	10.0	12.5	15.0
0.5	5.06	6.09	7.64	10.2	12.9	15.6
1.0	5.12	6.18	7.78	10.5	13.3	16.1
1.5	5.19	6.27	7.92	10.7	13.7	16.7
2.0	5.25	6.36	8.06	11.0	14.0	17.2
2.5	5.31	6.45	8.20	11.2	14.4	17.7
3.0	5.37	6.54	8.34	11.5	14.8	18.3
3.5	5.43	6.62	8.47	11.7	15.1	18.8
4.0	5.50	6.71	8.61	12.0	15.5	19.3
4.5	5.56	6.80	8.74	12.2	15.8	19.7
5.0	5.62	6.89	8.87	12.4	16.2	20.2
5.5	5.68	6.97	9.00	12.6	16.5	20.6
6.0	5.74	7.05	9.13	12.8	16.8	21.0
6.5	5.80	7.14	9.26	13.0	17.1	21.4
7.0	5.86	7.22	9.38	13.2	17.4	21.7
7.5	5.91	7.30	9.50	13.4	17.6	22.1
8.0	5.97	7.38	9.62	13.6	17.9	22.4
8.5	6.03	7.46	9.74	13.8	18.2	22.7
9.0	6.09	7.54	9.85	14.0	18.4	23.0
9.5	6.14	7.62	9.96	14.2	18.6	23.3
10.0	6.20	7.70	10.1	14.3	18.8	23.5
11.0	6.31	7.84	10.3	14.6	19.2	24.0
12.0	6.41	7.99	10.5	14.9	19.6	24.4
13.0	6.51	8.13	10.7	15.2	19.9	24.8
14.0	6.62	8.26	10.9	15.5	20.2	25.1
15.0	6.71	8.39	11.0	15.7	20.5	25.4
16.0	6.81	8.51	11.2	15.9	20.8	25.7
17.0	6.90	8.63	11.3	16.1	21.0	25.9
18.0	6.99	8.74	11.5	16.3	21.2	26.1
19.0	7.07	8.85	11.6	16.4	21.4	26.3
20.0	7.16	8.95	11.8	16.6	21.5	26.5
21.0	7.23	9.05	11.9	16.7	21.7	26.7
22.0	7.31	9.14	12.0	16.9	21.8	26.8
23.0	7.39	9.23	12.1	17.0	22.0	27.0
24.0	7.46	9.32	12.2	17.1	22.1	27.1
25.0	7.53	9.40	12.3	17.2	22.2	27.2
26.0	7.59	9.48	12.4	17.3	22.3	27.3
27.0	7.65	9.55	12.5	17.4	22.4	27.4
28.0	7.72	9.62	12.5	17.5	22.5	27.5

Here are some examples for using Table 9.4:

Example 9.13

Computer obsolescence

You purchase a $2000 computer system on store credit and agree to pay 15% interest for a three-year loan. When is half of the loan balance paid?

The time period at the intersection of the three-year column on Table 9.4 with the 15% interest rate is 1.67 years, or 20 months. Notice that computers typically become obsolete within one year and are worth much less than 50% of their purchase price at that time.

[Worksheet A4.a, Table 9.4: Rate = 15%, Duration = 3 years; Result is Time = 1.67 years]

Example 9.14

Home equity

You decide that your mortgage principal should be at least half-paid in 20 years. When shopping for a 30-year mortgage, what is the highest interest rate you can pay that will allow you to achieve your goal?

Look down the 30-year column in Table 9.4 to find a time closest to 20 years. That time 20.2 years in the 5% row. If you pay more than 5% annual interest it will take longer than 20 years to reduce the principal by half.

[Worksheet A4.b, Table 9.4: Time = 20 years, Duration = 30 years; Result is Rate = 5%]

Example 9.15

Automobile trade-ins

You decide that your car should be half-paid within three years so that the trade-in value will cover the new car loan. If finance rates are 8.5%, what is the longest duration loan that you can have and achieve your goal?

Look across the 8.5% row in Table 9.4 for the last number that is under 3 years. That time of 2.76 years is in the 5-year column. Your new car loan must not be structured for longer than 5 years.

[Worksheet A4.c, Table 9.4: Time = 3 years, Rate = 8.5%; Result is Duration = 5 years]

Payments on Intermediate-term Loans

Sometimes it is desirable to borrow money for a few months rather than a few years. Table 9.5 is analogous to Table 9.1 because it shows monthly payments per $1000 borrowed that are required to pay off a loan. The difference is that the duration of the loans are one to 12 months. Next are some examples for using Table 9.5.

Table 9.5: Monthly loan payments per $1000 borrowed on loans with less than a one-year duration. Rate is an annual percentage; interest is compounded monthly.

Monthly loan payments

Rate(%)	Loan Duration (months)					
	1	2	3	4	5	6
0.0	$1,000	$500	$333	$250	$200	$167
0.5	$1,000	$500	$334	$250	$200	$167
1.0	$1,001	$501	$334	$251	$201	$167
1.5	$1,001	$501	$334	$251	$201	$167
2.0	$1,002	$501	$334	$251	$201	$168
2.5	$1,002	$502	$335	$251	$201	$168
3.0	$1,003	$502	$335	$252	$202	$168
3.5	$1,003	$502	$335	$252	$202	$168
4.0	$1,003	$503	$336	$252	$202	$169
4.5	$1,004	$503	$336	$252	$202	$169
5.0	$1,004	$503	$336	$253	$203	$169
5.5	$1,005	$503	$336	$253	$203	$169
6.0	$1,005	$504	$337	$253	$203	$170
6.5	$1,005	$504	$337	$253	$203	$170
7.0	$1,006	$504	$337	$254	$204	$170
7.5	$1,006	$505	$338	$254	$204	$170
8.0	$1,007	$505	$338	$254	$204	$171
8.5	$1,007	$505	$338	$254	$204	$171
9.0	$1,007	$506	$338	$255	$205	$171
9.5	$1,008	$506	$339	$255	$205	$171
10.0	$1,008	$506	$339	$255	$205	$172
11.0	$1,009	$507	$339	$256	$206	$172
12.0	$1,010	$508	$340	$256	$206	$173
13.0	$1,011	$508	$341	$257	$207	$173
14.0	$1,012	$509	$341	$257	$207	$174
15.0	$1,013	$509	$342	$258	$208	$174
16.0	$1,013	$510	$342	$258	$208	$175
17.0	$1,014	$511	$343	$259	$209	$175
18.0	$1,015	$511	$343	$259	$209	$176
19.0	$1,016	$512	$344	$260	$210	$176
20.0	$1,017	$513	$345	$261	$210	$177
21.0	$1,018	$513	$345	$261	$211	$177
22.0	$1,018	$514	$346	$262	$211	$178
23.0	$1,019	$514	$346	$262	$212	$178
24.0	$1,020	$515	$347	$263	$212	$179
25.0	$1,021	$516	$347	$263	$213	$179
26.0	$1,022	$516	$348	$264	$213	$180
27.0	$1,023	$517	$348	$264	$214	$180
28.0	$1,023	$518	$349	$265	$214	$181

Observation: The difference in monthly payments between a 9-month loan and a 12-month loan is less than $30 per thousand borrowed.

Monthly loan payments

	Loan Duration (months)					
Rate (%)	7	8	9	10	11	12
0.0	$143	$125	$111	$100	$91	$83
0.5	$143	$125	$111	$100	$91	$84
1.0	$143	$125	$112	$100	$91	$84
1.5	$144	$126	$112	$101	$92	$84
2.0	$144	$126	$112	$101	$92	$84
2.5	$144	$126	$112	$101	$92	$84
3.0	$144	$126	$113	$101	$92	$85
3.5	$145	$127	$113	$102	$93	$85
4.0	$145	$127	$113	$102	$93	$85
4.5	$145	$127	$113	$102	$93	$85
5.0	$145	$127	$113	$102	$93	$86
5.5	$145	$128	$114	$103	$93	$86
6.0	$146	$128	$114	$103	$94	$86
6.5	$146	$128	$114	$103	$94	$86
7.0	$146	$128	$114	$103	$94	$87
7.5	$146	$129	$115	$103	$94	$87
8.0	$147	$129	$115	$104	$95	$87
8.5	$147	$129	$115	$104	$95	$87
9.0	$147	$129	$115	$104	$95	$87
9.5	$147	$129	$116	$104	$95	$88
10.0	$148	$130	$116	$105	$96	$88
11.0	$148	$130	$116	$105	$96	$88
12.0	$149	$131	$117	$106	$96	$89
13.0	$149	$131	$117	$106	$97	$89
14.0	$150	$132	$118	$107	$97	$90
15.0	$150	$132	$118	$107	$98	$90
16.0	$151	$133	$119	$107	$98	$91
17.0	$151	$133	$119	$108	$99	$91
18.0	$152	$134	$120	$108	$99	$92
19.0	$152	$134	$120	$109	$100	$92
20.0	$153	$135	$121	$109	$100	$93
21.0	$153	$135	$121	$110	$101	$93
22.0	$154	$136	$122	$110	$101	$94
23.0	$154	$136	$122	$111	$102	$94
24.0	$155	$137	$123	$111	$102	$95
25.0	$155	$137	$123	$112	$103	$95
26.0	$156	$137	$123	$112	$103	$96
27.0	$156	$138	$124	$113	$104	$96
28.0	$156	$138	$124	$113	$104	$97

Example 9.16

Credit card consolidation

Christmas is over and your three separate department store cards have balances totaling $5500. You decide to transfer them to a new credit card that offers a 7% introductory interest rate for the first year. To completely pay off the balance by the next Christmas, how much should you pay each month?

The intersection of the 7% row with the 12-month column in Table 9.5 has $86.53. The number of $1000 amounts you owe is $5500 divided by $1000, or 5.5. Therefore you must pay 5.5 x $86.53 or $476 per month for the next 12 months to pay off all the balances.

[Worksheet A2.a, Table 9.5: Rate = 7%, Duration = 12 months, Principal = $5500; Result is Monthly Payment = $476]

Example 9.17

Comparing offers for credit card consolidation

Consider the previous example of consolidating $5500 in Christmas debt, but you must choose between two introductory credit card offers. The second offer is for 2% annual rate but only for the first 6 months. What would your monthly payments be to pay off $5500 in six months with 2% annual interest?

According to Table 9.5 you must make payments of $168 for each $1000 borrowed per month for six months. Monthly payments are 5.5 x $168 or $924. This is $28 less than if you doubled the monthly payments in the previous example. The difference is a lower interest rate over a shorter time.

[Worksheet A2.a, Table 9.5: Rate = 2%, Duration = 6 months, Principal = $5500; Result is Monthly Payment = $924]

Total Cost of Intermediate-term Loans

When deciding to borrow money for a few months it is also useful to consider the total cost. Table 9.6 is analogous to Table 9.2 because it shows the total cost per $1000 borrowed but the time periods are for 1-12 months. Here are some examples for using Table 9.6:

Example 9.18

Chasing introductory teaser rates

Your current credit card has a 17% annual rate of interest. An offer arrives in the mail for a new credit card that advertises a 3% introductory rate for the first four months if you transfer your balance. Your current balance is $6500. How much will you save over the next four months if you make this switch?

According to Table 9.6, at 17% annual interest, if you make four equal monthly payments you will pay back $1036 for every $1000 borrowed. For a four-month loan of $6500, you will pay back 6.5 x $1036, or $6734. That amounts to $234 in finances charges. For 3% annual interest for the same four months you pay back $1006 for every $1000 borrowed. You pay back 6.5 x $1006, or $6539. Your total finance charge over four months will be $39. You save $234 minus $39, or $195 in finance charges by making this switch. Just be careful to read the fine print. Chapter 10 will explain that introductory "teaser rates" can often have other charges buried in the fine print that negate any savings. Also be aware that having too many credit cards can lower your overall credit score.

[Worksheet A3.a, Table 9.6: Rate = 17%, Duration = 4 months, Cash Price = $6500; Result is Total Cost = $6734]
[Worksheet A3.a, Table 9.6: Rate = 3%, Duration = 4 months, Cash Price = $6500; Result is Total Cost = $6539]

Table 9.6: Total cost per $1000 borrowed on loans with less than a one-year duration. Rate is an annual percentage; interest is compounded monthly.

Total cost of a loan

Rate (%)	Loan Duration (months)					
	1	2	3	4	5	6
0.0	$1,000	$1,000	$1,000	$1,000	$1,000	$1,000
0.5	$1,000	$1,001	$1,001	$1,001	$1,001	$1,001
1.0	$1,001	$1,001	$1,002	$1,002	$1,003	$1,003
1.5	$1,001	$1,002	$1,003	$1,003	$1,004	$1,004
2.0	$1,002	$1,003	$1,003	$1,004	$1,005	$1,006
2.5	$1,002	$1,003	$1,004	$1,005	$1,006	$1,007
3.0	$1,003	$1,004	$1,005	$1,006	$1,008	$1,009
3.5	$1,003	$1,004	$1,006	$1,007	$1,009	$1,010
4.0	$1,003	$1,005	$1,007	$1,008	$1,010	$1,012
4.5	$1,004	$1,006	$1,008	$1,009	$1,011	$1,013
5.0	$1,004	$1,006	$1,008	$1,010	$1,013	$1,015
5.5	$1,005	$1,007	$1,009	$1,011	$1,014	$1,016
6.0	$1,005	$1,008	$1,010	$1,013	$1,015	$1,018
6.5	$1,005	$1,008	$1,011	$1,014	$1,016	$1,019
7.0	$1,006	$1,009	$1,012	$1,015	$1,018	$1,021
7.5	$1,006	$1,009	$1,013	$1,016	$1,019	$1,022
8.0	$1,007	$1,010	$1,013	$1,017	$1,020	$1,023
8.5	$1,007	$1,011	$1,014	$1,018	$1,021	$1,025
9.0	$1,007	$1,011	$1,015	$1,019	$1,023	$1,026
9.5	$1,008	$1,012	$1,016	$1,020	$1,024	$1,028
10.0	$1,008	$1,013	$1,017	$1,021	$1,025	$1,029
11.0	$1,009	$1,014	$1,018	$1,023	$1,028	$1,032
12.0	$1,010	$1,015	$1,020	$1,025	$1,030	$1,035
13.0	$1,011	$1,016	$1,022	$1,027	$1,033	$1,038
14.0	$1,012	$1,018	$1,023	$1,029	$1,035	$1,041
15.0	$1,013	$1,019	$1,025	$1,031	$1,038	$1,044
16.0	$1,013	$1,020	$1,027	$1,034	$1,040	$1,047
17.0	$1,014	$1,021	$1,028	$1,036	$1,043	$1,050
18.0	$1,015	$1,023	$1,030	$1,038	$1,045	$1,053
19.0	$1,016	$1,024	$1,032	$1,040	$1,048	$1,056
20.0	$1,017	$1,025	$1,034	$1,042	$1,051	$1,059
21.0	$1,018	$1,026	$1,035	$1,044	$1,053	$1,062
22.0	$1,018	$1,028	$1,037	$1,046	$1,056	$1,065
23.0	$1,019	$1,029	$1,039	$1,048	$1,058	$1,068
24.0	$1,020	$1,030	$1,040	$1,050	$1,061	$1,071
25.0	$1,021	$1,031	$1,042	$1,053	$1,063	$1,074
26.0	$1,022	$1,033	$1,044	$1,055	$1,066	$1,077
27.0	$1,023	$1,034	$1,045	$1,057	$1,069	$1,080
28.0	$1,023	$1,035	$1,047	$1,059	$1,071	$1,083

Observation: Paying back a loan in less than one year keeps the cost of finances charges low.

Total cost of a loan

Rate (%)	Loan Duration (months)					
	7	8	9	10	11	12
0.0	$1,000	$1,000	$1,000	$1,000	$1,000	$1,000
0.5	$1,002	$1,002	$1,002	$1,002	$1,003	$1,003
1.0	$1,003	$1,004	$1,004	$1,005	$1,005	$1,005
1.5	$1,005	$1,006	$1,006	$1,007	$1,008	$1,008
2.0	$1,007	$1,008	$1,008	$1,009	$1,010	$1,011
2.5	$1,008	$1,009	$1,010	$1,011	$1,013	$1,014
3.0	$1,010	$1,011	$1,013	$1,014	$1,015	$1,016
3.5	$1,012	$1,013	$1,015	$1,016	$1,018	$1,019
4.0	$1,013	$1,015	$1,017	$1,018	$1,020	$1,022
4.5	$1,015	$1,017	$1,019	$1,021	$1,023	$1,025
5.0	$1,017	$1,019	$1,021	$1,023	$1,025	$1,027
5.5	$1,018	$1,021	$1,023	$1,025	$1,028	$1,030
6.0	$1,020	$1,023	$1,025	$1,028	$1,030	$1,033
6.5	$1,022	$1,025	$1,027	$1,030	$1,033	$1,036
7.0	$1,023	$1,026	$1,029	$1,032	$1,035	$1,038
7.5	$1,025	$1,028	$1,032	$1,035	$1,038	$1,041
8.0	$1,027	$1,030	$1,034	$1,037	$1,040	$1,044
8.5	$1,029	$1,032	$1,036	$1,039	$1,043	$1,047
9.0	$1,030	$1,034	$1,038	$1,042	$1,046	$1,049
9.5	$1,032	$1,036	$1,040	$1,044	$1,048	$1,052
10.0	$1,034	$1,038	$1,042	$1,046	$1,051	$1,055
11.0	$1,037	$1,042	$1,046	$1,051	$1,056	$1,061
12.0	$1,040	$1,046	$1,051	$1,056	$1,061	$1,066
13.0	$1,044	$1,049	$1,055	$1,061	$1,066	$1,072
14.0	$1,047	$1,053	$1,059	$1,065	$1,071	$1,077
15.0	$1,051	$1,057	$1,064	$1,070	$1,077	$1,083
16.0	$1,054	$1,061	$1,068	$1,075	$1,082	$1,089
17.0	$1,057	$1,065	$1,072	$1,080	$1,087	$1,094
18.0	$1,061	$1,069	$1,076	$1,084	$1,092	$1,100
19.0	$1,064	$1,073	$1,081	$1,089	$1,097	$1,106
20.0	$1,068	$1,076	$1,085	$1,094	$1,103	$1,112
21.0	$1,071	$1,080	$1,090	$1,099	$1,108	$1,117
22.0	$1,075	$1,084	$1,094	$1,104	$1,113	$1,123
23.0	$1,078	$1,088	$1,098	$1,108	$1,119	$1,129
24.0	$1,082	$1,092	$1,103	$1,113	$1,124	$1,135
25.0	$1,085	$1,096	$1,107	$1,118	$1,129	$1,141
26.0	$1,089	$1,100	$1,111	$1,123	$1,135	$1,146
27.0	$1,092	$1,104	$1,116	$1,128	$1,140	$1,152
28.0	$1,095	$1,108	$1,120	$1,133	$1,145	$1,158

Example 9.19

Early Christmas shopping

It is early July and the $80 toy you want to buy your child for Christmas is on sale for $60, a savings of 25%. Your budget is structured so that money to purchase the toy will not be available until December. If you make the purchase now and finance it for five months with your credit card at 19% annual interest, will you still save money?

According to Table 9.6, it costs $1048 to finance $1000 for five months at 19% annual interest. The number of $1000 amounts needed is $60 divided by $1000, or 0.06. Therefore your total cost is $1048 x 0.06 or $62.88 for your early Christmas purchase. You will save $80 minus $62.88 or $17.12 by making the purchase at the sale price in July.

[Worksheet A3.a, Table 9.6: Rate = 19%, Duration = 5 months, Cash Price = $60; Result is Total Cost = $62.88]

Total Cost of Short-term Loans

Lastly, consider loans of a few weeks duration. For these cases a structured payoff schedule is not considered. The money is borrowed and paid off in its entirety with one payment that includes the interest. Table 9.7 shows the total amount needed to pay off a $1000 loan at various annual interest rates for time periods of one to six weeks. For Table 9.7, interest is compounded daily and added to the total that will be paid once at the end of term. No partial payments are assumed for this table. The entire balance—interest plus principal—is paid all at once and only once.

An inspection of the overlap between Tables 9.7 and 9.6 shows slight discrepancies in the finance charges that accrue. For example, Table 9.6 shows that a one-month loan at 20% annual interest costs $17 per $1000 borrowed, while Table 9.7 shows a four-week (28-day) loan at 20% interest costs $15 per $1000 borrowed. The extra charge for the one-month loan occurs because on average a month is longer than four weeks (30.41 days). But a three-month loan at 20% interest costs $34 per $1000 borrowed, while a 12-week loan at 20% (84 days) costs $47 per $1000 borrowed. In this case the effect of making monthly payments on the three-month loan reduces that total finance charge, whereas no intermediate payments are assumed in the weekly loan table.

Most short-term loans charge exceptionally high annual interest rates. To avoid stating how high the interest actually is the word "interest" is not used. Finance charges are re-labeled as "service charges." Whatever language is used; the bottom line is still the same. You, the borrower, are paying for the use of somebody else's money. Some common scenarios for using Table 9.7 are as follows:

Example 9.20

Advances on tax refunds

Your tax preparer informs you that your refund is $1400 and the IRS will take about four weeks to process your return and issue a check. The tax preparer offers to advance the refund to you for a "fee" of $40. If you take this offer, what effective annual interest rate do you pay the tax preparer?

In this situation you are borrowing $1400 for four weeks and paying back $1440. The total cost per $1 borrowed is $1440 divided by 1400, or $1.02857. Multiply by 1000 to get $1028.57 paid back for each $1000 borrowed. Look down the four-week column in Table 9.7 and find the number closest to $1028.57. That number, $1027, falls in the row corresponding to a 35% annual interest rate. If you need the money that soon, it would be better to take a cash advance on a credit card that charges 19% annual interest than to take the tax preparer's offer.

[Worksheet A3.b, Table 9.7: Total Cost = $1440, Cash Price = $1400, Duration = 4 weeks; Result is Rate = 35%]

Table 9.7: Total one-time payment per $1000 borrowed. Rate is an annual percentage; interest is compounded daily.

Total cost of a loan

Rate (%)	Loan Duration (weeks)					
	1	2	3	4	5	6
0	$1,000	$1,000	$1,000	$1,000	$1,000	$1,000
1	$1,000	$1,000	$1,001	$1,001	$1,001	$1,001
2	$1,000	$1,001	$1,001	$1,002	$1,002	$1,002
3	$1,001	$1,001	$1,002	$1,002	$1,003	$1,003
4	$1,001	$1,002	$1,002	$1,003	$1,004	$1,005
5	$1,001	$1,002	$1,003	$1,004	$1,005	$1,006
6	$1,001	$1,002	$1,003	$1,005	$1,006	$1,007
7	$1,001	$1,003	$1,004	$1,005	$1,007	$1,008
8	$1,002	$1,003	$1,005	$1,006	$1,008	$1,009
9	$1,002	$1,003	$1,005	$1,007	$1,009	$1,010
10	$1,002	$1,004	$1,006	$1,008	$1,010	$1,012
11	$1,002	$1,004	$1,006	$1,008	$1,011	$1,013
12	$1,002	$1,005	$1,007	$1,009	$1,012	$1,014
13	$1,002	$1,005	$1,008	$1,010	$1,013	$1,015
14	$1,003	$1,005	$1,008	$1,011	$1,014	$1,016
15	$1,003	$1,006	$1,009	$1,012	$1,014	$1,017
16	$1,003	$1,006	$1,009	$1,012	$1,015	$1,019
17	$1,003	$1,007	$1,010	$1,013	$1,016	$1,020
18	$1,003	$1,007	$1,010	$1,014	$1,017	$1,021
19	$1,004	$1,007	$1,011	$1,015	$1,018	$1,022
20	$1,004	$1,008	$1,012	$1,015	$1,019	$1,023
22	$1,004	$1,008	$1,013	$1,017	$1,021	$1,026
24	$1,005	$1,009	$1,014	$1,019	$1,023	$1,028
26	$1,005	$1,010	$1,015	$1,020	$1,025	$1,030
28	$1,005	$1,011	$1,016	$1,022	$1,027	$1,033
30	$1,006	$1,012	$1,017	$1,023	$1,029	$1,035
35	$1,007	$1,014	$1,020	$1,027	$1,034	$1,041
40	$1,008	$1,015	$1,023	$1,031	$1,039	$1,047
45	$1,009	$1,017	$1,026	$1,035	$1,044	$1,053
50	$1,010	$1,019	$1,029	$1,039	$1,049	$1,059
55	$1,011	$1,021	$1,032	$1,043	$1,054	$1,065
60	$1,012	$1,023	$1,035	$1,047	$1,059	$1,071
65	$1,013	$1,025	$1,038	$1,051	$1,064	$1,078
70	$1,014	$1,027	$1,041	$1,055	$1,069	$1,084
75	$1,014	$1,029	$1,044	$1,059	$1,074	$1,090
80	$1,015	$1,031	$1,047	$1,063	$1,080	$1,096
85	$1,016	$1,033	$1,050	$1,067	$1,085	$1,103
90	$1,017	$1,035	$1,053	$1,071	$1,090	$1,109
95	$1,018	$1,037	$1,056	$1,075	$1,095	$1,115

Observation: Typical finance charges for many short-term loans correspond to extraordinarily high annual interest rates.

Total cost of a loan

Rate (%)	Loan Duration (weeks)					
	7	8	9	10	11	12
0	$1,000	$1,000	$1,000	$1,000	$1,000	$1,000
1	$1,001	$1,002	$1,002	$1,002	$1,002	$1,002
2	$1,003	$1,003	$1,003	$1,004	$1,004	$1,005
3	$1,004	$1,005	$1,005	$1,006	$1,006	$1,007
4	$1,005	$1,006	$1,007	$1,008	$1,008	$1,009
5	$1,007	$1,008	$1,009	$1,010	$1,011	$1,012
6	$1,008	$1,009	$1,010	$1,012	$1,013	$1,014
7	$1,009	$1,011	$1,012	$1,014	$1,015	$1,016
8	$1,011	$1,012	$1,014	$1,015	$1,017	$1,019
9	$1,012	$1,014	$1,016	$1,017	$1,019	$1,021
10	$1,014	$1,015	$1,017	$1,019	$1,021	$1,023
11	$1,015	$1,017	$1,019	$1,021	$1,023	$1,026
12	$1,016	$1,019	$1,021	$1,023	$1,026	$1,028
13	$1,018	$1,020	$1,023	$1,025	$1,028	$1,030
14	$1,019	$1,022	$1,024	$1,027	$1,030	$1,033
15	$1,020	$1,023	$1,026	$1,029	$1,032	$1,035
16	$1,022	$1,025	$1,028	$1,031	$1,034	$1,037
17	$1,023	$1,026	$1,030	$1,033	$1,037	$1,040
18	$1,024	$1,028	$1,032	$1,035	$1,039	$1,042
19	$1,026	$1,030	$1,033	$1,037	$1,041	$1,045
20	$1,027	$1,031	$1,035	$1,039	$1,043	$1,047
22	$1,030	$1,034	$1,039	$1,043	$1,047	$1,052
24	$1,033	$1,037	$1,042	$1,047	$1,052	$1,057
26	$1,036	$1,041	$1,046	$1,051	$1,056	$1,062
28	$1,038	$1,044	$1,049	$1,055	$1,061	$1,067
30	$1,041	$1,047	$1,053	$1,059	$1,065	$1,071
35	$1,048	$1,055	$1,062	$1,069	$1,077	$1,084
40	$1,055	$1,063	$1,071	$1,080	$1,088	$1,096
45	$1,062	$1,071	$1,081	$1,090	$1,100	$1,109
50	$1,069	$1,080	$1,090	$1,101	$1,111	$1,122
55	$1,077	$1,088	$1,100	$1,111	$1,123	$1,135
60	$1,084	$1,096	$1,109	$1,122	$1,135	$1,148
65	$1,091	$1,105	$1,119	$1,133	$1,147	$1,161
70	$1,098	$1,113	$1,128	$1,144	$1,159	$1,175
75	$1,106	$1,122	$1,138	$1,155	$1,171	$1,188
80	$1,113	$1,130	$1,148	$1,166	$1,184	$1,202
85	$1,121	$1,139	$1,158	$1,177	$1,196	$1,216
90	$1,128	$1,148	$1,168	$1,188	$1,209	$1,230
95	$1,136	$1,157	$1,178	$1,200	$1,222	$1,244

Example 9.21

Advances on paychecks

One week before your bi-weekly payday, the car that you need to get to work requires a major repair. You bring a pay stub to a service that provides advances on paychecks. For $20 the service advances your entire $1100 paycheck. What effective annual interest rate do you pay for this one-week loan?

For this loan you borrow $1100 and pay back $1120 one week later. The total cost per $1 borrowed is $1120 divided by $1100, or $1.18. Multiply this by 1000 to get $1018 paid back for each $1000 borrowed. In the one-week column of Table 9.7 the total cost of $1018 per $1000 borrowed is in the row corresponding to a 95% annual interest rate.

[Worksheet A3.b, Table 9.7: Total Cost = $1120, Cash Price = $1100, Duration = 1 week; Result is Rate = 95%]

Obviously short-term loans with the above conditions should be avoided. In order to avoid stating an annual interest rate the companies that provide these kinds of loans will not use the word "interest." The tactic of re-labeling finance charges with a term other than "interest" is actually widespread throughout the consumer-lending industry. You don't have to go to shady check-cashing services to find interest charges re-labeled as service fees. In the next chapter on evaluating loans, the practice of re-labeling will be examined in more detail.

Summary

As a borrower, you will find that financing assets that appreciate over time (homes, education, businesses) with long-term, high-interest rate loans is expensive but not risky. At all times in the future, the asset will usually be worth more than the loan balance. A house financed with a 30-year mortgage has little risk, even though the loan balanced is reduced over time at a slow rate, because the home usually appreciates in value. A student will take on a large long-term debt burden to fund the intangible non-transferable asset of an education. But the increased earning opportunities over an entire lifetime that result more than pay for the cost of the loan.

Borrowing to acquire assets that depreciate over time (cars, computers, furniture, clothes) with long-term, high-interest rate loans is risky. Almost immediately, the value of the asset is worth less than the balance on the loan and continues to be worth less for the life of the loan. If the asset needs to be replaced before the loan is paid, debt is piled on top of debt. Depreciating assets should be financed with short-term loans.

Lenders know that financing assets that depreciate entails more risk. To compensate for the additional risk, lenders charge higher interest rates. Interest rates for consumer credit (credit cards, store financing) are higher than for mortgages because of the additional risk. The borrower is taking on more risk when using consumer credit and is also paying extra to compensate the lender for that additional risk.

Yo-yo Financing

In 2004 a financing dispute between an automobile buyer and a dealership ended up before the United States Supreme Court. While the court case was highly unusual the events leading up to it were not. The fraudulent lending practices that touched off the legal dispute are so common, that it was in the financial interest of the car dealership with backing from the consumer lending industry to appeal the case all the way to the U. S. Supreme Court.

The case began when Bradley Nigh purchased a Chevrolet Blazer at a Fairfax, Virginia car dealership and used his old truck as a trade-in. He made a down payment, signed a contract, and drove away. Three weeks later the dealer called back to tell him that the financing would not go through unless he put down an additional $2000. Nigh tried to back out of the purchase, but the dealer told him that was not possible because his old truck had been sold. The dealership threatened to have him arrested for car theft If he did not agree to the new terms. Nigh sued and won $24,000 in damages plus $26,000 in court costs and attorney fees. The dealership appealed the ruling and after losing in the lower courts, the dealership took the case to the Supreme Court.

You might wonder how a car dealership could renege on a sales contract and then argue the case all the way to the U. S. Supreme Court? However, the dealer's position was that Nigh had breached the contract and technically that position was correct. It is a common practice in automobile sales for buyers to take "spot delivery." When a car buyer takes possession of a car "on the spot," and drives off immediately after negotiating the sale, the contract signed is usually contingent on credit approval. That means that the dealership can claim after the sale that the financing did not go through and demand changes in the loan agreement. The practice of changing the loan agreement after the buyer has possession of the vehicle is so common that it even has a special name—"yo-yo financing." My personal experience with "yo-yo financing" described at the beginning of this chapter is not unusual. Dealers can and often do demand changes in financing terms days or weeks after a sale.

Nigh could not sue for breach of contract. Instead his damage award rested on a federal law known as the "Truth in Lending Act," (TILA) and it is because of this law that the dispute became a federal case. Passed in 1968, the TILA law is a consumer protection bill that requires lenders to clearly explain the finance charges in a loan agreement so that consumers can understand and evaluate all the costs. Nigh sued the dealership under the TILA law and a jury agreed that the dealership had violated the law and awarded Nigh the $50,000 in damages.

But Nigh's success in court alarmed more than just car dealerships. The entire banking industry feared massive exposure to litigation. In the words of a lawyer for the American Banking Association, "There are technical violations of TILA all the time." The dealership, with support from the American Bankers Association, National Association of Auto Dealers and the American Financial Services Association, appealed the award on the grounds that the TILA law capped the damages allowed to no more than $1000.

Nigh prevailed in two lower court rulings. Finally the case came before the U. S. Supreme Court. Arguments hinged on the location of the commas in the TILA law. The majority on the U. S. 4th Circuit Court of Appeals ruled that because of the position of the commas, the word "subparagraph" applied to both section (i) and section (ii) of a particular clause in the TILA law that provided guidelines for damage awards. The American Bankers Association in a friend of the court brief argued that "by blindly following the punctuation of two subparagraphs" the 4th Circuit Court overlooked the potential harm to the consumer lending industry.

On November 30, 2004 the Supreme Court issued an 8 to 1 decision that overturned the lower court rulings and limited Nigh's damage award to just $1000. Justice Ruth Bader Ginsburg, writing for the majority, blamed a "less than meticulous drafting" of the law for the confusion. She argued that interpreting TILA to allow larger damages would lead to an absurd result because damages for car loans would be unlimited while damages for larger loans, such as mortgages, are capped at just $2000. The lone dissenter was Justice Antonin Scalia who essentially argued that the Supreme Court should not be in the business of cleaning up sloppy writing in laws passed by Congress. He wrote: "The Court should not fight the current structure of the statue merely to vindicate the suspicion that Congress actually made—but neglected to explain clearly—a different policy decision."

The bottom line is that Nigh lost and threats of $1000 damage awards for violating TILA are not going to change deceptive practices in the consumer lending industry. A consumer cannot afford to pay an attorney to sue for that small an amount.

Chapter 9 Resources

Appendix II contains the exact mathematical formulas used to generate Tables 9.1 through 9.7.

Morton D. Davis, *The Math of Money: Making Mathematical Sense of Your Personal Finances,* (New York: Copernicus Books, 2001) has a readable, although more mathematically sophisticated discussion of interest charges and mortgages.

The Web site http://www.bankrate.com has a variety of useful financial planning calculators that can be used online for free. You can test out different loan scenarios with any duration or interest rate. The site even has a calculator that determines the duration of your credit card balance if you only make the minimum payment.

For some practical guides on dealing with personal debt see:

Lynnette Khalfani, *Zero Debt: The Ultimate Guide to Financial Freedom* (South Orange, NJ: Advantage World Press, 2004)

Liz Pulliam Weston, *Deal with Your Debt: The Right Way to Manage Your Bills and Pay Off What You Owe* (New York, NY: Prentice Hall, 2005)

CHAPTER TEN

Evaluating Loans

Phantom Finance Charges

"You load sixteen tons and what do you get?
Another day older and deeper in debt.
Saint Peter don't call me cause I can't go
I owe my soul to the company store."

—Merle Travis, 1947
"Sixteen Tons"

Consumer lending has become a lucrative and aggressively marketed business. I get about ten solicitations per week for credit cards, mortgages, and auto loans; and I believe my household is typical. A generation ago, people who wanted to borrow money had to ask the bank. Today roles are reversed— banks constantly ask people to borrow money. The reason for this reversal is that a generation ago banks expected the money they lent to be paid back. Because state governments tightly regulated the amount banks could charge for interest on a loan, banks could only profit if people did pay the money back. Banks loathed lending money to people judged as poor financial risks.

That mathematics fundamentally changed in 1978 when interest rates became deregulated. Once banks could charge any amount of interest on a loan, *they discovered that more profit could be made from borrowers who did not pay the money back*. It seems counterintuitive, but today a bank's most sought after customers are the people who can least afford to pay back borrowed money. Financial institutions that provide consumer credit have become the modern day version of the company store. Workers who take on high-interest consumer loans can never climb out of debt, because subsisting and paying interest on the debt is all they can afford. In the previous chapter we learned how high-interest rates result in a "debt trap," because the mathematics of loan repayment shifts debt reduction further into the future as interest rates rise. Once a worker becomes permanently in debt, the wages from their labor effectively becomes profit for the bank. Short of bankruptcy there is no way out, and while bankruptcies have risen to record levels, banks have factored that in as a cost of doing business. Banks have determined that over the long run, it is more profitable to write off a certain fraction of their loans as bad debt than to lower interest rates to the point that allows people to get out of debt. During the early 2000s the Federal Reserve lowered the interest rates charged to banks to record low levels. But during this time, while banks paid customers who saved less than 1% annual interest, they continued to charge customers who borrowed on credit cards rates of 15% or higher. The banking industry also lobbied Congress heavily for a new bankruptcy bill that passed in 2005 and was signed into law. The new law makes it much more difficult for people to discharge their debts through bankruptcy.

Because competition to lend money to consumers is so fierce, banks have become creative at hiding charges when they structure loans. Hiding charges allows them to advertise lower interest rates than the borrower will effectively pay. Also, borrowers cannot comparison shop for financing in a meaningful way when advertisements tell only part of the story. Most of the techniques used by banks rely on the mathematical ignorance of their customers. Everyone can compare prices when they shop for goods, but few people understand how monthly payments and interest charges are determined in a loan agreement.

The techniques lenders use to hide charges follow recurring themes that include the following:

Emphasis on monthly payments: The total cost or the duration of the loan is not openly discussed. A salesman will never ask you how much you can afford to spend; he or she will instead ask what the highest monthly payment is that you can afford. A direct mail solicitation to loan you money has a low monthly payment highlighted. The number of years or decades you will be working to make that payment is hidden deep in the letter.

Bury details in fine print: Interest rates and additional charges are buried in the fine print. Lenders know that most of their customers will have no choice but to trust their monthly payment calculation. My car dealership experience described at the beginning of Chapter 9, where the interest rate was changed, is an example of this tactic. Most people sign loan documents that agree to a monthly payment. Few people know how to check the monthly payment calculation to see if any additional charges have been added and then search the fine print if the numbers do not add up.

Bait and switch: While my car dealership experience is a blatant example from 25 years ago of bait and switch, today's bait and switch tactics are much more sophisticated and rely on mathematical deception. The method today is to re-label finances charges in a loan agreement with a different term—transaction fee, rebate, service charge, etc., thereby allowing advertised finance charges to appear low and to make comparison shopping for the best interest rate impossible. The most egregious examples of the re-labeling tactic in today's marketing environment are the 0% loans from automobile companies, where the actual finance charge is re-labeled as a "rebate."

The Effective Interest Rate

To evaluate loan agreements, it helps to think in terms of an *effective finance charge*—that is the difference between the cash price of a purchase and the total amount of money you pay back if you finance the purchase. From the point of view of both parties, yours and the lending company's, that difference is your cost and their gain. By dividing the *total cost* by the *cash price,* we arrive at the total cost per dollar financed. With knowledge of the total cost per dollar and the total duration of the loan, Table 9.2 in Chapter 9 can be used to determine the *effective interest rate*. The method to do this is given in Worksheet A3.b and was already used for Examples 9.20 and 9.21. The steps are to multiply the total cost per dollar financed by 1000 and then look for the amount closest to that value in the column in Table 9.2 labeled with the loan's duration. The row that value appears in corresponds to the effective interest rate. When choosing between loan agreements the effective interest rates should be compared, not the advertised interest rate. Often the advertised interest rate is a meaningless number.

Example 10.1

Purchasing a new computer system

You are deciding whether to purchase a new computer system with cash or store financing. The cash price is $1500 and the store financing is $50 per month for 36 months. What effective interest is paid on this purchase if you take the store financing?

If you pay $50 per month for 36 months, your total cost is $1800. You are paying $1800 divided by $1500 or $1.20 for each $1.00 over the cash price. Multiply this by 1000 to get $1200 and in Table 9.2 look down the three-year column until you find the number closet to $1200; that number,

$1196, is in the 12% row. The effective interest rate for this purchase is about 12%.

[Worksheet A3.b, Table 9.2: Total Cost = $1800, Cash Price = $1500, Duration = 3 years; Result is Rate = 12%]

Rent-to-own agreements

Rent-to-own agreements charge high effective interest rates on purchases, but the company will argue that the cost includes services not available in a traditional loan agreement. The consumer is paying for a service, not financing. Consider a rent-to-own advertisement. I have one from Rent-A-Center that advertises a bedroom suite with a cash price of $935.48, or $17.99 per week over 104 weeks for a total cost of $1870.96. In other words, the rent-to-own agreement requires $2 to be paid back for every $1 in cash value over a two-year period. Multiply by 1000 and check the 2-year column of Table 9.2. You will not find $2000 in the two-year column because the table would have to include annual interest rates up to 78% to have $2000 appear in that column. Truth-in-lending laws do not apply because the consumer is not "financing" a purchase; the consumer is "renting to own." The difference between renting to own and borrowing to purchase is that because ownership is retained by the store, the customer is allowed to return the bedroom suite at any time and the store is responsible for normal wear and tear. It also means that the customer has no equity in the bedroom suite until all payments are made. A year into the agreement, if payments stop, the item goes back to the store and the customer loses everything invested.

From a financial standpoint, a consumer with no cash who wants a bedroom suite would be much better off shopping for the best available cash price, buying the item outright by charging it to a high-interest credit card, and paying an amount equal to the rental fee to the credit card. At $17.99 per week, even a full-priced $935 bedroom suite charged to a credit card with 25% annual interest would be completely paid for in 14 months. If temporary use is desired, have a yard sale and recoup some of the investment. Do not lose it all to the store. Notice that $17.99 per week is actually $78 per month.

Introductory Teaser Rates for Credit Cards

At my house credit card offers litter the mail table like confetti. All come in envelopes with a low introductory "teaser" rate written in large letters on the outside. If I open the offer to read the fine print, many times I find that the advertised teaser rate is a meaningless number. Credit card companies routinely employ the mathematical deception of re-labeling their finance charges as something other than interest. Often the term is "transaction fee."

Consider the following solicitation. I received a packet of cash advanced checks for one of my credit cards in April 2002. The enclosed brochure had large letters that stated "2.9% APR*" on money borrowed with the enclosed checks until October 2002. The asterisk referred to fine print on the back of the brochure that stated, "The Cash Access transaction fee for Convenience Checks is 3% of each transaction, with a minimum fee of $5, for the purpose of the attached checks only, the maximum fee shall be $50." The gist of the fine print means that it will cost more to borrow money with the checks than the stated 2.9% interest rate. What is the effective interest rate under these conditions? It depends on how much is borrowed and for how long. Consider these examples:

Example 10.2

Deciding on an immediate cash advance

Suppose I write a $1000 check to make a purchase in May and pay off the balance in four months, which would be in September, just before the promotional rate expires. What is the effective interest rate?

The "cash price" in this example is $1000. Next add up all the fees to get a total cost. In September I will owe the $1000 plus the 3% transaction fee, which is $30, plus the 2.9% interest for 1/3 of a year, which is approximately $10. The total cost is $1040 on a $1000 loan for 1/3 of a year (4 months). Look in the 4-month column of Table 9.6 (Total Cost for 1-12 Month Loans) for the value $1040. It is in the row corresponding to a 19% annual rate of interest.

[Worksheet A3.b, Table 9.6: Total Cost = $1040, Cash Price = $1000, Duration = 4 months; Result is Rate = 19%]

Example 10.3

Deciding on a delayed cash advance

Same conditions as in Example 10.2 but I decide to wait one month to use my cash advance check. If I still write a $1000 check and pay it back in 3 months, what is the effective interest rate?

The "cash price" is still $1000 and I still owe the $30 transaction fee. The total cost is $1000 plus $30 plus the 2.9% interest for 3 months (1/4 year), which is about $7, for a total of $1037. Look for $1037 in the 3-month column of Table 9.6. It is in the row corresponding to a 22% annual interest rate.

[Worksheet A3.b, Table 9.6: Total Cost = $1037, Cash Price = $1000, Duration = 3 months; Result is Rate = 22%]

Example 10.4

Minimizing the effective interest rate

What is the lowest effective interest rate that I can ever get under the conditions of this cash advance offer?

The lowest possible effective interest rate is obtained by maxing out the credit card for the longest period of time. My limit for this card is $10,000. If I write a $10,000 check, then the $50 cap on the transaction fee applies. Suppose I write the check immediately. In September I owe 2.9% interest on $10,000 for 1/3 of a year, or about $100. Total costs add to $10,150, or $1015 for each $1000 borrowed. In the 4-month column of Table 9.6, $1015 is in the row corresponding to a 7% annual rate of interest. That is the lowest effective interest rate possible under the terms of this offer.

[Worksheet A3.b, Table 9.6: Total Cost = $10,150, Cash Price = $10,000, Duration = 4 months; Result is Rate = 7%]

These examples show that the 2.9% teaser rate is a meaningless number. If I decide to transfer a balance to this credit card, the effective interest rate I pay depends on how much I transfer and for how many months I borrow the money. Banks and finance companies have become very creative with teaser rates. Here are some other deceptions to watch out for:

• I purchased a computer system from a store that advertised a 0% finance rate for the first three months of the loan. The contract fine print stated that at the end of the three-month period I would owe 18% APR interest *retroactively* from the date I made the purchase. The interest would even be assessed retroactively on the money already paid. In other words, this is a 0% loan only if the balance is paid in full at the end of three months. Otherwise it is an ordinary loan at 18% APR, starting from day one.

• I received a credit card offer with a 0% teaser rate for the first six months on balance transfers. However if one payment arrives even one day late, the interest rate changes immediately to the "default" rate of 24.67% APR and a $25 late payment fee applies. People who take this offer should hope that the company posts payments in a timely manner. There is a large incentive for them to run an inefficient mailroom and blame their customers.

The 0% Percent Financing Scam

Marketers have discovered that 0% financing promotions are one of their most effective sales tools. For example, automobile companies produce print ads and television commercials that abound with offers of "0% APR" on new models. The idea is to attract buyers for new cars by making it appear that compared to used cars, they will save money on financing. However, almost all 0% financing offers provide multiple options for the consumer. The ads usually read something like "0% financing for three years or a specified amount of cash back." The amount of cash back depends on the model, with expensive models receiving larger rebates. Further inquiries reveal that if you desire a longer loan, that option is also available for a reduced interest rate of 1% or 2%. Which option is best for you as an automobile buyer? Should you (a) take the cash back, (b) take the 0% offer, or (c) take the longer-term loan at a reduced interest rate.

The answer of course is—it depends. But before we analyze the situation to determine what your choice depends on, let us immediately dispense with the 0% financing myth. If you are considering a car with a $15,000 price tag and are told that you will get $2,000 back if you pay cash, that car costs $13,000. If you are told that the car cost $15,000 and instead of the cash back they will finance it at 0% for three years, the car still costs $13,000 and you are being asked to pay a $2000 financing charge up front. Car dealerships go through an elaborate charade to make the car appear to cost $15,000, but the bottom line is once all the money has changed hands, the net cost to you is $13,000. Like the examples with teaser rates for credit cards, we can calculate an effective interest rate if we label the "rebate" for what it really is—a prepaid finance charge. This is an example of the kind of "framing" described in Chapter 8 that marketers use to influence buying decisions. A finance charge, something that most people perceive as a loss, is re-framed as a "rebate" so that people will think of it as a gain. In fact many "0% finance" offers have the finance charge included in the purchase price. It is better to shop for the lowest price and then figure out if it is worth paying more for 0% financing. Often it is not.

Example 10.5

Deciding on 0% automobile financing

You must decide whether to pay $15,000 for a new car and receive 0% financing from the dealer, or take a $2000 rebate and finance the car with a loan from your bank that carries 8% annual interest. For either case it will be a three-year loan. What should you do?

The total cost if you take the 0% financing is $15,000. The cash price, $13,000, is the amount you will need to borrow from your bank. Divide $15,000 by $13,000 to get $1.15. That means it will cost $1.15 for every $1, or $1150 for every $1000 borrowed if you take the dealer financing. The value closest to $1150 in the 3-year column of Table 9.2 is in the row for 9.5% annual interest. Conclusion—you should go to your bank.

[Worksheet A3.b, Table 9.2: Total Cost = $15,000, Cash Price = $13,000, Duration = 3 years; Result is Rate = 9.5%]

This example shows that when deciding between a rebate and a 0% financing offer, you should use Worksheet A3.b and Table 9.2 to determine the effective interest rate and compare it to other sources of financing available. As in Example 10.5, depending on the size of the rebate and the cost of alternative financing, it might be better to finance the purchase at a non-zero annual interest rate and take the rebate. However, there are some additional considerations when making this decision.

•When you take the 0% financing offer, you are liable for the money even if the loan doesn't go for the full term. Suppose you decide to take the cash back and borrow from your bank to pay for the car. If three months later the car is totaled, you must pay off the balance of the loan, an amount that will be less than what you borrowed from the bank and you do not pay further interest. However, if you took the 0% finance offer, the payoff balance will include what remains on the full purchase price of the car. You cannot go back and ask for the rebate. Also the insurance company does not care whether or not you took the rebate, their settlement is always for the actual cash value of the car, not for the "sales price." As mentioned in Chapter 9, *when all things are equal, it is better to get the best cash price for a purchase, even if you have to pay a higher interest rate.* Then if for any reason you pay the loan off early you are responsible only for the principal that funded the purchase price and not for future interest charges. When automobile buyers choose not to take the rebate, they are effectively pre-paying the finance charge. It is a no-lose proposition for the automobile company because whatever happens in the future, the buyer is responsible for the entire purchase price.

•You should also consider the tax issues. Whether you take the cash back or the 0% financing, you will have to pay sales tax on the full purchase price without any adjustment for the rebate because that is the amount the dealer will list as the "sale price". By inflating the "sale price" to hide their financing charge, the automobile companies increase the sales tax liability for all their customers. They might also increase their customer's income tax liability if the rebate is considered taxable income. You should include the cost of taxes when computing the total costs of an automobile purchase in order to determine an effective interest rate. It might have an effect on your decision to take the rebate or reduced financing.

Table 9.2 is even useful for analyzing choices that involve reduced financing over longer terms. Consider Example 10.6:

Example 10.6

Deciding on reduced-rate financing for an automobile

You decide on a new car that costs $20,000 but you cannot afford the monthly payments on the three-year loan that is required for the 0% financing. The dealer counters with an offer of 2% annual interest on a five-year loan. If you reject the 2% financing and pay cash with money borrowed from your bank, there is a $2500 rebate. What is the effective interest rate for the five-year loan from the dealer?

If you finance $20,000 at 2% for five years, Table 9.2 indicates that you pay $1052 back for every $1000 borrowed on five-year loan. Your total cost is $1052 x 20 = $21,040. If you pay the cash price of $20,000 minus $2500, or $17,500, what interest rate results in a total cost of $21,040? Divide $21,040 by $17,500 to find that $1.202 is paid for every $1 borrowed, or $1202 for every $1000. In the five-year column of Table 9.2, you will find $1202 in the row corresponding to a 7.5% annual interest rate. Your decision depends on whether alternative sources of financing have annual interest rates that are better or worse than 7.5%.

[Worksheet A3.a, Table 9.2: Rate = 2%, Duration = 5 years, Cash Price = $20,000; Result is Total Cost = $21,040]
[Worksheet A3.b, Table 9.2: Total Cost = $21,040, Cash Price = $17,500, Duration = 5 years; Result is Rate = 7.5%]

Home Mortgages

A home mortgage is usually the largest single payment in a typical family budget. The standard mortgage is scheduled to pay off the loan over a 30-year time period. The long duration means that payments in the early years of the mortgage are almost entirely interest, private mortgage insurance (PMI), and escrow for insurance and taxes. Consider borrowing $100,000 at 7% annual interest rate to buy a house. A typical first monthly mortgage payment would consist of the following:

Interest	$583
Private mortgage insurance	$50
Hazard insurance	$40
Real Estate Taxes	$150
Principal	$82
Total	$905

That means of the first $905 monthly payment, less than 10% goes towards reducing the loan amount. Three years of payments are needed before the amount allocated to the principal reaches $100. During those first three years the new homeowner will pay a total of $20,678 in interest while reducing the initial $100,000 loan balance by just $3273. Tables 9.3 and 9.4 in Chapter 9 illustrate that for long-term loans, equity accrual is a slow process because in the early stages of the loan a large fraction of the payment goes towards interest. When the loan is the size of a typical mortgage, the borrower treads water for the first few years while the interest charges run into the tens of thousands of dollars.

To assist in mortgage planning Table 10.1 shows the fixed monthly payments required to pay off fixed-interest loans of $10,000 over 15, 18, 20, 22, 25, and 30 year terms. While Table 10.1 shows some of the same information as Table 9.1, the difference is that greater detail is shown for the lower interest rates and Table 10.1 lacks columns for 18 and 22-year terms.

In the interest rate column for Table 10.1, the rates between 3% and 10% are spaced at 0.25% intervals. No rates are given below 3% and above 20% in Table 10.1 because it is assumed no one's mortgage rate is lower than 3% and it hoped that no one's rate is higher than 20%. Monthly payments per $10,000 borrowed are given because mortgages are usually in the tens of thousands of dollars. For example, in Table 9.1, a 9.5% loan for 30 years requires monthly payments $8.41 per $1000 borrowed. In Table 10.1 a 9.5% loan requires $84.09 per $10,000 borrowed. Divide $84.09 by 10 and round to the nearest penny and the value from Table 9.1 is reproduced.

For mortgage rates quoted to the hundredth of a percent, Table 10.1 is still useful for determining the range in which a payment must fall. For example, if your mortgage rate is 9.59%, the monthly payments for principal and interest must fall between $84.09 and $85.92 (the value from Table 10.1 for a 9.75% rate) per $10,000 borrowed. If it does not some other charges are included. Escrow payments for taxes and insurance and PMI are always in addition to the principal and interest payments, but make sure you know what these numbers are and that everything adds up.* Sometimes mortgage brokers will tack on additional commissions and fees and roll them into the amount financed. These amounts show up as small increases to the monthly payments for a 30-year loan rather than itemized lump sum payments on the settlement sheet. If you think that you are financing a $100,000 loan at 9.59% interest and the principal and interest payments are $865.40, an amount that falls outside the range just given, then you are not being told everything. I have my own personal story, which is related at the end of this chapter, on how loan payments can be used to hide additional fees and interest charges. If you need an exact payment calculation for an interest rate not precisely

---

*Escrow refers to a special bank account that is used to pay property taxes, private mortgage insurance (PMI), and hazard insurance. The annual costs for each of these expenses are added and then divided by 12. Each month, lenders require the homeowner to put one-twelfth of the total costs of these expenses into the escrow account. Each time a tax or insurance bill comes due, the lenders pays it with money from the escrow account. Escrow payments are always in addition to the monthly loan payment for principal and interest.

Table 10.1: Monthly loan payments per $10,000 borrowed. Rate is an annual percentage; interest is compounded monthly.

Monthly loan payments

Rate (%)	Loan Duration (years)					
	15	18	20	22	25	30
3.00	$69.06	$59.97	$55.46	$51.79	$47.42	$42.16
3.25	$70.27	$61.21	$56.72	$53.07	$48.73	$43.52
3.50	$71.49	$62.47	$58.00	$54.37	$50.06	$44.90
3.75	$72.72	$63.74	$59.29	$55.68	$51.41	$46.31
4.00	$73.97	$65.02	$60.60	$57.02	$52.78	$47.74
4.25	$75.23	$66.32	$61.92	$58.37	$54.17	$49.19
4.50	$76.50	$67.63	$63.26	$59.74	$55.58	$50.67
4.75	$77.78	$68.96	$64.62	$61.12	$57.01	$52.16
5.00	$79.08	$70.30	$66.00	$62.53	$58.46	$53.68
5.25	$80.39	$71.66	$67.38	$63.95	$59.92	$55.22
5.50	$81.71	$73.03	$68.79	$65.38	$61.41	$56.78
5.75	$83.04	$74.42	$70.21	$66.84	$62.91	$58.36
6.00	$84.39	$75.82	$71.64	$68.31	$64.43	$59.96
6.25	$85.74	$77.23	$73.09	$69.79	$65.97	$61.57
6.50	$87.11	$78.66	$74.56	$71.29	$67.52	$63.21
6.75	$88.49	$80.10	$76.04	$72.81	$69.09	$64.86
7.00	$89.88	$81.55	$77.53	$74.34	$70.68	$66.53
7.25	$91.29	$83.02	$79.04	$75.89	$72.28	$68.22
7.50	$92.70	$84.50	$80.56	$77.45	$73.90	$69.92
7.75	$94.13	$85.99	$82.09	$79.03	$75.53	$71.64
8.00	$95.57	$87.50	$83.64	$80.62	$77.18	$73.38
8.25	$97.01	$89.01	$85.21	$82.22	$78.85	$75.13
8.50	$98.47	$90.55	$86.78	$83.84	$80.52	$76.89
8.75	$99.94	$92.09	$88.37	$85.47	$82.21	$78.67
9.00	$101.43	$93.64	$89.97	$87.12	$83.92	$80.46
9.25	$102.92	$95.21	$91.59	$88.78	$85.64	$82.27
9.50	$104.42	$96.79	$93.21	$90.45	$87.37	$84.09
9.75	$105.94	$98.38	$94.85	$92.13	$89.11	$85.92
10.00	$107.46	$99.98	$96.50	$93.82	$90.87	$87.76
10.50	$110.54	$103.22	$99.84	$97.25	$94.42	$91.47
11.00	$113.66	$106.50	$103.22	$100.72	$98.01	$95.23
11.50	$116.82	$109.83	$106.64	$104.24	$101.65	$99.03
12.00	$120.02	$113.20	$110.11	$107.79	$105.32	$102.86
13.00	$126.52	$120.04	$117.16	$115.02	$112.78	$110.62
14.00	$133.17	$127.04	$124.35	$122.39	$120.38	$118.49
15.00	$139.96	$134.17	$131.68	$129.89	$128.08	$126.44
16.00	$146.87	$141.42	$139.13	$137.50	$135.89	$134.48
17.00	$153.90	$148.79	$146.68	$145.21	$143.78	$142.57
18.00	$161.04	$156.27	$154.33	$153.00	$151.74	$150.71

Observation: Small differences in the annual interest rate make a significant difference in the monthly payments for a typical 30-year mortgage.

stated in Table 10.1 (or Table 9.1), use the formula in Appendix II or go online to http://www.TheTwoHeadedQuarter.com and use one of the financial planning calculators. Also most personal finance software packages such as Quicken have loan planning calculators built in.

Example 10.7

Monthly payments on a house

What would be the monthly payments on a 30-year mortgage to finance a $275,000 purchase if the annual interest rate is 7.25%?

The intersection of the 7.25% row with the 30-year column in Table 10.1 shows $68.22 paid for each $10,000 borrowed. Divide $275,000 by $10,000 and the result is 27.5. Monthly payments for principal and interest would be $68.22 x 27.5, or $1876. Monthly payments for property taxes, PMI, and hazard insurance must be added to this amount.

[Worksheet A5.a, Table 10.1: Rate = 7.25%, Duration = 30 years, Principal = $275,000; Result is Monthly Payment = $1876]

Example 10.8

Deciding how much you can afford for a house

You decide that your budget can support $1500 per month payments for a home. Your research shows that monthly payments for property taxes, PMI, and hazard insurance will cost about $200 per month. If the annual interest rate is 7.25%, how much can you afford to spend on a house?

The principal and interest portion of your home payment will be $1500 minus $200, or $1300 per month. Just as in

Example 10.7, the monthly payment per $10,000 borrowed on a 7.25%, 30-year loan is $68.22. Divide $68.22 into $1300 and the result is 19 for the number of $10,000 amounts you can afford to borrow. You can spend up to $190,000 on a house.

[Worksheet A5.d, Table 10.1: Rate = 7.25%, Duration = 30 years, Monthly Payment = $1300; Result is Principal = $190,000]

30-year Mortgages

In the modern mortgage market, lenders have concocted a dizzying array of choices — adjustable rate-mortgages, balloon mortgages, interest-only mortgages, etc. — to fit different needs and budgets. But before considering some of the more complicated financing options, it is useful to have a good understanding of the standard 30-year mortgage. The 30-year mortgage is often the safest option for financing a home, especially if you plan to own it for at least a decade.

The next series of tables — Tables 10.2, 10.3, 10.4 and 10.5 — refer specifically to *standard 30-year mortgages with a fixed interest rate and fixed monthly payments*. Tables 10.2 and 10.3 show the balance remaining and total interest paid on a 30-year loan after a given number of years have elapsed. For Table 10.2, the columns show the total number of years that payments have been made and the rows the annual interest rate. The balance per $10,000 borrowed that remains after the elapsed time is shown. Table 10.3 has the same layout as Table 10.2, interest rates for the rows and elapsed time for each column. The total interest paid per $10,000 borrowed to that point in time is listed in Table 10.3. Both Tables 10.2 and 10.3 assume that interest on the loan is charged monthly and fixed payments are made each month.

Tables 10.2 and 10.3 show that most of the money paid in the early years of a home mortgage goes to paying interest and not to reducing the principal. These two tables, 10.2 and 10.3 show that equity accrual on a 30-year loan is a deceptively slow

Table 10.2: Balance remaining per $10,000 borrowed on a 30-year loan after the number of years heading the column has ellapsed. Rate is an annual percentage rate.

Balance remaining on a 30-year loan

Rate (%)	Years into a 30-Year Loan					
	1	2	3	4	5	6
3.00	$9,791	$9,576	$9,354	$9,126	$8,891	$8,648
3.25	$9,800	$9,593	$9,379	$9,159	$8,931	$8,695
3.50	$9,808	$9,609	$9,404	$9,190	$8,970	$8,741
3.75	$9,816	$9,625	$9,427	$9,221	$9,008	$8,786
4.00	$9,824	$9,641	$9,450	$9,251	$9,045	$8,830
4.25	$9,831	$9,656	$9,472	$9,281	$9,081	$8,872
4.50	$9,839	$9,670	$9,493	$9,309	$9,116	$8,914
4.75	$9,846	$9,684	$9,514	$9,336	$9,150	$8,954
5.00	$9,852	$9,697	$9,534	$9,363	$9,183	$8,994
5.25	$9,859	$9,710	$9,554	$9,389	$9,215	$9,032
5.50	$9,865	$9,723	$9,573	$9,414	$9,246	$9,069
5.75	$9,871	$9,735	$9,591	$9,438	$9,276	$9,105
6.00	$9,877	$9,747	$9,608	$9,461	$9,305	$9,140
6.25	$9,883	$9,758	$9,625	$9,484	$9,334	$9,174
6.50	$9,888	$9,769	$9,642	$9,506	$9,361	$9,207
6.75	$9,893	$9,779	$9,657	$9,527	$9,388	$9,238
7.00	$9,898	$9,789	$9,673	$9,547	$9,413	$9,269
7.25	$9,903	$9,799	$9,687	$9,567	$9,438	$9,299
7.50	$9,908	$9,808	$9,701	$9,586	$9,462	$9,328
7.75	$9,912	$9,817	$9,715	$9,604	$9,485	$9,356
8.00	$9,916	$9,826	$9,728	$9,622	$9,507	$9,383
8.25	$9,921	$9,834	$9,741	$9,639	$9,528	$9,409
8.50	$9,924	$9,842	$9,753	$9,655	$9,549	$9,434
8.75	$9,928	$9,850	$9,764	$9,671	$9,569	$9,458
9.00	$9,932	$9,857	$9,775	$9,686	$9,588	$9,481
9.25	$9,935	$9,864	$9,786	$9,700	$9,606	$9,504
9.50	$9,938	$9,871	$9,796	$9,714	$9,624	$9,525
9.75	$9,941	$9,877	$9,806	$9,727	$9,641	$9,546
10.0	$9,944	$9,883	$9,815	$9,740	$9,657	$9,566
10.5	$9,950	$9,894	$9,833	$9,764	$9,688	$9,604
11.0	$9,955	$9,905	$9,849	$9,786	$9,716	$9,639
11.5	$9,960	$9,914	$9,863	$9,806	$9,742	$9,671
12.0	$9,964	$9,923	$9,877	$9,825	$9,766	$9,700
13.0	$9,971	$9,938	$9,900	$9,857	$9,808	$9,753
14.0	$9,977	$9,950	$9,919	$9,884	$9,843	$9,796
15.0	$9,981	$9,960	$9,935	$9,906	$9,872	$9,833
16.0	$9,985	$9,968	$9,948	$9,924	$9,896	$9,863
17.0	$9,988	$9,974	$9,958	$9,939	$9,916	$9,888
18.0	$9,991	$9,980	$9,967	$9,951	$9,932	$9,909

Observation: For a 30-year mortgage, reduction of the principal is a slow process.

Balance remaining on a 30-year loan

Rate (%)	Years into a 30-Year Loan					
	7	**8**	**9**	**10**	**12**	**15**
3.00	$8,398	$8,141	$7,875	$7,602	$7,030	$6,105
3.25	$8,452	$8,201	$7,941	$7,673	$7,110	$6,194
3.50	$8,504	$8,259	$8,006	$7,743	$7,189	$6,281
3.75	$8,556	$8,317	$8,069	$7,811	$7,266	$6,368
4.00	$8,606	$8,373	$8,131	$7,878	$7,343	$6,454
4.25	$8,655	$8,428	$8,191	$7,944	$7,418	$6,539
4.50	$8,703	$8,482	$8,251	$8,009	$7,492	$6,623
4.75	$8,749	$8,534	$8,309	$8,072	$7,564	$6,706
5.00	$8,795	$8,585	$8,365	$8,134	$7,636	$6,788
5.25	$8,839	$8,635	$8,421	$8,195	$7,706	$6,869
5.50	$8,882	$8,684	$8,475	$8,254	$7,775	$6,949
5.75	$8,923	$8,731	$8,528	$8,312	$7,842	$7,028
6.00	$8,964	$8,777	$8,579	$8,369	$7,908	$7,105
6.25	$9,003	$8,822	$8,629	$8,424	$7,973	$7,181
6.50	$9,042	$8,866	$8,678	$8,478	$8,036	$7,256
6.75	$9,079	$8,908	$8,725	$8,530	$8,098	$7,330
7.00	$9,115	$8,949	$8,772	$8,581	$8,158	$7,402
7.25	$9,150	$8,989	$8,817	$8,631	$8,217	$7,473
7.50	$9,183	$9,028	$8,860	$8,679	$8,275	$7,543
7.75	$9,216	$9,065	$8,903	$8,727	$8,331	$7,611
8.00	$9,248	$9,102	$8,944	$8,772	$8,386	$7,678
8.25	$9,278	$9,137	$8,984	$8,817	$8,440	$7,744
8.50	$9,308	$9,171	$9,022	$8,860	$8,492	$7,808
8.75	$9,336	$9,204	$9,060	$8,902	$8,543	$7,871
9.00	$9,364	$9,236	$9,096	$8,943	$8,592	$7,933
9.25	$9,391	$9,267	$9,131	$8,982	$8,640	$7,993
9.50	$9,416	$9,297	$9,165	$9,021	$8,687	$8,052
9.75	$9,441	$9,326	$9,198	$9,058	$8,733	$8,110
10.0	$9,465	$9,353	$9,230	$9,094	$8,777	$8,166
10.5	$9,510	$9,406	$9,290	$9,162	$8,862	$8,275
11.0	$9,552	$9,455	$9,347	$9,226	$8,942	$8,379
11.5	$9,590	$9,500	$9,399	$9,286	$9,017	$8,477
12.0	$9,626	$9,542	$9,448	$9,342	$9,087	$8,571
13.0	$9,689	$9,617	$9,535	$9,442	$9,215	$8,743
14.0	$9,743	$9,681	$9,610	$9,528	$9,327	$8,897
15.0	$9,787	$9,735	$9,674	$9,602	$9,424	$9,034
16.0	$9,825	$9,780	$9,727	$9,666	$9,509	$9,156
17.0	$9,856	$9,818	$9,773	$9,720	$9,581	$9,264
18.0	$9,882	$9,850	$9,811	$9,765	$9,644	$9,358

process, and interest charges are far greater than people realize, even on a comparatively low interest loan. When homeowners judged to be poor credit risks are saddled with "sub-prime" home mortgages, the reduction in the loan balance during the early years of the loan is barely noticeable.

Example 10.9

Sub-prime mortgages

Because of a poor credit rating, a sub-prime mortgage with a 14% annual interest rate is all that is available for financing your $180,000 home purchase. If you decide to accept this mortgage, how much principal will you owe after 10 years of payments? How much interest will you have paid to the lender during this 10-year time?

In Table 10.2 the intersection of the 14% row with the 10-year column shows that for every $10,000 borrowed $9528 is still owed. The number of $10,000 amounts borrowed is $180,000 divided by $10,000, or 18. That means that after 10 years of payments you will owe 18 x $9528, or $171,504 on the original $180,000 loan. In Table 10.3 the intersection of the 14% row and 10-year column shows that during those five years, you will have paid $13,747 in interest for each $10,000 borrowed, which is a total of 18 x $13,747, or $247,446. These figures are correct. After ten years of payments on the loan, the lender has received $247,446 in interest payments but only $180,000 minus $171,504, or $8496 towards the principal.

[Worksheet A6.a, Table 10.2: Rate = 14%, Time = 10 years, Principal = $180,000; Result is Balance = $171,504]
[Worksheet A7.a, Table 10.3: Rate = 14%, Time = 10 years, Principal = $180,000; Result is Interest Paid = $247,446]

Tables 10.2 and 10.3 are useful for making a variety of decisions. Some examples follow:

Example 10.10

Determining the break-even time on a real-estate sale

You purchase a home for $150,000 that costs you $3500 to close. You pay the closing costs yourself, but finance the entire purchase price at 7.5% annual interest. To sell the house, it will cost 5% of the value to pay the realtor, and an additional $2500 to close. If the price of your home stays flat, how long must you own it before you can sell it for $150,000 and have enough money to pay off the loan balance and your closing costs?

Your total costs, in addition to the purchase price, to buy and sell this home are $2500 + $3500 + (0.05 x $150,000), or $13,500. To walk away from the sale and break even requires having a loan balance of $150,000 minus $13,500, or $136,500 remaining at the time of the sale. That means you must owe no more than $136,500 divided by 15, or $9100 per $10,000 borrowed. In Table 10.2, look in the 7.5% row until you find a number closest to $9100. That number is $9028, which falls in the eight-year column. Assuming housing prices stay flat, you must own the home nearly eight years before you can walk away and break even at the close.

[Worksheet A6.c, Table 10.2: Principal = $150,000, Balance = $136,500, Rate = 7.5%; Result is Time = 8 years]

This example illustrates why lenders insist on either 20% down from the buyer or the purchase of private mortgage insurance. If the buyer defaults on the loan in the early years, before prices have had time to appreciate, the lender cannot recover enough money to pay the costs of foreclosure by selling the home.

Table 10.3: Total interest paid per $10,000 borrowed on a 30-year loan after the number of years heading the column has ellapsed. Rate is an annual percentage rate.

Interest paid on a 30-year loan

Rate (%)	Years into a 30-Year Loan					
	1	2	3	4	5	6
3.00	$297	$588	$872	$1,150	$1,420	$1,684
3.25	$322	$637	$946	$1,248	$1,542	$1,829
3.50	$347	$687	$1,020	$1,346	$1,664	$1,974
3.75	$372	$737	$1,094	$1,444	$1,786	$2,120
4.00	$397	$786	$1,169	$1,543	$1,909	$2,267
4.25	$422	$836	$1,243	$1,642	$2,032	$2,414
4.50	$447	$886	$1,318	$1,741	$2,156	$2,562
4.75	$472	$936	$1,392	$1,840	$2,280	$2,710
5.00	$497	$986	$1,467	$1,940	$2,404	$2,859
5.25	$522	$1,036	$1,542	$2,039	$2,528	$3,008
5.50	$547	$1,086	$1,617	$2,139	$2,653	$3,157
5.75	$572	$1,136	$1,692	$2,239	$2,778	$3,307
6.00	$597	$1,186	$1,767	$2,339	$2,903	$3,457
6.25	$622	$1,236	$1,842	$2,440	$3,028	$3,607
6.50	$647	$1,286	$1,917	$2,540	$3,154	$3,757
6.75	$672	$1,336	$1,992	$2,640	$3,279	$3,908
7.00	$697	$1,386	$2,068	$2,741	$3,405	$4,059
7.25	$722	$1,436	$2,143	$2,842	$3,531	$4,211
7.50	$747	$1,487	$2,219	$2,942	$3,657	$4,362
7.75	$772	$1,537	$2,294	$3,043	$3,783	$4,514
8.00	$797	$1,587	$2,370	$3,144	$3,910	$4,666
8.25	$822	$1,637	$2,445	$3,245	$4,036	$4,818
8.50	$847	$1,688	$2,521	$3,346	$4,163	$4,970
8.75	$872	$1,738	$2,596	$3,447	$4,289	$5,122
9.00	$897	$1,788	$2,672	$3,548	$4,416	$5,274
9.25	$922	$1,838	$2,747	$3,649	$4,542	$5,427
9.50	$947	$1,889	$2,823	$3,750	$4,669	$5,579
9.75	$972	$1,939	$2,899	$3,851	$4,796	$5,732
10.0	$997	$1,989	$2,974	$3,953	$4,923	$5,884
10.5	$1,048	$2,090	$3,126	$4,155	$5,177	$6,190
11.0	$1,098	$2,190	$3,277	$4,357	$5,430	$6,495
11.5	$1,148	$2,291	$3,428	$4,560	$5,684	$6,801
12.0	$1,198	$2,391	$3,580	$4,762	$5,938	$7,106
13.0	$1,298	$2,593	$3,882	$5,167	$6,445	$7,717
14.0	$1,399	$2,794	$4,185	$5,571	$6,952	$8,327
15.0	$1,499	$2,995	$4,487	$5,975	$7,459	$8,937
16.0	$1,599	$3,195	$4,789	$6,379	$7,965	$9,546
17.0	$1,699	$3,396	$5,091	$6,782	$8,470	$10,153
18.0	$1,799	$3,597	$5,392	$7,185	$8,974	$10,760

Observation: In the early years of a 30-year mortgage, most of the monthly payment is used to pay interest.

Interest paid on a 30-year loan

Rate (%)	Years into a 30-Year Loan					
	7	8	9	10	12	15
3.00	$1,940	$2,188	$2,429	$2,661	$3,101	$3,694
3.25	$2,108	$2,379	$2,641	$2,895	$3,377	$4,027
3.50	$2,276	$2,570	$2,855	$3,131	$3,655	$4,364
3.75	$2,446	$2,763	$3,070	$3,369	$3,935	$4,704
4.00	$2,616	$2,956	$3,287	$3,607	$4,217	$5,048
4.25	$2,787	$3,151	$3,504	$3,848	$4,502	$5,394
4.50	$2,959	$3,346	$3,723	$4,089	$4,788	$5,744
4.75	$3,131	$3,542	$3,942	$4,332	$5,076	$6,096
5.00	$3,304	$3,739	$4,163	$4,576	$5,366	$6,451
5.25	$3,477	$3,936	$4,385	$4,821	$5,658	$6,809
5.50	$3,651	$4,135	$4,607	$5,068	$5,951	$7,169
5.75	$3,825	$4,333	$4,830	$5,315	$6,245	$7,532
6.00	$4,000	$4,533	$5,054	$5,563	$6,541	$7,897
6.25	$4,175	$4,733	$5,279	$5,812	$6,839	$8,264
6.50	$4,351	$4,934	$5,504	$6,062	$7,138	$8,633
6.75	$4,527	$5,135	$5,730	$6,313	$7,438	$9,004
7.00	$4,703	$5,336	$5,957	$6,565	$7,739	$9,377
7.25	$4,880	$5,538	$6,184	$6,817	$8,041	$9,752
7.50	$5,057	$5,740	$6,412	$7,070	$8,344	$10,129
7.75	$5,234	$5,943	$6,640	$7,324	$8,648	$10,506
8.00	$5,411	$6,146	$6,868	$7,578	$8,952	$10,886
8.25	$5,589	$6,349	$7,097	$7,832	$9,258	$11,267
8.50	$5,767	$6,553	$7,327	$8,087	$9,564	$11,649
8.75	$5,945	$6,756	$7,556	$8,343	$9,871	$12,032
9.00	$6,123	$6,960	$7,786	$8,598	$10,179	$12,416
9.25	$6,301	$7,165	$8,016	$8,855	$10,487	$12,802
9.50	$6,480	$7,369	$8,247	$9,111	$10,796	$13,188
9.75	$6,658	$7,573	$8,477	$9,368	$11,105	$13,575
10.0	$6,837	$7,778	$8,708	$9,625	$11,414	$13,963
10.5	$7,194	$8,187	$9,170	$10,139	$12,034	$14,741
11.0	$7,551	$8,597	$9,632	$10,654	$12,655	$15,521
11.5	$7,909	$9,007	$10,094	$11,170	$13,277	$16,302
12.0	$8,266	$9,417	$10,557	$11,685	$13,899	$17,086
13.0	$8,981	$10,237	$11,482	$12,716	$15,144	$18,655
14.0	$9,696	$11,056	$12,407	$13,747	$16,389	$20,225
15.0	$10,409	$11,873	$13,330	$14,776	$17,632	$21,794
16.0	$11,121	$12,690	$14,251	$15,803	$18,873	$23,362
17.0	$11,832	$13,505	$15,170	$16,828	$20,111	$24,926
18.0	$12,542	$14,318	$16,088	$17,850	$21,346	$26,486

Example 10.11

Determining the break-even time for points paid

Your mortgage broker quotes rates on 30-year loans as 7.5% for 0 points and 7.0% for 2 points. You need to borrow $130,000 to buy a house. If you pay the 2 points for a lower rate, how long must you own the house before the interest savings equals the points paid?

In mortgage jargon, 1 point is equal to 1% of the amount financed and is paid up front in exchange for a lower interest rate. For this example, 2 points is equal to 2 x $1300, or $2600, which is equal to $200 extra for every $10,000 borrowed. Rather than use a worksheet for this example, just examine the 7.0% and 7.5% rows in Table 10.3. Look at how the *difference* in the values in these rows grows as time passes. After the first year the difference is $747 minus $697, or $50 per $10,000 borrowed. It is in year four that the difference becomes $2942 minus $2941, or $201 per $10,000 borrowed. At that point in time you have saved enough interest charges to get back the amount paid in points. If you keep the loan 20 years you will have saved $12,672 minus $11,697, or $975 per $10,000 borrowed, which is $12,675 for a $130,000 loan. After subtracting the $2600 cost of points, you have saved $10,075.

Are points a good deal? The concept is no different from forgoing a rebate on a new car in exchange for a lower interest rate. You take a risk that you will keep the loan long enough to realize a savings from paying points. Lenders are aware that many mortgages are kept only a few years and are happy to collect some of the interest up front rather than wait. If you plan on moving in a few years, do not pay points. Even if you don't plan on moving, be careful about investing in points. It is common to refinance and not move. Each time you refinance, you begin again, and the benefits of past paid points are lost.

Accelerated Mortgage Payments

Because mortgages are structured so that much of the interest is paid in the first few years, homeowners can greatly accelerate equity accrual by paying a small amount extra each month that goes directly towards the principal.

Table 10.4 is a guide to increasing equity by making extra payments each month towards the principal. The first column shows annual interest rates and the remaining columns show the duration of the loan when extra payments are made each month towards the principal. Each column is headed by the amount extra per $10,000 borrowed that is *added* towards the payments taken from the *30-year column* of Table 10.1.

Example 10.12

Reducing the duration of a 30-year mortgage

You finance a home with a 30-year, $100,000 loan that has 7% annual interest and monthly payments of $665.30 per month. You decide to add an additional $30 per month to payments towards the principal and interest, how long will it take the loan to be paid? How much interest will be saved?

Divide $100,000 by $10,000 to get 10 for the number of $10,000 amounts borrowed. If $30 per month extra is paid, that is $30 divided by 10, or an extra $3 per $10,000 borrowed. The intersection of the $3 column in Table 10.4 with the 7% row shows that the loan shortens to 26.2 years. Table 10.5 shows the total savings in interest charges that accrues by making these extra payments. At the intersection of 7% row and the $3 column is $2121 saved per $10,000 borrowed. Therefore, over the life of a $100,000 loan 10 x $2121, or $21,210 is saved.

[Worksheet A8.c, Table 10.4: Principal = $100,000, Rate = 7.0%, Additional Monthly Payment = $30; Result is Time = 26.2 years]
[Worksheet A9.c, Table 10.5: Principal = $100,000, Rate = 7.0%, Additional Monthly Payment = $30; Result is Interest Saved = $21,210]

Table 10.4: Duration in years of a 30-year loan when extra payments are made to the principal each month. Column heading is the amount extra per month per $10,000 borrowed. Rate is an annual percentage rate.

Loan duration in years

Rate (%)	\$1.00	\$2.00	\$3.00	\$4.00	\$5.00	\$6.00
	Monthly Addition per \$10,000 to a 30-Year Loan					
3.00	28.9	27.9	26.9	26.0	25.2	24.4
3.25	28.9	27.8	26.9	26.0	25.2	24.4
3.50	28.9	27.8	26.9	26.0	25.1	24.3
3.75	28.9	27.8	26.8	25.9	25.1	24.3
4.00	28.8	27.8	26.8	25.9	25.0	24.2
4.25	28.8	27.7	26.8	25.8	25.0	24.2
4.50	28.8	27.7	26.7	25.8	24.9	24.1
4.75	28.8	27.7	26.7	25.7	24.9	24.1
5.00	28.8	27.6	26.6	25.7	24.8	24.0
5.25	28.7	27.6	26.6	25.6	24.7	23.9
5.50	28.7	27.6	26.5	25.6	24.7	23.9
5.75	28.7	27.5	26.5	25.5	24.6	23.8
6.00	28.7	27.5	26.4	25.4	24.5	23.7
6.25	28.7	27.4	26.4	25.4	24.5	23.6
6.50	28.6	27.4	26.3	25.3	24.4	23.5
6.75	28.6	27.3	26.2	25.2	24.3	23.5
7.00	28.6	27.3	26.2	25.1	24.2	23.4
7.25	28.5	27.2	26.1	25.1	24.1	23.3
7.50	28.5	27.2	26.0	25.0	24.0	23.2
7.75	28.5	27.1	25.9	24.9	23.9	23.1
8.00	28.4	27.1	25.9	24.8	23.8	23.0
8.25	28.4	27.0	25.8	24.7	23.7	22.9
8.50	28.3	26.9	25.7	24.6	23.6	22.8
8.75	28.3	26.9	25.6	24.5	23.5	22.6
9.00	28.3	26.8	25.5	24.4	23.4	22.5
9.25	28.2	26.7	25.4	24.3	23.3	22.4
9.50	28.2	26.6	25.3	24.2	23.2	22.3
9.75	28.1	26.6	25.2	24.1	23.1	22.2
10.0	28.1	26.5	25.1	24.0	23.0	22.1
10.5	28.0	26.3	24.9	23.7	22.7	21.8
11.0	27.8	26.1	24.7	23.5	22.5	21.5
11.5	27.7	25.9	24.5	23.3	22.2	21.3
12.0	27.6	25.7	24.2	23.0	21.9	21.0
13.0	27.3	25.3	23.7	22.5	21.4	20.5
14.0	26.9	24.8	23.2	21.9	20.8	19.9
15.0	26.5	24.3	22.6	21.3	20.2	19.3
16.0	26.1	23.7	22.0	20.7	19.6	18.7
17.0	25.6	23.2	21.4	20.1	19.1	18.2
18.0	25.1	22.6	20.8	19.5	18.5	17.6

Observation: The higher the annual interest rate on a 30-year mortgage, the more it will shorten by making extra payments towards the principal.

Loan duration in years

Rate (%)	Monthly Addition per $10,000 for a 30-Year Loan					
	$7.00	$8.00	$9.00	$10.00	$12.00	$15.00
3.00	23.7	23.0	22.4	21.8	20.7	19.2
3.25	23.7	23.0	22.3	21.7	20.6	19.1
3.50	23.6	22.9	22.3	21.7	20.6	19.1
3.75	23.6	22.9	22.2	21.6	20.5	19.0
4.00	23.5	22.8	22.2	21.6	20.4	19.0
4.25	23.5	22.8	22.1	21.5	20.4	18.9
4.50	23.4	22.7	22.0	21.4	20.3	18.8
4.75	23.3	22.6	22.0	21.4	20.2	18.8
5.00	23.3	22.6	21.9	21.3	20.2	18.7
5.25	23.2	22.5	21.8	21.2	20.1	18.6
5.50	23.1	22.4	21.7	21.1	20.0	18.5
5.75	23.0	22.3	21.7	21.0	19.9	18.5
6.00	22.9	22.2	21.6	21.0	19.8	18.4
6.25	22.9	22.2	21.5	20.9	19.7	18.3
6.50	22.8	22.1	21.4	20.8	19.7	18.2
6.75	22.7	22.0	21.3	20.7	19.6	18.1
7.00	22.6	21.9	21.2	20.6	19.5	18.0
7.25	22.5	21.8	21.1	20.5	19.4	17.9
7.50	22.4	21.7	21.0	20.4	19.3	17.8
7.75	22.3	21.6	20.9	20.3	19.1	17.7
8.00	22.2	21.5	20.8	20.2	19.0	17.6
8.25	22.1	21.3	20.7	20.0	18.9	17.5
8.50	22.0	21.2	20.6	19.9	18.8	17.4
8.75	21.8	21.1	20.4	19.8	18.7	17.3
9.00	21.7	21.0	20.3	19.7	18.6	17.2
9.25	21.6	20.9	20.2	19.6	18.5	17.1
9.50	21.5	20.8	20.1	19.5	18.4	17.0
9.75	21.4	20.6	20.0	19.3	18.2	16.8
10.0	21.2	20.5	19.8	19.2	18.1	16.7
10.5	21.0	20.3	19.6	19.0	17.9	16.5
11.0	20.7	20.0	19.3	18.7	17.6	16.3
11.5	20.5	19.7	19.1	18.5	17.4	16.0
12.0	20.2	19.5	18.8	18.2	17.1	15.8
13.0	19.6	18.9	18.3	17.7	16.6	15.3
14.0	19.1	18.4	17.7	17.1	16.1	14.9
15.0	18.5	17.8	17.2	16.6	15.6	14.4
16.0	18.0	17.3	16.7	16.1	15.2	14.0
17.0	17.4	16.8	16.2	15.6	14.7	13.6
18.0	16.9	16.2	15.7	15.2	14.3	13.2

Table 10.5: Total interest saved for a 30-year loan when extra payments are made to the principal each month. Column heading is the amount extra per month per $10,000 borrowed. Rate is an annual percentage rate.

Interest saved on a 30-year loan

Rate (%)	Monthly Addition per $10,000 for a 30-Year Loan					
	$1.00	$2.00	$3.00	$4.00	$5.00	$6.00
3.00	$214	$410	$591	$758	$913	$1,057
3.25	$238	$456	$657	$842	$1,013	$1,173
3.50	$264	$505	$726	$930	$1,118	$1,293
3.75	$291	$556	$799	$1,022	$1,228	$1,419
4.00	$319	$609	$875	$1,118	$1,343	$1,550
4.25	$349	$666	$954	$1,219	$1,462	$1,687
4.50	$381	$725	$1,038	$1,324	$1,587	$1,830
4.75	$414	$787	$1,125	$1,434	$1,718	$1,978
5.00	$449	$852	$1,217	$1,549	$1,853	$2,133
5.25	$485	$920	$1,313	$1,670	$1,995	$2,294
5.50	$524	$992	$1,413	$1,795	$2,143	$2,461
5.75	$565	$1,067	$1,519	$1,926	$2,297	$2,635
6.00	$608	$1,147	$1,629	$2,063	$2,457	$2,816
6.25	$653	$1,229	$1,744	$2,206	$2,624	$3,004
6.50	$700	$1,316	$1,864	$2,354	$2,797	$3,200
6.75	$751	$1,408	$1,990	$2,510	$2,978	$3,402
7.00	$803	$1,503	$2,121	$2,671	$3,165	$3,613
7.25	$859	$1,604	$2,258	$2,840	$3,360	$3,831
7.50	$917	$1,709	$2,402	$3,015	$3,563	$4,056
7.75	$979	$1,819	$2,551	$3,197	$3,773	$4,290
8.00	$1,044	$1,934	$2,707	$3,387	$3,991	$4,532
8.25	$1,112	$2,055	$2,870	$3,584	$4,217	$4,783
8.50	$1,183	$2,182	$3,040	$3,789	$4,451	$5,041
8.75	$1,259	$2,314	$3,217	$4,002	$4,693	$5,309
9.00	$1,338	$2,452	$3,401	$4,222	$4,944	$5,585
9.25	$1,422	$2,597	$3,592	$4,451	$5,203	$5,869
9.50	$1,509	$2,748	$3,792	$4,688	$5,471	$6,163
9.75	$1,602	$2,906	$3,999	$4,934	$5,748	$6,465
10.0	$1,698	$3,071	$4,214	$5,188	$6,033	$6,776
10.5	$1,907	$3,422	$4,669	$5,723	$6,631	$7,425
11.0	$2,137	$3,803	$5,158	$6,293	$7,265	$8,110
11.5	$2,390	$4,216	$5,683	$6,900	$7,935	$8,831
12.0	$2,668	$4,663	$6,243	$7,543	$8,641	$9,587
13.0	$3,305	$5,661	$7,475	$8,940	$10,162	$11,204
14.0	$4,063	$6,806	$8,857	$10,483	$11,822	$12,954
15.0	$4,957	$8,103	$10,387	$12,166	$13,614	$14,828
16.0	$5,996	$9,554	$12,061	$13,982	$15,529	$16,817
17.0	$7,189	$11,155	$13,870	$15,920	$17,555	$18,908
18.0	$8,541	$12,899	$15,805	$17,968	$19,680	$21,089

Observation: Making relatively small extra payments towards the principal on an average size 30-year mortgage will save tens of thousands of dollars in finance charges.

Interest saved on a 30-year loan

Rate (%)	Monthly Addition per $10,000 for a 30-Year Loan					
	$7.00	$8.00	$9.00	$10.00	$12.00	$15.00
3.00	$1,191	$1,317	$1,435	$1,546	$1,748	$2,012
3.25	$1,321	$1,460	$1,589	$1,711	$1,933	$2,223
3.50	$1,456	$1,608	$1,750	$1,883	$2,126	$2,441
3.75	$1,597	$1,762	$1,917	$2,061	$2,325	$2,667
4.00	$1,743	$1,922	$2,090	$2,246	$2,532	$2,900
4.25	$1,896	$2,089	$2,270	$2,439	$2,745	$3,142
4.50	$2,054	$2,263	$2,457	$2,638	$2,967	$3,391
4.75	$2,219	$2,443	$2,650	$2,844	$3,196	$3,648
5.00	$2,391	$2,629	$2,851	$3,058	$3,432	$3,913
5.25	$2,569	$2,823	$3,060	$3,279	$3,677	$4,186
5.50	$2,754	$3,025	$3,275	$3,508	$3,929	$4,468
5.75	$2,946	$3,233	$3,499	$3,745	$4,190	$4,757
6.00	$3,146	$3,449	$3,730	$3,990	$4,458	$5,055
6.25	$3,353	$3,673	$3,969	$4,243	$4,735	$5,362
6.50	$3,567	$3,905	$4,216	$4,504	$5,021	$5,677
6.75	$3,790	$4,144	$4,471	$4,773	$5,314	$6,000
7.00	$4,020	$4,392	$4,735	$5,051	$5,616	$6,332
7.25	$4,258	$4,648	$5,006	$5,337	$5,927	$6,672
7.50	$4,504	$4,912	$5,286	$5,631	$6,246	$7,021
7.75	$4,758	$5,185	$5,575	$5,934	$6,574	$7,378
8.00	$5,021	$5,466	$5,872	$6,246	$6,910	$7,744
8.25	$5,293	$5,756	$6,178	$6,566	$7,255	$8,118
8.50	$5,573	$6,054	$6,493	$6,895	$7,609	$8,500
8.75	$5,861	$6,361	$6,816	$7,233	$7,971	$8,891
9.00	$6,159	$6,677	$7,148	$7,579	$8,341	$9,290
9.25	$6,465	$7,002	$7,489	$7,934	$8,720	$9,697
9.50	$6,780	$7,335	$7,839	$8,298	$9,108	$10,112
9.75	$7,103	$7,677	$8,197	$8,670	$9,503	$10,535
10.0	$7,436	$8,028	$8,564	$9,051	$9,907	$10,966
10.5	$8,128	$8,757	$9,323	$9,838	$10,740	$11,850
11.0	$8,855	$9,520	$10,117	$10,658	$11,604	$12,765
11.5	$9,618	$10,317	$10,944	$11,511	$12,499	$13,709
12.0	$10,415	$11,148	$11,803	$12,395	$13,424	$14,680
13.0	$12,109	$12,906	$13,616	$14,254	$15,359	$16,701
14.0	$13,930	$14,786	$15,545	$16,225	$17,398	$18,817
15.0	$15,870	$16,778	$17,581	$18,298	$19,532	$21,018
16.0	$17,916	$18,870	$19,712	$20,462	$21,748	$23,294
17.0	$20,057	$21,052	$21,927	$22,705	$24,038	$25,635
18.0	$22,282	$23,312	$24,216	$25,019	$26,391	$28,033

The most important pattern to note in Tables 10.4 and 10.5 is that *the benefits of putting extra money toward the principal each month are magnified for loans at high interest rates.* A 30-year, $100,000 mortgage at 6% annual interest shortens to 27.5 years if you pay an extra $20 per month towards the principal (or $2.00 per $10,000 borrowed) and saves $11,470 in finance charges. But, if the interest rate is 14%, the same extra $20 per month put towards a $100,000, 30-year mortgage shortens the duration to 24.8 years and saves $68,060 in finance charges. This effect is true for any loan, not just mortgages. If you have a $10,000 credit card balance with 18% annual interest, just adding an additional $5 to $10 per month above the required minimum payment can lead to dramatic savings in finance charges and greatly reduce the time it takes to pay off the debt.

Here are further examples for the use of Tables 10.4 and 10.5:

Example 10.13

Planning for college

You and your spouse purchase a new home and begin a family at the same time. Ideally, you would like the house paid for in 19 years so that when your child begins college, your monthly mortgage costs can go towards tuition payments. Your initial mortgage is for $110,000 with an 8% annual interest and monthly payments towards principal and interest are $807.18. How much extra should you pay each month to end the mortgage after 19 years?

Follow the 8% row in Table 10.4 until you find 19 years. That is under the $12 per $10,000 per month column. Divide $110,000 by $10,000 to get 11. If you add an additional 12 x $11, or $132 to the $807.18 monthly payment, bringing it to $939.18 per month, the mortgage will be paid off in 19 years. You can think of the $132 per month as a completely risk-free way of saving for college. In Table 10.5 go to the intersection of the $12 column with the 8% row, and you will

find that your total interest savings is 11 x $6910, or $76,010.
The savings alone pays for the college education.

**[Worksheet A8.a, Table 10.4: Rate = 8.0%, Time = 19 years, Principal =
$110,000; Result is Additional Monthly Payment = $132]**
**[Worksheet A9.c, Table 10.5: Principal = $110,000, Rate = 8.0%, Additional
Monthly Payment = $132; Result is Interest Saved = $76,010]**

Example 10.14

The real cost of PMI

*You need a $120,000 mortgage with a 7.75% annual interest
rate to buy a house. An additional $60 per month must be paid
for private mortgage insurance (PMI). If you did not have to
pay PMI, but instead applied the $60 per month towards the
loan balance, by how much would the loan shorten and how
much would you save?*

The number of $10,000 amounts you need to borrow is
$120,000 divided by $10,000, or 12. The $60 per month
divided by 12 equals $5 extra per $10,000 borrowed. In Table
10.4 the intersection of the 7.75% row with the $5 column
shows 23.9 years. The corresponding intersection in Table
10.5 shows $3773 per $10,000 saved. For this example, the
savings would be 12 x $3773, or $45,276.

**[Worksheet A8.c, Table 10.4: Principal = $120,000, Rate = 7.75%, Additional
Monthly Payment = $60; Result is Time = 23.9 years]**
**[Worksheet A9.c, Table 10.5: Principal = $120,000, Rate = 7.75%, Additional
Monthly Payment = $60; Result is Interest Saved = $45,276]**

If possible, PMI should be avoided because while you pay for
it, the lender's risk is insured, not yours. If you can put a down
payment equal to 20% of the purchase price PMI is not required,
and it is usually not required on second mortgages. If you do not
have 20% of the purchase price, one strategy to avoid PMI is to
get two mortgages. Have a primary mortgage equal to 80% of the
purchase price and a second mortgage equal to the difference.

Example 10.15

Avoiding PMI with a "piggyback" mortgage

As in Example 10.14, you need a $120,000 mortgage to buy a house. How would monthly payments compare for the following two options? (a) A single $120,000 mortgage with a 7.75% annual interest rate and $60 per month PMI, (b) A primary 30-year mortgage for 80% of $120,000, or $104,000 with a 7.75% annual interest rate and a second 15-year mortgage with a 9% annual interest rate for the remaining $16,000 and no PMI.

For the first option, if you get just one $120,000 30-year mortgage, Table 10.1 shows that you must pay 12 x $71.64, or $859 plus $60 PMI for a total of $919 per month. The second option requires monthly payments of 10.4 x $71.64, or $745 on the primary mortgage. For the second 15-year mortgage at 9% (second mortgages usually have higher interest rates) for the remaining $16,000, the monthly payments would be 1.6 x $101.43, or $162. Your principal and interest payment each month for the two mortgages would be $162 + $745, or $907. Getting two mortgages in this manner would lower your total monthly payments by $12 per month and build equity faster because no money would go towards PMI. Also, while home mortgage interest is tax deductible, PMI is not.

[Worksheet A5.a, Table 10.1: Rate = 7.75%, Duration = 30 years, Principal = $120,000; Result is Monthly Payment = $859]
[Worksheet A5.a, Table 10.1: Rate = 7.75%, Duration = 30 years, Principal = $104,000; Result is Monthly Payment = $745]
[Worksheet A5.a, Table 10.1: Rate = 9%, Duration = 15 years, Principal = $16,000; Result is Monthly Payment = $162]

Many lenders will work with cash-poor homebuyers to set up these so-called "piggyback" second mortgages. It is worth checking into, but be careful: if your credit isn't sterling, unfavorable terms might be worked into the second mortgage. It might have a variable interest rate and prepayment penalties. Shop around and ask lots of questions before signing any agreements.

Bi-weekly Mortgages

Many new mortgage holders receive a letter shortly after settlement that offers to convert their new monthly loan to a bi-weekly loan. For example, if your monthly payments are $1000, a bi-weekly loan requires $500 payments every two weeks. For people who are paid bi-weekly, converting to bi-weekly payments is an attractive way to budget money. The letter will also argue that bi-weekly payments will reduce a 30-year loan by seven to eight years, depending on the interest rate. I have received these letters and found the math to be absolutely correct and the arguments for converting the monthly loan to bi-weekly payments manipulative and deceptive.

One letter I received stated, "Bi-weekly payments will still pay off your loan years *faster* than adding extra to monthly payments." The emphasis on the word "faster" is theirs. To support this claim, the letter uses as an example borrowing $110,000 at 7.5% annual interest with total monthly payments for 30 years (including escrow) of $1000. If bi-weekly payments of $500 are made, the loan will be paid off in 22 years with a total savings of $51,310 in interest. If instead $50 is added each month to the $1000 payment, the loan term is reduced to 24 years with a total savings of $36,762.

The letter goes on to state that to switch to bi-weekly payments requires a "non-refundable origination fee of $395" and a "standard transfer fee of $3.50 that is added to each bi-weekly payment to cover processing charges." On the subject of these additional charges the letter states, "Compare this small charge to the tens of thousands of dollars you can save with bi-weekly payments."

Clearly the bank wants the reader to believe that there is some mathematical magic with bi-weekly payments that will accomplish more than making extra payments towards the principal each month. To access this magic the reader will gladly pay all the additional charges and fees. Actually this letter is deceptive because while the math is correct, it is comparing "apples to oranges" rather than "apples to apples." If a mortgage that requires 12 payments per year of $1000 is converted to 26 bi-weekly payments of $500 each, the yearly total becomes $13,000 rather than $12,000. An extra $1000 per year divided by 12 amounts to $83 per month put towards the principal, not $50. Of course putting $83 per month extra towards the principal will pay down a loan faster than putting an extra $50 per month.

The fact is anyone can realize the savings of bi-weekly payments without all the additional fees. Every two weeks, set aside money equal to one half of your mortgage payment. Every month pay the mortgage with an additional amount equal to one twelfth of one month's payment. For the example given in the letter, $500 would be set aside every two weeks, and $1083 would be paid every month. If this is done, $13,000 per year will be set aside for mortgage payments and $13,000 will be paid out.

It should also be noted that the escrow portion of a mortgage varies between locations and in time. Real estate taxes and hazard insurance depend on where you live and tend to increase as time passes. The bank's letter urging a switch to bi-weekly payments uses a "typical" escrow payment in their calculation. Nowhere in the letter does it state that the fixed portion of the monthly payment—the principal and interest—is $769 for $110,000 loan with 7.5% annual interest. (That fact can be calculated using Worksheet A5.a and Table 10.1.) That means that your payments would be $769 plus whatever escrow applies to your location. To know when the loan is paid off for your situation, determine the amount extra per month applied to the principal with bi-weekly budgeting and use Worksheet A8.a and Table 10.4.

Example 10.16

Bi-weekly budgeting

You have a 30-year, $110,000 mortgage with 7.5% annual interest and monthly payments towards the principal and interest of $769. Your monthly contribution to the escrow account is $151, bringing your total payment every month to $920. You decide to switch to bi-weekly budgeting where you pay $920 divided by 2, or $460 every two weeks. How long will it take to pay off the mortgage? How much interest will you save?

By doing this, you will pay an extra $920 divided by 12, or $77 extra each month. The number of $10,000 amounts borrowed is $110,000 divided by $10,000, or 11. That means you are paying $77 divided by 11, or $7 extra per $10,000 borrowed towards the principal. Look down the $7 column of Table 10.4 to the row for 7.5% annual interest. The new time is 22.4 years. In the $7 column of Table 10.5, the interest saved is $4504 per $10,000 borrowed. Total interest saved is 11 x $4504, or $49,544.

[Worksheet A8.c, Table 10.4: Principal = $110,000, Rate = 7.5%, Additional Monthly Payment = $77; Result is Time = 22.4 years]
[Worksheet A9.c, Table 10.5: Principal = $110,000, Rate = 7.5%, Additional Monthly Payment = $77; Result is Interest Saved = $49,544]

Low Interest Rates versus Low Prices

The psychology that makes 0% financing such an effective sales tool for automobile companies also influences home purchases. During the early 2000s a drop in mortgage rates to record lows spurred a furious bidding war on houses that drove prices to record highs. People feel compelled to pay almost any price for a house if they can lock in a "once in a generation" low interest rate. I find this behavior strange because homes can be re-financed if interest rates drop, but sale prices can never be renegotiated. For example, I purchased my house in the early 1990s when interest rates were in the high single digits. My first 30-year mortgage at 8.5% cost $76.89 per $10,000 borrowed (see Table 10.1). Less than 10 years later I was in the same house but with a different 15-year mortgage at 5% that costs $79.08 per $10,000 borrowed. Without substantially changing my monthly payments, I shortened the length of the mortgage by years by re-financing at the lower interest rates. During the first 10 years that I owned my house, its value increased by over 50% because of the strong demand for housing brought on by the lower interest rates. But homebuyers in the early 2000s, who receive record low financing, will never be able to lower their payments at a later date by re-financing when rates drop and they will always be responsible for the full purchase price paid. If demand for housing drops when rates rise, the homebuyer risks becoming trapped in the house because of negative equity.

I am not recommending that home buying be avoided when interest rates are low any more than I am recommending that you never accept a 0% finance offer on an automobile. My argument is that the total cost of the purchase, including both price and financing be considered together. There are limits to how much extra you should pay on a purchase to reduce the financing. *Paying extra at the time of purchase to reduce finance charges in the future always entails risk.* Many loans do not go for their full duration. The car or home must be sold; rates drop to trigger a refinancing; an unexpected bonus at work allows you to pay off the loan early. When the loan is paid off early, the benefit of a reduced finance charge that you paid extra for is lost.

Historically, homes purchased at any point in time are a good investment. Even if interest rates are high, a home can be a good investment if a "buyer's market" has resulted. But, take care to shop for the most competitive financing and avoid "sub-prime" mortgages. If you don't qualify for a competitive rate on a mortgage, consider waiting on a home purchase.

Summary

When evaluating loans, consider the total cost, not the monthly payment. The total cost of the loan is the amount paid out over the life of the loan minus the cash price. That difference might have many labels: interest, finance charge, rebate, points, transaction fee, origination fee, or service fee. Whatever the label, it amounts to the same thing, the payment for the use of someone else's money. Lenders use different labels for finance charges to make comparison-shopping for loans difficult. But if you add all the costs specified in a loan agreement, you can use the tables and worksheets in this book to determine an *effective interest rate* for any financing offer. *It is the effective interest rates that should be compared when shopping for financing.*

Do not fall into the monthly payment trap that amounts to working for the modern version of the company store. Lenders want their monthly payments to become a permanent part of your budget. Always plan on debt as being temporary. Learn to set aside money instead for savings and investments.

"We're required to by law."

If someone takes $200 out of your wallet, you would notice. But if a bank tacks on an extra $200 to a six-figure loan, few people notice. Mental accounting, discussed in Chapter 8, also applies to borrowing. A large sum of money paid back over many years goes into a different mental account than cash.

I was taken for an extra $200 in a mortgage refinancing in the following manner. I borrowed $134,000 at 6.95% for a 15-year loan. The bank deposited the entire amount I borrowed in my money market account (which was with the same bank) on the 29th of the month and wired the money needed to pay off my existing mortgage to my old lender. Thirty-three days later, on the first of the following month, I made my first payment of $1202 and I received a bank statement showing that I now owed $133,843.

I took the statement to the bank to question that figure. The daily interest accrued on the $134,000 I owed over that time period was $25.51; multiply that by 32 days and that's $841. My first payment should have reduced the principal by $361, not the $157 shown on the statement. Why the discrepancy?

There is a federal law concerning second mortgages and refinances that allows the borrower to call off the deal anytime within three business days *after* the settlement. Therefore banks must wait three business days before making any payoffs. I signed the bank note on Tuesday the 23rd; but three business days, followed by the weekend, meant no money changed hands until Monday the 29th. However the bank officer explained that I was obligated for the money the moment I signed the note. The conversation went like this:

"So during those six days I was paying interest on two mortgages?"

"Yes"

"So then I should receive six days of money market interest on the $134,000."

"No, it wasn't in your account until the 29th."

"But you're saying I owed you the money during those six days and it didn't go to pay off the old mortgage. Then the money must have been in my possession."

"No, we're required by law not to pay out the money until the end of the rescission period."

Talk about having something both ways. This is like flipping a two-headed quarter where the bank gets to call heads.

A large regional bank generates thousands of mortgages per year. That means this scam alone generates $200,000 for every thousand loans, enough to pay all the tellers at one branch for a year. Few people notice, and those like myself who do, find it not worth their time and effort to challenge any further.

How did they sneak this by in the loan documents? Some post-mortem mathematical analysis is even more revealing. Table 10.1 shows that for a 15-year, 7% loan, I should pay $89.88 per $10,000 borrowed, so for a $134,000 loan that payment would be $89.88 x 13.4, or $1204.39. Since the interest rate is 6.95%, a slightly lower payment of $1202.74 sounded reasonable when I signed the papers. However a precise calculation performed using the 6.95% interest rate shows that payments for such a loan should be $1200.68. It appears the bank added nine days of interest, $230, to the original loan and calculated monthly payments over 15 years assuming that I borrowed $134,230, which must be how they arrived at $1202.74. They lumped the extra $230 in with the total $82,495 finance charge stated on the promissory note so it would still look like I was only borrowing $134,000. Usually interest needed to finish a month is listed separately on the settlement sheet as a closing cost, but this loan was sold as a "bank pays closing costs" deal. Why the nine days of interest? The bank planned on settling on Monday the 22nd; it was my work schedule that prevented me from coming in until Tuesday the 23rd. It appears that I became obligated for the money the day the bank was ready for me to sign the note, not the day I actually did, because nine days after the 22nd is the 31st of the month. By the way, have I mentioned this happened in April?

Chapter 10 Resources

Elizabeth Warren and Amelia Warren Tyagi in *The Two Income Trap: Why Middle-Class Mothers and Fathers Are Going Broke* (New York: Basic Books, 2003) provide an account of how deregulated interest rates have resulted in predatory lending practices. The authors explain why banks make more money lending to the people who can least afford to borrow money. More frightening is that Congress, rather than limiting predatory lending, passed a bill in 2005 to make it more difficult for families to seek bankruptcy protection.

Robert D. Manning in *Credit Card Nation: The Consequences of America's Addiction to Credit* (New York: Basic Books, 2003) examines the profound social changes that have resulted from the increased reliance on credit cards by middle class families to maintain their life styles. Manning provides numerous case studies that profile the lives of people with out of control debt.

The Delphi Corporation's *Monthly Interest and Amortization Tables* (New York: McGraw-Hill Trade, 1994) has an extensive compilation of tables for loan payments and interest charges.

Part IV

Misunderstood Math

CHAPTER ELEVEN

Voting

Number-Dropping

"Look, the problem is that under Governor Bush's planned, $1.6 trillion tax cut, mostly to the wealthy, under his own budget numbers, he proposes spending more money for a tax cut just for the wealthiest 1% than all the new money he budgets for education, health care and national defense combined. Now under my plan we'll balance the budget every year. I'm not just saying this. I'm not just talking. I have helped to balance the budget for the first time in 30 years, paid down the debt, and under my plan, in four years, federal spending will be the smallest that it has been in 50 years."

—Al Gore
The Third 2000 Gore-Bush Presidential Debate
October 17, 2000

"The Vice President believes only the right people ought to get tax relief. I don't think that's the role of the president to pick you're right and you're not right. I think if you're going to have tax relief, everybody ought to get it. And therefore, wealthy people are going to get it. But the top 1% will end up paying one-third of the taxes in America and they get one-fifth of the benefits. And that's because we structured the plan so that six million additional American families pay no taxes. If you're a family of four making $50,000 in Missouri, you get a 50% cut in your federal income taxes. What I've done is set priorities and funded them. And there's extra money."

—George Bush
The Third 2000 Gore-Bush Presidential Debate
October 17, 2000

Here is a parlor game to play—count the numbers in a speech. In just the short exchange quoted, Gore cited five numbers (1.6 trillion, 1%, 30, four, 50) and Bush cited seven numbers (1%, one-third, one-fifth, 6 million, four, 50,000, 50%). Of course I had to read the transcripts of the debates carefully to figure that out. When I listened to the actual live debate it was not possible for me to digest all of their numerical data. Clearly both Bush and Gore did their homework in preparation for the debate. The level of numerical detail in each quote above is impressive. But making sense of all their numbers is another matter. I do not know the factual basis for any of the numbers in these quotes from Bush and Gore, and I do not believe that they know the basis themselves.

People, who give speeches, make presentations, engage in public debates, and market products, love to quote numbers and statistics. Sprinkle the speech with enough specific numerical details, and it appears to the listener that the speaker actually studied the issue and knows what he or she is talking about. Does the speaker actually know the factual basis for the numbers he or she is quoting? You will never know. The practice is similar to name-dropping. Try to determine exactly how well a name-dropper knows the people he or she mentions.

In the three chapters that form the last part of this book, I will discuss numbers and their use. I will explain how scientists use numbers and contrast the scientific understanding with how the general public makes sense of numbers. The topics I cover will move beyond purely personal financial decisions, to decisions such as voting that are still financially related. We do not usually think of voting as a financial decision, but politicians seeking votes often address "pocketbook issues." In the quotes at the beginning of this chapter, it is clear that Bush and Gore are trying to assure potential voters that their proposed tax and spending policies will benefit the family budget. Their reason for appealing to the financial self-interest of voters is that federal tax rates, social security benefits, and government-funded jobs do impact everyone's personal finances.

Voting is just one example of a personal decision with indirect financial consequences. In the final part of this book I will discuss other examples of personal decisions with indirect financial consequences. Topics will include: risk assessment, medical treatments, news reporting, and the testing of both legal and illegal drugs. Numbers appear repeatedly in all of these contexts and affect the personal decisions people make. Many of these decisions have financial consequences. People give great weight to numbers when making decisions because numerical data is assumed to be objective. An argument based on numerical comparison is hard to assail because who can argue with the principle that "more is better than less." It is for this reason that proponents for any issue love to "drop numbers" into their arguments. However, we will learn that many number-based arguments are deceptive and can easily be assailed once the context and factual basis for the numbers is understood.

In this chapter on voting, I will first explain the difference between numerical precision and accuracy. You will learn how and why scientists make a careful distinction between precision and accuracy when they consider numerical data. Once this distinction is understood I will discuss some recent high-stakes political events and show how controversies resulted because the legal system fails to distinguish between precision and accuracy. While the examples I use in this chapter are political, the concepts developed apply to *all* kinds of numerical data, including financial figures. Whenever you are asked to make any kind of a decision based on quantitative data you should question both the precision and accuracy of the numbers.

The Myth that Precise Means Accurate

Precision refers to the actual number of *meaningful* digits in the number. The scientific term for the number of meaningful digits is "significant figures." I will explain the criteria for determining how many figures are "significant" in the next section. First, let me begin with examples to show what "significant figures" means. The number 3 has one significant figure, while the number 3.049 has four significant figures. The latter number with four significant figures is more precise. As a general rule, the more precise a number, the more credibility people give it. Speakers usually avoid talking about quantities in general terms because they know that an audience is more impressed if the numbers quoted have at least two significant figures. In the debate quotes given, Gore does not say "more than a trillion dollar tax cut." He says, "$1.6 trillion tax cut." Bush does not say, "your taxes will be cut in half." He says, "you get a 50% cut." Bush also does not refer to a "typical" or "average" American family. Instead he refers to a "family of four making $50,000 in Missouri." But are these precise numbers also accurate? Many people would not understand this question because for many people precision and accuracy are synonymous. People assume that the more precise a number, the more effort and knowledge must have gone into the calculation or measurement that produced the number. Therefore, precision implies accuracy. This is a faulty line of reasoning and its widespread belief allows people to be manipulated by mathematically deceptive arguments.

Precision

Scientists do not use the terms "precision" and "accuracy" synonymously. The concept of precision can be illustrated by a joke a student of mine told me many years ago.

A man takes an underground tour inside a cave. The tour guide points to a large stalagmite and tells him, "That stalagmite is one million and four years old."

The man says, "Wow! How do they determine the age that exactly?"

"I don't know," replies the tour guide, "but four years ago when I started working here I was told the stalagmite was one million years old."

The humor in this joke arises because we know that when a geologist says that a stalagmite is one million years old, that does not mean the stalagmite is exactly 1,000,000 years old, and that next year the stalagmite will be exactly 1,000,001 years old. If geologists knew how to determine the age of a stalagmite to the nearest year, the tour guide would have been told something like that stalagmite is 1,050,302 years old and then adding the four additional years that elapsed since being told the age would make sense. But what exactly does it mean when a scientist says that a stalagmite is one million years old, or that the Earth is 93 million miles from the Sun, or that the world population is 6.4 billion people? None of these numbers is meaningful to the nearest year or mile or person because each of these numbers is the result of a measurement.

Every measuring technique ever devised has a finite *precision* associated with it. Different measuring techniques have different precisions, some more precise than others. Scientists are always careful to express numbers that result from a measurement in a way that communicates the precision. If a geologist claimed that the stalagmite is 1,050,302 years old, that is a precision of seven significant figures and means that the age measurement technique is known to the nearest year. All seven digits in this number are significant so adding four years, an operation that only affects the last digit in this number, is valid. But, if a geologist claims the stalagmite is one million years old, that is a precision of only one significant figure. Only the one digit in the millions place is significant so adding an additional four years of time makes no sense.

Notating significant figures

Setting the humor aside, the joke above does reveal a serious ambiguity that arises when writing about numbers. If the stalagmite is exactly 1,000,000 years old and all seven digits are significant, how is this number distinguished from the case of 1,000,000 years old when only the first digit is significant? In other words, if the number ends with many zeros, how do we indicate which zeros are significant? To indicate the numbers of zeros that are significant, it is necessary to have some conventions.

The approach most writers take is to use the standard Arabic numerals for the significant digits, and words for insignificant zeros. For example:

1 million years has one significant figure. That means that if this number were written out using all numerals, the six zeros following the one would not be significant.

1.00 million years has three significant figures. The first two zeros following the one are significant. If this number were written using all numerals by moving the decimal point six places to the right, the four zeros that need to be filled in are not significant.

1.000000 million years has seven significant figures. In this case the stalagmite is exactly 1,000,000 years old.

For decimal fractions, the zeros that appear between the decimal point and first non-zero digit are *not* significant figures. Zeros added at the end of the fraction are significant and indicate greater precision. For example:

0.003 seconds has one significant figure, the three. The zeros preceding the three are not significant.

0.00300 seconds has three significant figures. The three and the two zeros that follow the three are significant. Again the zeros preceding the three are not significant.

0.0035710 seconds has five significant figures. The four non-zero figures and the zero that follows are significant.

Words can also be used for decimal fractions. The numbers above can be written as 3 thousandths second, 3.00 thousandths second, and 3.5710 thousandths second respectively. Again Arabic numerals are used for the significant figures and the word "thousandths" indicates the location of the decimal point. But the use of words for decimal fractions is not as critical because zeros between the decimal point and the first non-zero digit to the right are *never* significant. In contrast, for numbers that are not decimal fractions, zeros between the decimal point and first non-zero digit to the left may or may not be significant. Therefore, combining numerals with words is a useful technique for indicating the number of significant digits for non-fractions. In the next chapter I will explain *scientific notation*, which is simply a compact mathematical notation to indicate the location of the decimal point and avoid the use of words and all their resulting ambiguities.

Determining the number of significant figures

The appropriate number of significant figures to use when writing a measured value is determined by the precision of the measuring technique. Most people have an innate understanding of the limited precision of all measurements, even though they do not know about the concept of significant figures. For example, consider measurements of distance. To know the distance that you drive to work each day, you use the odometer on your car. The odometer measures distances to the nearest tenth of a mile. Expressed as a decimal fraction, any distance measurement in miles that uses the odometer has just one significant figure following the decimal point. A distance measurement might be 5.2 miles, but it is not correct to write 5.20 miles because that implies that the distance is known to the nearest hundredth of a mile, a precision the odometer lacks.

A distance measurement that requires a much higher precision needs a different measuring device. A machinist fabricating metal parts on a lathe needs to measure distances to the nearest thousandth of an inch. For this level of precision, machinists use a device called a "caliper" for measuring the dimensions of the parts they fabricate. With a caliper, a machinist can measure the difference between a part that is 1.375 inches wide and one that is 1.373 inches wide, discernment to the nearest thousandth of an inch that justifies writing three significant figures after the decimal point (four total significant figures).

But does this mean that the more precise a measuring technique, the more credible and desirable it is? Actually, in most cases the highest possible precision is not desirable. It would be a waste of time and money to always use the highest possible precision in a measurement. For any measurement, the technique chosen has to have a level of precision that is appropriate and practical for the problem. Too much precision can be as impractical as too little. Consider measuring the length of your driveway to pour concrete. You would not use the odometer on your car to measure the length of your driveway. The precision of about one tenth of a mile is useless for determining lengths to even the nearest yard. But devising a technique to measure the length of the driveway to the nearest thousandth of an inch would be a complete waste of time. In this case the appropriate measuring device is a tape measure and the precision needed is to the nearest inch.

Most people know to use the correct measuring tool for the job and do not obsess over unnecessary levels of precision. But in this age of calculators with seven-digit displays, strange results occur when measurements are used in calculations. Consider a measurement of distance using an automobile odometer that results in 21 miles. This distance could be reported in inches. The result in inches would be 21 miles x 5280 feet per mile x 12 inches per foot, or 1.3 million inches. I would only write two digits of precision in the answer (1.3) because I only had two digits of precision in the measurement (21). But, many people would write the answer to this problem as 1,330,560 inches. However, 1,330,560 inches has a precision not present in the original measurement. Multiplying 21 miles by conversion factors to arrive at the same distance in inches does not increase its precision. You still only know the distance to the nearest tenth of a mile, not to the nearest inch. Therefore it is not correct to write more than two significant figures for the result. This observation can be stated as a general principle:

The Constancy of Precision

The use of conversion factors never increases the precision of a measurement.

The number of significant figures in a result is determined by the inherent limitations of the measurement technique used to obtain values that are the basis of the result. In fact we can generalize even further. *The number of significant figures for a value that results from any calculation is equal to the number of significant figures in the original measurement.*

Go back to our tour guide who adds 1 million + 4 to get 1,000,004, and note that each input for his calculation had one significant figure. That means the output can only have one significant figure, *which is always the leading digit*. The stalagmite is still 1 million years old. The remaining six digits that include the 4 are insignificant.

There is one final rule about significant figures. If the inputs to a calculation differ in their numbers of significant figures, it is the input with the fewest significant figures that determines the number in the output. When the tour guide retires after 35 years of service, the stalagmite is 1 million + 35 years, or 1 million years old. Despite two significant figures for the duration of service, the total time still has only one significant figure. The stalagmite remains 1 million years old.

Accuracy

Accuracy is a different concept from precision. If you put the wrong size tires on your car, you will not change the precision of your odometer. It will still record distance traveled to the nearest tenth of a mile. However, the distances recorded will be wrong. If you make an arithmetic mistake while subtracting purchases in your checkbook, the precision is still the same. The amounts are still in dollars and cents but the result is not accurate. Errors that produce inaccurate results do not change the precision. Scientists worry about two general types of errors that affect accuracy.

Systematic errors: Mistakes that bias the results in one direction. For example, if you put the wrong size tires on your car it will bias the odometer readings. If the tires are too large, the car travels farther forward with each tire revolution than the odometer records. As a result the odometer consistently under reports the mileage.

Random errors: Mistakes that could go in either direction. For example, subtraction errors in your checkbook result in a wrong balance that can be high or low.

Of these types of errors, systematic errors are the most worrisome and troubling. If a measurement is repeated numerous times, the random errors will tend to cancel out. An average of all the measurements will converge to an accurate result if the errors are random. But systematic errors are repeated the same way in each measurement and cannot average out. Taking an average of repeated measurements that are systematically biased will not improve accuracy. To understand systematic errors, consider another conversation I had with a student.

I did a problem on the board that ended with an answer of:

$$\frac{6.0}{1.9 \times 7.2} = 0.44$$

A student approached me after class and told me that his answer was 22.73684, not 0.44. He asked if I had made an error because his calculator had produced his result. Now the number 22.73684 is a very precise number, much more precise than the numbers in the equation can justify. Writing out 7 digits of precision when the equation only has 2 digits is equivalent to the tour guide in the cave adding 4 years to one million years and implying that the age of stalagmite is known to the nearest year.

But the student's result is nowhere close to accurate.

"Clearly your answer is wrong," I told him. "In the denominator you have a number a little less than 2 times a number a little more than 7 so the result must be close to 14. Divide six by a little more than 14 and the result must be slightly less than one half. It certainly cannot be greater than one."

"But I've checked it five times. I always get the same result."

"You are either using your calculator incorrectly or it is broken."

"No, that can't be; my calculator is working. The answer must be 22.7."

"Find the instruction manual for your calculator and read it. If you still get 22.7 after carefully following the instructions, then you need to have the calculator repaired or replaced."

"No the calculator is working. Let me show you."

He brought the calculator to me and pressed the keys: 6 / 1.9 x 7.2 = and the display lit up with the number 22.73684. "See," he said.

"Yes, I see your calculator is working fine. You need to use the parenthesis keys to enclose 1.9 x 7.2. Without the parentheses, the calculator is performing the operations in the order you entered them. 6 divided by 1.9 is 3.16. Multiply 3.16 by 7.2, and the result is 22.7. But that's not the problem you are trying to solve."

There are three points to note about this conversation:

- *The degree of precision in a result is not related to its accuracy.* Even if the calculator has seven significant digits of precision in the display, that means nothing if the problem is done incorrectly.

- *Repeating the same error reproduces the same wrong result.* This is what is meant by a systematic error. It does not matter that the calculation was repeated five times. A mistake will not become correct through the act of repetition.

•*Judging accuracy requires an understanding of the problem before it is undertaken.* I know before even picking up a calculator that the result must be less than one because I understand that any fraction with a denominator greater than its numerator represents a number less than one. My student did not have that understanding and was not able to make that judgment.

The ability to judge accuracy is most important, and it requires knowledge and understanding of the problem. Often highly precise numbers are used to cover up a lack of understanding. Scientists always worry about accuracy first and precision later. Once a scientist is confident that the measuring technique used is accurate, he or she will then refine the technique to obtain more precision. Putting in effort to be precise before it is certain that the technique is free of systematic errors can be an embarrassing waste of time and money. The refinement effort will be done later, and then only if greater precision is needed. Often high precision is not necessary. For many people it is the other way around. Precision comes first because it lends credibility. Few people want to put in the effort needed to understand whether the result is accurate.

Elections and Laws

The failure to understand the difference between precision and accuracy has resulted in laws that from a scientific and mathematical point of view make no sense. When a legal ruling depends on the precision and accuracy of measurements, bizarre legal reasoning can result if these concepts are not correctly considered. Let us go back to the year 2000, and consider two high-stakes political events that year and the legal issues that resulted. The outcome of each event depended on a measurement. In each case legal problems arose because the laws governing these events failed to adequately address issues of precision and accuracy.

2000 Florida Presidential Election

The chaos that followed the 2000 Florida presidential election occurred because the precision needed in the vote count to determine the winner did not exist. The election ended when the U.S. Supreme Court decision halted any further re-counting of votes. George Bush won the Florida election and with it the presidency. The final vote count was 2,912,790 for Bush and 2,912,253 for Gore. That means out of nearly 6 million votes cast, Bush won by 537. To discern such a slim margin of victory requires a precision in the vote count of at least five significant figures. The immediate question that followed the Florida election was the following: are vote counts that precise?

A fair question, but in the days following the election, a great deal of the rhetoric focused on issues of accuracy. The Democrats complained about the "butterfly ballot" with a confusing layout that they contended fooled people into voting for a different candidate than intended. Voter rolls had been purged of convicted felons prior to the election, and Democrats alleged that in the process many legally registered voters had also been dropped from the rolls. Inadequate voting equipment in traditionally Democratic areas had resulted in long lines that discouraged many people in those areas from voting. But none of these issues has anything to do with the precision of the vote count. All of these issues relate to the accuracy of the results because each of these problems produces a systematic bias in the measurement. However, an election is by law a one-time measurement, and the only way to fix an inaccurate measurement is to repeat the process with the systematic biases removed. Unless the inaccuracies result from widespread criminal behavior, there are no legal grounds for repeating an election.

Election officials can do nothing about accuracy once people have voted. Their job is to arrive at a precise count of the votes cast. But are the procedures for counting votes so precise that a re-count of nearly six million votes would lead to the exact same numbers as the first count? As election officials struggled with re-counts the answer to that question appeared to be "no." Machines that read and tabulate the votes from punch-card ballots fail to record everyone. When election officials examined the ballots by hand, it became apparent that a standard would be needed to define a vote. The bits of paper, called "chads" that are punched out of the ballot by the voter, were in various states. An entire lexicon for "chads" arose in the weeks following the Florida election. Officials referred to chads as being either "dimpled," "pregnant" or "hanging." No pre-defined standards existed. As a result, no one seemed to know what reasonable precision could be expected in a count of six million votes. Republicans worried that recounting would not lead to the exact same numbers and with the vote totals so close might even result in Gore having a lead. Bush's campaign appealed to the courts, and after failing in the Florida State courts, was able to get the U.S. Supreme Court to intervene.

The Supreme Court chose a practical solution to the problem. They simply stopped any vote recounting, which meant the original results stood. But the Supreme Court never addressed the real issue—what should happen when the precision in the vote count needed to determine the winner is unobtainable? Instead, the Supreme Court came up with utterly bizarre legal reasoning that borders on nonsense. The court decided that hand recounts of votes in selected areas of Florida violated the equal protection clause in the fourteenth amendment to the Constitution because recounted votes would be treated differently from other votes. The conservative *National Review* while lauding Bush's election questioned the Supreme Court's reasons. Because different vote tabulation systems are used throughout Florida, and throughout the country, the *National Review* asked why "this line of reasoning wouldn't render Florida's entire electoral system unconstitutional. Or, for that matter, the nation's electoral system." Conservative columnist George Will has referred to the *Bush v. Gore* decision as a "ticking bomb." He warns that in the next closely contested presidential election the parties might unleash thousands of lawyers in a closely contested state to "ferret out equal protection violations."

The fact is, the issue of precision in a vote count, which has to do with the technical limitations of the voting tabulation and has nothing to do with accuracy of the election, has never been adequately addressed in our election laws or courts. Politicians continue to parrot the "every vote should count" dictum while failing to face the fact that when millions of votes are cast, our election machinery does not have one-vote precision in counting them anymore than geologists have one-year precision in determining the age of a stalagmite.

Congressional representation

Every 10 years a nationwide census is conducted to determine how many people live in each U.S. state and congressional district. That count provides the basis for apportioning congressional representation, determining each state's electoral votes, and redrawing boundaries for congressional districts. Enormous amounts of money are at stake in the results of the census. As congressional representation shifts in response to population shifts, so do federally funded programs, assistance, jobs, and projects. Each state and locality wants its share of federal largesse.

The results of the 2000 census include the following. The U.S. Census Bureau reported in its nationwide count that as of April 1, 2000, 281,421,906 people lived in the United States, which was an increase of 32,712,033 people since the April 1, 1990, count. These numbers are provided in a report that is available on their website at http://www.census.gov. The report includes a breakdown by state of the U.S. population. In it I learned that on April 1, 2000, Maryland had 5,296,486 people, and Georgia 8,186,453 people. I presume from this data, that had I not moved my family in 1992 from Georgia to Maryland that these numbers would have been 5,296,481 and 8,186,458 respectively because we are a family of five.

The Census Bureau provides incredibly precise numbers for their population counts, which leads people to believe that the numbers are accurate. Actually accuracy is not the primary goal of the U.S. Census, and the precision of the numbers provided is clearly unobtainable. There is no technique for measuring the U.S. population that would provide the eight significant figures of precision given in the census tables. For a population as large as the United States', the exact number of people present fluctuates by the minute as births, deaths, immigrants and emigrants continuously add and subtract people from the population. Even if a technique existed with enough precision to exactly count every single person in the United States that measurement would need to be applied at a precise instant in time, say 12:00 a.m. EST on April 1, 2000. Specifying a single day, such as April 1, 2000, is not a short enough time to meaningfully report an exact population count, because numerous births and deaths occurred throughout that day. A scientist interpreting the report, as a scientific document, would laugh at all the effort spent tabulating numbers with eight significant figures when clearly no more than three or four are justified. But, the census is not a "measurement" of the U.S. population in the scientific sense; rather it is a political act mandated by the U.S. Constitution using procedures dictated by Congress and the courts. The immediate purpose of the census is to apportion representation in the U.S. House of Representatives and as a result political considerations are of greater importance than the accuracy of the numbers.*

To conduct the census, the bureau first mails census forms to every known household and asks the residents to complete the form and return it by mail. Only about 60 to 70 percent of households actually comply with this initial request. A census

*The founders of the United States intended that representation in the House be based on population and the census was mandated for that reason. Originally the U.S. Constitution stipulated that representatives should not exceed one for every 30,000 people. The intent was that as the U.S. population grew, so should the House of Representatives. However, even having one representative for every 30,000 people quickly became unworkable. By 1910 House membership had grown to 435 members but the U.S. population had increased to about one hundred million people, which meant that each member represented about 200,000 people. A 1911 law fixed House membership at 435 members. Although the U.S. Constitution was never amended, House membership has stayed at 435 ever since that law. By the way, applying the original 1 per 30,000 formula to today's population would result in a U.S. House of Representatives with nearly 10,000 members.

taker is sent to actually knock on the doors of those who do not return the forms and ask how many people live in the house. The precise head count based on the forms mailed in and the census takers' canvassing is the number reported for the U.S. Census. The procedure works much like taking attendance at a public meeting. If you don't sign in or raise your hand to indicate your presence, you are absent. A scientist would not consider methods that rely so heavily on self-reporting and finding people at home, as providing an accurate measure of the population. In a small town with a stable population, a simple self-reported head count might work well, but in a large, densely populated urban area with people constantly moving around, sorting out who lives where is difficult. Any measurement of the population that uses self-reporting is systematically biased towards counting people who take the time to self-report. People who don't receive mail, don't read mail, don't respond to mail, and don't talk to census takers are not counted.

Prior to the 2000 census, the Clinton administration attempted to the change the methodology used by the census bureau. The proposed change was to measure the U.S. population in a scientifically meaningful manner with modern sampling techniques coupled with statistical analysis to correct for undercounts. That means that rather than attempt to count every single person, a representative sample of people from each locality would be counted and statistical methods used to infer from that sample the total number of people. Sampling methods are widely used in political polling and market research. If a polling firm wants to know what the population as a whole thinks about an issue, the firm does not contact every single person. Instead small groups of people who are representative of the larger population are polled.

Republicans in a Congress moved to block any change in method, and a flurry of lawsuits resulted. Republicans argue that sampling is the equivalent of polling. Elections are not decided by polling, and neither should Congressional representation. People who desire representation should participate in the census. Democrats counter that the census should provide a scientifically accurate measure of the population, and Congressional representation should include everyone.

Both sides can back their respective positions with lofty rhetoric, but scientific truth and civic engagement are not the primary concerns. Each side has political motivations for their position. Democrats fear that a measurement technique that is systematically biased towards undercounting people in cities will miss Democratic voters and deprive their party of Congressional seats. Republicans fear that statistical sampling methods are open to manipulation and distrust a Democratic administration to conduct them in a manner that is not biased towards eliminating Republican Congressional seats. Neither side makes an effort to understand the available techniques for conducting an accurate population count and the inherent limitations for each technique. Statistics is a complex and technically demanding discipline. For the political parties, the issue is not the best method to choose for an accurate count, but what method to use that will best benefit the party.*

In the lawsuits that resulted over the census methods, the courts sided with the Republicans. The basis for the court decisions is found in Article I, Section 2 of the U.S. Constitution that mandates the census and states:

> *"The actual Enumeration shall be made within three Years after the first Meeting of the Congress of the United States, and within every subsequent Term of ten Years, in such Manner as they shall by Law direct."*

---

*The manipulation of census data for political purposes has a long history in the United States and is enshrined in the U.S. Constitution itself. The southern states wanted their slaves counted in the census, but the northern states saw this as wanting to have it both ways. If slaves had no voting or property rights, why should their population count when determining Congressional representation? But politics is about compromise and numbers can always be manipulated. The final language in the Constitution became *"...Numbers, which shall be determined by adding to the whole Number of free Persons, including those bound to Service for a Term of Years, and excluding Indians not taxed, three-fifths of all other Persons."* That effectively meant that when it came to apportioning Representatives, slaves counted as three-fifths of a person, but when it came to voting they counted as zero. The Fourteenth and Fifteenth Amendments to the Constitution abolished this formula for counting and voting.

The courts have held that when the writers of the Constitution used the word "enumeration" they meant an actual head count, not a measurement of the population based on a statistical sampling. Of course the courts are correct because sampling techniques and statistical analysis did not exist in 1789 when the Constitution was written. The court's job is not science-related either. Its job is to determine what the framers of the Constitution meant when they wrote the document. A head count was the only method the framers could imagine.

The next time you receive a census form, bear in mind that if you don't fill it out and return it, you are not counted when Congressional representation is determined. Participating in the census is similar to participating in an election. Whatever count results in the end is by law the outcome. The systematic errors in the measurement techniques and the eight significant figures in the results might not make any sense scientifically, but scientific truth is not the point.**

Summary

Often we are asked to make decisions—many with financial implications—on the basis of numerical data. When presented with a number, you should always ask two questions:

Is the number accurate?
Is the precision obtainable?

Accuracy should be questioned first, and to judge accuracy it is necessary to have knowledge of the actual measuring technique, how the technique was used, and knowledge beforehand of what a reasonable outcome should be.

People who never question the accuracy of calculations amaze me. In this age of calculators and computers, people have become enamored with precision. Numbers are reported to seven decimal

---

**The Census Bureau could adjust the census data for undercounting but a decision was made to use the unadjusted figures for the 2000 census. See the report "Census 2000 Basics" available from the Census Bureau's Web site at http://www.census.gov.

places, but if you asked the person doing the calculation, "How do you know that result is accurate?" The response is "that is what the computer/calculator gave. It must be right."

Even if the number is accurate, it might reflect an unobtainable precision. The precision issue might not matter if decisions based on the number do not depend on the precision. The one-person precision reported in the U.S. Census is not obtainable, but because Congressional representatives represent about 500,000 people, it is not necessary. However, in a close election one-vote precision might not be obtainable and yet it can be critical for determining the outcome.

In reality there is no way to answer the above questions unless the accuracy of the result can be judged beforehand and the inherent limitations of the measuring techniques that determined the precision understood. The reasonability analysis and questions outlined in Chapter 3 should be applied to any numerical result. Too often people never question the accuracy of numbers. Precision nonsense is written down and believed.

Negative Taxation?

My father owns a small business, and early in my working life, he had his accountant do my tax returns. I had not yet learned the intricacies of the 1040 form, so it was easy for me to turn over my W-2 to his accountant and receive a completed 1040 ready for my signature and mailing. One year his accountant informed me that I was due an especially large refund—$1207 to be precise. The forms arrived at my home for me to sign and one look immediately told me that the $1207 figure might be precise, but it was not accurate. In other words, his precise calculation was completely wrong.

How did I know the refund result was wrong without having to go through the 1040 form? While I did not know the details of the calculation, I did know the basic idea behind a tax refund. Part of each paycheck is sent to the government. At the end of the year, if the amount sent is greater than the amount actually owed the government, the overpayment is refunded. When I saw that my tax refund was greater than the total withholding listed on my W-2 form, I knew immediately that the accountant's precise result was not accurate. If the government refunded more than I paid, that would amount to a negative tax. I'm sure somewhere in the vast realm of the tax code, negative taxation is possible, but I knew I did not fit any special case that would cause the government to pay me money.

I looked through the 1040 form and found some simple arithmetic mistakes. After I corrected the mistakes, a tax refund resulted that made sense. Only then did I sign and mail my tax return.

Chapter 11 Resources:

For a more technical discussion on the difference between precision and accuracy see:

Ronald Lane Reese, *University Physics* (New York, NY: Brooks Cole, 1999)

For more information on the United States census visit: http://www.census. gov

CHAPTER TWELVE

Estimating

The Three Sizes of Numbers

"The purpose of computing is insight, not numbers!"

—R. W. Hamming
Mathematician and pioneer in early computing

After one of the worst natural disasters in modern history—the December 26, 2004 tsunami that devastated vast coastal areas along the Indian Ocean—the U.S. government pledged $35 million in aid to assist the recovery. Immediately U.S. government officials found themselves on the defensive. Condemnation poured in from around the world accusing the U.S. administration of "stinginess," of "not caring about Muslim countries," of shirking its responsibility as the world's wealthiest country to help those in need. An intended goodwill gesture had gone awry. Embarrassed administration officials quickly added an additional zero to the aid pledge to make it $350 million and assured everyone that the U.S. government did care.

What went wrong in this incident? Whoever came up with the initial $35 million figure for a pledge had no understanding of number size. It sounds like a generous pledge. After all, most people will never have access to that much personal wealth in their entire lifetime. But to put $35 million into perspective, consider some other stories that made the news that same week.

While the tsunami dominated the front page, a story on the sports page announced that the Fox TV network would charge $2.4 million to air a single 30-second ad during the 2005 Super Bowl broadcast. Anheuser-Busch had already purchased ten of these 30-second commercial time slots. That means that a single U.S. corporation had committed $24 million just to market beer during a single four-hour telecast on a single Sunday afternoon. Given that sports programming on television is popular every weekend in the United States and that Anheuser-Busch is a highly visible advertiser for many sports broadcasts, I shudder to think of the amount of money spent annually to encourage Americans to drink beer. I will pass on making an estimate of the marketing budget at Anheuser-Busch because I think this one news story about the Super Bowl makes the point that $35 million is not much money to a major U.S. corporation and certainly not much money to the U.S. government. Actually, the U.S. government didn't even need to specify such a low number in their aid pledge. Thousands of Navy and Air Force personnel equipped with ships, planes and helicopters had already swung into action delivering aid to the affected people. The cost *each week* to have the U.S. military on site supplying aid far exceeded $35 million, and the operation lasted for months.

For many people, all numbers that are too large to comprehend become equal to one another. The difference between $35 million and $350 million becomes irrelevant because both figures represent an incomprehensible amount of money. But this tendency to treat all large numbers as equally large not only leads to embarrassing misunderstandings, but costly misunderstandings as well. The same can be said of misunderstanding small numbers. Once a number becomes too small to comprehend people treat the number as insignificant. But like large numbers, differences in small numbers do matter.

In Chapter 3 I discussed financial planning and the need to examine business and investment proposals for mathematical reasonability. But many people are unable to do the kind of numerical analysis I described because they lack an understanding of the relative size of different numbers. The purpose of this chapter is to teach an understanding of number size so that you can make estimates and examine proposals and ideas for mathematical reasonability. Just as in the previous chapter that taught the concepts of numerical precision and accuracy, I will begin with a scientific detour to teach how scientists understand and communicate number size. Then I will apply this understanding to some current events and discuss in particular how to analyze risks when deciding on medical treatments and procedures.

Number Size

My observation is that for most people, numbers fall into three categories of size:

- •Ordinary numbers
- •Large numbers
- •Small numbers

Ordinary numbers are easily counted and understood. Examples include the number of people at a dinner party, the number of items on a grocery list, the number of hours in a day, the number of rooms in a house. Ordinary numbers can be counted using your fingers, and their relative size determined through simple observation. If some one asks you the number of people you ate dinner with, it is easy to imagine the people seated at table and mentally count each person. Your answer will be accurate because you are not likely to confuse the numbers 3 and 12. In fact, you won't mistake the number 3 for 4.

Large numbers cannot be mentally counted. It is not possible to go to a football game, scan the crowd and say, "The scoreboard attendance figure is correct. There are 64,507 people here." If the scoreboard operator mistakenly entered 59,507 instead of 64,507, you would not know the difference. Just imagine making an unintentional mistake, omitting 5000 people and you are completely unaware. As numbers get larger it becomes not only difficult to count them, but impossible to imagine them. No one can picture a million of something, let alone a billion or a trillion. Because large numbers cannot be imagined, it is difficult for people to understand the relative size of a million compared to a billion.

To communicate the relative size of large numbers, math and science writers usually resort to numerical analogies. They convert large numbers into ordinary numbers. What is the difference between a million, a billion, and a trillion? A million seconds is 12 days, a billion seconds is 33 years, and a trillion seconds is 33 millennia. In other words the difference between a million seconds, a billion seconds, and a trillion seconds, is the difference between two weeks, one generation, and about one-third of human history.

Likewise, incomprehensibly small numbers can also be expressed with analogies. Consider our modern understanding of atomic structure. The protons and neutrons are located in the center of an atom and make up a small densely packed nucleus that the electrons orbit. It is a picture most people are familiar with by the time they reach high school. However, it is a distorted picture that fails to adequately communicate the relative sizes of the objects involved. Drawings in grade-school science texts show an atom with a large massive nucleus surrounded by nearby electrons that are equal in size to the protons. Unlike these drawings in textbooks, atoms are mostly empty space. The size of the electrons, protons and neutrons that form an atom are tiny in comparison to the atom itself. But no one has any direct sensory experience with objects as small as an atom so again analogy helps.

Here is my analogy of an atom. Imagine the atomic nucleus is the size of a marble. Place that marble in the center of a football field on the 50-yard line. The closest electron would be in the end zone about 50 yards away. For a relatively light element such as carbon, the cloud of six orbiting electrons surrounding the marble-sized nucleus would fill the entire stadium. On the atomic scale, electrons are point particles that literally have no size. That means the electrons for our stadium-sized atom still have no size and occupy no measurable volume. A marble-sized nucleus for an atom the size of a football stadium and nothing else with any measurable size or volume is one way to imagine the relative size of an atomic nucleus in comparison to the size of the atom.

From this analogy we can understand that a picture to accurately represent the relative size of the electrons, protons and neutrons in an atom can never be presented in a textbook. If our stadium-sized atom has shrunk to the size of a page in a book, the marble-sized nucleus becomes invisible, and again the electrons have no size at all. You would be staring at a blank page. A "drawing" with nothing in it would be consistent with what modern physicists believe—that the atoms that make up you and all the solid material that surrounds you are almost entirely empty space. The sizes of an atom's constituents are tiny compared to the size of the atom itself. That thought is difficult to comprehend, but the mathematical analysis of experiments on atomic structure leads to the mostly empty space conclusion. Atomic diameter and nuclear diameter are measured in small units of distance, but the distance measurements are not equally small. These "small numbers" vary considerably in size.

Scientific Notation

If you understand scientific notation you might be able to skip this section and go directly to next section on language and scientific notation.

The purpose of a numerical analogy is to convert numbers that are too small or too large to comprehend into ordinary numbers that relate to familiar experiences. Instead of saying that an atomic nucleus is about 0.000000000000001 meter in diameter while an atom is about 0.00000000001 meter in diameter, we compare the size of a marble to the size of a football stadium. Marbles and football stadiums are familiar objects for most people. Because the relative size of familiar objects is understood, the analogy works when communicating number size to the public. But when scientists talk among themselves, they usually do not resort to analogies to compare numbers. The problem with analogies is that they always require a "unit conversion." Instead of measuring length in a standard scientific unit such as meters, nuclear diameters are now measured in "marble diameters" and atomic size is measured in "stadiums." The same problem occurs with my large number analogy of the difference between 1 million, 1 billion and 1 trillion seconds. When these times are converted to 12 days, 33 years and 33 millennia the numbers 12 and 33 are comprehensible but the units for time—day, years, millennia—are all different.

When comparing numbers of vastly different sizes, scientists prefer to work with a consistent set of units. If a scientist wants to compare two vastly different times, both times will be expressed in the same unit (seconds, for example) even if the numbers turn out to be incomprehensibly small or large. Also, scientists rarely write out incomprehensibly large or small numbers in decimal form. A scientific paper will never read that "the diameter of an atomic nucleus is 0.000000000000001 meter," because a number that small written in decimal form does not communicate any more to a scientist than it does to a non-scientist. To understand and compare number sizes, both large and small, scientists refer first to a number's *order of magnitude*, which is simply a count of the number of decimal places, either to the right or left of the decimal point, that are needed to write out the number in decimal form.

To see understand the "order of magnitude" concept, first consider some numbers and note the location of the decimal point. For ordinary numbers like 5 or 4.26 the decimal point is either explicitly written after the first digit (as in 4.26) or known to be immediately after the first digit without writing it (as in 5). These numbers have an order of magnitude of zero. All numbers greater than or equal to 1 (such 1.002) but less than 10 (such as 9.999) have an order of magnitude of zero. Numbers equal to or larger than 10 require more digits to the left of the decimal point. Each additional digit to the left of the decimal point increases the order of magnitude by one. That means that the number of digits between the first digit and decimal point is equal to the number's order of magnitude. For 72.3 there is one digit, the 2, between the first digit and the decimal point so it has an order of magnitude of one, while for 1,256,910 there are six digits after the first digit and before the decimal point so it has an order of magnitude of six.

For numbers between 0 and 1, when written in decimal form, the first non-zero digit will *always* appear to the right of the decimal point. It is for this reason the concept of a negative order of magnitude is useful.* Numbers, such as 0.043, that have their first non-zero digit appear to the right of the decimal point have a negative order of magnitude. The place to the right of the decimal point where the first non-zero digit occurs determines the order of magnitude. For the number 0.043 the first non-zero digit is two places to the right of the decimal point so the order of magnitude is –2. Using this convention, the number 0.375 has an order of magnitude of –1, while 0.000045 has an order of magnitude of –5.

Once you understand the way the order of magnitude works, it is easy to construct a concise "scientific notation" for writing and for comparing numbers of arbitrary size, no matter how large or small. Scientific notation expresses numbers using two factors that are multiplied together. That is, all numbers can be expressed as a product in the following form:

$$a \times 10^n$$

The first part—"*a*"—is the *numeric* factor, which is a number written in familiar decimal form. The second part, the *exponential* factor gives the actual location of the decimal point and is written in a form 10^n, where the superscript n represents an integer that can be positive, negative or zero.

---

*A number with a negative order of magnitude is not the same as a negative number. Any number less than zero is a negative number regardless of its order of magnitude. A negative or positive order of magnitude just refers to the location of the decimal point. For example: the number –115 is a negative number but has an order of magnitude of positive 2, while the number –0.088 is negative and has an order of magnitude of negative 2.

To understand the exponential factor, notice that in the conventional decimal system for writing numbers, multiplication by 10 moves the decimal point one place to the left; and division by 10 moves the decimal point one place to the right. In other words, multiplication by 10 increases a number's order of magnitude by 1, and division by 10 decreases a number's order of magnitude by 1. For repeated multiplication or division by 10, mathematicians use a simple notation where the number 10 is written with a superscript that indicates the number of times the multiplication/division is to be repeated. A positive number for the superscript means multiply while a negative number in the superscript means divide. Therefore 10^6 is an instruction to multiply by 10 six times, an action that shifts the decimal point six places to the right. The notation 10^{-3} is an instruction to divide by 10 three times, an action that would shift the decimal point three places to the left. In mathematical jargon, the superscript is called an "exponent."

Using this notational system, you can convert familiar decimal expressions for numbers of any size to "scientific notation" by counting places to the right or left of the decimal point, or in the language just introduced simply determining the number's order of magnitude. The conversion steps are as follows:

For numbers with orders of magnitude greater than one the first non-zero digit is always to the left of the decimal point.

1. Move the decimal point to the left until it is just to the right of the first non-zero digit. The new number that results from moving the decimal point is the numeric factor.
2. Count the number of places the decimal point moved and use this count as the *exponent*.
3. The number in scientific notation is the numeric factor times 10 with that exponent. See Table 12.1a for some examples.

Table 12.1a: Comparison of decimal and scientific notation for numbers with orders of magnitude greater than 1.

Numbers with positive orders of magnitude

Decimal Notation	Scientific Notation
1,024,000	1.024×10^6
−288,470,000	$−2.8847 \times 10^8$
1,000,000,000,000 (1 trillion)	1×10^{12} (1 trillion)

Observation: Conversion to scientific notation greatly compacts the expression of large numbers such as 1 trillion in the table above.

For numbers with orders of magnitude less than one the first non-zero digit is always to the right of the decimal point.

1. Move the decimal point to the right until it is just to the right of the first non-zero digit. The new number that results from moving the decimal point is the numeric factor.
2. Count the number of places the decimal point moved and use this count as a negative *exponent*.
3. The number in scientific notation is the leading number times 10 with that negative exponent. See Table 12.1b for some examples.

Table 12.1b: Comparison of decimal and scientific notation for numbers with orders of magnitude less than 1.

Numbers with negative orders of magnitude

Decimal Notation	Scientific Notation
0.0284	2.84×10^{-2}
0.00008307	8.307×10^{-5}
−0.000000000000001	$−1 \times 10^{-15}$

Observation: Conversion to scientific notation eliminates the need for long strings of zeros after the decimal point.

Language and Scientific Notation

English words for large and small numbers, such as one million or one millionth have an equivalent expression in scientific notation. For example one million is 1×10^6 or more concisely 10^6 because any number multiplied by one is equal to itself. That means that when the numeric factor is 1 its does not need to be explicitly written. Some exponential factors used in scientific notation also have an equivalent international prefix and abbreviation. All of these equivalences are useful to know and are summarized in Tables 12.2a and 12.2b. For example, one thousand of a quantity can be expressed as 1000, 1 kilo, 1K or 10^3. Each expression means the same thing.

Table 12.2a gives the equivalences for numbers where the decimal point is on the right. For decimal fractions, which are numbers where the decimal point is on the left, Table 12.2b lists the equivalences. A quantity of one millionth is equivalent to 0.000001, 1 micro, 1 μ, or 1×10^{-6}. The "μ" symbol is the letter in the Greek alphabet called "mu." It is the only non-Latin letter in Tables 12.1a and 12.1b. The letter is pronounced mew, as in the sound that cats make but scientists always say "micro" when the abbreviation is used to indicate the size of a number. The expression "5 μ-seconds" would be pronounced "5 microseconds."

Many of these international prefixes have found their way into everyday language in place of the usual English words. It is not uncommon for people to refer to salaries using an expression such as: "she makes \$45 K a year," rather than "she makes \$45,000." Computer specifications also use international prefixes. A computer with 256 megabytes of RAM (random access memory) has 256,000,000 bytes of RAM.

Note from these expressions that exponents used in scientific notation do not have to equal a number's order of magnitude. The decimal point can be shifted *any* number of places and that shift action notated with 10 with an exponent equal to the number of places moved. While it is often convenient to use a numeric factor between 1 and 10, a writer has choices. A distance such as 30,000 meters can be expressed using the number's order of magnitude as the exponent and the result is 3×10^4 meters. But the same distance can also be written as 30×10^3 meters where an exponent is used only for the last three zeros, or 30 kilometers where the last three zeros are replaced with the metric prefix "kilo." Often the reason to put some of the zeros in the numeric factor rather than the exponent is to show significant figures. The expression 3×10^4 implies one significant figure while the expression 30×10^3 implies two significant figures. (See Chapter 11 for a discussion of significant figures.)

Table 12.2a: Repeated multiplication by one thousand expressed in English words, decimal notation, the international prefix, international abbreviation, and scientific notation.

Multiples of one thousand

English	Decimal	Prefix	Abbreviation	Scientific
one thousand	1,000	kilo	K	10^3
one million	1,000,000	mega	M	10^6
one billion	1,000,000,000	giga	G	10^9
one trillion	1,000,000,000,000	tera	T	10^{12}

Table 12.2b: Repeated division by one thousandth expressed in English words, decimal notation, the international prefix, international abbreviation, and scientific notation.

Multiples of one thousandth

English	Decimal	Prefix	Abbreviation	Scientific
one thousandth	0.001	milli	m	10^{-3}
one millionth	0.000001	micro	μ	10^{-6}
one billionth	0.000000001	nano	n	10^{-9}
one trillionth	0.000000000001	Pico	p	10^{-12}

Observation: Many of the metric prefixes are now used in ordinary conversation.

Scientific notation has the following advantages for understanding numbers:

•*It communicates the number concisely:* While writing "A mile has 5.280×10^3 feet," takes slightly more space than "A mile has 5280 feet," scientific notation is a necessity once numbers become extremely large or small. For example, Avogadro's number—6.023×10^{23}—occurs frequently in chemistry calculations. To write it in decimal form requires moving the decimal point 23 places to the right of the 6. A fundamental constant of nature known as "Planck's constant," frequently appears in quantum mechanical calculations. That constant—6.63×10^{-34} Joule seconds—would require 33 zeros to appear between the decimal point on the left and the first 6 if you wrote it in decimal form.

•*It immediately communicates the number's size:* When the superscript is the number's order of magnitude, you don't need to count decimal places or groups of three zeros separated by commas to determine the size of the number. If I ask which is larger 0.000000000000327 or 0.00000000000942, you need to count the zeros carefully. If I ask which is larger 3.27×10^{-13} or 9.42×10^{-12} you can see immediately that the order of magnitude of the second number (−12) is one greater than the order of magnitude (−13) of the first number. Therefore the second number is greater. If this last claim confused you, remember that in the winter a temperature of −5° is much warmer than a temperature of −30°. In other words, when you count with negative numbers in the following manner −10, −11, −12, −13 etc., −10 is *largest* number.

•*It immediately communicates the precision of the number:* Scientists use numbers to report measurements, and as we discussed in the previous chapter, all measurement techniques have a finite *precision*. In the previous chapter when the topics of precision and significant figures were discussed, an ambiguity arose for numbers that end with zeros. How many significant figures are present for a number such as 20,000? Scientific notation allows for the easy expression of significant figures. The number 20,000 is equal to 2×10^4, or 2.0×10^4, or 2.00000×10^4. Mathematically, all these numbers are equal but each form implies a different precision. The first form means one significant figure of precision, the second form two significant figures, and the third form six significant figures.

•*It transforms the problem of multiplying and dividing large and small numbers into addition and subtraction:* This is the most compelling reason to use scientific notation for writing numbers. If you have ever wanted to know the trick scientists and engineers use to perform arithmetic on large numbers in their head with no use of a calculator or even pencil and paper, here it is: Consider the multiplication of 63,000 by 3,000,000. In scientific notation the problem becomes 6.3×10^4 multiplied by 3×10^6. All that needs to be multiplied are the numeric factors 6.3 and 3 to get 18.9. To arrive at the correct exponent for the answer simply add the exponents of the two numbers. Because 4 plus 6 equals 10 the final result is 18.9×10^{10}. Convert back to decimal notation by moving the decimal point to the right the number of times indicated by the new exponent. In this example the result is 189,000,000,000 or 189 billion. Notice from this example that positive exponents are instructions to move the decimal point to the right from wherever it is. If it is already shifted to the right after multiplication, you must shift it further right when converting to decimal form.

For division, simply divide the numeric factors and subtract the exponents. Therefore 63,000 divided by 3,000,000 is the same as 6.3×10^4 divided by 3.0×10^6. The numeric factor for the answer is 6.3 divided by 3, or 2.1, and the exponent is 4 minus 6, or -2. The final result is 2.1×10^{-2}, which in decimal form is 0.021. Note that when converting to decimal form, the -2 exponent means that you move the decimal point 2 places to the left from wherever it is. If it is already on the left, you have to move it further to the left.

With a little practice using scientific notation, you will find that multiplication and division of numbers of any size without using a calculator is easy. Once you learn to convert numbers to scientific notation, all you need to know are your grade school multiplication facts combined with addition and subtraction. Here are some further examples:

Comparing computer storage media

How many floppy disks are needed to back up a 60-gigabyte hard drive?

A high-density floppy disk holds about 1.5 megabytes of information. Using Table 12.2a for language equivalences, we see that the exponent equivalents for mega and giga are 10^6 and 10^9 respectively. In scientific notation the number of floppy disks needed is 60×10^9 bytes divided by 1.5×10^6 bytes. Divide the numeric factors 60 and 1.5 to get 40 and subtract the two exponents 9 minus 6 to get 3. The number of floppy disks needed is 40×10^3, or in decimal notation 40,000. From this calculation the reason that floppy disks have become obsolete is immediately apparent. A single backup of your hard drive using floppy disks would take a long time. In fact even CD-ROMs that hold about 600 megabytes of information are becoming unmanageable for backing up a typical hard drive. You would need 60×10^9 divided by 600×10^6 CD-ROMs to store all the information. The numeric factor 60 divided by 600 is 0.1 and subtracting the exponents 9 minus 6 still results in 3. The number of CD-ROMs needed is 0.1×10^3, or in decimal notation 100.

Federal debt in relation to the population

Suppose the federal government decided to levy a one-time tax on every person in the United States to eliminate its debt. How much would that tax be?

In the previous chapter we learned that the United States has a population of about 280,000,000 people, and in the Chapter 4 on graphs we learned that the projected debt held by the public for the year 2006 (Figure 4.2) is about \$5 trillion. Convert these numbers to scientific notation and divide. The problem becomes this: what is \$5x10^{12} divided by 2.8x10^8? For the numeric factors, 5 divided by 2.8 is 1.8 and for the exponents 12 minus 8 is 4. The answer is \$1.8x10^4. That means that if every person in the United States would put up \$18,000 all at one time, the entire federal debt could be eliminated. This figure is only valid for the year 2006. It is projected to increase every year for the foreseeable future.

Reasonable Number Sizes

The last two examples show how comparing number sizes is useful for answering questions of reasonability. Is it reasonable to use floppy disks to back up a 60-gigabyte hard drive? Is it reasonable to levy a one-time tax to eliminate the federal debt? The quick comparisons of number size just performed show immediately that the answer to these two questions is no. Chapter 3 had a discussion of "Fermi" problems, which is a method for answering questions based on a determination of mathematical reasonability. Examining questions and proposals for mathematical reasonability requires some knowledge of "typical" number sizes for the quantities involved. The difficulty that arises is that a particular quantity—population in some of Fermi problems—can vary considerably in size.

For example, Chapter 3 discussed how examining business proposals for feasibility depends on market size. The difference in population between a small town such as Concord, New Hampshire, and a large city such as Los Angeles is more than two orders of magnitude. That means more than 100 times more people live in Los Angeles than Concord. A major city like Baltimore has 25% more people within its city limits than the entire state of Wyoming. The feasibility of a business proposal critically depends on the proposed location of the business.

To give an idea of "typical" number sizes, I have compiled tables with approximate representative values for various: speeds (Table 12.3a), distances (Table 12.3b), masses (Table 12.3c), times (Table 12.3d), populations (Table 12.3e), wealth (Table 12.3f) and causes of death (Table 12.3g). In each table I have expressed the values using scientific notation and a single measurement unit. All times are in seconds, distances in meters, masses in kilograms, speeds in meters per second, populations in numbers of people, wealth in dollars, and causes of death in incidences in the United States for the year 2002. By using scientific notation and a single unit of measurement for each table, we can see differences in orders of magnitude immediately. I have also expressed some of the measurements in familiar units (miles, feet, miles per hour, pounds etc.) so that you can get a sense of the relative size of the units of measure that are more customary. The examples chosen show a wide range in the orders of magnitude for each quantity. Often people are deceived when comparing two quantities because they fail to understand that the difference in the orders of magnitude of the quantities might be so great that a comparison makes no sense. Much distorted thinking results from such failures to understand number size. Here are some random comparisons of number sizes taken from each of the tables. When orders of magnitude are compared, some surprising discoveries appear. Consider the following observations.

Speeds: To orbit the Earth, the space shuttle needs to travel at 7.5×10^3 meters per second: that is 23 times the speed of sound (3.3×10^2 meters per second). If the space shuttle were to break free of the earth's orbit and travel to the star nearest our sun, it would take 4×10^{16} m divided by 7.5×10^3 meters per second, or 5.5×10^{12} seconds. Look in Table 12.1a and you will find that time is nearly twice as long as all of human history (3×10^{12} seconds). Travel time could be improved considerably if the space shuttle could be accelerated to 1/10 the speed of light times 3×10^8 meters per second. That would shorten travel time to 1.3×10^9 seconds, which is only 41 years. For those who think that this might be achieved one day, I should mention that there is a formula in physics that states that the energy required for a vehicle to reach a given speed increases as the speed squared. That means that if the space shuttle were to travel one-tenth the speed of light (400 times faster than its current speed), it would require 400^2 or 160,000 times more energy than the space shuttle currently has. Storing and releasing that much energy in a controlled manner in the confines of a single vehicle is difficult to imagine. Fantasies of interstellar space travel are just that, fantasies.

Distance: The diameter of a hydrogen atom—about 1×10^{-11} m— is about four orders of magnitude (10,000 times) greater than its nuclear diameter 1×10^{-15} m, hence the origin of my marble in the center of the football field analogy. A marble's diameter is about 1 centimeter (1×10^{-2} m) while the length of a football field at 92 m is close to 1×10^2 m (100 m). Again this is a four order-of-magnitude difference because 2 minus –2 is equal to 4. The solar system actually has similar proportions because the diameter of the solar system (about 1×10^{13} m) is almost four orders of magnitude greater than the diameter of the sun (1.4×10^9 m). That means that all those drawings in grade-school science texts of planets circling the sun are just as out of proportion as the drawings of electrons orbiting an atomic nucleus. Interstellar distances are truly unimaginable. The distance to the closest star to our sun is 4000 times the diameter of the solar system, and the diameter of our galaxy is 25,000 times this sun-to-closest-star distance. Intergalactic distances are greater still, and there are millions of galaxies spread throughout the universe.

Masses: Scientists have measured mass over an enormous range of scale. The mass of a single electron has been measured to be 9.1×10^{-31} kg, while measurements of the mass of the earth result in 6×10^{24} kg. The difference in these two numbers is almost 55 orders of magnitude. That means the mass of the Earth is almost 1×10^{55} times the mass of an electron. The number 1×10^{55} has no equivalent expression in words; in decimal notation, the number would be a 1, followed by 55 zeros. Scientific notation

Table 12.3a: Speeds (meters per second).

Speed	Object	Miles per hour
7×10^{-8}	Growth rate of human hair	1.6×10^{-7}
1×10^{-2}	Speed of a garden snail	0.22
1.5	Human walking	3.4
30	Automobile on a highway	67
2.5×10^{2}	Commerical jet aircraft	560
3.3×10^{2}	Speed of sound in air	740
7.5×10^{3}	Space shuttle in orbit	17,000
3.0×10^{4}	Orbital speed of the Earth around the Sun	67,000
3.0×10^{8}	Speed of light	670,000,000

Table 12.3b: Distances (meters).

Distance	Object	Comparison
1×10^{-15}	Diameter of an atomic nucleus	
1×10^{-11}	Diameter of a hydrogen atom	
1×10^{-10}	Distance between atoms in a sodium chloride crystal (salt)	
1×10^{-6}	Size of a bacterium	0.001 millimeter
1×10^{-4}	Thickness of a human hair	0.1 millimeter
1.8	Height of an average human	70 inches
92	Length of a football field	100 yards
1.6×10^{3}	One mile	1.6 kilometers
4.3×10^{6}	New York to San Francisco	2700 miles
4×10^{7}	Circumference of Earth	25,000 miles
3.8×10^{8}	Distance from the Earth to Moon	240,000 miles
1.4×10^{9}	Diameter of Sun	900,000 miles
1.5×10^{11}	Distance from the Earth to Sun	93 million miles
1×10^{13}	Diameter of Solar System	6 billion miles
1×10^{16}	One light-year	6.2 trillion miles
4×10^{16}	Nearest star to the Sun	4 light years
1×10^{21}	Diameter of Milky Way Galaxy	100,000 light years
2×10^{22}	Distance to the Andromeda Galaxy	2 million light years
1×10^{26}	Most distant object in the visible universe	10 billion light years

Table 12.3c: Masses (kilograms).

Mass	Object	Comparison*
9.1×10^{-31}	Electron	
1.7×10^{-27}	Proton	
1.7×10^{-27}	Neutron	
3.3×10^{-25}	Gold atom	
1×10^{-19}	Virus	
1×10^{-12}	Living cell	
6×10^{-8}	Grain of salt	60 millionths of a gram
4×10^{-4}	Paper clip	0.014 oz (0.4 gram)
1.5×10^{-1}	Baseball	0.33 lbs (5.3 oz)
7×10^{1}	Human	150 lbs
1×10^{3}	Automobile	2200 lbs (1.1 tons)
1×10^{5}	Wide body jet (empty)	110 tons
3×10^{8}	Aircraft carrier	330,000 tons
7×10^{22}	Moon	
6×10^{24}	Earth	
2×10^{30}	Sun	

* In everyday language the terms "mass" and "weight" are used interchangeably. It is common to see on a box of crackers the words "packed by weight, not volume" and a label in grams (a unit of mass) and ounces (a unit of weight). To a physicist the terms "mass" and "weight" mean two different things. Physicists would not usually use units of weight (pounds, ounces, tons) in a table of masses as I have done here. I do this only to help relate these quantities of mass to the familiar. Most people know their weight in pounds but have no idea what their mass is.

The reason why physicists are so careful in distinguishing between mass and weight is that it is easy to imagine situations—such as a ride on the space shuttle—where a person would have all of their mass and none of their weight. That is because weight is a measure of the force of gravity on an object, which will change if you leave the surface of the Earth, and mass is measure of an object's inertia, which will not change just by leaving the Earth's surface. Inertia is the property that objects have that makes them resist changes in motion. You need to apply a force to move objects because of their inertia.

On the surface of the Earth mass and weight are directly proportional. That means if you double an object's mass you double its weight. It is for this reason that we can interchange the terms mass and weight in everyday language and not have problems. You would have big problems if you confused these terms while planning any kind of space mission.

Table 12.3d: Times (seconds).

Time	Event	Comparison
1×10^{-15}	Shortest laser pulses	
5.3×10^{-6}	Time for light to travel one mile	5.3 microseconds
1 to 20×10^{-3}	Camera flash durations	1 - 20 milliseconds
0.2	Time for sound in air to travel one mile	one-fifth second
9.8	Human record for 100 meter sprint	
8.6×10^4	One day	
3.2×10^7	One year	
3.2×10^9	One century	100 years
6.4×10^{10}	Time since Christ's birth	2000 years
3×10^{12}	Age of earliest human fossils (homo sapiens)	100,000 years
2 to 8×10^{15}	Ages of dinosaur fossils	60-250 million years
1.6×10^{17}	Age of Solar System	5 billion years
4×10^{17}	Age of Universe	13 billion years

Table 12.3e: Populations (number of people in the year 2000)

Population	Place	Fraction of World (%)
3.1×10^4	Concord, New Hampshire	0.00048
1.1×10^5	Peoria, Illinois	0.0017
4.9×10^5	Wyoming	0.0076
6.5×10^5	Baltimore, Maryland	0.010
3.7×10^6	Los Angeles, California	0.058
8.0×10^6	New York City	0.125
2.1×10^7	New York Metropolitan Area	0.33
3.4×10^7	California	0.53
2.9×10^8	United States	4.5
1.0×10^9	India	15
1.3×10^9	China	20
6.4×10^9	**World**	**100**

Table 12.3f: Wealth (dollars in year 2004).

Amount	Asset	Comparison
1.1×10^3	Per capita GDP* (Kenya)	$1100
5.6×10^3	Per capita GDP (China)	$5600
1.9×10^4	U. S. poverty threshold (family of four)	$19,000
2.8×10^4	Per capita GDP (Germany)	$28,000
4.0×10^4	Per capita GDP (U. S.)	$40,000
4.4×10^4	U. S. median household income	$44,000
1.8×10^5	Median home price in U. S. (single family)	$180,000
2.3×10^6	Average major league baseball salary	$2.3 million
4.0×10^7	Earnings of Elvis Presley's estate in 2004 (He died in 1977.)	$40 million
2.2×10^8	Oprah Winfrey's estimated 2004 earnings	$220 million
1.8×10^9	Baltimore County Maryland's operating budget	$1.8 billion
3.0×10^9	George Lucas' net worth	$3 billion
1.2×10^{10}	Nicaragua GDP	$12 billion
3.0×10^{10}	Apple Computer market capitalization**	$30 billion
3.5×10^{10}	Kenya GDP	$35 billion
4.8×10^{10}	Bill Gate's net worth	$48 billion
3.0×10^{11}	Microsoft market capitalization	$300 billion
4.8×10^{11}	U. S. federal deficit for 2004	$480 billion
1.0×10^{12}	Mexico GDP	$1 trillion
2.4×10^{12}	U. S. federal budget for 2004	$2.4 trillion
3.7×10^{12}	NASDAQ market capitalization	$3.7 trillion
4.4×10^{12}	U. S. federal debt owed to the public	$4.4 trillion
1.1×10^{13}	U. S. (GDP)	20% of world GDP
1.3×10^{13}	NYSE market capitalization	$13 trillion
5.5×10^{13}	World (GDP)	$55 trillion

* GDP is an abbreviation for "gross domestic product." See Chapter 4 for an explanation of this term. Per capita GDP is the GDP divided by the total population.

**See Chapter 3 for an explantion of "market capitalization."

Table 12.3g: Causes of death in the United States (number in year 2002).

Number of Deaths	Cause	Fraction of Total (%)
55	Tornados	0.0023
100	Lightning*	0.0042
618	Aircraft accidents**	0.026
3.5×10^3	Drowning (accidental)	0.15
1.7×10^4	Homicides	0.71
1.7×10^4	AIDS	0.71
3.2×10^4	Suicide	1.3
3.6×10^4	Influenza	1.5
4.2×10^4	Motor vehicle accidents	1.8
7.1×10^4	Diabetes	3.0
1.6×10^5	Stroke	6.7
5.6×10^5	Cancer	23
7.0×10^5	Heart disease	29
7.7×10^5	All other causes	32
2.4×10^6	**All Causes**	**100**

* Typical year. Exact number not known.

** In 2002 there were no fatalities on scheduled passenger aircraft. All of these fatalities involved general aviation and other uses of aircraft.

is a necessity for working with a number like this. Electrons, despite being responsible for an atom's chemical interactions, are extraordinarily light particles. A proton is 1800 times more massive than an electron. Neutrons have about the same mass as a proton. The protons and neutrons that form the compact atomic nucleus account for almost all of an atom's mass.

Time: The expression "it's a dinosaur" is a derogatory statement meaning "obsolete." But dinosaurs lasted for an extraordinary long period of time. The age of dinosaurs occurred from 2×10^{15} to 8×10^{15} seconds ago. The total time dinosaurs lived is the difference between these times — 6×10^{15} seconds. In comparison, our own species — *Homo sapiens* — has only been on the planet for about 3×10^{12} seconds. Divide these two times, and you find that dinosaur history is 2000 times longer than all of human history. And the last two millennia (the past 6×10^{10} seconds) — that has seen the rise of Western civilization and its accompanying technology that greatly stresses global resources — is only a small fraction (1/50) of all of human history. Humans have been around for such a short period of time that there is no basis for judging our long-term sustainability as a species. We have a long way to go to catch up to the dinosaurs.

Population: Human population is unevenly distributed on all scales. Combined, the Asian countries of China and India have 35% of the world's population. The United States in comparison has about 4.5% of the world's population. Within the United States, there are great disparities in populations. More than 10% of the U.S. population lives in the state of California; and combined, the New York City metropolitan area and California are home to about one of every five Americans. More people live within the city limits of Baltimore, Maryland, than in the vast state of Wyoming. The population of the capital of New Hampshire — Concord — would be considered a neighborhood in Baltimore and might only represent a few square blocks of New York City.

Wealth: The distribution of wealth throughout the world is more uneven than the population distribution. The United States with 4.5% of the world's population accounts for 20% of the world's gross domestic product (GDP). The market capitalization of some major U.S. corporations is greater than the GDP of some countries. Bill Gates' net worth is about equal to the combined 2004 GDP of Kenya and Nicaragua. Not all billionaires are created equal. Billionaire George Lucas, the creator of Star Wars, is only worth about one-sixteenth of what Bill Gates is worth. And consider the disparities in the millionaire circle. An average major league baseball player would have to work almost a hundred years to earn what Oprah Winfrey earned in 2004. Elvis Presley continues to top *Forbes'* list of highest earning dead celebrities. His 2004 earnings were about 1000 times the median household income in the United States, and yet he died in 1977.

Deaths: The causes of death that make for big news stories—like airplane crashes and tornados—are few compared to mundane causes like the flu. Deaths that result from heart disease, cancer, stroke, and diabetes account for more than half (62%) of all deaths in the United States. These diseases, which kill large numbers of people, are sometimes related to lifestyle. If the 20% of the U.S. population who smoke would quit, life expectancy would increase considerably. In an average year about 36,000 people die of the flu, almost as many as the number of people killed in motor vehicle accidents. Yet companies that manufacture flu vaccine do not find it profitable. Only a fraction of the population bothers to get vaccinated. But because the media prefers stories that contain ordinary numbers over stories with large numbers, the unusual causes of death get more coverage. Deaths resulting from storms, homicides, and airplane crashes are major front-page news, even though deaths from these causes are a tiny fraction of the total number of deaths each year. As a result we develop a distorted sense of risk. Many people who are afraid to fly will still smoke.

Number Size and Risk Analysis

"If one wishes to emphasize the severity of a problem, one will usually talk about the number of people afflicted nationally. If one wants to downplay the problem, one will probably speak about the incidence rate."

—John Allen Paulos
A Mathematician Reads the Newspaper
(New York, NY: Anchor Books, 1995) p. 79

Armed with a scientific understanding of number size and how to compare large and small numbers meaningfully, we can now turn a critical eye on the use of numbers in assessing risk. It is my observation that because most people sort numbers into "large," "small" and "ordinary" categories, those who write about risks tend to use the following techniques, depending on their motives.

Manipulating People with Number Size

•If the motive is to engage the reader/listener, the writer uses an ordinary number.

•If the motive is to alarm or impress the reader/listener, the writer uses a large number.

•If the motive is to reassure or calm the reader/ listener, the writer uses a small number.

What might surprise you is that writers can choose to use an ordinary, large, or small number for just about any topic related to risk. The trick lies in the choice of context for the number and the choice of other numbers for comparison. Here are some examples:

Highway safety

In *USA Today* on March 3, 2005, the opening sentence of a front page article on highway fatalities reads as follows: "The death rate for motorists on rural roads was more than 2 1/2 times the rate for driving on all other roads in 2003, a study to be released today shows." Notice the use of an ordinary number in the first sentence to engage the reader. Later in the article a spokesman is quoted as saying, "The nation's rural roads... are exposing rural residents and visitors to an unacceptable level of risk." To reinforce that dire warning the writer switches to large numbers. Readers learn that although rural roads account for 28% of total miles driven, 52% of the 42,301 average annual traffic deaths from 1999 to 2003 happened on rural roads. So should you be frightened to drive your car on a rural road? Let me take some numbers from the same study and construct some reassuring statements that use small numbers. A motorist who travels 100,000 miles on all roads other than rural has a probability of being killed of 1×10^{-3}, or about a 1 in a 1000 chance. For motorists traveling rural roads the probability of being killed is 2.7×10^{-3} for every 100,000 miles traveled or a chance of 2.7 in a 1000. Because both 2.7×10^{-3} and 1×10^{-3} are small numbers, the reader does not notice the "more than 2 1/2 times" difference between them and is less compelled to demand action on rural road improvements.

Smallpox vaccination

Smallpox is a deadly and disfiguring disease that kills about 30% of its victims. People born in the United States before 1972 (including me) received a smallpox vaccination as a child. But mass vaccinations performed worldwide eradicated the disease, and after 1972 vaccinations were discontinued in the United States. The last known case of smallpox was reported in Somalia in 1977. The end of smallpox as a naturally occurring disease has not ended the fear. There is concern that samples of smallpox have been secretly stockpiled and could be used in a bio-terrorism attack. After the September 11, 2001, attacks, the U.S. government updated its preparations for the event of a smallpox attack.

It might appear that the simplest solution to avoid a deadly smallpox attack would be to vaccinate everyone. After all, prior to 1972 everyone was vaccinated, so why not return to that practice? The problem is that the smallpox vaccine is one of the least safe of all the vaccines. It is estimated that about one out every one million recipients would die from the vaccine. Some health authorities think the death rate might be higher, but with no current statistics, an accurate estimate of the death rate is difficult to perform. When considering the problem of mass smallpox vaccinations, we again encounter issues of number size. An individual's chance of dying from a smallpox vaccine is extremely low, about 1×10^{-6}, but that small number when multiplied by the entire U.S. population, about 2.9×10^8 people means that a significant number of deaths (290) will result. No public health official would recommend an action that would kill hundreds of people as a preventive action for a disease that has killed no one in the past three decades.

This example is another manifestation of the "risk paradox" first encountered in Chapter 8 in a discussion of financial risks. The risk paradox can now be generalized to include all risks, not just those that are financial.

The Risk Paradox

Groups have different priorities than individuals when exposed to the same risk.

Public health officials deal with large groups and think in terms of total numbers. A health official compares the total number of people who will die from a specific action to the total number of people saved. If more people are expected to die than be saved, the action will not be recommended. Individuals deal with risks to only one person—themselves. A person either dies from the action or does not. There is no comparison of total deaths versus lives saved for an individual. It is often in the individual's interest to dismiss the small risk and take the vaccine. But a policy maker cannot dismiss a small risk and recommend mass vaccinations unless there is a measurable benefit for the group.

Down's syndrome

Down's syndrome (trisomy 21) is a chromosomal abnormality that on average occurs for roughly one out of every 900 births. The risk increases with the mother's age. A woman at age 35 is at least four times more likely to have a Down's syndrome child than a woman at age 20. A woman age 45 is about 40 times more likely to give birth to a Down's syndrome child than a woman age 20. Again the use of ordinary numbers such as "four times" and "40 times" engages the reader and causes pregnant women over the age of 35 to worry about the possibility of a Down's syndrome child. A more reassuring statement can be constructed with small numbers. For a pregnant woman age 25, the chance of having a child with Down's syndrome is one in 1300 (0.077%); for a woman age 35, the chance is one in 270 (0.37%); and for a woman age 45, it is one in 30 (3.3%). In other words, the vast majority of pregnancies for women of any age do not result in Down's syndrome.

The incidence of Down's syndrome can also be expressed with large numbers, but when this is done some surprises appear. You might conclude from the above statistics that most children with Down's syndrome have older mothers. Actually 70-80% of all Down's syndrome children have mothers under the age of 35. The reason is that women under the age of 35 account for more than 90% of all pregnancies. For 100,000 births, we expect roughly 90 children with Down's syndrome; but if 90% of those births (90,000) are to women under the age of 35 where the overall incidence rate is about 1 per 1300 births, they account for 95,000/1300, or 69 of the 90 children (about 77%). Women over the age of 35, even though they have a higher incidence rate, have far fewer pregnancies and account for the remaining 23% of Down's syndrome babies.

Because the risk of Down's syndrome increases with age, pregnant women aged 35 and older are often advised to undergo screening for Down's syndrome using amniocentesis, a procedure where amniotic fluid is taken and fetal cells are examined for chromosomal abnormalities. But why do medical doctors recommend amniocentesis only for women over the age of 35 if that only addresses 20 to 30% of the problem? What is special about age 35? One medical paper explains the reason in this manner:

"At age 35, the second-trimester prevalence of trisomy 21 (1/270) approaches the estimated risk of fetal loss due to amniocentesis (1/200). Therefore, age 35 was chosen as the screening cutoff—the risk threshold at which diagnostic testing is offered."

—David S. Newberger
American Family Physician
vol. 62, no. 4 (2000) pp. 825-832

Here we see two small numbers (1/200) and (1/270) being compared, but how do these numbers translate into actual numbers of cases? Imagine performing amniocentesis on 100,000 pregnant women who are age 25. That action will result in 100,000/200, or 500 random miscarriages. Because the incidence rate for Down's syndrome for mothers age 25 is one out of 1300, doctors expect to find only 77 cases in this 100,000 population. From a risk/reward perspective, sacrificing 500 healthy pregnancies to search for 77 problems does not make medical sense. For older mothers, the risk/reward balance changes. If 100,000 pregnant women of age 35 undergo amniocentesis, the same 500 random miscarriages will result; but 100,000/270, or 370 cases of Down's syndrome will be found. The risk/reward ratio is more in balance; and for populations of women older than 35, the reward will become greater than the risk. Note the medical reasoning is same as encountered in the discussion of the smallpox vaccine. The medical authorities are comparing the total effect of a proposed action—using amniocentesis to screen for Down's syndrome—on populations. The age 35 cutoff is chosen simply because at that age, a statistical crossover occurs and one risk becomes greater than another.

But in such a case, the interests of the individual might have nothing to do with the statistics. A woman could feel that keeping her pregnancy is more important to her than anything else and be willing to accept the risk of a Down's syndrome child. In that case, taking the one in 200 chance of a miscarriage associated with amniocentesis makes no sense no matter what her age is. Or a woman could feel that knowing if she is pregnant with a Down's syndrome child is most important. In that case testing using amniocentesis might be appropriate even if she is under the age of 35. Again doctors dealing with populations have a different set of criteria than individuals weighing risks to themselves from one-time events. Just because two events are equally probable — miscarriage versus identifying Down's syndrome — doesn't mean that the individual undergoing the procedure ranks the impact of each event equally.

Summary

"I'm an excellent poker player. If I had to be more specific, my guess would be that I'm in the top .1 percentile in the world. That's a fancy statistic if you're talking about SATs or something like archery, but when it comes to poker, it can create an enormous problem. With somewhere in the neighborhood of 135 million people across the planet who play the game, a little eighth-grade math will tell you that there are about 135,000 people shuffling cards at this very moment who are better than me."

— Andy Bellin
Opening lines to *Poker Nation*
(New York, NY: HarperCollins, 2002) p. 1

Questions of feasibility often depend on the size of the numbers involved. Whether the proposal involves computer usage, public health, taxation, marketing, or interstellar space travel, naïve ideas can often be immediately rejected after a quick examination of the numbers. Knowledge of typical number sizes and the ability to make rough estimates is useful for separating out fantasies from real solutions to problems.

But vast discrepancies in number size can also be used hide important facts. When numbers are too large or too small to imagine, we often fail to consider the numbers in an appropriate context. Numbers that are too small to comprehend are all mentally grouped as equally insignificant. Numbers that are too large to comprehend all fall in the "more than enough" category. Scientific notation is useful for avoiding these mental pitfalls because it clearly communicates the relative size of a number by emphasizing its order of magnitude. When comparing numbers, always look first at orders of magnitude before looking at the precise digits.

In the examples covered in this chapter, note the following principles at work:

Small Numbers Are Significant

No matter how small a number, it can become significant
if it is multiplied by a sufficiently large number.

The quote about poker that introduced this section is an example of this principle, but it applies to any popular competitive activity that requires skill—baseball, football, golf, soccer, music, SATs, writing, and so on. No matter what level of skill you attain, there will always be a significant number of people who are better. This property of numbers is especially important when assessing risks. No matter how small the risk of a certain disease, accident, or medical condition, if a large enough population is considered a significant number of cases will be found. You can be assured that the news media will always find and report on the unusual cases. News is by definition an event that is out of the ordinary. But that does not mean that individuals should constantly worry or alter their behavior based on reports of unusual cases.

Order of Magnitude Comes First

Multiplying or dividing any number by an ordinary number between 1 and 10 will not change its order of magnitude by more than 1.

That means that a large number multiplied by an ordinary number is still a large number, and a small number multiplied by an ordinary number is still a small number. Expressions such as "2 times more likely," "3 times as often," "your chances double," "a 40% improvement seen," etc. are impressive but meaningless if the order of magnitude is the real issue. If you purchase two lottery tickets, your chances of winning the lottery are doubled, but those chances are so remote that the doubling that occurs is meaningless. A new medical treatment that shows a 40% improvement in comparison to the old treatment sounds impressive, but that might not mean anything if the old treatment rarely worked.

Taken together these principles form the foundation of the "risk paradox." Those who provide advice and make policies and rules for large groups have different priorities from an individual person. They are acutely aware of the measurable effects on the entire population of their decisions. Laws, policies, and practices for highway safety, public health, and medicine are made for the benefit of the group, not the individual.

Blondi © 2004 Reprinted with special permission, King Features Syndicate, Inc.

Making Sense of Safety

During my childhood, my parents moved to a new suburb in upstate New York. An idyllic rural area carpeted with farms suddenly sprouted hundreds of new homes with accompanying cars that soon overwhelmed the existing road system. My family attended what had been a small church located at the intersection of a narrow country road and a major four-lane highway. Every Sunday morning dozens of cars stood in line to cross the highway. As you can imagine, close calls with high-speed oncoming traffic were frequent. Members of the church organized and petitioned the state highway administration to install a traffic light. The state did not find merit in the proposal because from its point of view, the intersection posed no problem. The reason given—no deaths had been reported.

The state's position makes a certain amount of mathematical sense. It would not be practical or desirable to put a traffic light at every location where a country road intersected with the highway. Traffic light installation needs a compelling reason and fatal accidents are certainly compelling reasons. Without fatalities the intersection was not a priority for the state. But from the point of view of the community, the state's position is macabre. It means that lives of members of the community, people that everyone will know, need to be sacrificed before the intersection can be made safe for all. Some serious accidents did occur. The mother of a friend of mine suffered serious internal injuries when her car was broadsided while crossing the highway. Church members continued to petition, and the state finally relented and installed a light before actual fatalities occurred.

At that time my parents owned the family car of their generation—a station wagon. Once a year we made a ten-hour trip to the city of my birth—Detroit—to visit relatives. The back seats were all folded down, and my brother and two sisters and I, stretched out in back, played board games, read, or slept. I don't know if my parents wore the seatbelts in front because those were a novel item at the time. The first station wagon my parents owned had no seatbelts. In Detroit, my older cousin had a small Volkswagen convertible. It had cramped seating for four; but with the top down, we could stack people on top of one another. Seven or eight of my siblings and cousins would pile in and go speeding down the Detroit freeways. Hair flapping in the breeze would sting our faces as we traveled, but we all got to where we wanted to go.

Today the actions of my parents and cousin would be blatantly illegal. They would be stopped and ticketed for violating seatbelt usage laws. Obviously I survived my childhood, as did millions of other people who can recount similar experiences. To many people, the laws compelling seatbelt usage are a massive invasion of privacy. The existence of such laws raises the question of how far the government should go towards compelling people to act in their own best interest. But from the government's point of view, seatbelt usage saves lives. Each year about 40,000 Americans die in automobile accidents, a little more than 1 out of every 10,000 Americans. That is not a high enough incident rate to keep people from driving, but the U.S. population is so large that the measurable reduction in the fatality rate that results from compulsory seatbelt usage translates into thousands of lives saved every year. In all probability it will not be your life, but it will be someone's.

Chapter 12 Resources

For useful books on putting numbers into perspective:

John Allen Paulos, *A Mathematician Reads the Newspaper* (New York, NY: Anchor Books, 1996)

John Allen Paulos, *Innumeracy: Mathematical Illiteracy and Its Consequences* (New York, NY: Hill and Wang, 1988)

For comprehensive national health statistics visit the Website for the Center for Disease Control: http://www.cdc.gov.

CHAPTER THIRTEEN

Measuring

Is it valid?

"We have looked at the data and the data that we have been able to see has all been statistical data that has not convinced me that smoking causes death."

—Andrew H. Tisch
Chairman and CEO, Lorillard Tobacco Company
Testimony before House Subcommittee on Health and the Environment
April 14, 1994

One day during my senior year of high school, I took a note from my mother to the school office that gave me permission to leave early for an appointment. Of course, students turn in notes for excused absences every day, and my school had the usual policy of calling the parent to verify their authenticity.

"Your phone number?" the receptionist asked.

Silence followed. My mind was elsewhere this particular morning, and I was not thinking about my upcoming first period math class, rather about issues with my then girlfriend.

"What is your phone number?"

"Huh?"

"Your phone number?"

"Oh…. Yes, my phone number….. uh.."

"Do you have a phone?"

"My number, yeah…… it is ….um ….."

I finally blurted out my phone number. Ten minutes later, the

Dean, who witnessed this exchange from her office, arrived at my first period math class. She insisted I come with her to the nurse's office where they confronted me with questions on drinking and drug use. What had I been taking that morning? What drug was I on? Did I feel OK? My mind came into focus very quickly, and they saw that I was in fact lucid. After the questioning I was allowed to return to class.

I believe that today, if an incident happened that caused a school administrator to suspect drug use, answering a few questions would not be enough. Drug testing would be demanded. In fact many schools and organizations debate whether or not routine testing should be required of everyone, not just suspected users. Many employers insist that job applicants be tested for drugs as a condition of employment. The reasoning is that no one other than a drug user should have cause to fear a drug test, and no drug users should ever be tolerated. Many schools and employers have implemented "zero tolerance" policies for drug use, policies that take away all discretion from administrators. Zero tolerance is a politically popular concept, and even better, if no discretion is available, those in charge bear no responsibility for their actions.

Zero tolerance is a wonderful aspiration. We should all be perfect people, raising perfect children in a perfect world. Why tolerate anything short of perfection? However, there is a serious scientific problem with the zero tolerance idea. The problem is determining zero. The concept of nothing, represented by the number zero, seems simple, and in the abstract it is—no person should ever use illegal drugs. But the problem of determining through testing, that a school has zero drug use is not as straightforward as it appears.

The Signal-to-Noise Ratio

My high school had 2000 students. Suppose a decision was made to test each student with a test that was 99% accurate. Further suppose that the test is free of systematic errors—no laboratory contamination, no legal substances such as poppy seeds that would cause a test to appear positive, etc. Assume that the test errors are all random and when it is in error, half of the errors are false positives and half are false negatives.* A false positive means that a non-drug user tests positive for drugs. A false negative means that a person on drugs passes the test. All 2000 students are tested for drugs, and 20 individuals test positive. What has been learned from this expensive and invasive exercise? The surprising answer is "not much." If the school had zero drug use, we would still expect that, on average, 0.5% of the students, or 10, would test positive for drugs. Again we have to use that troublesome "on average" qualifier that appeared throughout Chapter 7 on probabilities. The reason is that the error rate is a random process so we cannot even say that it will be exactly 10, even if we test 2000 drug-free students. It could be more than 10 or less than 10 every time we test a drug-free school with 2000 students because the error rate is just an average of a random process.

In this case we identified 20 individuals with positive drug tests, which is more than 10. But who among this 20 are the drug users and who are the false positives? We cannot even say that we have exactly 10 of each, but on average we expect that half of the 20 are drug users and the other half, false positives. Of course we have no way to know which individuals are in which group. We encounter another paradox. Even though the test is 99% accurate, the chance that one of these individuals who test positive is a drug user is only 50%. This example illustrates the measurement problem. The problem is this:

The Measurement Problem

Confidence in a test is not necessarily equal to confidence
in the results of the test.

---

* The distinction between random errors and systematic errors is explained in Chapter 11.

To understand this discrepancy, we need to consider two quantities when performing a measurement—the *signal* and the *noise*. The signal is the quantity being measured, in this case the number of drug users. The noise is the background that is always present whether a signal exists or not. In this case, the noise is the number of random errors. For a *single* test to be useful, the signal has to be greater than the noise. I emphasize the word "single" because I will explain later that the problem of finding a small signal amongst greater noise can be addressed by using multiple tests. But first we need to understand the problem with single tests.

Imagine that there is only one drug user in the entire school. We have no hope of identifying that person through one test of all 2000 students because approximately 10 false positive tests are expected before the process is even begun. If after conducting all the tests, some number that is close to 10—such as six or nine or eleven—are positive, it is not possible to even know that there is a drug user, let alone identify the individual. And, if it is not possible to know whether there is a drug user from mass testing, does that mean the school has zero drug use? That conclusion is not valid either. All that can be stated is that there is an upper limit on drug use in the school of about 0.5%. That means the rate of drug use does not exceed that number. The actual rate might be 0%, but the test lacks the sensitivity for us to know for certain.

What if there are substantially more than 10 positive test results? Suppose the 2000 tests are conducted, and 50 positives result. The number 50 is substantially greater than 10 and indicates a signal that is greater than the noise. It is reasonable to conclude that the school has drug users. Scientists often refer to a quantity called the "signal-to-noise ratio." It is the actual measured signal divided by the random background noise. Because the signal-to-noise ratio is now five, confidence in the results has increased. We now expect that approximately 40 of the 50 positive tests are real, which means that the chance that someone who tested positive for drugs is a user has increased to 80%. It also means that we still do not know for sure who the drug users are.

At this point, you might wonder whether use of a drug test will ever identify a drug user with the 99% confidence advertised? That would be the case if we tested the school and only 10 tests came back negative. At this extreme, the number of false negatives becomes an issue. If the population tested consists entirely of 2000 drug users, we expect that 0.5% or about 10 tests will come back falsely negative. Because 10 is the expected number of false negatives if everyone used drugs, our confidence is now about 99% that a positive drug test means that the person actually uses drugs.

The issue of sample size

When signals are small and comparable to the noise, an additional and related measurement problem appears. The size of the sample tested might be too small to even know the signal-to-noise ratio accurately. My wife went to a much smaller high school than I did. There were only about 200 students in her school. Suppose the same drug test is applied to all 200 students and two test positive. It is expected that about one false positive would result. Does that mean that the signal-to-noise ratio is 2 to 1? Although we expect that on average there will be one false positive, there have not been enough tests for the "average" to be meaningful. In Chapter 7 we learned about the law of large numbers and a consequence of this law that results from small samples do not always reflect the actual average. When the sample is small and the signal weak, only repeated measurements will arrive at an accurate determination of the signal-to-noise ratio.

Signal Averaging

The signal-versus-noise problem can be reduced, although never entirely eliminated, but doing so costs testers greater expense and effort. If the signal is less than or comparable to the noise, we can use a technique called "signal averaging" to increase our confidence that a person the test identifies as a drug user is actually using drugs. Let's go back to high school drug testing.

Imagine all 2000 students are tested and 10 positives result, the number expected from the random failure rate of the test. The 2000 tests are performed again, and 8 positives are found. Again everyone is tested, and 11 positives result. The question to ask is "Does each pass pick out different people or do one or two people consistently appear in the group?" Positives that result from randomly occurring errors would most likely identify a different group of people each time the test is performed. But if a particular individual always appears in the positive test group, it becomes much less probable that the result is a random error. The first positive test can be attributed to a random error; the second positive test might still be an error; but if the same individual continues to appear in the positive test group, the probability of that being a random occurrence becomes progressively smaller. Suppose we test the entire school five times and always get between 8 and 11 positives, but two individuals are always in that group. We now have our "signal." Even though that signal is still less than the noise, the probability that these two individuals are using drugs is better than 99%. The process of repeatedly testing the same sample to see if a pattern will emerge despite the presence of random noise is known as signal averaging. This process relies on repetition. Noise is always present, but confidence that the emerging pattern is real increases with the number of repetitions.

Statistical models

But once repetition is introduced to the measuring process and different outcomes result, the tester needs some way of making sense of the differences in the data sets. If a tester finds 50 drug users on the first measurement, 57 on the second, 44 on the third and so on, what can be concluded from these different results? Clearly errors are occurring that hide the truth. To make sense of differing outcomes, the tester needs a statistical model to explain the variability that results from errors. The act of performing a measurement carries with it an assumption—that the quantity being measured has a true value. The crux of the measurement problem is as follows: the unavoidable randomness inherent in the measurement process results in a measured value that is not necessarily the true value. In fact, it is unlikely that the measured value and the true value will ever be exactly the same. The question becomes: How "close" is the measured value to the true value? Articulating what is meant by "close" requires some care. When scientists report a measurement, they usually report a "confidence interval" along with the measurement. The confidence interval is a range of values surrounding the measured value and is often called the "margin of error."

Suppose a scientist is asked to measure the number of drug users in a school. After careful testing, the result reported is: 52 ±7 students use drugs where ±7 is the confidence interval associated with the measurement. There are two significant figures in the measurement, meaning that the measurement method has a precision of one student. But the reported confidence interval, expressed as ±7 students indicates a range of uncertainty and is a reflection of the accuracy of the measurement.* It would be tempting to think that ±7 range of uncertainty means that the true value lies between 52 – 7 and 52 + 7 students, or that somewhere between 45 and 59 students are drug users. Actually, interpreting a confidence interval is more complicated. Remember the errors in the test occur randomly, so that means the confidence associated with the measurement must be stated in terms of a probability. In fact a confidence interval is a probability statement. It gives the *probability* that the true value lies within the range of the confidence interval. That probability is known as the "confidence level" and depends on the statistical model used to analyze the data.

For example, a common statistical model for random errors is the so-called "bell curve," which is named because of its shape. This model is known synonymously as a *normal* or *Gaussian* distribution in the mathematical literature. The idea is that repeated measurements of the same value—the number of drug

*The difference between *precision* and *accuracy* is explained in Chapter 11.

users in our example—will yield different values because of measurement errors. But if the errors are random, the average of many measurements should converge to the true value and if a chart is made of each measurement the picture that results should resemble a bell curve centered about the true value. By computing the average, and how far each measurement deviates from the average, a statistician can determine both the confidence interval and the confidence level. For measurements modeled using a bell curve it is common to report a "standard error" which is the confidence interval that has a 95% confidence level. If the measurement of drug users is 52 ± 7 students where the ±7 is a standard error that means the probability is 95% that the number of drug users is between 45 and 59 students.

To summarize, a measured value has three attributes.

Attributes of a Measured Value

- *The value:* Which is the outcome of the measurement.
- *The confidence interval:* Which is a range of uncertainty about the value.
- *The confidence level:* Which is the probability that the true value lies within the confidence interval.

But there is big catch to all of this, which is that the assumptions that went into the statistical model might not be valid. For example, if the errors are not random a bell curve is not the correct statistical model. Statisticians actually have a multitude of models for interpreting the variability in a set of measurements and it is not always obvious which is the correct model to use.* Worse, unless the signal-to-noise ratio is high or the number of measurements made is large, the assumptions

---

* The computation of margins of error associated with measurements is a rich and complex area of statistics. There are a many different methods for modeling the errors inherent in a measurement. A statistician must use judgment when choosing a model.

associated with *any* statistical model will not be valid. Statistical modeling relies on the law of large numbers. A "bell curve" will not look like a bell curve unless a large number of measurements have been made and now the problem we had in Chapter 7 of how large is large enough appears again. The "large" requirement depends on the variability of the outcomes, or in terminology just introduced—the signal-to-noise ratio. The smaller the signal to noise ratio the more measurements are needed before it is known if the statistical model is valid. The law of large numbers implies that for any measurement to be valid the following is required:

Conditions for a Valid Measurement

- A large signal-to-noise ratio
- A large sample
- Repeated measurements on the sample

If all three of these criteria are met, it is likely that the statistical model used and the resulting measurement, confidence interval, and confidence level are all valid. If one of the criteria is missing, for example the signal-to-noise ratio is small then increasing the number of measurements—the process called "signal averaging" will still result in a valid measurement. If none of these criteria are met, for example a one-time measurement on a small sample with a weak signal, the measured value that results is meaningless.

The media fosters misunderstandings and deceptive claims occur as a result, because it is always possible to compute an average, a confidence interval, and a confidence level from *any* set of data. The question is: Have enough measurements been made for any of these values to be meaningful? Consider the constant confusion surrounding health and dietary studies. Newspapers report measurements and sometimes confidence intervals (margins of error). But it is rare to see a report of a confidence level or an explanation of the statistical model used. Sometimes the size of a sample is reported but rarely is the signal-to-noise ratio reported so that it would be possible to know if the sample size is adequately large. News reporters are quick to report impressive sounding statistics but rarely is the context provided for those statistics so that it is possible for the reader/listener to judge the validity of the conclusions.

When interpreting the results of a study, a reader must decide if the sample size and signal-to-noise ratio are acceptable. But the "acceptable" condition is always a judgment call. And, a person who acts on the results of a study must judge how much certainty is required for him or her to have confidence in the action taken. For example, consider the "zero tolerance" idea mentioned at the beginning of this chapter. Because all tests have an uncertainty associated with them, a rate of drug use that is undetectable is not necessarily zero. It is a judgment call as to how much expense and effort devoted to testing for drugs is warranted to insure that drug use is as close to zero as possible.

Dilbert: © Scott Adams/Dist. by United Feature Syndicate, Inc.

Correlations and Causes

Chapter 7 discussed how patterns are always found within randomness but pointed out that these patterns are not predictive. Now, to confound matters further, we have learned that real predictive patterns—signals in scientific jargon—are always muddled to a certain degree by randomness. People study patterns because they want to predict the future. But random sequences have patterns, and patterns have random sequences. If a pattern is found, does that mean it is predictive or is it part of the randomness? In other words, when does a pattern become predictive? We now have a criterion for determining whether a pattern is real. We can repeat the measurement until the standard error is so small that the probability that the pattern is real approaches 100%.

But the real world is rarely so simple that patterns just appear. Often there are many *variables* to sort through. A variable is a condition or circumstance that differs among the subjects studied. For example, suppose I want to study rates of drug use in high schools. I might start by testing the student populations for drugs in many different schools. I would examine conditions that varied among schools — variables such as location, economic backgrounds, student grades, SAT scores, and so on — and look for "correlations." A correlation is a type of pattern that exists between the variables. When two or more variables change together in a predictable manner, those variables are "correlated." I would look for correlations between drug use and some of the variables I mentioned. Are some, if any, of the correlations that emerge, predictive of drug use in a school? But what happens once I have performed all the measurements, or "acquired all the data," as a scientist would say? I would then want to use the data to construct a model that would predict how likely it is that a school would have a drug problem. Once I have a model, a second related question arises, suppose I find correlations that are real and predictive of drug use, does that imply a cause? Knowing the causes would be the ultimate goal because I would want to do more than just predict drug use, I would want to identify and eliminate the causes.

To answer these questions requires first separating real patterns with randomness from randomness with apparent patterns. Second, once the separation is made, causal pathways must be identified. Scientific measurement and interpretation can be difficult for two reasons:

•Determining if a correlation is real requires large samples and repeated measurements.
•Understanding causes is a separate issue from identifying correlations.

Many people mistake correlations for causes. This is easy to do because sometimes an exceptionally strong correlation can actually hide the true cause, and correlations are usually easy to find. For example a study of high school drug use might find that drug users have low SAT scores. But what would a strong correlation between the effect studied (drug use) and the variable (SAT scores) mean? Does drug use cause low SAT scores or do low SAT scores cause drug use? Could there be a third variable that causes both drug use and low SAT scores? Is a correlation between drug use and SAT scores even meaningful or is it just a coincidence? Much of the challenge and creativity that comes in science involves identifying which correlations are meaningful and which are not and explaining the actual causes of an effect, not just how the effect correlates with other variables. In searching for correlations and causes, there are many logic traps that are easy to fall into. Here is a survey of some of the common logic pitfalls.

Correlations that are not real

News media often revel in finding completely meaningless correlations that arise entirely from coincidence. For example, prior to the 1980 presidential election, several commentators noted that the outcome of the World Series had "predicted" nine out the last 10 presidential elections. When a National League team won in October, a Democrat won in November; when an American League team won in October, a Republican won in November. Truman's stunning upset in 1948 was the only exception. Truman didn't know that he also had the World Series going against him. Of course this pattern of World Series and Presidential winners had just begun in 1940. A National League team won in 1980, but that result didn't help Jimmy Carter. He lost to the Republican Ronald Reagan.

Beginning in the year 1840, all presidents elected in a year ending in zero have died in office either through illness or assassination, the one exception being Ronald Reagan who nearly died after being struck by a would-be assassin's bullet. Only one president, Zachary Taylor, has died in office and not been elected in a year ending in zero. This widely noted observation even has a name—Tecumseh's curse. Folklore arose that the Native American Chief Tecumseh, defeated by William Harrison at the battle of Tippecanoe, cursed Harrison's later presidency. Harrison became the first U.S. president to die in office after falling ill on his inauguration day. He died one month later, which is the shortest time served for any U.S. president. Reagan's survival 140 years later caused some people to claim that he "broke the curse." Lucky for George W. Bush who was elected in the year 2000, that Reagan did so. As of this writing, President Bush is alive and well, although still in office. Or maybe the curse doesn't apply if the year ends in three zeros? We will have to wait until the 2020-30 decade to know.

Look for correlations between completely unrelated events, and you will find them. Use qualifiers like "nine of the past 10" or "beginning in the year 1840" or "nearly died" and the number of such correlations is essentially infinite. Sometimes writers will search for silly correlations like the examples above as a source for humorous pieces. My personal favorite is the late columnist Mike Royko's observation of "the Cub factor." Royko, a long-time columnist for Chicago newspapers, claimed that the team entering the World Series with the most former Chicago Cubs on its roster would lose. He of course had the statistics to "prove" his claim and by using the "Cub factor" he "predicted" events such as the spectacular collapse of the Boston Red Sox in the 1986 World Series against the New York Mets. And everyone remembers the final play of game six of the 1986 World Series when the ball went through the legs of ex-Cub Bill Buckner. That one play alone provided tangible evidence of the "Cub factor" at work. However, most sportswriters blamed the Red Sox collapse on the "curse of the Bambino." The Red Sox had not won a World Series since their owner sold Babe Ruth to the New York Yankees in 1920. Prior to 1920, the Red Sox had won more World Series than any other team and the Yankees had never won. Since 1920 the Yankees have won more World Series than any other team. The Red Sox finally broke their "curse" in 2004 by sweeping the St. Louis Cardinals in four straight World Series games.

All of these correlations are entirely coincidental and examples of the tendency of people to find patterns in random events that was discussed in Chapter 7. These correlations are always observed with the benefit of hindsight and tend to disappear as soon as they are noticed. None of these coincidences has any predictive value. Unless the writing is intended to be humorous, e.g. Royko's "Cub factor," it is silly that editors even allow such drivel to appear in print. You know that these correlations are not real because of the absence of repetition. There simply are not enough events to state with confidence that the above correlations are real, and I can assure you that there never will be.

Correlations that are real but without causes

But once a real correlation is found, that does not automatically mean that there is a causal relationship. Many times there are events that are *conditionally* probable. In the Chapter 7 on the subject of probability, the discussion was limited to *independent* probabilities. Flipping coins, rolling dice, spinning roulette wheels, shuffling decks of cards—all are independent events. Past outcomes do not affect the future because each event is independent, completely unconnected to the past. Despite many false claims to the contrary that were examined in that chapter, it is not possible for a coin, die, wheel, or card deck, to remember its past. Therefore the probabilities are the same for every event.

But for some random events, additional knowledge is available to use in computing the probabilities. In these instances the probabilities become "conditional" on that knowledge. Players of card games, such as poker and bridge, and card counters who play blackjack make decisions based on conditional probabilities all the time. Pick one card off the top of a randomly shuffled, standard 52-card deck, and the probability is one in 13 that it is an Ace. Deal out 26 cards from the deck, and *observe* each one of them. If no Aces are seen, the probability that the next card is an Ace has doubled to two out of 13. In this case the probability that the next card is an Ace is conditional on the number of Aces that have already been dealt.

The act of observation is critical for computing conditional probabilities. If you do not observe the cards as they are dealt, the probability that the next card is an Ace remains one out of 13 for every card in the deck, including the very last one. That means probabilities change when cards are observed, not because the deck has a "memory," but because the person doing the observing has a memory. The Aces are still randomly placed throughout the deck, which means that no cause is associated with their location.

Conditional events lead to correlations that are impressively strong. A poker player who needs to draw an Ace to win but sees that all the Aces are already in play knows to fold his or her hand. The player knows that this situation has a 100% probability of losing. But while conditional correlations might be of great use to a card player, there are many instances in science where a conditional correlation is of little use. Consider the following correlations:

- 100% of the deaths from ovarian cancer occur for females.
- 100% of the deaths from prostate cancer occur for males.

Of course being male does not cause prostate cancer. It is simply a condition for the disease. Likewise, ovarian cancer is conditional on being female. These probabilities are strong but of no help if you are studying and trying to understand the causes of these diseases.

Correlations such as these—that are strong because of conditions—are a favorite with advertisers. For example, the cliché "doctor recommended" appears in many ads for drugs and medical treatments. That correlation is meant to impress, but it has little meaning because almost no drug or medical treatment is marketed unless a doctor recommends it.

Correlations that are real but have underlying causes

"Dad, why does swimming in the pool make the water warmer?" my eight-year- old daughter asked.
"What makes you think the water gets warmer when you swim in it?"
"When we swim everyday, the water gets warm, but when we don't swim for a week, the water is very cold when we get back in."

That exchange with my daughter illustrates a classic logic flaw when analyzing correlated events. The flaw is to mistake strong correlations for causes. Does swimming cause warm water or does warm water cause swimming? Despite the strong correlation between warm water and swimming, there is no causal relationship in either direction between them. If my daughter does not swim for an entire week, it is because the weather was too cold. The water will be cold when she goes back into the pool because of the cold weather. In this case the correlation exists because not swimming and cold water have the same underlying cause—cold weather.

While the logic flaw above might appear obvious, many adults fall into the same logic trap when it occurs in other contexts. They believe that if a strong correlation exists between two variables, there must be a causal relationship between them. For example, consider the following correlation: People with more education earn more money. According to the U.S. Census Bureau, the correlation between income level and education is extraordinary. Consider these statistics from a July 2002 report that relate the average annual earnings for years 1997-1999 of all workers age 25 to 64 years to their educational attainment.

Highest Level of Education	Average Annual Earnings
Professional Degree	$99,300
Doctoral Degree	$81,400
Masters Degree	$54,500
Bachelors Degree	$45,400
Associates Degree	$33,000
Some College	$31,200
High School Graduate	$25,900
Not High School Graduate	$18,900

Because of this correlation, many people believe that a degree is a "cause" of increased income. Many college students believe that it is a cause and focus entirely on fulfilling the requirements for a degree without necessary focusing on the meaning of a degree. This same logic carried to the extreme leads to the conclusion that all that matters is having a piece of paper that states that you have a degree. Apparently that logic has existed for some time because "diploma mills" existed long before the creation of the Internet and the proliferation of spam offering people "degrees" for a modest fee.

But a degree is not a cause of income. For many professions, it is a necessary condition. You will not become a doctor, lawyer, engineer, scientist, or teacher without a degree. But no employer will ever cut someone a paycheck simply because that person has a degree. To earn money it is necessary to perform work that is of sufficient value to an employer that it becomes in his or her financial interest to pay for the work. A strong correlation exists between education and income because of an underlying cause. The knowledge, skills, and insights that a person acquires through the process of education are of greater value to employers. But educated people still have to use their acquired abilities in order to be paid. Simply having those abilities is not enough to cause an increased income. In fact there are many highly paid people without college degrees. A college degree might be a condition to enter some professions, but it is not a condition for being highly paid.

Consider another strong correlation: Children of the affluent read better. This correlation is so strong that it makes it extremely difficult to do research on effective methods of reading instruction. If you study the reading ability of children, you learn more about their family background than the methods of reading instruction used. For example, studies have shown that children from families that have many books in their home read better than those who don't. No surprise there, you might think; if you are going to learn to read, you need books. But this correlation is so strong that it is tempting to believe that books cause reading ability. For example, in 2004 Illinois Governor Rod Blagojevich proposed a $26 million state program that would send 12 free books each year to every child in the state under the age of five. In proposing the program, Governor Blagojevich was quoted as saying, "Studies show reading to children is the greatest factor in helping them to read at an early age."

I find the governor's intentions and initiative admirable, but the logical basis for his program, the conclusion that simply sending children books will cause them to read is equivalent to my daughter's belief that swimming every day warms the water. Imagine if someone filled my house with books written in a language that I did not know and every day read the books to me. Would that cause me to learn to read the language? Obviously I would not learn to read this way because the acquisition of reading ability is an active process. It will not happen by osmosis. Action by the learner is required. The existence of books, parents reading books to children, a high-income level, living in an affluent neighborhood, etc., all correlate strongly with high reading ability, but none of these factors *cause* children to learn to read. The strong correlation exists because of underlying causes. Affluent people possess certain expectations and attitudes for themselves and their children that are the root cause of success when it comes to both income and reading levels. It is the attitudes and expectations that cause children to take the actions needed to learn to read, not the mere presence of books in the house.

While I have used some examples where the logic is straightforward, in doing real science it is not always easy to recognize when a strong correlation between two variables has an underlying cause. Consider the great Spanish flu epidemic of 1918-19 that circled the globe killing tens of millions of people. Desperate medical researchers worked to find a treatment or vaccine, but first they needed to identify the pathogen that caused the illness. While many suspected a flu virus, the disease was unlike any previous influenza. After extensive studies of tissue samples taken from victims, the researchers identified a specific bacterium that they believed to be the most likely cause of the disease. The bacteria were so strongly correlated with the influenza deaths that researchers who reported not finding the bacterium in a victim were assumed to be doing shoddy work. Enormous resources were allocated to culturing the bacterium and devising possible treatments. But eventually research showed that the strong correlation was not because the bacterium caused influenza. The bacterium was a common secondary infection made possible by damage to the victim's lungs that resulted from the influenza. The great influenza epidemic did indeed have a viral cause. But at that time, before antibiotics had been developed, before DNA was recognized, and before mutations in viral DNA were understood, a bacterial cause was a reasonable conclusion to make, given the facts. The correlation between the bacterium and the illness was strong and therefore might be causal, although the medical researchers were well aware that a strong correlation does not automatically mean a cause, and debated the issue fiercely.

Causes with weak correlations

To complicate matters further, it is possible to have events that are not perfectly correlated with their cause. Sometimes that correlation is so weak that a purely statistical analysis would have difficulty identifying the cause. The most obvious example is pregnancy. Sexual intercourse causes pregnancy, but not all acts of sexual intercourse result in pregnancy. In fact the statistical correlation would be extremely weak. For most people, the acts of sexual intercourse engaged in far outnumber pregnancies that result. If a statistician, with no knowledge of the workings of human reproduction, attempted to deduce the cause of pregnancy purely from statistical methods, it would be a difficult undertaking. Not only is there a weak correlation between sexual intercourse and pregnancy, but the probability that an act of sexual intercourse will result in pregnancy varies greatly from couple to couple. There are also many other behaviors associated with human mating—kissing, hand holding, sleeping together—that are not causal to pregnancy but would be just as correlated as intercourse. To know for certain that sexual intercourse causes pregnancy requires understanding how it causes pregnancy. Statistics alone will not answer the question how.

Now consider a less obvious example. Smoking causes lung cancer but not all smokers get lung cancer. In the case of smoking and lung cancer, the correlation is not perfect. There are many elderly life-long smokers without lung cancer. The imperfect correlation between the cause (smoking) and the effect (lung cancer) makes possible the following bizarre exchange in a House of Representatives subcommittee hearing. The following is from a transcript of an April 14, 1994, hearing of the House Energy & Commerce Committee Subcommittee on Health and the Environment. Representative Henry Waxman questions Andrew H. Tisch, Chairman and CEO, Lorillard Tobacco Company.

Rep. Waxman: Mr. Tisch, I want to move to you for a moment. In a deposition last year you were asked whether cigarette smoking causes cancer. Your answer was "I don't believe so." Do you stand by that answer today?

Mr. Tisch: I do, sir.

Rep. Waxman: Do you understand how isolated you are in the belief from the entire scientific community?

Mr. Tisch: I do, sir.

Rep. Waxman: You're the head of a manufacturer of a product that's been accused by the overwhelming scientific community to cause cancer. You don't know? Do you have an interest in finding out?

Mr. Tisch: I do, sir, yes.

Rep. Waxman: And what have you done to pursue that interest?

Mr. Tisch: We have looked at the data and the data that we have been able to see has all been statistical data that has not convinced me that smoking causes death.

Despite his testimony to the contrary, Mr. Tisch clearly has no interest in identifying the causal mechanisms of lung cancer. His position is that his company has looked at the statistical data and from that data it cannot be concluded that smoking causes lung cancer. Of course, statistics alone are not enough to conclude that smoking causes cancer so, while mathematically his position is correct, his statement is meaningless. He is avoiding responsibility for his actions by hiding behind a true but trite fact on the limitations of statistics. By the way this is the same hearing where all seven of the tobacco company executives present stated that cigarettes are not addictive. James Johnson, CEO of the RJR Tobacco Company, testified that cigarettes and nicotine do not fit the "classic definition" of addiction because "there is no intoxication."

The fact is cigarettes are addictive and smoking causes lung cancer. The vast majority of people with lung cancer would not have the disease if they did not smoke and scientists do understand the causal pathways. The carcinogenic chemicals in cigarette smoke have been identified. Because the correlation between cancer and smoking is not perfect that does not mean that smoking is not a cause of cancer. The reasoning employed by the tobacco executives is identical to that of a young couple who claim that they do not think that sexual intercourse will cause pregnancy because they have been having sex for two years without a pregnancy occurring.

Causes with correlations

There are of course causes that produce strong consistent correlations. While I have argued that the issue of a cause is separate from the issue of a correlation I do not mean to imply that causes are unlikely to result in correlations. A strong correlation might not be a sign of a cause, but often a cause does produce a strong correlation. The law of "cause and effect" is powerful and it works. But because strong correlations do not always result from causes, some people see that as an opening to turn scientific thinking completely on its head and deny obvious cause and effect situations.

For example, over the past decade an extremely dangerous line of thinking has arisen that HIV (human immunodeficiency virus) does not cause AIDS (acquired immune deficiency syndrome). One of the more vocal proponents of this view Dr. Mohammed Ali Al-Bayati has even authored a published book—*Get All The Facts: HIV does not cause AIDS* (Dixon, CA: Toxi-Health International, 1999). He writes that he is a toxicologist and pathologist and has conducted extensive research showing that HIV is "harmless virus" and does not cause AIDS. A Google search will turn up thousands of Websites promoting this point of view. What does cause AIDS, according to Al-Bayati and others that subscribe to his point of view? Among the causes he attributes to AIDS are drug-use, malnutrition, and drugs used to treat AIDS such as AZT. This is a fascinating piece of twisted logic. He points to conditions that strongly correlate with having AIDS, such as receiving drug treatment for the disease, and claims that those are the causes while discounting the overwhelming scientific evidence built up over two decades of research that AIDS is caused by HIV.

It would be easy to ignore people who think this way except for the fact that some of these views on AIDS have become dangerously influential. Thabo Mbeki, who became president of South Africa in 1999, has stated that AZT is too dangerous to give to HIV-infected pregnant women, even though the drug is commonly used to prevent transmission of the virus to newborns. President Mbeki appointed members to a government AIDS advisory panel that believe that HIV does not cause AIDS and he stated in an interview with the *Washington Post* that he personally does not know anyone infected with HIV. These are the words and actions of a man who leads a country where about one out of every 10 people are infected with HIV and hundreds die from AIDS related illnesses every day.

AIDS is a preventable disease. Unfortunately people who succumb to this massive denial of reality could face deadly consequences. The scientific evidence for HIV infection as the cause of AIDS is conclusive. It cannot be dismissed as just a strong correlation.

Summary

"Whenever new research fails to replicate early claims for efficacy or suggests that efficacy is more limited than previously thought, it is not necessary that the original studies were totally wrong and the newer ones are correct simply because they are larger or better controlled. Alternative explanations for these discrepancies may include differences in disease spectrum eligibility criteria, or the use of concomitant interventions. Different studies on the same question are typically not replicas of each other. In fact discrepancies may be interesting on their own because they require careful scrutiny of the data and reappraisal of our beliefs."

—John P. A. Ioannidis
"Contradicted and Initially Stronger Effects in Highly Cited Clinical Research"
Journal of the American Medical Association
vol. 294, no. 2 (2005)

This quote is from a medical paper that examined 49 highly cited clinical research studies and discovered that for nearly one-third of those studies, the effects found were either contradicted or found not to be as strong in subsequent studies. But notice that the author of this medical paper does not draw the conclusion that many people would—that science has no firm ground and no results can be trusted.

There are many areas of medicine where the conclusions are not in doubt. For example, the research showing that smoking causes lung cancer and that HIV causes AIDS is conclusive. The reason for such a high level of confidence in these conclusions is that the studies have been replicated many times and the causal mechanisms are known. The number of patients in studies on smoking and AIDS is in the millions and the number of research papers is in the thousands. The studies have been conducted over decades and repeated in laboratories all over the world. These conclusions are so rock-solid that the popular press no longer notices much of the ongoing research.

What the popular press does notice are any new studies that hint at some new beneficial effect from a drug, or diet, or medical treatment. But often the new studies have not been replicated, the causes for the new effect have not been understood, and the number of subjects in the study is small. This is not to say that the new studies are wrong, only that the uncertainties in the results are large. In some studies numerous variables are tracked, and many different correlations are found. It is not easy to figure out which correlations result from causes and which result from conditions associated with the study. But the press rarely reports on the uncertainties or nuances associated with a study. Only the conclusions and their implications are broadcast. The overall effect is a distortion of how science goes about acquiring knowledge.

As a result, many people take extreme positions on the validity of measurements. There are those who have unquestioning faith in any measurement, regardless of the method used. For example, the people who advocate spending millions of dollars on testing for illegal drugs because they believe all instances of illegal drug use should be found and eradicated. The fact that uncertainties inherent in any test make this impossible does not discourage their quest for zero drug use. At the other extreme are people who argue that because measurements can be wrong and have been wrong, no measurement is believable. Tobacco company executives have used this argument for years as a way of avoiding responsibility for the enormous amount of suffering and deaths their product causes.

Neither of these extremes is justifiable. Yes, performance of a valid measurement is a hard problem. Even harder is drawing valid conclusions from a valid measurement. But every measurement has an uncertainty associated with it, and a context in which it was conducted. The strength of any conclusion based on a measurement rests on the uncertainties and the context. Those must be carefully considered when deciding to act on the basis of a measurement.

Metal Legs at the Airport

My first airline trip in the post-9/11 world was a short one-hour flight from Baltimore to Indianapolis to give a talk at a physics conference. On the return flight, I was one of the passengers "randomly" pulled from the line for a more extensive search and screening. The security guards rifled every pocket and side pocket of my briefcase, searched my billfold, made me take off my shoes, and scanned my body with a metal detector. I had to remove my belt because the buckle set off the metal detector, and I was then asked to sit in a chair with my legs held out parallel to the floor, while the guard scanned their entire length with the metal detector. During the leg scan, the metal detector went off the entire time. It was as if my leg bones were made of metal. As the guard moved from one leg to the next, he looked up to see a quizzical expression on my face.

"Oh, don't worry," he said. "It's just the re-bar in the floor."

I wanted to mention that in my business of experimental physics, there is a concept known as the signal-to-noise ratio. I wanted to ask how the "signal" of a possible knife in my pant legs, would stand out above the background "noise" caused by the metal bars used in the construction of the floor. But, there are times when it is best to say nothing. When he was done, I put my shoes back on and boarded the flight.

Chapter 13 Resources

Steven D. Levitt and Stephen J. Dubner, *Freakonomics: A Rogue Economist Explores the Hidden Side of Everything* (New York, NY: Harper Collins, 2005) examines the relationship between causes and correlations for selected current events, including Governor Rod Blagojevich's proposal to send all young children in the State of Illinois books.

David S. Moore, *Statistics: Concepts and Controversies,* fifth edition (New York, NY: W. H. Freeman, 2001) has a clear explanation at the beginner's level of many important statistical concepts and relates statistics to current events.

John M. Barry, *The Great Influenza: The Epic Story of the Deadliest Plague In History* (New York, NY: Viking, 2004) describes the difficulty scientists in 1918 had identifying the cause of the deadly influenza epidemic.

Appendix I

Worksheets

These worksheets are for use with the tables in Chapters 5, 6, 9, and 10. See the numbered examples in those chapters for the kinds of questions that those tables and these worksheets can be used to answer. Photocopy these worksheets as needed or visit http://www.TheTwoHeadedQuarter.com for additional ones.

Worksheets A1.a-d: For use with Table 5.2 (Fixed-rate growth), Table 5.3 (Integrated Fixed-rate growth) and Table 6.1 (Fixed-rate inflation).

(a) Determining a Final Value
Inputs Needed: *Rate, Duration, Initial Value*
1. Enter *Rate* (in annual percent):
2. Enter *Duration* (in years):
3. Locate row with *Rate*.
4. Locate column with *Duration*.
5. Enter value from box at the row-column intersection:
6. Enter *Initial Value* (in dollars):
7. Multiply Box 6 by Box 5 for the *Final Value*:

(b) Determining a Rate
Inputs Needed: *Final Value, Initial Value, Duration*
1. Enter *Final Value* (in dollars):
2. Enter *Initial Value* (in dollars):
3. Divide Box 1 by Box 2.
4. Enter *Duration* (in years):
5. Locate column with *Duration*.
6. Find the value in the duration column closest to the value in Box 3.
7. Result is the *Rate* for the corresponding row:

For examples see Chapter 5: Examples 5.1 through 5.13; Chapter 6: Examples 6.1 through 6.9.

(c) Determining a Duration
Inputs Needed: *Final value, Initial Value, Rate*
1. Enter *Final Value* (in dollars):
2. Enter *Initial Value* (in dollars):
3. Divide Box 1 by Box 2.
4. Enter *Rate* (in annual percent):
5. Locate row with the *Rate*.
6. Find the value in the rate row closest to the value in Box 3.
7. Result is the *Duration* for the corresponding column:

(d) Determining an Initial Value
Inputs Needed: *Rate, Duration, Final Value*
1. Enter *Rate* (in annual percent):
2. Enter *Duration* (in years):
3. Locate row with *Rate*.
4. Locate column with *Duration*.
5. Enter value from box at the row-column intersection:
6. Enter *Final Value* (in dollars):
7. Divide Box 6 by Box 5 for the *Initial Value:*

Worksheets A2.a-d: For use with Table 9.1 (Monthly loan payments:2-30 years) and Table 9.5 (Monthly loan payments:1-12 months).

(a) Determining a Monthly Payment
Inputs Needed: *Rate, Duration, Principal*
1. Enter *Rate* (in annual percent):
2. Enter *Duration*:
3. Locate row with *Rate*.
4. Locate column with *Duration*.
5. Enter value from box at the row-column intersection:
6. Enter *Principal* (in dollars):
7. Divide Box 6 by 1000.
8. Multiply Box 5 by Box 7 for the *Monthly Payment*:

(b) Determining a Rate
Inputs Needed: *Principal, Monthly Payment, Duration*
1. Enter *Principal* (in dollars):
2. Divide Box 1 by 1000.
3. Enter *Monthly Payment* (in dollars):
4. Divide Box 3 by Box 2.
5. Enter *Duration*:
6. Locate column with *Duration*.
7. Find the value in the duration column closest to the value in Box 4.
8. Result is the *Rate* for the corresponding row:

For examples see Chapter 9: Examples 9.1 through 9.4, 9.16 and 9.17.

(c) Determining a Duration	
Inputs Needed: *Principal, Monthly Payment, Rate*	
1. Enter *Principal* (in dollars):	
2. Divide Box 1 by 1000.	
3. Enter *Monthly Payment* (in dollars):	
4. Divide Box 3 by Box 2.	
5. Enter *Rate* (in annual percent):	
6. Locate row with the *Rate*.	**Rate**
7. Find the value in the rate row closest to the value in Box 4.	
8. Result is the *Duration* for the corresponding column:	**Duration**

(d) Determining a Principal	
Inputs Needed: *Rate, Duration, Monthly Payment*	
1. Enter *Rate* (in annual percent):	
2. Enter *Duration*:	
3. Locate row with *Rate*.	**Rate**
4. Locate column with *Duration*.	**Duration**
5. Enter value from box at the row-column intersection:	
6. Enter *Monthly Payment* (in dollars):	
7. Divide Box 6 by Box 5.	
8. Multiply Box 7 by 1000 for the *Principal*:	

Worksheets A3.a-d: For use with Table 9.2 (Total cost of a loan:2-30 years), Table 9.6 (Total Cost of a loan:1-12 months), and Table 9.7 (Total cost of a loan:1-12 weeks).

(a) Determining a Total Cost
Inputs Needed: *Rate, Duration, Cash Price*
1. Enter *Rate* (in annual percent):
2. Enter *Duration*:
3. Locate row with *Rate*.
4. Locate column with *Duration*.
5. Enter value from box at the row-column intersection.
6. Enter *Cash Price* (in dollars).
7. Divide Box 6 by 1000.
8. Multiply Box 5 by Box 7 for the *Total Cost*:

(b) Determining a Rate
Inputs Needed: *Total Cost, Cash Price, Duration*
1. Enter *Total Cost* (in dollars):
2. Enter *Cash Price* (in dollars):
3. Divide Box 1 by Box 2.
4. Multiply Box 3 by 1000.
5. Enter *Duration*:
6. Locate column with *Duration*.
7. Find the value in the duration column closest to the value in Box 4.
8. Result is the *Rate* for the corresponding row.

For examples see Chapter 9: Examples 9.6 through 9.9 and Examples 9.18 through 9.21; Chapter 10: Examples 10.1 through 10.6.

(c) Determining a Duration

Inputs Needed: *Total Cost, Cash Price, Rate*

1. Enter *Total Cost* (in dollars):	
2. Enter *Cash Price* (in dollars):	
3. Divide Box 1 by Box 2.	
4. Multiply Box 3 by 1000.	
5. Enter *Rate* (in annual percent):	
6. Locate row with the *Rate*.	**Rate**
7. Find the value in the rate row closest to the value in Box 4.	
8. Result is the *Duration* for the corresponding column.	**Duration**

(d) Determining a Cash Price

Inputs Needed: *Rate, Duration, Total Cost*

1. Enter *Rate* (in annual percent):	
2. Enter *Duration*:	
3. Locate row with *Rate*.	**Rate**
4. Locate column with *Duration*.	**Duration**
5. Enter value from box at the row-column intersection:	
6. Divide Box 5 by 1000.	
7. .Enter *Total Cost* (in dollars):	
8. Divide Box 7 by Box 6 for the *Cash Price*:	

Worksheets A4.a-d: For use with Table 9.3 (Time required to pay 20% of the principal), and Table 9.4 (Time required to pay 50% of the principal).

(a) Determining a Time	
Inputs Needed: *Rate, Duration*	
1. Enter *Rate* (in annual percent):	
2. Enter *Duration* (in years):	
3. Locate row with *Rate*.	**Rate**
4. Locate column with *Duration*.	**Duration**
5. Result is *Time* (in years) from box at the row-column intersection:	

(b) Determining a Rate	
Inputs Needed: *Time, Duration*	
1. Enter *Time* (in years):	
2. Enter *Duration* (in years):	
3. Locate column with *Duration*.	
4. Find the value in the duration column closest to the value in Box 1.	**Duration**
5. Result is the *Rate* for the corresponding row.	**Rate**

For examples see Chapter 9: Examples 9.10 through 9.15.

(c) Determining a Duration	
Inputs Needed: *Time, Rate*	
1. Enter *Time* (in years):	
2. Enter *Rate* (in annual percent):	
3. Locate row with the *Rate*.	
4. Find the value in the rate row closest to the value in Box 1.	**Rate**
5. Result is the *Duration* for the corresponding column:	**Duration**

Worksheets A5.a-d: For use with Table 10.1 (Monthly loan payments:15-30 years).

(a) Determining a Monthly Payment

Inputs Needed: *Rate, Duration, Principal*

1. Enter *Rate* (in annual percent):	
2. Enter *Duration*:	
3. Locate row with *Rate*.	Rate
4. Locate column with *Duration*.	Duration
5. Enter value from box at the row-column intersection:	
6. Enter *Principal* (in dollars):	
7. Divide Box 6 by 10,000.	
8. Multiply Box 5 by Box 7 for the *Monthly Payment*:	

(b) Determining a Rate

Inputs Needed: *Principal, Monthly Payment, Duration*

1. Enter *Principal* (in dollars):	
2. Divide Box 1 by 10,000.	
3. Enter *Monthly Payment* (in dollars):	
4. Divide Box 3 by Box 2:	
5. Enter *Duration*:	
6. Locate column with *Duration*.	Duration
7. Find the value in the duration column closest to the value in Box 4.	
8. Result is the *Rate* for the corresponding row:	Rate

For examples see Chapter 10: Examples 10.7, 10.8, and 10.15.

(c) Determining a Duration	
Inputs Needed: *Principal, Monthly Payment, Rate*	
1. Enter *Principal* (in dollars):	
2. Divide Box 1 by 10,000.	
3. Enter *Monthly Payment* (in dollars):	
4. Divide Box 3 by Box 2.	
5. Enter *Rate* (in annual percent):	
6. Locate row with the *Rate*.	**Rate**
7. Find the value in the rate row closest to the value in Box 4.	
8. Result is the *Duration* for the corresponding column:	**Duration**

(d) Determining a Principal	
Inputs Needed: *Rate, Duration, Monthly Payment*	
1. Enter *Rate* (in annual percent):	
2. Enter *Duration*:	
3. Locate row with *Rate*.	**Rate**
4. Locate column with *Duration*.	**Duration**
5. Enter value from box at the row-column intersection:	
6. Enter *Monthly Payment* (in dollars):	
7. Divide Box 6 by Box 5.	
8. Multiply Box 7 by 10,000 for the *Principal*:	

Worksheets A6.a-d: For use with Table 10.2 (Balance remaining on a 30-year loan).

(a) Determining a Balance	
Inputs Needed: *Rate, Time, Principal*	
1. Enter *Rate* (in annual percent):	
2. Enter *Time (in years)*:	
3. Locate row with *Rate*.	Rate
4. Locate column with *Time*.	Time
5. Enter value from box at the row-column intersection:	
6. Enter *Principal* (in dollars):	
7. Divide Box 6 by 10,000.	
8. Multiply Box 5 by Box 7 for the *Balance*:	

(b) Determining a Rate	
Inputs Needed: *Principal, Balance, Time*	
1. Enter *Principal* (in dollars):	
2. Divide Box 1 by 10,000.	
3. Enter *Balance* (in dollars):	
4. Divide Box 3 by Box 2.	
5. Enter *Time*:	
6. Locate column with *Time*.	Time
7. Find the value in the time column closest to the value in Box 4.	
8. Result is the *Rate* for the corresponding row:	Rate

For examples see Chapter 10: Examples 10.9 and 10.10.

(c) Determining a Time	
Inputs Needed: *Principal, Balance, Rate*	
1. Enter *Principal* (in dollars):	
2. Divide Box 1 by 10,000.	
3. Enter *Balance* (in dollars):	
4. Divide Box 3 by Box 2.	
5. Enter *Rate* (in annual percent):	
6. Locate row with the *Rate*.	**Rate**
7. Find the value in the rate row closest to the value in Box 4.	
8. Result is the *Time* for the corresponding column:	**Time**

(d) Determining a Principal	
Inputs Needed: *Rate, Time, Balance*	
1. Enter *Rate* (in annual percent):	
2. Enter *Time (in years)*:	
3. Locate row with *Rate*.	**Rate**
4. Locate column with *Time*.	**Time**
5. Enter value from box at the row-column intersection:	
6. Enter *Balance* (in dollars):	
7. Divide Box 6 by Box 5.	
8. Multiply Box 7 by 10,000 for the *Principal*:	

Worksheets A7.a-c—For use with Table 10.3 (Interest paid on a 30-year loan).

(a) Determining Interest Paid	
Inputs Needed: *Rate, Time, Principal*	
1. Enter *Rate* (in annual percent):	
2. Enter *Time (in years)*:	
3. Locate row with *Rate*.	
4. Locate column with *Time*.	
5. Enter value from box at the row-column intersection:	
6. Enter *Principal* (in dollars):	
7. Divide Box 6 by 10,000.	
8. Multiply Box 5 by Box 7 for the *Interest Paid:*	

(b) Determining a Rate	
Inputs Needed: *Principal, Interest Paid, Time*	
1. Enter *Principal* (in dollars):	
2. Divide Box 1 by 10,000.	
3. Enter *Interest Paid* (in dollars):	
4. Divide Box 3 by Box 2.	
5. Enter *Time*:	
6. Locate column with *Time*.	
7. Find the value in the time column closest to the value in Box 4.	
8. Result is the *Rate* for the corresponding row:	

For an example see Chapter 10: Example 10.9.

(c) Determining a Time	
Inputs Needed: *Principal, Interest Paid, Rate*	
1. Enter *Principal* (in dollars):	
2. Divide Box 1 by 10,000.	
3. Enter *Interest Paid* (in dollars):	
4. Divide Box 3 by Box 2.	
5. Enter *Rate* (in annual percent):	
6. Locate row with the *Rate*.	**Rate**
7. Find the value in the rate row closest to the value in Box 4.	
8. Result is the *Time* for the corresponding column:	**Time**

Worksheets A8.a-c—For use with Table 10.4 (30-year Mortgage Acceleration Table).

(a) Determining an Additional Monthly Payment	
Inputs Needed: *Rate, Time, Principal*	
1. Enter *Rate* (in annual percent):	
2. Enter *Time:*	
3. Locate row with *Rate*.	Rate
4. Find value in the rate row closest to the value in Box 2.	
5. Enter value from the column heading:	Column Heading
6. Enter *Principal* (in dollars):	
7. Divide Box 6 by 10,000.	
8. Multiply Box 7 by Box 5 for the *Additional Monthly Payment:*	

(b) Determining a Rate	
Inputs Needed: *Principal, Additional Monthly Payment, Time*	
1. Enter *Principal* (in dollars):	
2. Divide Box 1 by 10,000.	
3. Enter *Additional Monthly Payment:*	
4. Divide Box 3 by Box 2.	
5. Enter *Time* (in years):	
6. Find a column with a heading closest to the value in Box 4.	Column Heading
7. Find the value in the column closest to the value in Box 5.	
8. Result is the *Rate* for the corresponding row:	Rate

For examples see Chapter 10: Examples 10.12 through 10.14 and 10.16.

(c) Determining a Time
Inputs Needed: *Principal, Additional Monthly Payment, Rate*
1. Enter *Principal* (in dollars):
2. Divide Box 1 by 10,000.
3. Enter *Additional Monthly Payment*:
4. Divide Box 3 by Box 2.
5. Enter *Rate* (in annual percent):
6. Find a column with a heading closest to the value in Box 4.
7. Find the value in the row closest to the value in Box 5.
8. Result is the *Time* in the box at the row-column intersection:

Column Heading

Rate

Time

Worksheets A9.a-c: For use with Table 10.5 (Interest Saved on a 30-year Mortgage).

(a) Determining an Additional Monthly Payment

Inputs Needed: *Principal, Interest Saved, Rate*

1. Enter *Principal* (in dollars):	
2. Divide Box 1 by 10,000.	
3. Enter *Interest Saved* (in dollars):	
4. Divide Box 3 by Box 2.	
5. Enter *Rate* (in annual percent):	
6. Locate row with *Rate*.	Rate ⟶
7. Find value in the rate row closest to the value in Box4.	
8. Enter value from the column heading:	Column Heading
9. Multiply Box 7 by Box 2 for the *Additional Monthly Payment*:	

(b) Determining a Rate

Inputs Needed: *Principal, Additional Monthly Payment, Interest Saved*

1. Enter *Principal* (in dollars):	
2. Divide Box 1 by 10,000.	
3. Enter *Additional Monthly Payment*:	
4. Divide Box 3 by Box 2.	
5. Enter *Interest Saved* (in dollars):	
6. Divide Box 5 by Box 2.	
7. Find a column with a heading closest to the value in Box 4.	Column Heading
8. Find the value in the column closest to the value in Box 6.	
9. Result is the *Rate* for the corresponding row:	Rate ⟶

For examples see Chapter 10: Examples 10.12 through 10.14 and 10.16.

(c) Determining Interest Saved	
Inputs Needed: *Principal, Additional Monthly Payment, Rate*	
1. Enter *Principal* (in dollars):	
2. Divide Box 1 by 10,000.	
3. Enter *Additional Monthly Payment*:	
4. Divide Box 3 by Box 2.	
5. Enter *Rate* (in annual percent):	
6. Find a column with a heading closest to the value in Box 4.	**Column Heading**
7. Locate the row with *Rate*.	**Rate**
8. Enter value from the row-column intersection:	
9. Multiply Box 7 by Box 2 for the *Interest Saved*:	

Appendix II

Mathematical Formulas

For completeness, here are the underlying formulas used to generate the tables and figures in the book.

A. Time Value of Money

The formula for the time value of money relates five variables:

N = number of periods
I = interest rate per period in percent
P = payment per period
V = initial value in dollars
F = final value in dollars

To simplify writing the formula first define a variable:

$$S = \left(1 + \frac{I}{100}\right)^{-N}$$

Then the relationship between all the variables is:

$$V + \left(\frac{100}{I}\right)(1-S)\,P = -S\,F$$

where it is assumed that payments are made at the end of each period. This is the underlying relationship behind all of the tables in Chapters 5, 6, 9, and 10.

For example, to calculate the monthly payments on a $1000 loan for 3 years with a 6% annual interest rate, the known variables would be:

N = 3 x 12 = 36 periods
I = (6/12) = 0.5% per period
V = –$1000
F = $0

Then S = 0.8356449 and solving the formula for the unknown P results in $30.42 per period, which is the amount that needs to be paid each month to pay off the loan.

The same formula works to compute the final value for investments that result from fixed-rate or integrated fixed-rate growth. For example, to calculate the final value from investing $1000 per year for 10 years with an 8% annual return, the known variables would be:

N =10 periods
I = 8% per period
P = –$1000 per period
V = $0

Then S = 0.4631935 and solving the formula for the unknown F results in $14,487.

B. Combinatorics

The formula for computing the number of possibilities (N) for choosing a specified number of objects (R) from a total number of objects (T) is:

$$N = \frac{T!}{R!\,(T-R)!}$$

In this notation the exclamation point (!) means "factorial," which is an instruction to multiply the number by *all* of the whole numbers below it. This means that 3! = 3 x 2 x 1 = 6; 4! = 4 x 3 x 2 x 1 = 24; 5! = 5 x 4 x 3 x 2 x 1 = 120; etc.

For example, to calculate the number of five-card poker hands possible when choosing 5 cards from a 52-card deck use:

T = 52
R = 5

Solving for N results in:

$$N = \frac{52!}{5!\,(47)!} = 2,\,598,\,960$$

C. Gaussian Distribution

A Gaussian or normal distribution (also known as a "bell curve"), is a function (F) of a variable (x) defined as:

$$F(x) = \frac{1}{\sigma\sqrt{2\pi}}\,\exp\left(\frac{-(x-\mu)^2}{2\sigma^2}\right)$$

where μ is the mean (or average) and σ is called the standard deviation. A graph of this function will show a symmetrical bell-shaped curve centered at the value for μ with a width that depends on the value for σ.

For example with $\mu=10$ and $\sigma = 2$, a graph of F(x) is shown below.

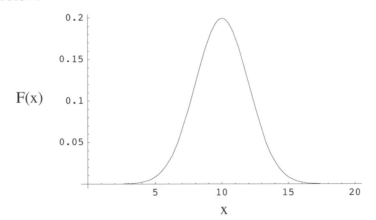

Acknowledgments

It was a great pleasure to work with all of the people who assisted with this book. I am grateful to all of them.

I want to thank my editor, Judith Dobler, for her hard work on the manuscript and enthusiasm for the project. I enjoyed working with her and I valued her feedback. She required clarity throughout and identified any lapses into jargon on my part.

Preston Athey, a fund manager for T. Rowe Price, read many of the chapters on investing and provided insightful comments and suggestions.

Christopher Morrell, a statistician and the chair of Loyola's Mathematical Sciences Department, read the chapters related to probability and statistics. He took the time to discuss with me how to better explain many of these concepts.

My friend and colleague in Loyola's Physics Department, Randall Jones read the entire manuscript and provided many useful suggestions. His feedback was especially helpful in shaping and focusing the final manuscript.

Mark Levine proofread the entire book and provided very helpful comments and suggestions on selling the book.

Graham Van Dixhorn of Write To Your Market, Inc. worked with great enthusiasm on the book cover writing.

I am grateful for the support and encouragement my wife Sharon provided throughout the three years that this project took.

Any errors found in this book are mine. Do not hesitate to call errors to my attention or provide any other feedback. I enjoy hearing from my readers. Send e-mail to comments@ JosephGanem.com or write to me to care of Chartley Publishing at P. O. Box 6705, Baltimore, MD 21285.

Examples Index

Tables and Figures Index

Index

About the Author

Joseph Ganem is currently an associate professor at Loyola College in Maryland where he teaches physics and mathematical methods for physics. He is an author on numerous scientific papers in the fields of laser development and magnetic resonance and has received grants from: Research Corporation, the Petroleum Research Fund and the National Science Foundation for his research on solid-state laser materials.

Ganem received a Ph.D. from Washington University in Saint Louis, an M. S. from the University of Wisconsin-Madison and a B. S. from the University of Rochester. He did postdoctoral work at the University of Georgia-Athens and at the United States Naval Research Laboratory in Washington, DC.

His interest in deceptive numbers arose from applying his knowledge of math to his own financial decisions.

Among his other interests is chess. He is an expert at correspondence chess and since 1991 has been the editor of *The Chess Correspondent*. This is a magazine devoted to correspondence chess that has been published by The Correspondence Chess League of America since 1940, making it one of the oldest chess magazines in the United States.

In his spare time he enjoys playing a wide variety of music on the piano. Currently he resides in Baltimore County Maryland with his wife and three children and is seen frequently in his neighborhood walking their dog Magnet.

You can visit his Website at http://www.JosephGanem.com.